Dictionary of Radio and Television Terms
English-German, German-English
Fachwörterbuch Hörfunk und Fernsehen
Englisch-Deutsch, Deutsch-Englisch

Dictionary of Radio and Television Terms

English - German, German - English

Fachwörterbuch Hörfunk und Fernsehen

Englisch - Deutsch, Deutsch - Englisch

HEYDEN

London · New York · Rheine

Heyden & Son Ltd., Spectrum House, Alderton Crescent, London NW4 3XX.

Heyden & Son Inc., 225 Park Avenue, New York, N.Y. 10017, U.S.A.

Heyden & Son GmbH, 4440 Rheine/Westf., Münsterstrasse 22, Germany.

ISBN 0 85501 250 1 Heyden & Son Ltd., London
ISBN 3 920730 05 4 Heyden & Son GmbH, Rheine

Printed in Great Britain by The Whitefriars Press Ltd., London and Tonbridge.

Dictionary of Radio and Television Terms

Compiled and Edited by the ARD
(Study group of the broadcasting corporations licensed by public law in the Federal Republic of Germany)

in collaboration with the BBC
(British Broadcasting Corporation)

and the ZDF
(Second German Television System)

Fachwörterbuch Hörfunk und Fernsehen

Herausgegeben von der ARD
(Arbeitsgemeinschaft der öffentlich-rechtlichen Rundfunkanstalten der Bundesrepublik Deutschland)

in Zusammenarbeit mit der BBC
(British Broadcasting Corporation)

und dem ZDF
(Zweites Deutsches Fernsehen)

Vorwort

Dieses Fachwörterbuch entstand auf Initiative der ARD und in Zusammenarbeit mit der BBC und dem ZDF. Es gründet auf das 1970 erschienene deutsch-französische Wörterbuch für Hörfunk und Fernsehen und umfaßt im deutsch-englischen Teil rund 12.000 und im englisch-deutschen Teil rund 17.000 Einträge. Die erste Auflage von 7.400 Exemplaren, die 1972 zu den Olympischen Spielen in München vorgelegt wurde, war schnell vergriffen. Diese zweite unveränderte Auflage möge in gleicher Weise der internationalen Zusammenarbeit auf dem Gebiet des Rundfunks dienen.
Dank für mühevolle, beharrliche Arbeit gebührt den ständigen Mitgliedern der Arbeitsgruppe: Frau Dr. Christa Schulze-Rohr, die das Team im Auftrage der ARD leitete, Herrn Anthony Powell von der BBC und Herrn Helmut Rinke vom ZDF, ebenso denjenigen Mitarbeitern der BBC, der ARD (insbesondere des Norddeutschen Rundfunks) und des Instituts für Rundfunktechnik in Hamburg, die jeweils für bestimmte Fachgebiete ihr Wissen und ihre Erfahrung eingebracht haben.

Für die ARD

KARL SCHNELTING

Programmdirektor Fernsehen
Saarländischer Rundfunk

Foreword

The compilation of this dictionary was initiated by the Arbeitsgemeinschaft der öffentlich-rechlichen Rundfunkanstalten der Bundesrepublik Deutschland (ARD) in collaboration with the British Broadcasting Corporation (BBC) and the Second German Television System (ZDF). It is based on the German-French dictionary for Radio and Television which was published in 1970, and comprises about 12,000 items in the German-English part and about 17,000 items in the English-German part.

The 1st edition which was presented at the time of the Olympic Games in Munich in 1972, was quickly sold out. I trust that this new edition will similarly further the cause of international cooperation in the field of broadcasting.

Gratitude for their painstaking and untiring work is due to all the permanent members of the teams, especially Frau Dr. Christa Schulze-Rohr, who led the ARD team as commissioned by that corporation; Mr. Anthony Powell of the BBC, and Herr Helmut Rinke of the ZDF. Our thanks also to those members of the staff of the BBC, the ARD (in particular North-German Radio) and the Institute for Broadcasting Techniques in Hamburg who applied their knowledge and experience within their respective areas of expertise.

For the ARD
KARL SCHELTING

Programming Director Television
Saarland Broadcasting System

Erläuterungen

Dieses Fachwörterbuch ist nach Gesichtspunkten des täglichen Gebrauchs in Rundfunk- und Fernsehhäusern zusammengestellt. Es berücksichtigt nur die Berufs- und Organisationsbezeichnungen deutscher und britischer Rundfunkanstalten. Dabei ist zu beachten, daß die unterschiedlichen Organisationsformen — föderalistische, zentrale und kommerzielle — in den meisten Fällen nur eine annähernde Übersetzung erlauben. So ist z.B. das Wort „Sendeleiter" mit „head of presentation" annähernd, der Definition nach jedoch unzureichend übersetzt.
Als Stichwörter gelten hier generell das erste (evtl. einzige) Wort einer Benennung. Benennungen, die dasselbe Stichwort enthalten, werden zu Gruppen zusammengefaßt. Innerhalb dieser Gruppen wird das Stichwort durch eine Tilde ersetzt. Die Sortierung wird so durchgeführt, daß hierbei zuerst die Benennungen, in denen das Stichwort (und damit die Tilde) am Anfang steht, angeführt werden, danach diejenigen Benennungen, in denen es in der Mitte oder am Ende erscheint.
Geschlecht oder Wortart sind nach jedem Stichwort angegeben; ausgenommen sind englische Mehrwortbenennungen. Ein Hinweis auf den Plural wird auf der englischen Seite auch in diesem Fall gegeben, wenn klargemacht werden soll, daß es sich hier im Gegensatz zum deutschen Singular um einen Plural handelt. Partizipien des Perfekts werden, da sie hier nur adjektivisch gebraucht sind, als Adjektive aufgeführt. Ein Sternchen bedeutet, daß die dazugehörige Benennung für eine Abteilung, Dienststelle o.ä. steht, z.B. Störungsannahme* = radio interference group.

In der englischen Technik wird häufig mit Abkürzungen gearbeitet, die hier nicht immer als Synonyme aufgeführt sind. Das Abkürzungsverzeichnis am Anfang des Wörterbuches dient unter anderem dazu, die abgekürzte Benennung in ihrer voll ausgeschriebenen Form aufzufinden.

Klammern schließen Abkürzungen, Erklärungen und Hinweise auf das Sachgebiet ein. Unterschiedliche Übersetzungen einer Benennung werden durch Komma getrennt, wenn sie sinnverwandt sind, durch Semikolon, wenn der Sinn sich ändert.

Amerikanismen sind mit dem Vermerk (US) gekennzeichnet; sie stehen meistens nur beim Grundwort, nicht jedoch in Zusammensetzungen, um Wiederholungen zu vermeiden.

Da es bei einigen Benennungen anstaltsverschiedene Begriffsverständnisse gibt, wurde die jeweils geläufigste Version als Standardbenennung aufgenommen. Dem zunehmenden Einsatz von Rechenanlagen in den Rundfunkanstalten trägt das eingefügte Vokabular aus der elektronischen Datenverarbeitung (EDV) Rechnung, das von der Siemens AG beigesteuert wurde.

Explanatory Note

This dictionary was compiled to meet the everyday requirements of radio and television organisations. It covers only professional and operational designations current in German and British broadcasting bodies; in view of the difference in their structure and organisation (some being centralised, some regional, others commercial), it should be borne in mind that the translations given can seldom be absolute equivalents. For example, »Sendeleiter« has been rendered into English as »head of presentation«, although this does not entirely convey the German connotation.

A keyword is always the first (and sometimes the only) word of a term. Terms containing the same keyword are grouped together. Within these groups keywords are replaced by a swung dash (~). Items are so ordered that terms in which the keyword (and thus the swung dash) appears at the beginning are listed first, followed by those in which the keyword appears in the middle or at the end.

Genders or parts of speech are shown after all keywords. They do not appear after English terms consisting of two words or more. Use of the plural, on the other hand, is invariably indicated on the English side when a term is singular in German. Past participles have been listed as adjectives, since this is the only form in which they appear in the dictionary.

An asterisk means the expression in question stands for a department, group, section or service. In view of the wide use in English of technical abbreviations which do not always figure here as synonyms, a table is provided at the beginning of the dictionary to help trace relevant terms.

Abbreviations, explanations and references to special meanings are enclosed in brackets. Alternative translations of a term are separated by commas when synonymous, by semicolons when there is a change of sense.

Americanisms are identified by the symbol (US). They usually occur only after a root word, having in most cases been omitted from compound forms in order to avoid repetition.

A number of terms relating to electronic data processing (EDP) and contributed by Siemens AG have been included because it was felt the dictionary should take account of the ever-increasing use of computers by broadcasting organisations.

Abbreviations Used in this Dictionary
Im Wörterbuch verwendete Abkürzungen

acoust.	acoustic
adj	adjective/Adjektiv
adv	adverb/Adverb
advert.	advertisement
akust.	akustisch
ampl.	amplifier
Ant.	Antenne
appar.	apparatus
approx.	approximately/approximativ, annähernd
bcast.	broadcast
cam.	camera
col.	colour
coll.	colloquial
compp.	in compounds
dub.	dubbing
elec.	electrical
elek.	elektrisch
elektron.	elektronisch
F	film/Film
f	feminine/Femininum
fam.	familiär, umgangssprachlich
FP	film-processing
f pl	feminine plural/Femininum Plural
freq.	frequency
imp.	impulse
in Zus.	in Zusammensetzungen
journ.	journalism
journal.	journalistisch
m	masculine/Maskulinum
mag.	magnetic
mech.	mechanical/mechanisch
micr.	microphone
m pl	masculine plural/Maskulinum Plural
Mus.	Musik
mus.	music
n	(English) noun/(deutsch) Neutrum (German) neuter/(englisch) Substantiv
neg.	negative
n pl	(English) plural noun / (deutsch) Neutrum Plural (German) neuter plural / (englisch) Substantiv Plural
OB	outside broadcast
opt.	optical/optisch
perf.	performer
phys.	physikalisch
pict.	picture
pl	plural/Plural
plt	Pluraletantum
PO	post office
Prod.	Produktion
prod.	production
Progr.	Programm
prog.	programme
Proj.	Projektor
proj.	projector
R	radio/Radio
rec.	receiver
recepn.	reception
repro.	reproduction
s.	see/siehe
s.a.	see also/siehe auch
Sat.	Satellit
sat.	satellite
sig.	signal

s.o.	someone	thea.	theatre
s.th.	something	TV	television/Television Fernsehen
sync.	synchronism		
tech.	technical/technisch	US	United States/ Amerikanismus
tel.	telephone		
Thea.	Theater	v	verb/Verb

Abbreviations from the Broadcasting Field
Fachsprachliche Abkürzungen

A	Austastung
ABC	American Broadcasting Companies, Inc. (USA)
ABC	Australian Broadcasting Commission (AUS)
ABERT	Associacão Brasileira de Emissoras de Radio e Televisão (BR)
ABU	Asian Broadcasting Union, Union der Asiatischen Rundfunkorganisationen
AC	alternating current
ACR	acceptable contrast ratio
AD	assistant director
ADC	analog-to-digital converter
ADU	Analog-Digital-Umsetzer
AF	audio-frequency
AFC	automatic frequency control
AGC	automatic gain control
ALR	automatische Lautstärkeregelung
ALU	arithmetic and logical unit
AM	amplitude modulation Amplitudenmodulation
ANL	automatic noise-limiting
APC	automatic phase control
AR	aspect ratio
ARD	Arbeitsgemeinschaft der öffentlich-rechtlichen Rundfunkanstalten der Bundesrepublik Deutschland
ASBU	Arab States Broadcasting Union, Union der Rundfunkorganisationen in den Arabischen Staaten
ASC	automatic sensitivity control
ASN	aural sensitivity network
AÜ	Außenübertragung
AV	audiovision, Audiovision audio-visual, audio-visuell
AVC	automatic volume control
AVR	automatic voltage regulator

B-	Bild- (in Zus.)
BA	Bildaustastung
BAS-Signal	Bildaustastsynchronsignal
BASP-Signal	Bildaustastsynchronsignal mit Prüfzeile
BBC	British Broadcasting Corporation
BC	bayonet cap
BCS	big close shot
BCU	big close-up
BEVR	Broadcasting Electronic Video Recording
BIEM	Bureau International de l'Edition Mécanique, International Bureau of the Societies Administering the Rights of Mechanical Recording and Reproduction, Internationale Verwertungsgesellschaft für mechanische Vervielfältigungsrechte
BIT	binary digit
BL	Bildleitung
BOC	broadcast operations control
BP	back projection
BR	Bayerischer Rundfunk (D)
BRT/RTB	Belgische Radio en Televisie/Radiodiffusion-Télévision Belge (B)
BS	Betriebssystem

BSS	British Standards Specification
B/W	black-and-white
CaBC	Caribbean Broadcasting Corporation (BDS)
CAR	central apparatus room
CAT	Clear Air Turbulence
CATV	central aerial television
CB	common-battery
CBC	Canadian Broadcasting Corporation (CDN)
CBS	Columbia Broadcasting System, Inc. (USA)
CCIR	Comité Consultatif International des Radiocommunications, International Radio Consultative Committee, Internationaler Beratender Ausschuß für den Funkdienst
CCITT	Comité Consultatif International Télégraphique et Téléphonique, International Telegraph and Telephone Consultative Committee, Internationaler Beratender Ausschuß für den Telegraphen- und Fernsprechdienst
CCR	central control room
CCTV	closed-circuit television
CCU	camera control unit
CeBC	Ceylon Broadcasting Corporation (CL)
CEM	centre d'écoute et de mesure receiving and measuring station
CEPT	Conférence Européenne des Administrations des Postes et des Télécommunications, European Conference of Postal and Telecommunication Administrations, Europäische Konferenz der Verwaltung für das Post- und Fernmeldewesen
CETS	Conférence Européenne des Télécommunications par Satellites, European Conference on Satellite Telecommunications, Europäische Konferenz für Fernmeldeverbindungen mittels Satelliten
CICP	Centre International de Coordination des Programmes, International Programme Coordination Centre, Internationale Programmkoordinationszentrale
CISAC	Confédération Internationale des Sociétés d'Auteurs et de Compositeurs, International Confederation of Societies of Authors and Composers, Internationale Vereinigung der Autoren und Komponisten
CISPR	Comité International Spécial des Perturbations Radioélectriques, International Special Committee on Radio Interference, Internationaler Sonderausschuß für Rundfunkstörungen
CLT/RTL	Compagnie Luxembourgeoise de Télédiffusion/ Radio-Télé-Luxembourg(L)
CMCR	colour mobile control

	room
CMS	close-medium shot
CMTT	Commission Mixte de Transmissions Télévisuelles, Joint CCIR/CCITT Study Group for Television and Sound Transmissions, Gemischte CCIR/CCITT-Kommission für Fernseh- und Tonübertragungen
CMVTR	colour mobile video tape recorder
COMMAG	combined magnetic sound kombinierter Magnetton
COMOPT	combined optical sound kombinierter Lichtton
COMP.SIG.	composite signal
COMSAT	Communications Satellite Corporation, Betriebsgesellschaft für Fernmeldesatelliten
CPB/PBS/NPR	Corporation for Public Broadcasting/Public Broadcasting Service/National Public Radio (USA)
CPR	Companía Peruana de Radiodifusión SA (PE)
CPS	cycles per second
CPU	central processing unit
CR	control room
CRO	cathode-ray oscillator cathode-ray oscilloscope
CRT	cathode-ray tube
CS	close shot
CSC	colour subcarrier
CT	colour temperature
CTV	community television
CTV	CTV Television Network Ltd. (CDN)
CU	close-up
CvD	Chef vom Dienst
CW	carrier wave
CyBC	Cyprus Broadcasting Corporation (CY)
CYC	cyclorama
DC	direct current
DE	de-emphasis
DFS	Deutsches Fernsehen
DIN	Deutsche Industrie-Norm
DLF	Deutschlandfunk
DOZ	Deutsches Olympia Zentrum German Olympic Centre
DPTR	Dioptrie
DR	Danmarks Radio (DK)
DSB	double sideband Doppelseitenband
DW	Deutsche Welle
EB	end board
EBC	Educational Broadcasting Corporation (USA)
EBU	European Broadcasting Union
E-Cam	electronic camera
ECO	electron-coupled oscillator
ECU	extreme close-up
EDP	electronic data processing
EDV	elektronische Datenverarbeitung
EFR	electronic film recording
EHF	extra-high frequency Millimeterwellenbereich
EID	Engineering Information Department (BBC)
EIRT	Ethnikon Idryma Radiophonias-Tileoraseos (GR)
ELA	Elektroakustik, Elatechnik
ELDO	European Launcher Development Organisation, Europäische Organisation für die Entwicklung und den Bau von Raumfahr-

	zeugträgern
ELS	extreme long shot
ENR	Emossora Nacional de Radiodifusão (P)
EOJ	end of job
ER	editor's report
ERP	effective radiated power effektive Strahlungsleistung
ESB	Einseitenband
ESC	European Space Conference, Europäische Weltraumkonferenz
ESRO	European Space Research Organisation, Europäische Weltraumforschungsorganisation
ETV	educational television
EV~	error voltage
EVC	Eurovision Control Centre, Eurovisionskontrollzentrale
EVR	electronic video recording
FACTS	Federation of Australian Commercial Television Stations (AUS)
FAZ	Filmaufzeichnung
FBA-Signal	Farbbildaustastsignal
FBAS-Signal	Farbbildaustastsynchronsignal
FER	film editor's report
FET	field effect transistor Feldeffekttransistor
FIAV	Fédération Internationale des Artistes de Variétés, International Federation of Variety Artists, Internationaler Verband der Unterhaltungskünstler
FIM	Fédération Internationale des Musiciens, International Federation of Musicians, Internationale Musiker-Föderation
FI-Schalter	Fehlerstromrelais
FLS	full-length shot
FM	frequency modulation Frequenzmodulation
FO	fade-out
FPS	frames per second
FS	Fernsehen
F-Signal	Farbartsignal
FTC	Fuji Telecasting Company Ltd. (J)
FU-Schalter	Fehlerspannungsrelais
GBC	Ghana Broadcasting Corporation (GH)
GEMA	Gesellschaft für musikalische Aufführungs- und mechanische Vervielfältigungsrechte
GVL	Gesellschaft zur Verwertung von Leistungsschutzrechten
H-	Horizontal- (in Zus.)
HA	Hauptabteilung
H a. D curve	Hurter and Driffield curve
HA	Hauptleitung
H a. D	Hurter and Driffield curve
HF	high frequency Hochfrequenz
HI	high intensity Hochintensität
Hi-Fi	high fidelity hohe Wiedergabegüte
HK	high key
HK-TVB	Television Broadcasts Ltd. (HK)
HR	Hessischer Rundfunk (D)

HT	high tension
HV	high voltage
Hz	Hertz
IBA	Israel Broadcasting Authority (IL)
IBAR	Internationaler Beratender Ausschuß für Radiokommunikation
IC	integrated circuit
ICCR	International Consultative Committee for Radio Communication
IEC	International Electrotechnical Commission, Internationale Elektrotechnische Kommission
IF	intermediate frequency
IFA	International Federation of Actors, Internationaler Schauspielerverband
IFM	Impulsfrequenzmodulation
IFPI	International Federation of the Phonographic Industry, Internationaler Verband der Schallplattenindustrie
ILO	International Labour Organisation, Internationales Arbeitsamt
INTELSAT	International Telecommunications Satellite Consortium, Internationales Fernmeldesatelliten-Konsortium
IO	image orthicon Image-Orthikon
IOC	International Olympic Committee
IOK	Internationales Olympisches Komitee
IRT	Institut für Rundfunktechnik
IRV	Instituto Nacional de Radio y Televisión-Inravisión (CO)
ISF	International Sporting Federations
ISO	International Standardisation Organisation, Internationale Organisation für Standardisierung
ISV	Internationale Sportverbände
IT	internationaler Ton
ITA	Independent Television Authority (GB)
ITCA	Independent Television Companies Association Ltd. (GB)
ITN	Independent Television News (GB)
ITU	International Telecommunication Union
IV	Intervision
IvD	Ingenieur vom Dienst
JBC	Jamaica Broadcasting Corporation (JA)
JRT	Jugoslovenska Radiotelevizija (YU)
JTV	Jordan Television (HKJ)
K	Kopierer
K	Klirrfaktor
K	degrees Kelvin
KB	Kathodenbasis
KBTS	Kuwait Broadcasting and Television Service (KWT)
KKG	Kamerakontrollgerät
KÜF	Kontrastübertragungsfunktion
KW	Kurzwelle
LB	local battery
LBC	Liberian Broadcasting Corporation (LB)

LC	inductance capacitance Eigenschwingung
LCT	low colour temperature
LF	low frequency
LOPT	line output transformer
LP	long-playing
LP	Langspielplatte
LR	Lautstärkeregler
LS 82 TV	LS 82 TV canal 7 (RA)
L-Signal	Linkssignal
LTS	Libyan Television Service
LvD	Leiter vom Dienst
LW	Langwelle long wave
MAZ	Magnetbildaufzeichnung
MBA	Malta Broadcasting Authority (M)
MBC	Malawi Broadcasting Corporation (MW)
MBS	Mainichi Broadcasting System Inc. (J)
MC	main control, master control
MCPS	Mechanical Copyright Protection Society
MCR	master control room, main control room
MCR	mobile control room
MCU	medium close-up
MDF	main distributing frame
M and E	music and effects
MF	modulation frequency Modulationsfrequenz
MF	medium frequency
MLS	medium long shot
MO	master oscillator
MS	manuscript Manuskript
MS	mid-shot, medium shot
MTV	Malta Television Service Ltd. (M)
MÜF	Modulationsübertragungsfunktion
MVTR	mobile video tape recorder
MW	Mittelwelle

NAB	National Association of Commercial Broadcasters in Japan (J)
NAB	National Association of Broadcasters (USA)
NAEB	National Association of Educational Broadcasters (USA)
NBC	National Broadcasting Company, Inc. (USA)
NDR	Norddeutscher Rundfunk (D)
NE	Nachentzerrung
NET	Nippon Educational Television Company Ltd. (J)
NF	Niederfrequenz
NHK	Nippon Hoso Kyokai (J)
NiBC	Nigerian Broadcasting Corporation (WAN)
NK	Nichtkopierer
NOS	Nederlandse Omroep Stichting (NL)
NRK	Norsk Rikskringkasting (N)
NSC	network switching centre
NTC	negative temperature coefficient
NTI	National Iranian Television (IR)
NTSC	National Television System Committee (USA)
NTV	Nippon Television Network Corporation (J)
NZBC	New Zealand Broadcasting Corporation (NZ)
OB	Ortsbatterie
OB	outside broadcast
ÖBL	öffentlicher beweglicher Landfunk
OIRT	Organisation Internationale de Radiodiffusion et

	Télévision, International Radio and Television Organisation, Internationale Rundfunk- und Fernsehorganisation
OOV	out of vision
ORF	Österreichischer Rundfunk (A)
ORTF	Office de Radiodiffusion-Télévision Française (F)
ORTN	Office de Radiodiffusion-Télévision du Niger (NIG)
OS	operating system
OSV	off-screen voice
O-Ton	Originalton
PA	public address
PA	personal assistant
PAL	phase alternating line
PAS	public address system
PAT	Panamericana Televisión SA (PE)
PBU	photo blow-up
PBX	private branch exchange
PCB	printed circuit board
PEC	photoelectric cell
PEM	Eichpegel für Monitor
PFM	pulse frequency modulation
PG	pulse generator
PI	programmed instruction
PL	Produktionsleiter
PM	phase modulation Phasenmodulation
POA	programme operations assistant
PPM	peak programme meter
PPS	pictures per second
PPS	pulses per second
PRF	pulse repetition frequency pulse recurrence frequency
PRS	Performing Right Society
PSC	programme switching centre
PTC	Pakistan Television Corporation Ltd. (PAK)
PTC	positive temperature coefficient positiver Temperaturkoeffizient
PU	programmierte Unterweisung
PWA	Programmwahlanlage
RAI	Radiotelevisione Italiana (I)
RB	Radio Bremen (D)
RBC	Rhodesia Broadcasting Corporation (RSR)
RBR	rebroadcasting reception
RBW	red-blue-white rot-blau-weiß
RC	resistance/capacitance Widerstand/Kapazität
RDY	Radiodiffusion du Dahomey (DY)
RF	radio frequency Radiofrequenz
RGB	red-green-blue rot-grün-blau
RH	relative humidity
RI	Radio Iran (IR)
RIAS	Rundfunk im amerikanischen Sektor von Berlin
RIFU	Richtfunk
RL	Radiodiffusion Libanaise (RL)
RMC	Radio Monte Carlo (MC)
RMS	root-mean-square
RNE/TVE	Radio Nacional de España/Televisión Española (E)
RNS	Radiodiffusion Nationale du Sénégal (SN)
RNT	Radiodiffusion Nationale Tchadienne
RP	rear projection
RPT	Rio de la Plata TV, SA (Canal 13) (RA)
PRI	Radio Republik Indonesia (RI)

R-Signal	Rechtssignal
RT	reverberation time
RT	radiotelephony
RT	Radio Tanzania (EAT)
RTA	Radiodiffusion-Télévision Algérienne (DZ)
RTB/BRT	Radiodiffusion-Télévision Belge/Belgische Radio en Televisie (B) Belge (B)
RTE	Radio Telefís Eireann (IRL)
RTG	Radiodiffusion-Télévision Gabonaise
RTI	Radiodiffusion-Télévision Ivoirienne (CI)
RTM	Radiodiffusion-Télévision Marocaine (MA)
RTMg	Radiodiffusion-Télévision de Madagascar (RM)
RTP	Radiotelevisão Portuguesa S.A.R.L. (P)
RTT	Radiodiffusion-Télévision Tunisienne (TN)
RTVM	Radio and Television Malaysia (PTM)
RUV	Rikisutvarpid-Sjonvarp(IS)
RV	Radio Vaticana (V)
S-	Synchron- (in Zus.)
SABC	South African Broadcasting Corporation (ZA)
SACD	Société des Auteurs et Compositeurs Dramatiques, Society of Dramatic Authors and Composers, Gesellschaft für Bühnenautoren und Komponisten
SCU	semi-close-up
SDR	Süddeutscher Rundfunk (D)
SEPDU-MAG	two separate magnetic sound tracks, separater Magnetton auf zwei Spuren
SEPMAG	separate magnetic sound separater Magnetton
SEPOPT	separate optical sound separater Lichtton
SFB	Sender Freies Berlin (D)
SHF	super-high frequency
SK	Schlußklappe
SM	studio manager, stage manager
SMM	Slowmotion-Maschine
S/N ratio	signal-to-noise ratio
SOF	sound on film
SPG	synchronised pulse generator
SPM	scratchpad memory
SR	Saarländischer Rundfunk (D)
SR	Sveriges Radio (S)
SRC	Société Radio Canada (CDN)
SRG	Schweizerische Radio- und Fernsehgesellschaft (CH)
SSB	single sideband
SSR	Société Suisse de Radiodiffusion et Télévision (CH)
STD	subscriber trunk dialling
STLSA	Sociedad Televisora Larranaga SA (U)
SWF	Südwestfunk (D)
TARIF	television apparatus for the rectification of indifferent film
TBS	Tokyo Broadcasting System, Inc. (J)
TCM	Tele-Cadena Mexicana SA (MEX)
TDM	time-division multiplex
TF	Trägerfrequenz
TIM	Televisión Independiente de México SA (MEX)
TK	telecine
TOM	technical operations manager

TR	telerecording
TRT	Türkiye Radyo-Televizyon Kurumu (TR)
TSM	Telesístema Mexicano SA (MEX)
TUPI	Sirta-Rede Tupi de Televisão (BR)
TV	Television
TVC	TV Chile (RCH)
TVRI	Televisi Republik Indonesia (RI)
TWT	travelling-wave tube
UCCTV	Universidad Católica de Chile (RCH)
Ü-Dienst	Übertragungsdienst
UER	Union Européenne de Radiodiffusion, Union der Europäischen Rundfunkorganisationen
UHF	ultra-high frequency ultrahohe Frequenz
UIE	Union Internationale des Editeurs, International Publishers' Association, Internationale Verleger-Union
UIT	Union Internationale des Télécommunications, Internationale Fernmelde-Union
UKW	Ultrakurzwelle
URTI	Université Radiophonique et Télévisuelle Internationale, International Radio-Television University, Internationale Rundfunk- und Fernsehuniversität
URTNA	Union des Radiodiffusions et Télévisions Nationales d'Afrique, Union of National Radio and Television Organisations of Africa, Union der Nationalen Rundfunk- und Fernsehorganisationen Afrikas
URSI	Union Radio Scientifique Internationale, International Scientific Radio Union, Internationale Wissenschaftliche Radio-Union
USIA	United States Information Agency (US)
V-	Vertikal- (in Zus.)
VCS	very close shot
VCU	variable correction unit
VDR	voltage dependent resistor
VF	video frequency Videofrequenz
VFR	video film recording
VHF	very high frequency
VLF	very low frequency
VLS	very long shot
VOK	The Voice of Kenya (EAK)
VTR	video tape recorder video tape recording
VTVM	vacuum-tube voltmeter
VU	volume unit
VZ	La Voix de Zaïre (CGO)
WDR	Westdeutscher Rundfunk (D)
WT	wireless telegraphy
YLE	Oy. Yleisradio (SF)
ZB	Zentralbatterieanschluß
ZD	Zentraldisposition
ZDF	Zweites Deutsches Fernsehen
ZF	Zwischenfrequenz

Dictionary of Radio and Television Terms

English - German

Fachwörterbuch Hörfunk und Fernsehen

Englisch - Deutsch

Lists of abbreviations used in this dictionary and in the general field of broadcasting will be found on pages XI and XIII respectively.

Im Wörterbuch verwendete Abkürzungen und fachsprachliche Abkürzungen siehe Seite XI und XIII.

A

A roll A-Rolle *f*; **~ side** (disc) A-Seite *f*
A and B printing A/B Kopierverfahren *n*
AB stereophonic recording process Stereoaufnahmeverfahren AB
A-battery *n* Heizbatterie *f*
aberration *n* Abweichung *f*, Abbildungsfehler *m*, Fehler *m*; ~ *n* (opt.) Streuung *f*; **chromatic ~** chromatischer Fehler
abrasion *n* Abrieb *m*
abrasive *n* (FP) Schleifmittel *n*
abridged version Kurzfassung *f*
absence of colour Farblosigkeit *f*
absorption *n* Absorption *f*; **~ coefficient** Absorptionsgrad *m*; **~ factor** Absorptionsgrad *m*; **~ rate** Aufnahmegeschwindigkeit *f*
abstract *n* Kurzfassung *f*; ~ *n* (script) Auszug *m*
AC *s.* alternating current
acceleration voltage Beschleunigungsspannung *f*
accelerator *n* Beschleuniger *m*
accentuate *v* anheben *v*
accentuation *n* Anhebung *f*
accept *v* (F, script) abnehmen *v*
acceptable contrast ratio (ACR) Kontrastumfang *m*
acceptance *n* (F, script) Abnahme *f*, Endabnahme *f*; **~ of production** Produktionsabnahme *f*; **~ of script** Buchabnahme *f*; **~ of story** Stoffzulassung *f*; **~ report** Abnahmebericht *m*, Abnahmeprotokoll *n*
acceptor circuit (filter) Saugkreis *m*
access *n* (EDP) Zugriff *m*; **~ time** Zugriffszeit *f*; **direct ~** wahlfreier Zugriff, direkter Zugriff; **immediate ~** Sofortzugriff *m*; **multiple ~** Vielfachzugriff *m*; **random ~** wahlfreier Zugriff, direkter Zugriff; **sequential ~** sequentieller Zugriff
accessories *n pl* Zubehör *n*
accessory equipment Zubehörgerät *n*; **~ instrument** Zusatzgerät *n*
accidental printing (F) Kopiereffekt *m*
accompaniment *n* (mus.) Begleitung *f*
accompanist *n* Begleitmusiker *m*
accounting *n* Rechnungswesen *n*; **~ department** Abrechnungsstelle *f* **~ -machine operator** Maschinenbuchhalter *m*; **~ services** *n pl* Finanzbuchhaltung* *f*
accumulator cell Akkumulatorenzelle *f*
accuracy of return Wiederkehrgenauigkeit *f*
AC/DC equipment Allstromgerät *n*
achromatic *adj* achromatisch *adj*, farblos *adj*, unbunt *adj*; **~ locus** Unbuntbereich *m*; **~ region** Unbuntbereich *m*
achromatism *n* Farblosigkeit *f*
achromatopsy *n* Farbenblindheit *f*
acidity *n* Säuregrad *m*
acid-proof *adj* säurefest *adj*
acid-resisting *adj* säurefest *adj*
acknowledgement signal (sat.) Quittungssignal *n*
acoustic *n* Raumklang *m*; ~ *adj* akustisch *adj*; **~ baffle** Schallwand *f*; **~ brilliance** Raumhelligkeit *f*; **~ carpet** Geräuschteppich *m*; **~ coloration** Raumkulisse *f*; **~ energy** Schallenergie *f*; **~ field** Hörfeld *n*; **~ flat** Gesangsbox *f*, Instrumentalbox *f*; **~ frequency** Hörfrequenz *f*; **~ gramophone**

Trichtergrammofon *n*; ~ **horn** Schalltrichter *m*; ~ **oscillation** Schallschwingung *f*; ~ **output** Schalleistung *f*; ~ **pattern** Klangbild *n*; ~ **pick-up** akustischer Tonabnehmer; ~ **pressure** Schalldruck *m*; ~ **radiator** Schallstrahler *m*; ~ **screen** Schallschirm *m*; ~ **vibration** Schallschwingung *f*

acoustically dead schalltot *adj*

acoustics *n* Akustik *f*, Raumakustik *f*, Raumklang *m*

acquisition of rights Rechteerwerb *m*

act *v* spielen *v*; ~ *n* (thea.) Akt *m*

acting *n* Spiel *n*; ~ *adj* stellvertretend *adj*

action chart (EDP) Funktionsdiagramm *n*

actor *n* Darsteller *m*, Ausführender *m*, Schauspieler *m*, Mime *m* (fam.) **professional** ~ Berufsschauspieler *m*; **to feature an** ~ einen Darsteller herausstellen

actuate *v* betätigen *v*

acuity *n* (opt.) Schärfe *f*; ~ **of colour image** Farbauflösungsvermögen *n*

acuteness of hearing Hörschärfe *f*

acyclic process (EDP) azyklischer Vorgang

ad *n* (coll.) Reklame *f*

adapt *v* anpassen *v*; ~ *v* (script) bearbeiten *v*

adaptation *n* Adaption *f*; ~ *n* (script) Bearbeitung *f*; ~ **fee** Bearbeitungshonorar *n*

adapter *n* Adapter *m*, Umrüstteil *n*, Anpaßglied *n*; ~ *n* (EDP) Anpassungseinrichtung *f*; ~ **ring** Zwischenring *m*; ~ **socket** Umrüstbuchse *f*

adaption *n* Anpassung *f*; ~ *n* (elec.) Adaption *f*

adaptor *n* (script) Bearbeiter *m*

add *v* überblenden *v*

addendum *n* Zusatz *m*

addition *n* Zusatz *m*

additional programme Zusatzprogramm *n*

additive *adj* additiv *adj*

address *n* (EDP) Adresse *f*; ~ **code** Adressen-Code *m*; ~ **selection** Adressenansteuerung *f*, Adressenauswahl *f*; **indirect** ~ indirekte Adresse *f*; **second level** ~ indirekte Adresse *f*

adhesive cardboard Aufklebekarton *m*; ~ **tape** Lassoband *n*, Klebeband *n*

adjacent-channel *adj* kanalbenachbart *adj*

adjacent sound carrier Nachbartonträger *m*; ~ **sound channel rejector** Nachbartonfalle *f*; ~ **vision carrier** Nachbarbildträger *m*

adjust *v* einstellen *v*, justieren *v*, regeln *v*, regulieren *v*, richten *v*, verstellen *v*, abgleichen *v*; ~ *v* (col.) abstimmen *v*

adjusting *n* Richten *n*; ~ **wedge** Justierkeil *m*

adjustment *n* Einstellung *f*, Justierung *f*, Regelung *f*, Abgleichung *f*; ~ **for definition** (opt.) Scharfeinstellung *f*; ~ **of white balance** Weißtonregelung *f*; ~ **of white level** Weißwertregelung *f*

ad-libbing *n* Improvisierung *f*

administration *n* Verwaltung *f*

administrative council Verwaltungsrat *m*

admission tax (US) Vergnügungssteuer *f*

admittance *n* (elec.) komplexer Leitwert, Scheinleitwert *m*

admixture *n* Zumischung *f*

adult education Erwachsenenbildung *f*; ~ **education television programme** Studienfernsehen *n*

advance *n* Vorschuß *m*; ~ **of travel expenses** Reisekostenvorschuß *m*

~ sales *n pl* Vorverkauf *m*; **~ script** Vorabtext *m*; **~ showing** (F) Vorpremiere *f*; **~ time** Vorgabezeit *f*
adventure film Abenteuerfilm *m*
advertise *v* anzeigen *v*
advertisement *n* Reklame *f*
advertising *n* Anzeigenwerbung *f*, Reklame *f*, Werbung *f*; **~ block** Werbeblock *m*; **~ break** Werbeeinblendung *f*; **~ campaign** Werbekampagne *f*; **~ consultant** Werbefachmann *m*; **~ medium** Werbeträger *m*; **~ revenue** Werbeeinnahmen *f pl*; **~ tariff** Einschaltpreis *m*; **brand ~** Markenwerbung *f*, Firmenwerbung *f*; **unfair comparative ~** Wettbewerbsverzerrung *f*
advisory council Beirat *m*
aerial *n* Antenne *f*; **~** *n* (radiator) Strahler *m*; **~ array** Antennengruppe *f*; **~ beam width** Richtkeulenöffnungswinkel *m*; **~ cable** Antennenkabel *n*; **~ change-over switch** Antennenumschalter *m*; **~ combining unit** Antennenweiche *f*; **~ connection box** Antennenanschlußdose *f*; **~ coupling** Antennenkopplung *f*, Antennenanpassung *f*; **~ coupling filter** Antennenanpassungsfilter *m*; **~ diplexer** Antennenweiche *f*; **~ distribution box** Antennenverteilerdose *f*; **~ down lead** Antennenniederführung *f*; **~ element** Antennenelement *n*; **~ equipment** Antennenanlage *f*; **~ feeder** Antennenkabel *n*, Antennenleitung *f*, Energieleitung *f*, Feeder *m*, Antennenzuleitung *f*; **~ gain** Antennengewinn *m*; **~ -image printer** optische Bank, Trickkopiermaschine *f*; **~ installation** Antennenanlage *f*; **~ junction box** Antennenabzweigdose *f*, Antennenanschlußdose *f*; **~ lead** Antennenleitung *f*; **~ lead-in** Antennenzuleitung *f*; **~ mast** (carrier) Antennenmast *m*; **~ matching** Antennenanpassung *f*; **~ matching filter** Antennenanpassungsfilter *m*; **~ outlet** Antennensteckdose *f*; **~ photograph** Luftaufnahme *f*; **~ plug** Antennenstecker *m*; **~ polar diagram** Antennendiagramm *n*; **~ pole** Antennenstandrohr *n*; **~ radiation pattern** Antennendiagramm *n*; **~ radiator** Antennenstrahler *m*; **~ rod** Antennenstab *m*; **~ socket** Antennensteckdose *f*; **~ spur box** Antennenabzweigdose *f*; **~ stack** Antennenebene *f*; **~ switch** Antennenumschalter *m*; **~ system** Antennenanlage *f*; **artificial ~** künstliche Antenne; **built-in ~** eingebaute Antenne; **buried ~** Erdantenne *f*; **collapsible ~** zusammenklappbare Antenne; **dummy ~** künstliche Antenne; **internal ~** Innenantenne *f*; **non-directional ~** ungerichtete Antenne; **omnidirectional ~** Rundempfangsantenne *f*, Rundstrahlantenne *f*, ungerichtete Antenne
afterglow *v* nachleuchten *v*; **~** *n* Nachleuchten *n*, Nachziehen *n*, Fahnenziehen *n*; **~ compensation** Nachleuchtkompensation *f*; **~ period** Nachleuchtdauer *f*
after-image *n* Nachleuchten *n*, Nachziehen *n*
afternoon programme Nachmittagsprogramm *n*
after-sales service Kundendienst *m*, Service *m*
aftertreatment *n* Nachbearbeitung *f*
agency *n* Agentur *f*; **~ coverage** Agenturberichterstattung *f*; **~ report** Agenturbericht *m*;

~ **reporting** Agenturberichterstattung *f*; ~ **story** Agenturbericht *m*
agent *n* (chem.) Mittel *n*
aging *n* Alterung *f*
agitator *n* (FP) Rührwerk *n*
agreement *n* Vertrag *m*
agricultural programmes* *n pl* Landfunk* *m*
aim *v* (cam.) einstellen *v*
air *n* Luft *f*; ~ **circulation** Luftumwälzung *f*; ~ **filter** Luftfilter *m*; ~ **intake** Luftansauger *m*, Zuluft *f*; ~ **supply** Zuluft *f*; ~ **time** Sendezeit *f*; ~ **trimmer** Lufttrimmer *m*; **to be off the** ~ (transmitter) außer Betrieb sein; **to be on the** ~ auf Sendung sein; **to be on the** ~ (transmitter) in Betrieb sein; **to come on the** ~ auf Sendung gehen, auf Sendung schalten, zu senden beginnen; **to go off the** ~ zu senden aufhören; **to go on the** ~ auf Sendung gehen, auf Sendung schalten, zu senden beginnen; **to put on the** ~ durch Rundfunk übertragen; **to put on the** ~ Sendung fahren; **to stay on the** ~ auf Sendung bleiben
airborne link Luftverbindung *f*
air-conditioning *n* Klimatechnik *f*; ~ *n* Klimatisierung *f*; ~ **engineer** Klimatechniker *m*; ~ **plant** Klimaanlage *f*
alarm message (EDP) Fehlermeldung *f*; ~ **signal input device** (EDP) Alarmeingabe *f*; **dynamic** ~ **signal input device** (EDP) dynamische Alarmeingabe; **static** ~ **signal input device** (EDP) statische Alarmeingabe
album *n* (disc) Kassette *f*
align *v* justieren *v*, abgleichen *v*
alignment *n* Justierung *f*, Abgleichung *f*; ~ **of heads** Einmessen der Köpfe, Kopfeinmessen *n*; **out of** ~ dejustiert *adj*
alkali *n* Alkali *n*
Allen-type wrench Inbusschlüssel *m*
alligator clip Alligatorklammer *f*, Alligatorklemme *f*, Krokodilklammer *f*, Krokodilklemme *f*
all-in *adj* pauschal *adj*; ~ **fee** Pauschalgage *f*, Pauschalhonorar *n*; ~ **figure** Pauschale *f*; **payment of** ~ **fee** Pauschalierung *f*
all-inclusive *adj* pauschal *adj*
allocation *n* Zuordnung *f*; ~ **of production facilities** Produktionsmittelbereitstellung *f*; ~ **sheet** Zuteilungsblatt *n*
allowances *n pl* Spesen *plt*
all-rights fee Pauschalgage *f*, Pauschalhonorar *n*
all-weather lamp Allwetterlampe *f*; ~ **protection** Allwetterschutz *m*
alphameric *s.* alphanumeric
alphanumeric *adj* (EDP) alphanumerisch *adj*, alphamerisch *adj*
alter *v* (saturation) abstufen *v*
alternately *adv* wechselweise *adv*
alternating current (AC) Wechselstrom *m*; ~ **current erase head** Wechselstromlöschkopf *m*; ~ **current magnetic biasing** Wechselstromvormagnetisierung *f* ~ **current motor** Wechselstrommotor *m*; ~ **current power** Wechselstromleistung *f*; ~ **current resistance** Wechselstromwiderstand *m*; ~ **current supply filter** Netzverdrosselung *f*; ~ **current supply operation** Netzspeisung *f*; ~ **current voltage** Wechselspannung *f*; ~ **current voltage regulator** Netzspannungsgleichhalter *m*; ~ **current voltage stabiliser** Netzspannungsgleichhalter *m*; ~ **voltage** Wechselspannung *f*

alternator *n* Zerhacker *m*
amateur actor Laienschauspieler *m* **~ band** Amateurband *f*; **~ cinematographer** Filmamateur *m*; **~ film** Amateurfilm *m*; **~ filmmaker** Filmamateur *m*; **~ frequency band** Amateurband *n*; **~ sound recordist** Tonjäger *m*
ambience *n* Raumkulisse *f*
ambient brightness Umfeldhelligkeit *f*; **~ field** Umfeld *n*; **~ light** Umlicht *n*; **~ lighting** Raumbeleuchtung *f*; **~ noise** Nebengeräusch *n*; **~ sound** Begleitton *m*; **~ temperature** Raumtemperatur *f*
amendment sheet Änderungsblatt *n*
ammeter *n* Strommesser *m*
ampex *n* (coll.) Magnetbildaufzeichnungsanlage *f*
amplification *n* Verstärkung *f*; **~ factor** Verstärkungsfaktor *m*; **~ stage** Verstärkungsstufe *f*; **selective ~** selektive Verstärkung
amplifier *n* Verstärker *m*; **~ bay** Verstärkergestell *n*; **~ chain** Verstärkerzug *m*; **~ data** Verstärkerdaten *n pl*; **~ room** Verstärkerzentrale *f*; **~ tube** Verstärkerröhre *f*; **~ valve** Verstärkerröhre *f*; **~ with regeneration** rückgekoppelter Verstärker; **carrier-frequency ~** trägerfrequenter Verstärker; **differential ~** Differenzverstärker *m*; **differentiating ~** Differenzierverstärker *m*; **feedback ~** gegengekoppelter Verstärker, rückgekoppelter Verstärker; **negative-feedback ~** gegengekoppelter Verstärker; **parametric ~** parametrischer Verstärker
amplify *v* (elec.) verstärken *v*
amplitude *n* Amplitude *f*; **~ distortion** Amplitudenverzerrung *f*; **~ error** Amplitudenfehler *m*; **~ filter** Amplitudensieb *n*; **~ frequency characteristic** Amplituden-Frequenzgang *m*, Amplitudengang *m*, Frequenzgang *m*; **~ frequency response** Amplituden-Frequenzgang *m*, Amplitudengang *m*, Frequenzgang *m*: **overall ~ frequency response** Frequenzgang über alles; **~ limitation** Amplitudenbegrenzung *f*; **~ modulation (AM)** *n* (electronics) Amplitudenmodulation (AM) *f*; **~ modulator** Amplitudenmodulator *m*
analog input (EDP) Analogeingabe *f* **~ input device** (EDP) Analogeingabe *f*; **~ output** (EDP) Analogausgabe *f*; **~ output device** (EDP) Analogausgabe *f*; **~ signal** (EDP) analoges Signal
analog-to-digital converter (ADC) (EDP) Analog-Digital-Umsetzer (ADU) *m*
analyser *n* Abtaster *m*
analysis *n* Analyse *f*; **brief ~** (journ.) Kurzkommentar *m*
anamorphic *adj* anamorphotisch *adj*; **~ lens** Anamorphot *m*
anamorphosis *n* Anamorphose *f*
anastigmatic *adj* anastigmatisch *adj*; **~ lens** Anastigmat *m*
anastigmatism *n* Anastigmatismus *m*
anchor *v* verankern *v*; **~ man** Diskussionsleiter *m*, Gesprächsleiter *m*, Moderator *m*; **~ man** (news) Studioredakteur *m*
ancillary apparatus Zusatzgerät *n*; **~ unit** Zusatzgerät *n*
Ancor machine Titelschreiber *m*
AND circuit (EDP) UND-Gatter *n*, Koinzidenzgatter *n*; **~ element** (EDP) UND-Gatter *n*, Koinzidenzgatter *n*; **~ gate** (EDP)

UND-Gatter *n*, Koinzidenzgatter *n*; **~ operation** (EDP) UND-Verknüpfung *f*
anechoic *adj* schalltot *adj*
angle *n* Winkel *m*; **~** *n* (cable) Knick *m*; **~** *n* (opt.) Einstellung *f*; **~ of acceptance** Auffangwinkel *m*, Einfangwinkel *m*; **~ of dispersion** (lighting) Streuwinkel *m*; **~ of divergence** (scanning) Streuwinkel *m*; **~ of emergence** Austrittswinkel *m*; **~ of image** Bildwinkel *m*; **~ of incidence** Einfallswinkel *m*; **~ of inclination** Neigungswinkel *m*; **~ of pitch** Gewindesteigung *f*; **~ of scatter** (scanning) Streuwinkel *m*; **~ of spread** (scanning) Streuwinkel *m*; **~ of view** Blickwinkel *m*, Gesichtswinkel *m*; **~ piece** Winkelstück *n*; **~ plate** Winkelstück *n*; **fixed ~** feste Einstellung; **maximum ~ of dispersion** maximaler Streuwinkel; **to find a new ~** (coll.) aufmöbeln *v*
angular field of lens Bildwinkel *m*
anhydrous *adj* wasserfrei *adj*
animated caption Trickgrafik *f*; **~ caption** (title) Tricktitel *m*; **~ cartoon** Zeichentrick *m*; **~ cartoon film** Zeichentrickfilm *m* **~ diagram** Zeichentrick *m*; **~ film** Trickfilm *m*; **~ intercut** (F) Trickeinblendung *f*; **~ puppet film** Puppentrickfilm *m*; **~ title** Tricktitel *m*
animation *n* Zeichentrick *m*, Trick; **~** *n* Trickfilm *m*; **~ board** Tricktisch *m*, Trickbank *f*; **~ camera trigger** Tricktaste *f*; **~ cameraman** Trickkameramann *m*; **~ department** Trickabteilung *f*; **~ desk** Trickpult *n*; **~ mixer** Trickmischer *m*; **~ model** Trickmodell *n*; **~ motor** Einzelbildmotor *m*; **~ phase** Phasenbild *n*; **~ picture** Trickaufnahme *f*; **~ stand** Tricktisch *m*, Trickbank *f*; **~ studio** Trickstudio *n*; **~ superimposition** Tricküberblendung *f*; **cartoon ~** figürlicher Trick; **mechanical ~** mechanischer Trick; **suspended ~** Standbildverlängerung *f*, Standkopie *f*
animator *n* Phasenzeichner *m*, Trickzeichner *m*, Zeichner *m*
announce *v* anzeigen *v*; **~** *v* (R, TV) ansagen *v*
announcement *n* Mitteilung *f*, Verlautbarung *f*, Durchsage *f*; **~** *n* (R, TV) Ansage *f*
announcer *n* Ansager *m*, Rundfunksprecher *m*, Sprecher *m* **~ booth** Ansagestudio *n*; **~ studio** Ansagestudio *n*
annular magnet Ringmagnet *m*; **~ nut** Ringmutter *f*
anode *n* Anode *f*; **~ battery** Anodenbatterie *f*; **~ bend detector** Anodengleichrichter *m*; **~ circuit tuning** Anodenkreisabstimmung *f* **~ current** Anodenstrom *m*; **~ detector** Anodengleichrichter *m*; **~ load resistance** (tube) Außenwiderstand *m*; **~ modulation** Anodenmodulation *f*; **~ tuning** Anodenkreisabstimmung *f*; **~ voltage** Anodenspannung *f*; **~ voltage-current characteristic** Anodenspannungsdiagramm *n*
anode to-grid capacitance Gitteranodenkapazität *f*
anodised *adj* eloxiert *adj*
answer print Erstkopie *f*, erste Kopie, Schnittkopie *f*; **first ~ print** erste Schnittkopie; **second ~ print** zweite Schnittkopie
answering machine (tel.) Telefonbeantworter *m*, Telefonrufbeantworter *m*

antenna *n* (US) Antenne *f*; ~ *n* (US) (radiator) Strahler *m*
anthology of radio plays Hörspielbuch *n*
anti-clockwise *adj and adv* gegen den Uhrzeigersinn
anti-halation *n* Lichthofschutz *m*; ~ *adj* lichthoffrei *adj*; ~ **backing** Lichthofschutzschicht *f*; ~ **layer** Lichthofschutzschicht *f*
anti-halo *adj* lichthoffrei *adj*
anti-hum potentiometer Entbrummer *m*
anti-interference *n* Entstörung *f*
anti-jamming *n* Entstörung *f*
antinode *n* Spannungsbauch *m*, Wellenbauch *m*
antiphase *n* Gegenphase *f*; ~ **feedback** Gegenkopplung *f*
anti-scratch treatment (F) Drop-out-Unterdrückung *f*
anti-static device Feuchtabtastung *f* ~ **treatment** Feuchtabtastung *f*
aperiodic *adj* aperiodisch *adj*
aperture *n* (opt.) Blende *f*, Blendenöffnung *f*, Öffnung *f*; ~ **angle** Öffnungswinkel *m*; ~ **correction** Aperturkorrektur *f*; ~ **defect** Öffnungsfehler *m*; ~ **error** Öffnungsfehler *m*; ~ **number** Öffnungszahl *f*; ~ **of diaphragm** Blendenöffnung *f*; ~ **plate** Bildfensterplatte *f*; ~ **ratio** Öffnungsverhältnis *n*, relative Öffnung; ~ **setting** Blendeneinstellung *f*; ~ **time** Öffnungszeit *f*; **critical** ~ kritische Blende; **geometric** ~ geometrische Blende; **maximum** ~ maximale Öffnung; **photometric** ~ fotometrische Blende; **relative** ~ relative Öffnung; **to close** ~ Blende schließen; **to open** ~ Blende öffnen
apogee *n* Apogäum *n*, Fernpunkt *m*
apparatus *n* Gerät *n*, Apparat *m*; ~ **room** Geräteraum *m*; ~ **workshop** Gerätewerkstatt *f*
apparent power Scheinleistung *f*
appear *v* (perf.) auftreten *v*
appearance *n* Auftritt *m*
appliance *n* Apparat *m*, Gerät *n*
application for travel allowances Reisekostenantrag *m*; ~ **for travel authorisation** Dienstreiseantrag *m*
approval of production budget Produktionsbewilligung *f*; ~ **of rough cut** Rohschnittabnahme *f*
apron *n* (thea.) Schürze *f*
arc *n* Bogenlampe *f*, HI-Scheinwerfer (HI) *m*, Lichtbogen *m*; ~ **feeding** Kohlenlampennachschub *m*; ~ **lamp** Lichtbogenlampe *f*, Kohlenlampe *f*; ~ **-over** *n* Überschlag *m*
architectural and civil-engineering department Bauabteilung *f*
archives *n pl* Archiv *n*
archivist *n* Archivar *m*
area *n* Bereich *m*, Raum *m*, Zone *f*; ~ *n* (prog.) Ressort *n*, Sparte *f*; ~ *n* Zone *f*; ~ **coverage** (US) regionale Berichterstattung; ~ **covered** Sendebereich *m*, Sendegebiet *n*, Anstaltsbereich *m*; ~ **news** (US) Regionalnachrichten *f pl*; ~ **served** Sendebereich *m*, Sendegebiet *n*, Anstaltsbereich *m*
arithmetic and logical unit (ALU) (EDP) Rechen- und Leitwerk *n*; ~ **unit** (EDP) Rechenwerk *n*
arrange *v* (mus.) bearbeiten *v*; ~ *v* (book) einrichten *v*
arrangement *n* Arrangement *n*; ~ *n* (mus.) Bearbeitung *f*; **technical** ~ technische Disposition, technische Planung
arranger *n* Arrangeur *m*; ~ *n* (mus.) Bearbeiter *m*
arranging fee (mus.) Bearbeitungshonorar *n*
arrival angle Einfallswinkel *m*
art and literary critic

Kulturkritiker *m*; **~ board** Titelkarton *m*, Zeichenkarton *m*; **~ cinema** Filmkunsttheater *n*; **~ direction** (credits) Bühnenbild *n*, Bauten *m pl*; **~ director** Bühnenbildner *m*, Szenenbildner *m*, Filmarchitekt *m*; **~ house** (US) Filmkunsttheater *n*; **~ supervision** künstlerische Oberleitung

article *n* Artikel *m*, Aufsatz *m*

articulated arm (lighting) Gelenkarm *m*

artificial *adj* künstlich *adj*; **~ light** Kunstlicht *n*; **~ light filter** Kunstlichtfilter *m*; **~ reverberation device** Echomaschine *f*

artist *n* Darsteller *m*, Künstler *m*; **performing ~** ausübender Künstler; **professional ~** ausübender Künstler

artistic *adj* künstlerisch *adj*; **~ programme** Nummernprogramm *n*

artists' bookings Besetzungsbüro *n*

artist's contract Honorarvertrag *m*

artists' contracts* Honorarabteilung *f*

artist's dressing-room Künstlergarderobe *f*, Darstellergarderobe *f*

artists' fees Darstellergagen *f pl*; **~ foyer** Künstlerfoyer *n*, Künstlerzimmer *n*; **~ index** Besetzungskartei *f*

arts feature Kulturbericht *m*; **~ features*** *n pl* Kultur* *f*; **~ features editor** Kulturredakteur *m*; **~ item** Kulturbericht *m*; **~ review** Kulturkritik *f*

asbestos *n* Asbest *m*

aspect ratio (AR) Bildformat *n*, Bildseitenverhältnis *n*, Filmformat *n*, Format *n*, Größe *f*

assemble *v* montieren *v*; **~** *v* (F) zusammenschneiden *v*

assembly *n* Aufbau *m*; **~** *n* (batch) Satz *m*; **~** *n* (editing) Vormontage *f*, Rohschnitt *m*, Schnittrolle *f*; **~ programme** (EDP) Assembler *m*; **~ routine** (EDP) Assembler *m*

assign *v* (journ.) ansetzen *v*

assignment *n* (journ.) Auftrag *m*; **~ sheet** Projektauftrag *m*

assistance *n* Hilfeleistung *f*

assistant *n* Assistent *m*; **~** *adj* stellvertretend *adj*; **~ cameraman** Kameraassistent *m*; **~ director (AD)** Regieassistent *m*; **~ editor** (news) leitender Redakteur; **~ film editor** Cutterassistent *m*

associate *n* Mitarbeiter *m*

astigmatism *n* Astigmatismus *m*

asynchronism *n* Asynchronität *f*

asynchronous *adj* asynchron *adj*; **~ working** (EDP) Asynchronbetrieb *m*

atmosphere *n* Atmosphäre *f*, Atmo *f* (fam.), Grundton *m*, Nebengeräusch *n*; **~ noise** Geräuschatmosphäre *f*

atmospherics *n pl* atmosphärische Störung, Rauschen *n*

attachment *n* (staff) Zuordnung *f*; **~** *n* (appar.) Zusatzgerät *n*; **~ lens** Vorsatzlinse *f*

attachments *n pl* Zubehör *n*

attack time Ansprechzeit *f*; **~ time** (ampl.) Anstiegzeit *f*

attendance *n* (thea.) Besuch *m*

attenuate *v* abschwächen *v*, dämpfen *v*

attenuation *n* Abschwächung *f*, Dämpfung *f*; **~ as a function of frequency** Frequenzgangabsenkung *f*; **~ equaliser** Dämpfungsentzerrer *m*; **~ loss** Dämpfungsverlust *m*; **~ of erasure** Löschdämpfung *f*

attenuator *n* Abschwächer *m*, Dämpfungsglied *n*; **~ circuit** Dämpfungskreis *m*; **~ pad** Dämpfungsglied *n*; **~ resistance** Dämpfungswiderstand *m*; **calibrated ~** geeichter Abschwächer

audibility *n* Hörbarkeit *f*, Verständigung *f*; ~ **range** Hörbereich *m*; ~ **threshold** Hörschwelle *f*

audible *adj* hörbar *adj*; ~ **calling signal** Rufsignal *n*; ~ **frequency** Hörfrequenz *f*, Niederfrequenz (NF) *f*

audience *n* Hörergemeinde *f*, Hörerschaft *f*, Zuhörerschaft *f*, Publikum *n*; ~ *n* Besuch *m*; ~ **fall-off** Besucherrückgang *m*; ~ **figure** Hörerzahl *f*; ~ **microphone** Geräuschmikrofon *n*; ~ **-puller** *n* (coll.) Zugnummer *f*, Knüller *m* (fam.), Lokomotive *f* (fam.); ~ **rating** Zuschauermessung *f*, Teilnehmermessung *f*; ~ **rating** (figure) Einschaltquote *f*, Hörbeteiligung *f*; ~ **research** (R) Hörerforschung *f*; ~ **research*** (TV) Zuschauerbefragung* *f*, Zuschauerforschung* *f*; ~ **research survey** (R) Hörerbefragung *f*; (TV) Zuschauerbefragung *f*; ~ **studio** Unterhaltungsstudio *n*, Sendesaal *m*; ~ **survey** (R) Höreranalyse *f*, Hörerbefragung *f*; ~ **survey** (TV) Zuschauerbefragung *f*; **size of** ~ Zuschauerzahl *f* (TV), Hörerzahl *f* (R)

audio *n* Niederfrequenz (NF) *f*; ~ **circuit** Tonleitung *f*; ~ **disc** Tonplatte *f*; ~ **engineer** Toningenieur *m*; ~ **engineering** Tontechnik *f*; ~ **frequency (AF)** Hörfrequenz *f*, Niederfrequenz *f* (NF), Tonfrequenz *f*; ~ **-frequency amplifier** Niederfrequenzverstärker *m*; ~ **-frequency level** Niederfrequenzpegel *m*; ~ **-frequency peak limiter** Tonfrequenzspitzenbegrenzer *m*; ~ **-frequency protection ratio** Niederfrequenzschutzabstand *m*; ~ **-frequency range** Hörfrequenzbereich *m*; ~ **-frequency signal** Niederfrequenzsignal *n*; ~ **-frequency signal generator** Tongenerator *m*; ~ **-frequency signal-to-interference ratio** Niederfrequenzstörabstand *m*; ~ **-frequency transformer** Niederfrequenztransformator *m*, Übertrager *m*; ~ **-frequency variation factor** Tonfrequenzschwankungsfaktor *m*; ~ **information** Toninformation *f*; ~ **interference** Tonstörung *f*; ~ **oscillator** Tongenerator *m*; ~ **range** Hörfrequenzbereich *m*; ~ **record** Tonplatte *f*; ~ **signal** Niederfrequenzsignal *n*; ~ **tape** Tonband *n*

audio-visual (AV) *adj* audio-visuell (AV) *adj*, optisch-akustisch *adj*, Bild-Ton- (in Zus.)

audit *n* Revision *f*

audition *v* (part) vorsprechen *v*; ~ *n* Vorsprechen *n*

auditioning *n* Vorsprechen *n*

auditor *n* Rechnungsprüfer *m*, Revisor *m*

auditorium *n* Hörsaal *m*; ~ **noise** Saalgeräusch *n*

auditory acuity Hörschärfe *f*; ~ **impression** Höreindruck *m*; ~ **sensation area** Hörfeld *n*

aural sensitivity network (ASN) Ohrkurvenfilter *m*; ~ **threshold** Hörschwelle *f*

aurally compensated gehörrichtig *adj*

author *n* Autor *m*, Urheber *m*, Verfasser *m*

author's rights Autorenrechte *n pl*

auto changer automatischer Plattenwechsler; ~ **release** Selbstauslöser *m*

automatic chroma control Autochroma *n*; ~ **control system** Regelkreis *m*; ~ **cut-out** Sicherungsautomat *m*; ~ **frequency control (AFC)**

automatische Frequenznachsteuerung, automatische Scharfabstimmung; **~ gain control (AGC)** automatische Verstärkungsregelung; **~ interrupter** Sicherungsautomat *m*; **~ lacing** (proj.) Selbsteinfädelung *f*; **~ locking** Verriegelungsautomatik *f*; **~ noise-limiting (ANL)** automatische Störbegrenzung; **~ phase control (APC)** automatische Phasenregelung; **~ release** Selbstauslöser *m*; **~ sensitivity control (ASC)** automatische Empfindlichkeitsregelung; **~ switching** Schalterautomatik *f*; **~ switching gear** Schalterautomatik *f*; **~ voltage regulator (AVR)** Spannungskonstanthalter *m*; **~ volume control (AVC)** automatische Lautstärkeregelung (ALR)

automation *n* Automation *f*

automaton *n* Automat *m*

autotransformer *n* Autotransformator *m*, Spartransformator *m*

auxiliary channel Hilfskanal *m*; **~ code** (EDP) Hilfscode *m*; **~ equipment** Hilfsgerät *n*; **~ finder** Mehrfachsucher *m*; **~ lens** Zwischenabbildungsobjektiv *n*; **~ set** Hilfsgerät *n*; **~ transmitter** Hilfssender *m*

avalanche voltage Durchbruchspannung *f*

average value Mittelwert *m*

axis *n* (pl. axes) Achse *f*; **movement about the ~** Bewegung auf der Achse; **optical ~** optische Achse; **principal ~** optische Achse

azimuth *n* Breitenwinkel *m*; **~ loss** Spaltdämpfung infolge Schiefstellung

B

B roll B-Rolle *f*

baby-legs *n pl* Kleinstativ *n*

baby spot Babyspot *m*, Liliput *m*, Pipifax *m* (fam.), Schnipex *m* (fam.)

back *n* Rückwand *f*; **~ announcement** Programmabsage *f*; **~ contact** Ruhekontakt *m*; **~ cue** kurze Absage; **~ face** Rückwand *f*; **~ focal distance** Auflagemaß *n*; **~ indication** Rückmeldung *f*; **~ light** Gegenlicht *n*, Hinterlicht *n*; **~ lighting** Gegenlicht *n*; **~ of receiver** Abdeckblech *n*; **~ panel** Rückwand *f*; **~ projection (BP)** Rückprojektion *f*, Rückpro *f* (fam.), Durchprojektion *f*; **~ projection screen** Rückproschirm *m*; **~ projector** Rückprojektor *m*; **~ -type set** Tornistergerät *n*; **~ wall** Rückwand *f*; **to ~ off one colour** verschwärzlichen *v*

backcloth *n* Prospekt *m*; **painted ~** gemalter Prospekt

back-drop *n* Hintergrund *m*

background *n* Hintergrund *m*, Background *m*; **~ atmosphere** akustische Untermalung; **~ brightness** Grundhelligkeit *f*; **~ colour** Grundierfarbe *f*; **~ fog** Grundschleier *m*; **~ illumination** Hintergrundausleuchtung *f*; **~ light** Dekorationslicht *n*, Hintergrundlicht *n*; **~ lighting** Hintergrundausleuchtung *f*; **~ mood light** Hintergrundlicht *n*; **~ music** Hintergrundmusik *f*, musikalische Kulisse, untermalende Musik,

Untermalung *f*; **~ noise** Grundgeräusch *n*, Grundrauschen *n*, Grundton *m*, Rauschton *m*; **~ painter** Kunstmaler *m*; **~ processing** (EDP) Hintergrund-Verarbeitung *f*; **~ projection** (design) Hintergrundprojektion *f*; **~ projector** Hintergrundprojektor *m*; **~ research** Recherche *f*; **~ set** Hintergrunddekoration *f*; **~ sound effects** Geräuschkulisse *f*; **non-stop ~ music** Musikberieselung *f*

backing *n* Rückschicht *f*; **~** *n* (set) Hintergrunddekor *n*, Hintersetzer *m*, Rücksetzer *m*; **~ film** Filmträger *m*; **~ programme** Rahmenprogramm *n*; **~ singer** Refrainsänger *m*

back-track *n* Kamerafahrt rückwärts, Rückfahrt *f*

backward-acting regulation Rückwärtsregelung *f*

badge reader (EDP) Ausweisleser *m*

baffle *n* Schallwand *f*; **~** *n* (light) absorbierende Wand; **~ board** Schallwand *f*

bag *n* Koffer *m*

balance *v* ausgleichen *v*, symmetrieren *v*; **~** *v* (bridge) abgleichen *v*; **~** *n* Ausgleich *m*; **~ adjustment** Balanceregelung *f*; **~ out** *v* (meas.) entkoppeln *v*

balanced transformer Symmetrieübertrager *m*

balanced-to-unbalanced transformer Symmetrierglied *n*

balancing *n* Auswuchtung *f*, Ausgleich *m*; **~** *n* (bridge) Abgleichung *f*; **~ battery** Pufferbatterie *f*; **~ magnetic stripe** Magnetausgleichsspur *f*; **~ microphone** Kompensationsmikrofon *n*; **~ resistor** (bridge) Abgleichwiderstand *m*; **~ stripe** Magnetausgleichsspur *f*

balancing-out *n* Neutralisation *f*; **~** *n* (meas.) Entkopplung *f*

ball-and-socket joint Kugelgelenk *n*

ballast triode Ballasttriode *f*; **~ tube** Ballaströhre *f*

ball-bearing *n* Kugellager *n*

ballet company Ballettkorps *n*, Balletttruppe *f*

ballet-master *n* Ballettmeister *m*

balun *n* Symmetrierglied *n*

balustrade *n* Brüstung *f*

banana jack Bananenbuchse *f*; **~ plug** Bananenstecker *m*

band *n* Band *f*, Orchester *n*; **~** *n* (wave) Band *n*, Bereich *m*; **~** *n* (prog.) Leiste *f*; **~ aerial** Bereichsantenne *f*; **~ amplifier** Bereichsverstärker *m*; **~ diplexer** Bereichsweiche *f*; **~ pass** Bandfilter *m*, Bandpaß *m*, Bandpaßfilter *m*; **~ -pass filter** Bandfilter *m*, Bandpaß *m*, Bandpaßfilter *m*; **~ -rejection filter** Bandsperre *f*; **~ -stop filter** Bereichssperrkreis *m*, Bandsperre *f*; **magic ~ valve** magisches Band

bandmaster *n* Kapellmeister *m*

bandwidth *n* (freq.) Bandbreite *f*; **~ at 50 % down** Halbwertsbreite *f*; **critical ~** Frequenzgruppe *f*; **3-db ~** Halbwertsbreite *f*; **occupied ~** (transmitter) übertragenes Frequenzband

bank of lamps Flächenleuchte *f*

bar *n* Balken *m*, Stange *f*; **~ generator** Balkengeber *m*; **~ pattern** Strichrastertestbild *n*; **~ test pattern** Strichrastertestbild *n*; **~ tilt** (imp.) Dachschräge *f*

barndoor *n* Lichtblende *f*, Blende *f*, Tor *n*, Torblende *f*, Scheuklappe *f* (fam.), Scheunentor *n* (fam.)

barrel *n* Stange *f*; **~ shutter** Trommelblende *f*

barrel-shaped *adj* tonnenförmig *adj*

barretter *n* (US) Kaltleiter *m*

barrier layer Sperrschicht *f*

barrier-layer cell Sperrschichtzelle *f*; **~ photocell** Sperrschichtzelle *f*

base *n* Basis *f*, Sockel *m*. Untergestell *n*; ~ *n* (aerial) Fußpunkt *m*; ~ *n* (F, tape) Schichtträger *m*, Trager *m*, Tonträger *m*; ~ **feed** Fußpunkteinspeisung *f*; ~ **-feeding** *n* Basiseinspeisung *f* ~ **impedance** Fußpunktwiderstand *m*; ~ **light** Grundlicht *n*; ~ **-light intensity** Grundleuchtdichte *f* ~ **material** Schichtträger *m*; ~ **of a bay** Rahmenträgeruntergestell *n*; ~ **plate** Bodenplatte *f*; ~ **side** (F) Blankseite *f*, Schichtträgerseite *f*, Trägerseite *f*; ~ **veil** Grundschleier *m*; **earthed ~** geerdeter Fußpunkt; **insulated ~** isolierter Fußpunkt; **to be away from ~** Außendienst haben

basic circuit diagram Prinzipschaltbild *n*, Prinzipschaltplan *m*; ~ **fee** Grundgage *f*; ~ **signals** Signalaufbauimpulse *m pl*; ~ **unit** Grundeinheit *f*

bass *n* Tiefen *f pl*; ~ *n* Tiefton *m*; ~ **boost** Baßanhebung *f*, Tiefenanhebung *f*; ~ **control** Baßregelung *f*; ~ **cut** Tiefenabschwächung *f*, Tiefensperre *f*; ~ **lift** Tiefenanhebung *f*; ~ **loudspeaker** Tieftonlautsprecher *m*; ~ **notes** Tiefen *f pl*; ~ **roll-off** Tiefenabschwächung *f*

batch *n* Satz *m*; ~ *n* (F) Charge *f*; ~ **number** (stock) Chargennummer *f*; ~ **processing** (EDP) Stapelverarbeitung *f*

bath *n* (F) Bad *n*; **it's in the ~** (coll.) der Film schwimmt; **to prepare a ~** (F) Bad ansetzen

batten *n* Latte *f*

battery *n* Batterie *f*; ~ **attendant** Batteriewart *m*; ~ **charger** Batterieladegerät *n*; ~ **lamp** Batterieleuchte *f*; ~ **light** Batterieleuchte *f*; ~ **-operated device** Batteriegerät *n*; ~ **operation** Batteriebetrieb *m*, Batteriespeisung *f*; ~ **room** Akkuraum *m*; ~ **service** Batteriedienst *m*, Batteriewartung *f*; ~ **tape recorder** Batterietonbandgerät *n*

bay *n* Rahmengestell *n*, Rahmenträger *m*; ~ **support** Rahmenträger *m*

bayonet cap (BC) (tube) Bajonettsockel *m*; ~ **connection** Bajonettverschluß *m*; ~ **fitting** Bajonettfassung *f*; ~ **socket** Bajonettsockel *m*

be, to ~ on (perf.) dran sein (fam.); **to ~ on a story** (journ.) dran sein (fam.)

beacon *n* Beleuchtungsfeuer *n*; ~ **frequency** (sat.) Bakenfrequenz *f*

beaded screen Perlleinwand *f*

beam *v* (to)ausstrahlen *v* (nach); ~ *v* richten *v* (auf); ~ *n* Strahl *m*; *n* (set) Träger *m*; ~ **aerial** Richtantenne *f*, Richtfunkantenne *f*, Richtstrahlantenne *f*; ~ **alignment** Strahlausrichtung *f*; ~ **convergence** Strahldeckung *f*; ~ **current** Strahlstrom *m*; ~ **-current adjustment** Strahlstromjustierung *f*; ~ **-current blanking** Strahlstromaustastung *f*; ~ **-current control** Strahlstromsteller *m*; ~ **-current focusing** Strahlstrombündelung *f*; ~ **-current limiting** Strahlstrombegrenzung *f*; ~ **-current noise** Strahlstromrauschen *n*; ~ **deflection** Strahlablenkung *f*; ~ **direction** Strahlungsrichtung *f*; ~ **focus** Strahlschärfe *f*; ~ **gate** Strahlstromsperre *f*, Strahlunterdrückung *f*; ~ **splitter** Strahlenteiler *m*; **optical ~ splitter** optischer

Strahlenteiler;
~ **splitting** Strahlenteilung *f*;
~ **wobble** Strahlwobbeln *n*; **coarse control of ~ current** Strahlstrom IK grob; **fine control of ~ current** Strahlstrom IK fein; **focused ~** gebündelter Lichtstrahl; **scattered ~** gestreuter Lichtstrahl
beamwidth *n* Strahlbreite *f*
beard line Bartschatten *m*
bearing *n* Peilung *f*, Anpeilung *f*; ~ *n* (tech.) Lager *n*; ~ **casing** Lagergehäuse *n*; **to take a ~ on** anpeilen *v*
beat *n* Takt *m*; ~ *n* Interferenz *f*; ~ *n* Schwebung *f*; ~ *n* (US) Ressort *n*;
~ **frequency** Mischfrequenz *f*, Schwebungsfrequenz *f*;
~ **frequency oscillator** Überlagerer *m*; ~ **note** Differenzton *m*;
~ **oscillator** Überlagerer *m*
beating *n* (freq.) Überlagerung *f*
begin, to ~ the interiors ins Atelier gehen
bellows *n* Balgen *m*
belt *n* Gurt *m*
bench camera Trickkamera *f*; **optical ~** optische Bank
bend *v* knicken *v*; ~ *n* Krümmung *f*; ~ *n* Knick *m*
bevel gear Kegelrad *n*; ~ **pinion** Kegelrad *n*; ~ **wheel** Kegelrad *n*
bias *n* Gitterspannung *f*, Arbeitspunkt *m*; ~ **current** Vormagnetisierungsstrom *m*
bifilar *adj* bifilar *adj*
bifurcation *n* Abzweigung *f*; ~ **box** Verzweigungsdose *f*; ~ **stub** Stichleitungsabzweigung *f*;
~ **system** Verzweigungssystem *n*
big close shot (BCS) ganz groß, ganz nah; ~ **close-up (BCU)** ganz groß, ganz nah
bilateral *adj* bilateral *adj*
bill *v* terminieren *v*; ~ *n* Plakat *n*
billboard *n* (US) Ansage *f*
billed, to be auf dem Spielplan stehen
billing *n* Plakatanschlag *m*; ~ *n* (prog.) Programmanzeige *f*
bimetallic contact Bimetallkontakt *m*
binary *n* bistabiler Multivibrator; ~ *adj* (EDP) binär *adj*, dual *adj*;
~ **code** Binärcode *m*;
pure ~ code reiner Binärcode, reiner Dualcode;
~ **-coded address** binär codierte Adresse; ~ **-coded decimal notation** BCD-Darstellung *f*; ~ **-coded decimal representation** BCD-Darstellung *f*
~ **counter** Binärzähler *m*; ~ **digit** Binärstelle *f*, Binärziffer *f*, Bit *n*;
~ **number** Binärzahl *f*, Dualzahl *f*
binaural *adj* binaural *adj*
bipack *n* Bipack *n*
bipolar *adj* zweipolig *adj*
bird *n* (US) Satellit *m*
birdies *n pl* Zwitschern *n*
bird's-eye view Vogelperspektive *f*, Luftperspektive *f*
bistable *adj* (EDP) bistabil *adj*
bit *n* (EDP) Binärstelle *f*, Binärziffer *f*, Bit *n*; ~ **actor** Chargenspieler *m*, Charge *f*;
~ **configuration** (EDP) Binärmuster *n*; ~ **density** (EDP) Schreibdichte *f*, Zeichendichte *f*;
~ **pattern** (EDP) Binärmuster *n*;
~ **player** Kleindarsteller *m*; ~ **rate** (EDP) Impulsfolge *f*
bit-part actor Chargenspieler *m*, Charge *f*
bivibrator *n* bistabiler Multivibrator
black *n* Schwarz *n*; ~ *adj* schwarz *adj*; ~ **-crushing** *n* Schattenschwärzung *f*, Schatten *m*, Schwarzwertstauchung *f*;
~ **flashing** Schwarzblende ziehen;
~ **leader** Schwarzfilm *m*; ~ **level** Schwarzwert *m*, Schwarzpegel *m*;
~ **-level adjustment** Schwarzwertsteuerung *f*; ~ **-level clamping**

Schwarzschulterklemmung *f*, Schwarzwerthaltung *f*, Schwarzwertfesthaltung *f*; ~ **-level control** Schwarzwertsteller *m*, Schwarzwertregler *m* (fam.); ~ **-level signal voltage** Signalspannung für Szenenschwarz; ~ **non-linearity** Schwarzkrümmung *f*; ~ **out** *v* Schwarz ziehen, Schwarzblende ziehen; ~ **spacing** Blindfilm *m*, Schwarzfilm *m*; ~ **stretch** Schwarzdehnung *f*; ~ **stretch and white stretch** multiplikatives Gamma; **absolute** ~ reines Schwarz; **clear** ~ gesättigtes Schwarz; **fade to** ~ Schwarzblende *f*; **pure** ~ reines Schwarz; **to clip** ~ **level** Schwarzwert begrenzen; **to fade down to** ~ Schwarz ziehen, Schwarzblende ziehen; **to fade to** ~ Schwarz ziehen, Schwarzblende ziehen; **to go to** ~ Schwarzblende ziehen; **to set down** ~ **level** Schwarzwert aufsetzen, Schwarzpegel aufsetzen; **to set up** ~ **level** Schwarzwert absetzen, Schwarzpegel absetzen

black-and-white (B/W) *adj* schwarzweiß *adj*; ~ **film** Schwarzweißfilm *m*; ~ **negative film** Schwarzweißnegativfilm *m*; ~ **negative stock** Schwarzweißnegativfilm *m*; ~ **positive film** Schwarzweißpositivfilm *m*; ~ **positive stock** Schwarzweißpositivfilm *m*; ~ **print** Schwarzweißabzug *m*; ~ **production** Schwarzweißproduktion *f*; ~ **receiver** Schwarzweißempfänger *m*; ~ **reversal film** Schwarzweißumkehrfilm *m*; ~ **stock** Schwarzweißfilm *m*; ~ **stock** Schwarzweißumkehrfilm *m*; ~ **television** Schwarzweißfernsehen *n*

blacken *v* schwärzen *v*; ~ *v* verschwärzlichen *v*

blackening *n* Schwärzung *f*; ~ *n* Verschwärzlichung *f*

blacker than black ultraschwarz *adj*

blacking *n* Schwarzfilm *m*, Blindfilm *m*

black-out *n* Schwarzblende *f*; ~ *n* (US) Austastung *f*; ~ **level** (US) Austastniveau *n*; ~ **pulse** (US) Austastgemisch *n*; ~ **signal** (US) Austastsignal (A-Signal) *n*

black-to-white step Schwarzweißsprung *m*; ~ **transition** Schwarzweißsprung *m*

blade *n* (light) Blende *f*

blank *v* austasten *v*, zutasten *v*; ~ *n* Weiß *n*; ~ *adj* weiß *adj*; ~ **film** Weißfilm *m*, Blankfilm *m*; ~ **tape** Leerband *n*

blanked picture signal Bildaustastsignal (BA-Signal) *n*, Bildsignal mit Austastung

blanking *n* Austasten *n*, Austastung *f*, Rücklaufaustastung *f*, Schwarztastung *f*, Zutastung *f*; ~ **amplifier** Austastverstärker *m*; ~ **interval** Austastlücke *f*; ~ **level** Austastpegel *m*, Austastniveau *n*, Austastwert *m*; ~ **level stability** Austastpegelfesthaltung *f*; ~ **pulse** Austastimpuls (A-Impuls) *m*, Bildaustastimpuls *m*; ~ **signal** Austastsignal (A-Signal) *n*, Rücklaufsignal *n*; **field** ~ **pulse** Vertikalaustastimpuls *m*; **vertical** ~ **pulse** (US) Vertikalaustastimpuls *m*

blasting *n* (micr.) Übersteuerung *f*

bleach *v* (FP) ausbleichen *v*, bleichen *v*; ~ **bath** Bleichbad *n*; ~ **out** *v* (col.) ausbleichen *v*

bleaching *n* Bleichen *n*, Bleichung *f*

bleeder *n* Belastungswiderstand *m*;

~ **current** Nebenschlußstrom *m*
bleeper *n* Funkrufdienst *m*, Rufanlage *f*
blend *v* (pict.) mischen *v*; ~ **in** *v* überblenden *v*; ~ **out** *v* (F) abblenden *v*
blimp *n* Blimp *m*, schalldichte Hülle, Schallschutzhaube *f*
blimped camera selbstgeblimpte Kamera, Blimp-Kamera *f*
blind booking Blindbuchen *n*
blinker unit Blinkgeber *m*
blip *n* (tape) Kennimpuls *m*, Hilfssynchronsignal *n*, Piep(s)er *m* (fam.), Tonblitz *m*; ~ **generator** Synchronzeichengenerator *m*
block *v* (scene) durchstellen *v*; ~ **and tackle** Flaschenzug *m*; ~ **booking** Blockbuchen *n*; ~ **diagram** Blockdiagramm *n*, Blockschaltbild *n*, Blockschaltplan *m*
blocking *n* Sperrung *f*, Blockierung *f*; ~ **capacitor** Kopplungskondensator *m*; ~ **layer** Sperrschicht *f*; ~ **oscillator** Sperrschwinger *m*; ~ **signal** Sperrsignal *n*
bloom *n* Überstrahlung *f*
blooming *n* Antireflexbelag *m*, Blooming *n*
bloop *v* Klebestellen abdecken
blooping ink Klebestellenlack *m*; ~ **patch** Tonpopel *m*, Fliege *f* (fam.)
blow *v* durchbrennen *v*; ~ *v* durchschlagen *v*; ~ **up** *v* aufblasen *v*; ~ **up** *v* (pict.) vergrößern *v*
blower *n* Gebläse *n*; ~ *n* Windmaschine *f*
blown *adj* (fuse) durchgebrannt *adj*
blow-up *n* Vergrößerung *f*, Vergrößerungskopie *f*
blue screen Blaustanzverfahren *n*, Farbschablonentrick *m*, Stanztrick *m*
blueprint *n* (drawing) Pause *f*
blur *v* (pict.) verwackeln *v*
blurred *adj* (pict.) unscharf *adj*, weich *adj*; ~ **edges** *n pl* Randunschärfe *f*; **to grow** ~ (pict.) abschwächen *v* (sich)
blurring *n* Unschärfe *f*
board of governors Aufsichtsrat *m*; ~ **of management** Geschäftsleitung *f*
boat-truck *n* Bühnenwagen *m*
bobbin *n* Bobby *m*, Spule *f*, Spulenkörper *m*
body colour Körperfarbe *f*; **black** ~ schwarzer Körper
bolt *n* Sperriegel *m*; ~ *n* Bolzen *m*
bond *n* Sicherungsleine *f*
bonus *n* Zugabe *f*
book *v* bestellen *v*; ~ *v* (contract) engagieren *v*; ~ *n* (thea.) Textbuch *n*; ~ **programme** literarisches Magazin; ~ **review** Buchbesprechung *f*
booking section Besetzungsbüro *n*
book-keeper *n* Buchhalter *m*
Boolean algebra (EDP) Boolesche Algebra; ~ **complementation** (EDP) Inversion *f*; ~ **operation table** (EDP) Funktionstabelle *f*, Wertetabelle *f*, Wahrheitstabelle *f*
boom *n* Galgen *m*; ~ *n* (cam.) Kran *m*; ~ **arm** Tonangel *f*, Angel *f*; ~ **operator** Tonangler *m*; ~ **shadow** Galgenschatten *m*
boominess *n* Dröhnen *n*
booming *n* Schwenk *m*; ~ **drone** Dröhnen *n*
booming-down *n* Senkrechtschwenk nach unten, senkrechter Schwenk nach unten
booming-up *n* Senkrechtschwenk nach oben, senkrechter Schwenk nach oben
boost *v* (tech.) anheben *v*; ~ *n* (tech.) Anhebung *f*
booster light Zusatzlicht *n*; ~ **voltage** Boosterspannung *f*
booth *n* Kabine *f*; ~ **shutter** (F) Feuerschutzklappe *f*; ~ **window** Kabinenfenster *n*

border *n* (pict.) Kontur *f*; ~ *n* (light) Soffitte *f*; ~ *n* (cam.) Maske *f*; ~ **light** Rampenbegrenzungslicht *n*

bouncing *n* Pumpen *n*

bowl-fire *n* Heizsonne *f*

box *n* Kasten *m*, Koffer *m*; ~ *n* (coll.) (TV) Flimmerkiste *f* (fam.)

box-office hit Kassenschlager *m*, Schlager *m*

brace *n* Blendenstrebe *f*, Blendenstütze *f*

bracket *n* Halterung *f*; ~ *n* (set) Träger *m*

braking field Bremsfeld *n*; ~ **relay** Bremsrelais *n*

branch distributors *n pl* Verleihfiliale *f*

branching amplifier Verzweigungsverstärker *m*

branching-off *n* Abzweigung *f*

brand advertising Markenwerbung *f*, Firmenwerbung *f*

brass band Blasorchester *n*; ~ **band music** Blasmusik *f*

breadboard circuit (EDP) Brettschaltung *f*

break *v* abschalten *v*; ~ *v* (news) anfallen *v*; ~ *n* Unterbrechung *f*; ~ *n* (prog.) Pause *f*; ~ *n* (bcast.) beabsichtigte kurze Unterbrechung; ~ *n* (F) Riß *m*, Filmriß *m*; ~ **contact** Ruhekontakt *m*; ~ **in programme** (unintentional) Programmunterbrechung *f*; ~ **in programmes** (intentional) Programmunterbrechung *f*; ~ **in transmission** (prog.) Umschaltpause *f*; ~ **into** *v* unterbrechen *v*; ~ **jack** Trennklinke *f*; ~ **of current** Stromunterbrechung *f*; ~ **of picture sequence** Bildsprung *m*; ~ **off** *v* (oscillator) abreißen *v*; ~ **up** *v* (pict.) durchfallen *v*; **momentary** ~ kurzzeitige Unterbrechung; **to** ~ **down** eine Panne haben, durchschlagen *v*

breakdown *n* Ausfall *m*, Panne *f*, Betriebsstörung *f*, Störung *f*; ~ **voltage** Durchbruchspannung *f*, Durchschlagspannung *f*, Überschlagspannung *f*

breaker *n* Unterbrecher *m*

breaking capacity Schaltvermögen *n*

break-off time Abreißzeit *f*

breakpoint instruction (EDP) Stoppbefehl *m*

break-through *n* Störsignal *n*

breathe *v* (tech.) atmen *v*

breathing *n* (tech.) Atmen *n*, Pumpen *n*

bridge *n* Brücke *f*; ~ **across** *v* einschleifen *v*; ~ **circuit** Brückenschaltung *f*; ~ **-connected rectifier** Brückengleichrichter *m*; ~ **connection** Brückenschaltung *f*; ~ **network** Brückenglied *n*; ~ **rectifier** Brückengleichrichter *m*, Graetzgleichrichter *m*

bridging amplifier Knotenpunktverstärker *m*

bridging-type filter Durchschleiffilter *m*

brief analysis (journ.) Kurzkommentar *m*

bright spot Leuchtfleck *m*

brighten up *v* aufhellen *v*

brightness *n* (intensity) Leuchtdichte *f*, Beleuchtung *f*; ~ *n* (TV) Helligkeit *f*; ~ **contrast** Helligkeitskontrast *m*; ~ **control** Helligkeitssteuerung *f*; ~ **distribution** Helligkeitsverteilung *f*; ~ **flicker** Helligkeitsflimmern *n*; ~ **impression** Helligkeitseindruck *m*; ~ **meter** Leuchtdichtemesser *m* ~ **of image** Bildhelligkeit *f*; ~ **range** (TV) Helligkeitsbereich *m*, Helligkeitsumfang *m*; ~ **range of object** (light) Objektumfang *m*; ~ **signal** Helligkeitssignal *n*; ~ **step** Helligkeitssprung *m*; ~ **value**

Helligkeitswert *m*
brilliance *n* Brillanz *f*; ~ *n* (TV) Helligkeit *f*
bring in *v* (profit) einspielen *v*; ~ **up** *v* (sound, light) anheben *v*; **to ~ into step** synchronisieren *v*; **to ~ out a film** Film herausbringen
Bristo wrench Inbusschlüssel *m*
brittle *adj* spröde *adj*
brittleness *n* Sprödigkeit *f*
broad *n* (coll.) (light) Fläche *f*, Lichtwanne *f*; ~ **band** Breitband *n* ~ **source** Lichtwanne *f*; **flooded ~** geflutete Fläche
broadcast *v* senden *v*, ausstrahlen *v*, übertragen *v*, durch Rundfunk übertragen; ~ *v* (announcement, message) durchsagen *v*; ~ *n* (bcast.) Sendung *f*, Rundfunksendung *f*, Übertragung *f*; ~ **fee** Sendehonorar *n*; ~ **operations control** (US) (BOC) Endkontrolle *f* ~ **series** Sendereihe *f*; **deferred ~** zeitversetzte Sendung; **educational ~** Lehrsendung *f*; **joint ~ by ...** angeschlossen waren ...; **sponsored ~** Sponsorsendung *f*, gesponsorte Sendung; **to ~ live** direkt senden, live senden
broadcaster *n* Rundfunkschaffender *m*
broadcasters *n pl* Rundfunkleute *plt*, Fernsehleute *plt*
broadcasting *n* Rundfunk *m*; ~ *n* (tech.) Ausstrahlung *f*; ~ **act** Rundfunkgesetz *n*; ~ **archives** *n pl* Rundfunkarchiv *n*; ~ **area** Sendebereich *m*, Sendegebiet *n*, Anstaltsbereich *m*, Verbreitungsgebiet *n*; ~ **by satellite** Satellitenrundfunk *m*; ~ **centre** Rundfunkkomplex *m*, Sendekomplex *m*, Sendezentrum *n*; ~ **charter** Rundfunkstatut *n*; ~ **company** Rundfunkgesellschaft *f*, Rundfunksendegesellschaft *f*, Sendegesellschaft *f*; ~ **corporation** Rundfunkgesellschaft *f*, Sendegesellschaft *f*; ~ **engineer** Rundfunktechniker *m*; ~ **house** Funkhaus *n*, Rundfunkhaus *n*; ~ **network** Sendenetz *n*; ~ **operations** *n pl* Sendeabwicklung *f*; ~ **organisation** Rundfunkorganisation *f*, Rundfunkanstalt *f*, Rundfunkträger *m*, Sendeanstalt *f*, Sender *m*; ~ **rights** *n pl* Senderechte *n pl*; ~ **satellite** Rundfunksatellit *m*; ~ **-satellite service** Rundfunkdienst mit Satelliten; ~ **sector** Sendesparte *f*; ~ **service** Rundfunkversorgung *f*; ~ **station** Rundfunkanstalt *f*, Rundfunkstation *f*, Sendeanstalt *f*, Sendestation *f*, Sender *m*; ~ **studio** Senderaum *m*, Sendestudio *n*; ~ **time** Sendezeit *f*; ~ **transmitter** Rundfunksender *m*; **history of ~** Rundfunkgeschichte *f* **ready for ~** zur Sendung; **wired ~** Drahtfunk *m*
broadside *n* Streulichtscheinwerfer *m*; ~ **array** Dipolebene *f*
brochure *n* Prospekt *m*
brushes *n pl* Bürsten *f pl*
brush-holder *n* Bürstenhalter *m*
brut *n* (coll.) Brut *n*
BSS corresponds to DIN-Norm
bubbling *n* (tech.) Tonblubbern *n*, Blubbern *n*
buckle *v* knicken *v*; ~ *n* Tragöse *f*
buckling *n* (tape) Verziehen *n*
budget breakdown Kostenvoranschlag *m*; ~ **estimate** Kostenvoranschlag *m*
budgeting *n* Haushaltswesen* *n*; ~ *n* Mittelbewirtschaftung* *f*
buffer amplifier Trennverstärker *m*; ~ **battery** Pufferbatterie *f*; ~ **battery operation** Pufferbetrieb *m*; ~ **choke** Pufferdrossel *f*; ~ **operation** Pufferbetrieb *m*; ~ **store** (EDP) Pufferspeicher *m*,

Puffer *m*
buffered *adj* (EDP) gepuffert *adj*
build up *v* aufbauen *v*, errichten *v*
building team Baustab *m*, Baukolonne *f*
build-up *n* Einschwingen *n*; **~ and delay distortion** Verzerrung durch Ein- und Ausschwingvorgänge; **~ time** Anstiegzeit *f*, Einschwingzeit *f*
built background Hintergrundaufbauten *m pl*; **~ piece** (design) Baueinheit *f*; **~ set** Aufbauten *m pl*
built-in aerial eingebaute Antenne
bulb *n* Birne *f*; **~** *n* Röhrenkolben *m*
bulk-erase noise Raumstatik *f*
bulk eraser (tape) Löschdrossel *f*, Löschgerät *n*; **~ erasure cubicle** Bandlöschkabine *f*
buried aerial Erdantenne *f*
burn out *v* (FP) durchbrennen *v*
burnt-out *adj* (FP) durchgebrannt *adj*; **~** *adj* (coll.) (pict.) knallig weiß
burst keying pulse Burst-Auftastimpuls *m*
bus bar Schiene *f*, Verbindungsleiste *f*
bush *n* (mech.) Buchse *f*
business manager Filmmanager *m*
bust shot Halbnahe *f*
busy signal Besetztzeichen *n*
butt joiner Stumpfklebelade *f*, Stumpfklebepresse *f*
butt-join *n* (F) Aneinanderhängen *n*
button *n* Taste *f*
buying* *n* Einkauf* *m*
buzz *v* brummen *v*, summen *v*; **~** *n* Brumm *m*, Brummton *m*
buzzer *n* Brummer *m*, Summer *m*, Schnarre *f*
buzz-track film Lichttonwobbelfilm *m*
B/W production Schwarzweißproduktion *f*
by-pass *n* Nebenschluß *m*
byte *n* (EDP) Byte *n*

C

cabaret *n* Kabarett *n*; **~ group** Kabarettensemble *n*; **~ programme** Kabarettsendung *f*
cabin *n* Kabine *f*; **~ window** Kabinenfenster *n*
cabinet *n* (appar.) Truhe *f*; **~** *n* (loudspeaker) Zarge *f*
cable *n* Kabel *n*, Leitung *f*, Schnur *f*, Strecke *f* (fam.); **~ amplifier** Kabelverstärker *m*; **~ assembly** Kabelbaum *m*; **~ box** Kabelkasten *m*; **~ circuit** Kabelleitung *f*, Kabelverbindung *f*; **~ clamp** Kabelschelle *f*, Kabelhalterung *f*, Kabelbefestigung *f*; **~ clip** Kabelschelle *f*; **~ connecting box** (aerial) Kabelanschlußdose *f*; **~ connecting sleeve** Kabelverbindungsmuffe *f*; **~ connection** Kabelverbindung *f*; **~ contribution circuit** Kabelzubringerleitung *f*; **~ core** Kabelseele *f*, Kabelkern *m*; **~ deflector** Kabelabweiser *m*; **~ -delay equalisation** Kabellaufzeitausgleich *m*; **~ distribution box** Kabelverteilerkasten *m*; **~ distributor** Kabelverteiler *m*; **~ drum** Kabeltrommel *f*; **~ duct** Kabeldurchgang *m*, Kabelkanal *m*; **~ entry** Kabeleinführung *f*; **~ film** Kabelüberspielung *f*; **~ fixing** Kabelbefestigung *f*; **~ form** Kabelbaum *m*; **~ harness** Kabelbaum *m*; **~ head** Kabelkopf *m*; **~ jacket** Kabelmantel *m*; **~ joint** Kabelspleißstelle *f*, Verbindungsstelle *f*; **~ jointing box** Kabelanschlußkasten *m*, Kabelkasten *m*; **~ jointing cabinet** Kabelanschlußkasten *m*; **~ -laying**

n Kabelverlegung *f*; ~ **-length compensator** Kabellängenentzerrer *m*; ~ **-length equaliser** Kabellängenentzerrer *m*; ~ **link** Kabelbrücke *f*, Kabelverbindung *f* ~ **man** Kabelhilfe *f*; ~ **reel** Kabeltrommel *f*; ~ **release** Drahtauslöser *m*; ~ **run** Kabelweg *m*; ~ **serving** Kabelmantel *m*; ~ **sheath** Kabelmantel *m*, Kabelschlauch *m*; ~ **socket** Kabelschuh *m*; ~ **splice** Kabelspleißstelle *f*; ~ **-stripping knife** Kabelmesser *n*; ~ **support** Kabelhalter *m*; ~ **television** Kabelfernsehen *n*, Drahtfernsehen *n*; ~ **terminal plug** Kabelschuh *m*; ~ **termination** Kabelende *n*; ~ **thimble** Kabelschuh *m*; ~ **tray** Kabelhalter *m*; **coaxial** ~ konzentrisches Kabel; **connecting** ~ Verbindungskabel *n*; **four-core** ~ vieradriges Kabel; **three-core** ~ dreiadriges Kabel; **to lay** ~ Kabel verlegen; **two-core** ~ zweiadriges Kabel

cabled dispatch Kabelbericht *m*

cabling *n* Verkabelung *f*

cadence *n* Takt *m*

calculate *v* berechnen *v*

calculation *n* Berechnung *f*

calendar day Kalendertag *m*; ~ **week** Kalenderwoche *f*; ~ **year** Kalenderjahr *n*

calibrate *v* eichen *v*, kalibrieren *v*

calibrated attenuator geeichter Abschwächer; ~ **fader** geeichter Abschwächer

calibrating *n* Kalibrieren *n*

calibration *n* Eichung *f*, Kalibrieren *n*; ~ **accuracy** Abgleichgenauigkeit *f*; ~ **film** Meßfilm *m*; ~ **mark** Eichmarke *f*; ~ **resistor** (bridge) Abgleichwiderstand *m*; ~ **tape** Bezugsband *n*, Magnetbezugsband *n*; **logarithmic** ~ logarithmische Teilung; **photometric** ~ fotometrische Eichung

call *v* abrufen *v*

call-back signal Rückrufzeichen *n*

calling signal Rufsignal *n*

cam *n* Kontaktnase *f*, Schaltkerbe *f*

camera *n* Kamera *f*

camera! Achtung! Aufnahme!

camera accessories *n pl* Kamerazubehör *n*; ~ **alignment** (F) Kameraeinstellung *f*; ~ **amplifier** Kameraverstärker *m*; ~ **angle** Aufnahmewinkel *m*, Gesichtswinkel *m*; ~ **aperture** Bildfenster *n*; ~ **assistant** Kameraassistent *m*; ~ **axis** Kameraachse *f*; ~ **balancing** Auswiegen der Kamera; ~ **base-plate** Kameragrundplatte *f*; ~ **boom** Kamerakran *m*; ~ **boom arm** Kameraarm *m*; ~ **cable** Kamerakabel *n*; ~ **car** Filmwagen *m*, Kamerawagen *m*; ~ **card** Kameranotiz *f*; ~ **case** Kamerakoffer *m*; ~ **chain** Kamerakette *f*; ~ **channel** Kamerazug *m*; ~ **control** Kamerakontrolle *f*; ~ **control amplifier** Kamerakontrollverstärker *m*; ~ **control desk** Kamerakontrollschrank *m*; ~ **control operator** Bildoperateur *m*, Kamerakontrollbedienung *f*; ~ **control unit (CCU)** Kamerakontrollgerät (KKG) *n*; ~ **cover** Kameradeckel *m*; ~ **crane** Kamerakran *m*; ~ **crew** Filmtrupp *m*, Kamerateam *n*; ~ **cue-card** Kameranotiz *f*; ~ **cut** Bildwechsel *m*; ~ **days** Kameratage *m pl*; ~ **dolly** Dolly *m*, Kamerafahrgestell *n*; ~ **door** Kameradeckel *m*; ~ **equipment** Kameraausrüstung *f*, Aufnahmegerät *n*; ~ **fade** Kamerablende *f*; ~ **harness**

Schultertragriemen *m*; ~ **head** Kamerakopf *m*; ~ **heating** Kameraheizung *f*; ~ **housing** Kameragehäuse *n*; ~ **lead** Kamerakabel *n*; ~ **levelling** Auswiegen der Kamera; ~ **maintenance engineer** (TV) Kameratechniker *m*; ~ **maintenance man** (F) Kameratechniker *m*; ~ **matte** Blendenschablone *f*, Schablonenblende *f*; ~ **monitor** Kamerakontrollgerät (KKG) *n*; ~ **mounting** Kamerastand *m*; ~ **mounting-plate** Kameragrundplatte *f*; ~ **movement** Kamerabewegung *f*; ~ **notes** *n pl* Klappenliste *f*; ~ **objective** Aufnahmeobjektiv *n*; ~ **operations centre** Kamerazentralbedienung *f*; ~ **operator** Kameramann *m*, Filmkameramann *m*, erster Kameraassistent, Schwenker *m*; ~ **pan** Kameraschwenk *m*; ~ **panning** Kameraschwenk *m*; ~ **placing** (TV) Kameraeinstellung *f*; ~ **plug** Kamerastecker *m*; ~ **position** Kamerastandort *m*; ~ **pulse** Kamerasignal *n*; ~ **rehearsal** Kameraprobe *f*, Kamerastellprobe *f*; ~ **report** Kamerabericht *m*; ~ **running!** Kamera läuft!; ~ **script** (VTR) Kamerafahrplan *m*; ~ **script** Bildscript *n*, Kamerascript *n*; ~ **set-up** Kameraeinrichtung *f*; ~ **set-up** (position) Kamerastandort *m*; ~ **sheet** Aufnahmebericht *m*, Klappenliste *f*; ~ **shooting** Kameraaufnahme *f*; ~ **shot** Kameraaufnahme *f*; ~ **shutter** Kameraverschluß *m*; ~ **-shy** *adj* kamerascheu *adj*; ~ **signal** Kamerasignal *n*; ~ **signal control** Kamerasignalüberwachung *f*; ~ **speed** Aufnahmegeschwindigkeit *f*; ~ **stand** Kamerastand *m*; ~ **stock** (F) Aufnahmematerial *n*; ~ **store** Filmgerätestelle *f*, Kameraabstellraum *m*; ~ **tape** Lassoband *n*, Klebeband *n*; ~ **team** Kamerateam *n*; ~ **test** Prüfzeile für Kamera; ~ **test line** Kameraprüfzeile *f*; ~ **tracking** Kamerafahrt *f*; ~ **trap** Sprungwand *f*; ~ **tripod** Kamerastativ *n*, Schwenkstativ *n*; ~ **truck** Kamerawagen *m*, Kamerafahrgestell *n*; ~ **tube** Kameraröhre *f*, Aufnahmeröhre *f*, Bildaufnahmeröhre *f*; ~ **unit** Aufnahmegruppe *f*; ~ **weight adjustment** Auswiegen der Kamera, Kameragewichtsausgleich *m*; ~ **workshop** Kamerawerkstatt *f*; **blimped** ~ selbstgeblimpte Kamera, Blimp-Kamera *f*; **clear ~s!** (TV) Kamera klar!; **concealed** ~ versteckte Kamera; **electronic** ~ elektronische Kamera (E-Cam); **fine for** ~ **!** (positioning) für Kamera in Ordnung; **finished with ~s!** (TV) Kamera klar!; **fixed** ~ fest eingestellte Kamera; **motion-picture** ~ Filmkamera *f*; **mute** ~ stumme Kamera; **o.k. for** ~ **!** (F) Kamera klar!; **radio** ~ drahtlose Kamera; **remote-controlled** ~ ferngesteuerte Kamera; **rigid** ~ fest eingestellte Kamera; **to be on-** ~ im Bild sein; **to be on the** ~ Kamera fahren; **to hog the** ~ kamerageil sein (fam.); **to perform on-**~ vor der Kamera auftreten; **vertical** ~ senkrechte Kamera

cameraman *n* Filmkameramann *m*, Kameramann *m*; ~ *n* (press) Pressefotograf *m*; **second** ~ zweiter Kameraassistent, Schärfeassistent *m*, Schärfezieher *m*

cameramen *n pl* Kameraleute *plt*
camerawork *n* Kameraführung *f*
can *n* (coll.) Konserve *f* (fam.); **in the ~** ! gestorben! (fam.); **to be in the ~** im Kasten sein
canard *n* (false report) Ente *f*
canaries *n pl* Zwitschern *n*
cancel *v* abbestellen *v*, abmelden *v*, annullieren *v*, widerrufen *v*
cancellation fee Ausfallgage *f*
cancelled *adj* gestrichen *adj*; **to be ~** (prog.) ausfallen *v*
candle-power *n* Lichtstärke *f*
canned programme Programmkonserve *f*
cans *n pl* (coll.) Kopfhörer *m*, Hörer *m*
canteen *n* Kantine *f*
cantilever aerial Holmantenne *f*
cap *v* (opt.) abdecken *v*; **~** *n* Kappe *f*; **~** *n* (opt.) Abdeckung *f*
capable of being stored speicherfähig *adj*
capacitance *n* Kapazität *f*; **~ bridge** Kapazitätsmeßbrücke *f*; **~ calibration** Kapazitätseichung *f*; **~ diode** Kapazitätsdiode *f*, Kapazitätsvariationsdiode *f*, Nachstimmdiode *f*; **~ regulation** Kapazitätsregelung *f*
capacitive *adj* kapazitiv *adj*
capacitor *n* Kondensator *m*; **bead-type ~** Perlkondensator *m*; **disc ~** Scheibenkondensator *m*; **tubular ~** Rohrkondensator *m*
capacity *n* Leistungsfähigkeit *f*, Kapazität *f*
capstan *n* Bandtransportrolle *f*; **~ idler** Andruckrolle *f*; **~ motor** Tonmotor *m*
caption *n* Einblendtitel *m*, Titel *m*, Titelinsert *n*, Insert *n*; **~** *n* (subtitle) Bildunterschrift *f*, Untertitel *m*; **~** *n* (station identification) Kennung *f*, Kennzeichen *n*; **~ artist** Titelanfertiger *m*, Titelzeichner *m* **~ changer** Insertwechsler *m*; **~ desk** Insertpult *n*; **~ easel** Grafikständer *m*, Insertpult *n*; **~ generator** (video) Setzmaschine *f*; **~ insertion** Schrifteinblendung *f* **~ lettering** Titelschrift *f*; **~ mixer** Schrifteinblender *m*, Schriftsetzer *m*; **~ positioning** Schriftaustastung *f*; **~ scanner** Diaabtaster *m*, Insertabtaster *m*; **~ shooting** Titelaufnahme *f*; **~ stand** Grafikständer *m*, Insertpult *n*, Titelständer *m*; **~ superimposition** Schrifteinblendung *f*; **black-on-white ~** positiver Titel; **roller ~** Rolltitel *m*, rollender Ttiel; **static ~** unbeweglicher Titel; **to run ~s** Titel aufziehen; **white-on-black ~** negativer Titel
captions artist Schriftgrafiker *m*
car radio Autoempfänger *m*, Autoradio *n*
carbon arc Kohlenbogen *m*; **~ arc lamp** Kohlenlampe *f*; **~ brush** Kohlenbürste *f*; **~ electrode** Kohlenelektrode *f*; **~ lamp** Kohlenlampe *f*; **~ microphone** Kohlemikrofon *n*; **~ resistor** Schichtwiderstand *m*
card column (EDP) Lochkartenspalte *f*; **~ index** Kartei *f*; **~ punch** (EDP) Kartenlocher *m*; **~ reader** (EDP) Kartenleser *m*
cardioid *n* Kardioide *f*; **~ characteristic** Nierencharakteristik *f*; **~ microphone** Nierenmikrofon *n*, Niere *f* (fam.); **~ pattern** Nierencharakteristik *f*
carpenter *n* Tischler *m*
carpenter's shop Tischlerei *f*
carrier *n* (HF) Träger *m*; **~ circuit** Trägerfrequenzstrecke *f*; **~ energy** Trägerenergie *f*; **~ -frequency** *adj* trägerfrequent *adj*; **~ frequency** Trägerfrequenz (TF) *f*; **~ -frequency equipment**

Trägerfrequenzanlage *f*; **~ -frequency line** Trägerfrequenzstrecke *f*; **~ pulse** Trägerimpuls *m*; **~ voltage** Trägerspannung *f*; **~ wave (CW)** Trägerwelle *f*, Träger *m*; **suppressed ~** unterdrückter Träger

carrying strap Tragriemen *m*

cartoon animation figürlicher Trick **~ camera bench** Tricktisch *m*, Trickbank *f*; **~ effect** Trickeffekt *m*

cartoon-film artist Trickzeichner *m*

cartoonist *n* Trickzeichner *m*

cartridge *n* Magazin *n*, Kassette *f*; **~ recorder** Kassettenrecorder *m*

cascaded rectifiers *n pl* Gleichrichter-Kaskadenschaltung *f*

cascode circuit Kaskodeschaltung *f*

case *n* Koffer *m*; **~** *n* (cam.) Hülle *f*

cash office Kasse *f*

cashier *n* Kassierer *m*

casing *n* Gehäuse *n*; **~ short-circuit** Gehäuseschluß *m*

cassette *n* Magazin *n*, Kassette *f*; **~ amplifier** Kassettenverstärker *m*; **~ case** Kassettenkoffer *m*; **~ motor** Kassettenmotor *m*; **~ recorder** Kassettenrecorder *m*; **~ video tape recorder** Bildbandkassettengerät *n*

cast *v* (perf.) besetzen *v*, verpflichten *v*; **~** *n* (perf.) Besetzung *f*, Rollenbesetzung *f*, Darstellerbesetzung *f*; **~** *n* (col.) Stich *m*; **~ list** Besetzungsliste *f*, Darstellerliste *f*; **change of ~** Umbesetzung *f*; **member of ~** Mitwirkender *m*

casting *n* (perf.) Besetzung *f*, Rollenbesetzung *f*, Darstellerbesetzung *f*

castor *n* (mech.) Rolle *f*

castored base Fahrspinne *f*

catch light Augenlicht *n*; **~ on** *v* einschlagen *v*

catchline *n* Schlagzeile *f*

cathode *n* Kathode *f*; **~ -coupled circuit** Anodenbasisschaltung *f*, Kathodenverstärker *m*; **~ current** Kathodenstrom *m*; **~ follower** Anodenbasisschaltung *f*, Kathodenfolgeschaltung *f*, Kathodenverfolger *m*; **~ potential** Kathodenpotential *n*; **~ ray oscilloscope (CRO)** Kathodenstrahloszilloskop *n*; **~ ray store** (EDP) Kathodenstrahlspeicherröhre *f*; **~ ray tube (CRT)** Kathodenstrahlröhre *f*, Wiedergaberöhre *f*; **~ resistor** Kathodenwiderstand *m*; **directly-heated ~** direkt geheizte Kathode; **filament-type ~** direkt geheizte Kathode; **hot ~** Glühelektrode *f*; **indirectly-heated ~** indirekt geheizte Kathode

cathodyne circuit Kathodynschaltung *f*

catwalk *n* Beleuchtergang *m*

cavity resonator Topfkreis *m*

cell *n* Zelle *f*; **~ side** (coll.) Schichtträgerseite *f*; **photoelectric ~ (PEC)** fotoelektrische Zelle, Fotoelement *n*, Fotozelle *f*

celluloid film Zellhornfilm *m*; **~ scratch** Blankschramme *f*; **~ side** Schichtträgerseite *f*

cellulose disc Tonfolie *f*

cemented surface of lens gekittete Objektivfläche

censor's certificate Zensurkarte *f*

censorship *n* Zensur *f*

central aerial television (CATV) Gemeinschaftsantennenanlage *f*; **~ apparatus room (CAR)** Bild- und Tonschaltraum *m*, Hauptgeräteraum *m*, Kamerazentralbedienung *f*, Zentralgeräteraum *m*; **~ axis** Mittelachse *f*; **~ control room (CCR)** Hauptschaltraum *m*, Endkontrolle *f*; **~ field of vision**

Mittelgrund *m*; ~ **operation position** Zentralbedienplatz *m*; ~ **processing unit (CPU)** (EDP) Zentraleinheit *f*, Prozessor *m*; ~ **registry** Zentralregistratur *f*; ~ **research*** Dokumentation* *f*; ~ **services*** *n pl* Hausverwaltung* *f*, Innenverwaltung* *f*; ~ **services group*** Betriebsverwaltung* *f*

centre *v* Bild einstellen; ~ *n* (F) Bobby *m*, Filmkern *m*; ~ *n* (building) Komplex *m*; ~ **desk** Zentralredaktion *f*; ~ **of dispersion** Zerstreuungspunkt *m*; ~ **of frame** (F) Bildmitte *f*, Bildmittelpunkt *m*; ~ **of gravity of aerial** Antennenschwerpunkt *m*; ~ **of interest** bildwichtiger Teil; ~ **of picture** (TV) Bildmitte *f*, Bildmittelpunkt *m*; ~ **on** *v* in die Bildmitte setzen; ~ **positioning** Mittenstellung *f*; ~ **tap** Mittelanzapfung *f*

centrifugal switch Fliehkraftschalter *m*

centring, bad fehlerhafte Bildeinstellung

centring-up *n* Bildeinstellung *f*

ceramic *adj* keramisch *adj*

chain *n* Kette *f*; ~ **amplifier** Kettenverstärker *m*; ~ **control** Kettenüberwachung *f*; ~ **hoist** Kettenzug *m*

chairman *n* (prog.) Diskussionsleiter *m*, Gesprächsleiter *m*

chamber *n* Raum *m*; ~ **music** Kammermusik *f*; ~ **orchestra** Kammerorchester *n*; **free-field ~** schalltoter Raum

change *n* Übergang *m*; ~ **around** *v* umschneiden *v*; ~ **of angle** (script) Einstellungswechsel *m*; ~ **of cast** Umbesetzung *f*; ~ **of focal length** Brennweitenänderung *f*; ~ **of focus** Einstellungswechsel *m*; ~ **of programme** Programmänderung *f*, Programmwechsel *m*; ~ **of scene** Bildwechsel *m*; ~ **of scenery** Szenenwechsel *m*; ~ **over** *v* umschalten *v*; ~ **over** *v* (pict.) überblenden *v*

change-over *n* Übergang *m*; ~ *n* (tech.) Umschaltung *f*; ~ *n* (proj.) Überblendung *f*, Überblenden *n*, Überblender *m*; ~ **contact** Umschaltkontakt *m*; ~ **cue** Stanze *f*, Überblendzeichen *n*; ~ **cue punching machine** Überblendzeichenstanze *f*; ~ **cues** Koppelzeichen *n pl*, Aktüberblendzeichen *n pl*, Bildüberblendzeichen *n pl*; ~ **identification** Umschaltkennung *f*; ~ **mark** Überblendzeichen *n*; ~ **point** (elec.) Kippunkt *m*; ~ **signal** Überblendzeichen *n*; ~ **switch** Umschalter *m*, Umschaltgerät *n*, Wechselschalter *m*; ~ **switch** (breakdown) Pannenschalter *m*; ~ **time** Umschaltzeit *f*

changing bag Dunkelsack *m*, Kassettenwechselsack *m*, Wechselsack *m*; ~ **frame** Wechselrahmen *m*; ~ **magazine** Wechselkassette *f*

channel *n* Kanal *m*, Signalweg *m*, Übertragungskanal *m*; ~ *n* (prog.) Programm *n*, Kanal *m*; ~ **amplifier** Kanalverstärker *m*; ~ **-balancing** *n* Kanalanpassung *f*; ~ **combining unit** Kanalweiche *f*; ~ **diplexer** Kanalweiche *f*; ~ **rejector circuit** Kanalsperrkreis *m*; ~ **selector** Kanalwähler *m*, Kanalschalter *m*; ~ **selector switch** Kanalschalter *m*; ~ **separation** Kanaltrennung *f*; ~ **signal generator** Kanalmeßsender *m*; **adjacent ~** Nachbarkanal *m*; **incoming ~** ankommende Leitung; **outgoing ~** abgehende Leitung; **to change ~s** auf einen anderen Kanal schalten

channels in tête-bêche spiegelbildliche Fernsehkanäle
character *n* (perf.) Rolle *f*; ~ *n* (EDP) Zeichen *n*; ~ **actor** Charakterdarsteller *m*; ~ **part** Charakterrolle *f*; ~ **type** Rollenfach *n*
characteristic curve Kennlinie *f*; ~ **frequency** (acoust.) Eigenfrequenz *f*; ~ **impedance** Wellenwiderstand *m*; ~ **oscillation** Eigenschwingung (LC) *f*; **falling ~** fallende Kennlinie; **linear part of ~** linearer Teil einer Kennlinie; **rising ~** steigende Kennlinie
characteristics *n pl* Kenndaten *n pl*, Daten *n pl*
charge *v* laden *v*; ~ *v* (elec.) speisen *v*; ~ *n* Ladung *f*; ~ *n* (fee) Gebühr *f* ~ **image** Ladungsbild *n*; ~ **pattern** Ladungsbild *n*; **static ~** (F) statische Aufladung
chargeable *adj* gebührenpflichtig *adj*
charge-hand electrician Oberbeleuchter *m*
charging capacitor Ladekondensator *m*; ~ **condenser** Ladekondensator *m*; ~ **current** Ladestrom *m*; ~ **rate** Stromaufnahme *f*; ~ **resistor** Ladewiderstand *m*
chart *n* Grafik *f*, grafische Darstellung, Kurve *f*, Schaubild *n*, Schautafel *f*, Tafel *f*
chassis, mobile fahrbarer Untersatz
check *v* nachprüfen *v*, checken *v*; ~ *n* Probe *f*, Prüfung *f*; ~ **bit** (EDP) Prüf-Bit *n*; ~ **character** (EDP) Prüfzeichen *n*; ~ **list** Prüfbericht *m*; ~ **point** Meßpunkt *m*; ~ **switch** Meßstellenschalter *m*
check-girl *n* (US) Garderobiere *f*
checking *n* Prüfung *f*
checkout *n* (EDP) Funktionsprüfung *f*
chemical compound chemische Verbindung; ~ **fade** chemische Blende; ~ **veiling** (FP) Niederschlag *m*
chequerboard cutting (FP) Nachschneiden *n*; ~ **pattern** Schwarzweißraster *m*; ~ **test pattern** Schachmustertestbild *n*
chicken-wire *n* Kükendraht *m*
chief *n* Leiter *m*; ~ **announcer** Chefansager *m*, Chefsprecher *m*; ~ **architect** Chefarchitekt *m*; ~ **conductor** Chefdirigent *m*; ~ **electrician** Oberbeleuchter *m*; ~ **engineer** leitender Ingenieur; ~ **librarian** Archivleiter *m*; ~ **reporter** Chefreporter *m*
children's broadcasts *n pl* Kinderfunk *m*; ~ **film** Kinderfilm *m*; ~ **hour** Kinderstunde *f*; ~ **news programme** Kindernachrichten *f pl*; ~ **performance** Jugendvorstellung *f*; ~ **programme** Kinderprogramm *n*; ~ **television** Kinderfernsehen *n*
chinagraph pencil Fettstift *m*
chirping *n* Zwitschern *n*
chocolate block (coll.) Lüsterklemme *f*
choice *n* Auswahl *f*; ~ **of programme** Programmauswahl *f*
choir *n* Chor *m*
choke *n* Drossel *f*, Drosselspule *f*, Sperrdrossel *f*
choose *v* auswählen *v*
chopper *n* Zerhacker *m*
choral music Chormusik *f*
choreographer *n* Choreograf *m*
choreography *n* Choreografie *f*
chorus *n* Chor *m*; ~ **director** Chorleiter *m*; ~ **manager** Chorwart *m*; ~ **master** Chorleiter *m*; ~ **singer** Chorist *m*, Chorsänger *m*; ~ **supervisor** Chorinspektor *m*; **member of a ~** Chorist *m*, Chorsänger *m*
chrom. sig. (coll.) Chrominanzsignal *n*
chroma (compp.)(coll.) Farb- (in Zus.); ~ **key** Blaustanzverfahren *n*,

Farbschablonentrick *m*, Stanztrick *m*
chromatic *adj* Farb- (in Zus.); **~ aberration** Farbabweichung *f*; **~ chain** Farbartkanal *m*; **~ channel** Farbartkanal *m*; **~ coefficient** Farbkoeffizient *m*; **~ component** Farbauszug *m*; **~ coordinate** Farbkoordinate *f*; **~ defect** Farbfehler *m*, chromatischer Fehler; **~ difference** Farbdifferenz *f*; **~ flicker** Farbartflimmern *n*; **~ resolution** Farbkonturschärfe *f*; **~ sensitivity** Farbempfindlichkeit *f*; **~ separation** Farbaufteilung *f*; **~ splitting** Farbaufteilung *f*; **~ tristimuli** trichromatische Farbkoeffizienten
chromaticity *n* Farbigkeit *f*, Farbart *f*, Farbwert *m*; **~ coordinates** Farbwertkoordinaten *f pl*; **~ diagram** Farbtafel *f*, Spektralfarbenzug *m*
chromatics *n* Farblehre *f*
chrominance *n* Chrominanz *f*; **~ channel** Chrominanzkanal *m*; **~ component** Chrominanzkomponente *f*, Farbwertbild *n*; **~ demodulator** Farbdemodulator *m*; **~ equaliser** Farbkanalentzerrer *m*; **~ information** Farbinformation *f*; **~ modulator** Chrominanzmodulator *m*, Farbmodulator *m*; **~ resolution** Farbauflösung *f*; **~ signal** Chrominanzsignal *n*, Farbartsignal (F-Signal) *n*, Farbwertsignal *n*; **~ sync pulse** Farbsynchronimpuls *m*
chromoscope *n* Farbbildröhre *f*
cinch *n* (tape) Bandwickelfehler *m*
cine (compp.) Film- (in Zus.); **~ camera** Filmkamera *f*, Aufnahmekamera *f*; **~ turret** Objektivrevolver *m*
cinefilm *n* (material) Kinofilm *m*
cinema *n* Filmtheater *n*, Lichtspieltheater *n*, Kino *n*; **~ circuit** Theaterring *m*; **~ film** Kinofilm *m*; **~ manager** Filmtheaterleiter *m*, Theaterleiter *m*; **~ publicity** Kinoreklame *f*; **~ screen** Bildwand *f*; **96-perforation ~ film** Kinefilm /96 Perforationslöcher
cinema-goer *n* Besucher *m*, Zuschauer *m*
cinematic *adj* filmisch *adj*
cinematics *n pl* Filmkunst *f*
cinematography *n* Film *m*, Filmkunst *f*, Kinematografie *f*
cinemicrography *n* Mikrokinematografie *f*
circle of confusion Zerstreuungskreis *m*
circuit *n* (elec.) Kreis *m*, Leitung *f*, Schaltkreis *m*, Schaltung *f*, Stromkreis *m*, Verbindung *f*; **~ allocation unit** Leitungsbüro *n*; **~ board** Schaltplatte *f*; **printed ~ board** gedruckte Schaltplatte, gedruckte Platte; **~ -breaker** *n* Ausschalter *m*, Sicherungsautomat *m*, Trennschalter *m*, Leistungsschalter *m*, Schütz *n*; **time-delayed ~ -breaker** Schütz mit Schaltverzögerung; **~ capacitance** Schaltkapazität *f*; **~ capacity** Schaltungskapazität *f*; **~ conference** Schaltkonferenz *f*; **~ diagram** Schaltplan *m*, Schaltschema *n*, Schaltbild *n*, Schaltung *f*, Stromlaufplan *m*; **~ down!** Leitung ist tot!; **~ section** Leitungsabschnitt *m*; **~ termination** Leitungsabschluß *m*; **~ up!** Leitung steht!; **~ with combined coupling** Zwischenbasisschaltung *f*; **active ~** (EDP) aktive Schaltung; **closed ~** geschlossener Stromkreis; **coil-loaded ~** bespulte Leitung; **incoming ~** ankommende Leitung

integrated ~ (IC) integrierter Schaltkreis, integrierte Schaltung, integrierter Baustein; **one-way ~** gerichtete Leitung; **open ~** offener Stromkreis; **out of ~** stromlos *adj*; **outgoing ~** abgehende Leitung; **permanent ~** stehende Leitung; **printed ~** gedruckter Schaltkreis, gedruckte Schaltung, Steckleiterplatte *f*; **to put in ~** zuschalten *v*; **to record over a ~** über Leitung aufnehmen, über Leitung aufzeichnen; **to set up a ~** Leitung einrichten; **unidirectional ~** gerichtete Leitung

circuitry *n* Schaltung *f*

circular radiation Rundstrahlung *f*, Rundumstrahlung *f*

circulation-system lubrication Umlaufschmierung *f*

circus performer Artist *m*

civil engineer Bauingenieur *m*

claim for remuneration Vergütungsanspruch *m*

clamp *v* klemmen *v*; ~ *n* Klemme *f*, Klemmhalterung *f*; ~ *n* (circuit) Klemmschaltung *f*, Clamp *m*; **~ pulse** Klemmimpuls *m*; **~ voltage** Klemmpotential *n*

clamping circuit Klemmschaltung *f*, Clamp *m*; **~ diode** Schwarzwertdiode *f*; **~ on front/back porch** Schwarzschulterklemmung *f*; **~ pulse** Klemmimpuls *m*, Nulltastimpuls *m*; **~ strip** Verriegelungslasche *f*; **~ voltage** Klemmpotential *n*

clapper *n* Synchronklappe *f*, Klappe *f*; **~ board** Synchronklappe *f*, Klappe *f*; **~ boy** Klappenschläger *m*

clarity of vowels Vokalverständlichkeit *f*

class A circuit (transmitter) A-Schaltung *f*; **~ B circuit** B-Schaltung *f*; **~ C circuit** C-Schaltung *f*

classroom reception Klassenempfang *m*

claw *n* Greifer *m*; **~ arm** Greiferarm *m*; **~ feed system** Greifersystem *n*

clean feed n-minus-eins-Schaltung *f*; **~ tape** Leerband *n*

Clear Air Turbulence (CAT) Strudelbewegung *f* (Luft)

clear film Blankfilm *m*; **~ film with frame line** Blankfilm mit Bildstrich; **~ leader** Blankfilm *m*; **~ run** Durchlauf *m*; **to ~ interference** entstören *v*; **to ~ the throat** (micr.) abhusten *v*

clearance *n* Spielraum *m*, Toleranz *f*; **~ of rights** Freistellung von Rechten

clearing *n* Klären *n*; **~ bath** Klärbad *n*

clearness *n* (opt.) Schärfe *f*

cleat *n* Blendenklammer *f*, Kulissenklammer *f*

clerical operator Vervielfältiger *m*

cliché *n* Klischee *n*, Schablone *f*

click *n* Knacken *n*; **~ setting** Blendenraste *f*

clip *v* abschneiden *v*, clippen *v*; ~ *n* Filmausschnitt *m*; **~ on** *v* aufstecken *v*

clip-on probe Stromzange *f*, Amperezange *f*

clipper *n* (TV) Abschneidestufe *f*, Clipperstufe *f*, Begrenzer *m*; **symmetrical ~** symmetrische Abschneidestufe

clipping *n* Abschneiden *n*, Amplitudenbegrenzung *f*, Begrenzung *f*; ~ *n* (press) Zeitungsausschnitt *m*; **~ circuit** (TV) Abschneidestufe *f*, Clipperstufe *f*

cloakroom *n* Garderobe *f*; **~ attendant** Garderobiere *f*

clock *v* die Zeit nehmen; ~ *n* (EDP) Taktgeber *m*; **~ frequency** (EDP) Taktfrequenz *f*; **~ generator** (EDP) Taktgeber *m*; **~ marker track**

(EDP) Taktspur *f*; ~ **pulse** Zeitimpuls *m*; ~ **pulse** (EDP) Taktimpuls *m*; ~ **rate** (EDP) Taktfrequenz *f*; ~ **signal** (EDP) Taktimpuls *m*; ~ **track** (EDP) Taktspur *f*
clockwise *adj and adv* im Uhrzeigersinn
clockwork *n* Federwerk *n*
clog wipe Kreiselblende *f*
close *v* abschließen *v*; ~ *v* (circuit) zuschalten *v*; ~ **contrast** Nahkontrast *m*; ~ **of transmission** Sendeschluß *m*; **to ~ a programme** absagen *v*; **too ~** (pict.) zuwenig Luft; **very ~ shot (VCS)** ganz groß, ganz nah
closed circuit (system) Kurzschlußempfangsverfahren *n*, Kurzschlußverfahren *n*; ~ **circuit** (line) Überspielleitung *f*; **to transmit over ~ circuit** überspielen *v*
closed-circuit current Ruhestrom *m* ~ **system** Kurzschlußempfangsverfahren *n*, Kurzschlußverfahren *n*; ~ **television (CCTV)** Betriebsfernsehen *n*, industrielles Fernsehen, Kabelfernsehen *n*; ~ **transmission** Überspielung *f*; ~ **TV camera** Fernauge *n*
close-down *n* Sendeschluß *m*
close-medium shot (CMS) Halbnahe *f*
close-perspective recording Nahaufnahme *f*, Naheinstellung *f*
close-range fading area (transmitter) Nahschwundzone *f*
close shot (CS) Großaufnahme *f*, Nahaufnahme *f*, Naheinstellung *f*
close statement (EDP) Abschlußbefehl *m*
close-talking microphone Nahbesprechungsmikrofon *n*
close-up (CU) *n* Großaufnahme *f*, Nahaufnahme *f*, Naheinstellung *f*; ~ *adj* groß *adj*, nah; ~ **adapter** Zwischenring für Nahaufnahme; ~ **view** (US) Großaufnahme *f*, Nahaufnahme *f*, Naheinstellung *f*; **extreme ~ (ECU)** Makroaufnahme *f*
closing *n* Abschluß *m*; ~ **announcement** Absage *f*, Programmabsage *f*, Stationsabsage *f*; ~ **captions** *n pl* Nachspann *m*; ~ **credits** *n pl* Nachspann *m*; ~ **-down** *n* Endabschaltung *f*; ~ **procedure** Schlußablauf *m*; ~ **scene** Schlußszene *f*; ~ **titles** *n pl* Endtitel *m*, Nachspann *m*, Schlußtitel *m*
cloth light Kleidungslicht *n*
clue *n* (US) Hinweis *m*
clutch *n* (mech.) Kupplung *f*
coarse-grained *adj* grobkörnig *adj*
coarse setting Grobeinstellung *f*
coat *n* Überzug *m*
coated tape Schichtband *n*
coating *n* (opt.) Antireflexbelag *m*, Beschichtung *f*; ~ *n* (F) Guß *m*, Schicht *f*, Überzug *m*; ~ **of lens** Vergütung *f*; **photosensitive ~** lichtempfindliche Schicht
co-author *n* Mitautor *m*
coax *n* (coll.) Koaxialkabel *n*, Koaxkabel *n* (fam.)
coaxial *adj* konzentrisch *adj*; ~ **cable** Koaxialkabel *n*, Koaxkabel *n* (fam.); ~ **line** Koaxialkabel *n*, Koaxkabel *n* (fam.)
cobweb gun Spinnwebmaschine *f*
co-channel service Gleichkanalbetrieb *m*
code *v* kodieren *v*, verschlüsseln *v*; ~ *n* Kode *m*; ~ **bar** Wahlschiene *f*, Schiene *f* (fam.); ~ **conversion** (EDP) Kode-Umwandler *f*; ~ **of practice** Betriebsanleitung *f*, Betriebsanweisung *f*
coder *n* Koder *m*, Enkoder *m*; ~ **network** (EDP) Kodiermatrix *f*
coding *n* Kodierung *f*

coefficient of re-emission Remissionsverhältnis *n*; **~ of reflectance** Remissionsverhältnis *n*
coercitivity *n* Koerzitivkraft *f*
cog wheel Zahnrad *n*
coil *v* (elec.) spulen *v*; ~ *n* (elec.) Spule *f*; **~ current** Spulenstrom *m*; **~ form** Spulenkörper *m*; **~ of cable** Kabelring *m*; **~ turret** Spulentrommel *f*; **~ (up)** *v* aufspulen *v*, aufwickeln *v*
coil-driven loudspeaker elektrodynamischer Lautsprecher
coiling *n* Wicklung *f*
coincidence circuit Koinzidenzschaltung *f*; **~ circuit** (EDP) UND-Gatter *n*, Koinzidenzgatter *n*; **~ detector** Koinzidenzgleichrichter *m*; **~ gate** (EDP) UND-Gatter *n*, Koinzidenzgatter *n*; **~ pulse** Koinzidenzimpuls *m*
coincident *adj* gleichzeitig *adj*; **~ image** kongruentes Teilbild
coincident-microphone stereo Intensitätsstereofonie *f*
cold light Kaltlicht *n*
collaborator *n* Mitarbeiter *m*
colleague *n* Mitarbeiter *m*
collecting lens Sammellinse *f*
collective product advertising Branchenwerbung *f*; **~ telephone number** Telefonsammelnummer *f*
collector *n* Kollektor *m*, Sammelelektrode *f*; **~ current** Kollektorstrom *m*; **~ electrode** Sammelelektrode *f*
collector-load resistance (transistor) Außenwiderstand *m*
collinear array of dipoles Dipolreihe *f*
coloration *n* Farbgebung *f*; ~ *n* (sound) Tonverfremdung *f*
colorimetric *adj* farbmetrisch *adj*; **~ purity** Farbdichte *f*
colorimetry *n* Farbmessung *f*, Farbmetrik *f*; ~ *n* Farblehre *f*
colortran lamp Colortranlampe *f*; **~ light** Colortranlicht *n*
colour *n* Farbe *f*; ~ (compp.) Farb- (in Zus.); **~ adviser** Farbberater *m*; **~ analysis** Farbanalyse *f*; **~ balance** Farbabstimmung *f*, Farbabgleich *m*, Farbbalance *f*, Farbgleichgewicht *n*; **~ balance filter** Farbausgleichfilter *m*; **~ banding** Farbbänder *n pl*; **~ bar** Farbbalken *m*; **~ bar pattern** Farbbalkentestbild *n*; **~ blending** Farbmischung *f*; **~ blindness** Farbenblindheit *f*; **~ break-up** Farbaufbrechen *n*; **~ broadcasting** Farbfernsehen *n*; **~ burst** Burst *m*; **~ -capable** *adj* farbtüchtig *adj*; **~ carrier** (coll.) Farbhilfsträger *m*, Farbträger *m*; **~ cast** Farbstich *m*; **~ chart** Farbtafel *f*; **~ cinex test** Farbbestimmungsprobe *f*; **~ circle** Farbkreis *m*; **~ coder** Farbkoder *m*; **~ compensating filter** Farbausgleichfilter *m*; **~ compensation filter** Farbkompensationsfilter *m*; **~ component** Farbkomponente *f*; **~ composition within picture** Farbdramaturgie *f*; **~ contamination** Farbübersprechen *n*; **~ contrast** Farbkontrast *m*; **~ correction mask** Farbkorrekturmaske *f*; **~ decoder** Farbdekoder *m*; **~ defect** Farbfehler *m*, chromatischer Fehler; **~ demodulator** Farbdemodulator *m*; **~ density** Farbdichte *f*; **~ developing** Farbentwicklung *f*; **~ deviation** Farbabweichung *f*; **~ difference** Farbunterschied *m*, Farbdifferenz *f*; **~ difference sensitivity** Farbunterscheidungsvermögen *n*; **~ difference signal** Farbdifferenzsignal *n*; **~ difference threshold** Farbunterscheidungsschwelle *f*;

~ distortion Farbabweichung *f*, Farbverschiebung *f*; **~ dupe neg** (coll.) Farbduplikatnegativ *n*; **~ duplicate negative** Farbduplikatnegativ *n*; **~ effect** Farbeindruck *m*; **~ electronics** Farbelektronik *f*; **~ encoder** Farbkoder *m*; **~ error** Farbfehler *m*, chromatischer Fehler; **~ fidelity** Farbtreue *f*; **~ film** Farbfilm *m*; **~ film leader** Farbvorlauffilm *m*; **~ film system** Farbfilmverfahren *n*; **~ filter** Farbfilter *m*; **~ flicker** Farbflimmern *n*, Farbartflimmern *n*, Farbvalenzflimmern *n*; **~ frame** Farbbild *n*; **~ fringing** Farbsaum *m*; **~ grader** Farblichtbestimmer *m*; **~ grey-scale chart** Farbgrauwerttafel *f*; **~ head leader** Farbvorlauffilm *m*; **~ hue banding** Farbtonstreifigkeit *f*; **~ -ident sync pulse** Koder-Kennimpuls *m*; **~ identification** Farbkennung *f*; **~ information** Farbinformation *f*; **~ intensity control** Farbstärkeregler *m*, Farbtonknopf *m*; **~ intermediate positive** Farbzwischenpositiv *n*; **~ killer** Colorkiller *m*, Farbabschalter *m*, Farbsperre *f*; **~ kinescope** (US) Farbbildröhre *f*; **~ lavender** Farblavendel *n*; **~ matcher** Farbkuppler *m*; **~ matching** Farbanpassung *f*; **~ matrix** Farbmatrix *f*; **~ matrix circuit** Farbmatrixschaltung *f*; **~ matrix unit** Farbmatrixschaltung *f*; **~ matrixing** Farbanpassung *f*; **~ memory** Farberinnerungsvermögen *n*; **~ mixing** Farbmischung *f*; **~ mixture** Farbmischung *f*; **~ mobile control room (CMCR)** Farb-Ü-Wagen *m*; **~ mobile video tape recorder (CMVTR)** Farb-MAZ-Wagen *m*; **~ modulator** Farbmodulator *m*; **~ negative** Negativfarbfilm *m*; **~ negative film** Farbnegativfilm *m*; **~ OB vehicle** Farb-Ü-Wagen *m*; **~ of light** Lichtfarbe *f*; **~ of object** Gegenstandsfarbe *f*; **~ of tone** (musical instrument) Tonfarbe *f*; **~ picture** Farbbild *n*; **~ picture and waveform monitor** Farbbildkontrollgerät *n*; **~ picture signal** Farbbildaustastsignal (FBA-Signal) *n*, Farbbildsignal *n*; **~ picture tube** Farbbildröhre *f*; **~ positive film** Farbpositivfilm *m*, Positivfarbfilm *m*; **~ print** Farbabzug *m*, Farbkopie *f*; **~ print film** Positivfarbfilm *m*; **~ process** Farbverfahren *n*; **~ production** Farbproduktion *f*; **~ programme** Farbsendung *f*; **~ purity** Farbreinheit *f*; **~ quality** Farbqualität *f*; **~ range** Farbbereich *m*; **~ receiver** Farbfernsehempfänger *m*, Farbempfänger *m*; **~ reception** Farbempfang *m*; **~ reference** Farbbezugspunkt *m*; **~ rendering** Farbwiedergabe *f*, Farbtreue *f*; **~ rendition** Farbwiedergabe *f*, Farbtreue *f*; **~ reproduction** Farbwiedergabe *f*, Farbtreue *f*; **~ reversal film** Farbumkehrfilm *m*; **~ reversal print** Farbumkehrduplikat *n*; **~ run-out leader** Farbnachlauffilm *m*; **~ saturation** Farbsättigung *f*; **~ saturation adjustment** Farbsättigungsregelung *f*; **~ saturation control** Farbsättigungsregler *m*; **~ -selective** *adj* farbselektiv *adj*; **~ sensitivity** Farbempfindlichkeit *f*; **~ separation** Farbteilung *f*, Farbauszug *m*; **~ separation overlay** Blaustanzverfahren *n*; **~ separation signal** Farbauszugssignal *n*; **~ separator** Farbteiler *m*; **~ -servicing signal**

generator Farbservicegenerator *m*; ~ **shade** Farbton *m*; ~ **shading** Farbtonverfälschung *f*; ~ **signal** Farbsignal *n*; ~ **slide** Farbdia *n*; ~ **splitting** Farbteilung *f*; ~ **splitting system** Farbzerlegungssystem *n*; ~ **stimulus** Farbreiz *m*; ~ **stimulus specification** Farbvalenz *f*; ~ **stock** Farbfilmmaterial *n*; ~ **subcarrier (CSC)** Farbhilfsträger *m*, Farbträger *m*; ~ **subcarrier oscillation** Farbträgerschwingung *f*; ~ **synchronising burst** Farbsynchronsignal *n*; ~ **synchronising signal** Farbsynchronsignal *n*; ~ **synthesis** Farbsynthese *f*; ~ **tail leader** Farbnachlauffilm *m*; ~ **television** Farbfernsehen *n*; ~ **television camera** Farbfernsehkamera *f*; ~ **television receiver** Farbfernsehempfänger *m*, Farbempfänger *m*; ~ **temperature (CT)** Farbtemperatur *f*; ~ **temperature meter** Farblichtbestimmer *m*, Farbtemperaturmesser *m*, Lichtfarbmeßgerät *n*; ~ **threshold** Farbschwelle *f*; ~ **tinge** Farbstich *m*; ~ **transition** Farbübergang *m*; ~ **transmission** Farbsendung *f*, Farbübertragung *f*; ~ **triad** Farbtripel *m*; ~ **triangle** Farbdreieck *n*; ~ **tube** Farbbildröhre *f*; ~ **value** Farbwert *m*; ~ **video signal** Farbbildaustastsynchronsignal (FBAS-Signal) *n*, Farbbildsignalgemisch *n*; **additive ~ process** additives Farbverfahren **additive ~ synthesis** additive Farbsynthese; **additive ~ system** additives Farbverfahren; **desaturated ~** verwaschene Farbe, **garish ~** schreiende Farbe; **impure ~** unreine Farbe; **loud ~** schreiende Farbe: **muted ~** gedämpfte Farbe; **pale ~** blasse Farbe; **pure ~** reine Farbe; **subdued ~** gedämpfte Farbe; **subtractive ~ process** subtraktives Farbverfahren; **subtractive ~ synthesis** subtraktive Farbsynthese; **subtractive ~ system** subtraktives Farbverfahren; **washed-out ~** verwaschene Farbe

coloured filter Farbfilter *m*; ~ **lighting** Effektfarbe *f*; ~ **noise** Farbrauschen *n*

colouring *n* Farbgebung *f*; ~ **matter** Farbstoff *m*

colourless *adj* farblos *adj*

colourlessness *n* Farblosigkeit *f*

column *n* (press) Spalte *f*; ~ **loudspeaker** Schallsäule *f*, Tonsäule *f*

coma *n* Zerstreuungskreis *m*

combination aerial Kombinationsantenne *f*; ~ **shot** Simultanaufnahme *f*; ~ **tone** Kombinationston *m*

combined aerial Kombinationsantenne *f*; ~ **magnetic sound (Commag)** kombinierter Magnetton (COMMAG); ~ **optical sound (Comopt)** kombinierter Lichtton (COMOPT); ~ **print** Magoptical-Kopie *f*; ~ **recording/reproducing head** kombinierter Aufnahme-Wiedergabekopf, Kombikopf *m*

combining unit Koppelweiche *f*, Senderweiche *f*, Weiche *f*

come off *v* (prog.) ankommen *v*

comedian *n* Komiker *m*

comedy *n* Komödie *f*; ~ **film** Lustspielfilm *m*; ~ **play** Komödie *f*; ~ **show** Familienserie *f*

Commag system Einstreifenverfahren *n*

command *n* (EDP) Befehl *m*

comment *v* kommentieren *v*; ~ *n* Kommentar *m*; ~ **on** *v*

kommentieren *v*; **marginal ~** Glosse *f*
commentary *n* Kommentar *m*, Sprechertext *m*; ~ *n* (sport) Bericht *m*, Reportage *f*; ~ *n* (F) Filmtext *m*; ~ **circuit** Kommentarleitung *f*; ~ **line** Kommentarleitung *f*; ~ **sound** Kommentarton *m*; **off-tube ~** Kommentar am Monitor
commentator *n* Berichterstatter *m*, Kommentator *m*, Sprecher *m*; ~ *n* (F) Sprecher *m*; ~ **unit** Kommentatoreinheit *f*
commentator's booth Sprecherkabine *f*; ~ **microphone** Sprechermikrofon *n*; ~ **position** Kommentatorplatz *m*, Kommentatorstelle *f*, Sprecherplatz *m*, Sprecherstelle *f*
commercial *n* kommerzielle Sendung, Spot *m*, Werbespot *m*; ~ *n* (TV) Fernsehspot *m*, Werbeeinblendung *f*; ~ *adj* kommerziell *adj*; ~ **advertising** Wirtschaftswerbung *f*; ~ **radio** Werbefunk *m*; ~ **record** Industrieschallplatte *f*; ~ **sound studio** Tonstudiobetrieb *m*; ~ **spot** Werbespot *m*, Spot *m*; ~ **station** Privatsender *m*; ~ **television** kommerzielles Fernsehen, Werbefernsehen *n*; ~ **use** kommerzielle Verwertung
commercialisation *n* Verwertung *f*
commission *n* Auftrag *m*; ~ *n* (mus.) Kompositionsauftrag *m*, Auftragskomposition *f*
commissionaire *n* Pförtner *m*
commissioned film Auftragsfilm *m*; ~ **production** Auftragsproduktion *f*; ~ **work** Auftragsarbeit *f*, Auftragswerk *n*
common-battery connection (CB) Zentralbatterieanschluß (ZB) *m*; ~ **exchange** Zentralbatterievermittlung *f*
common-channel service Gleichkanalbetrieb *m*
common chord Dreiklang *m*
common-wave operation Gleichwellenbetrieb *m*, Synchronbetrieb *m*
communal aerial Gemeinschaftsantenne *f*
communication *n* Kommunikation *f*, Nachricht *f*; ~ *n* (tel.) Verbindung *f*; ~ **check** Verständigungsprobe *f*; ~ **research** Kommunikationsforschung *f*; ~ **system** Verständigungsanlage *f*
communications* *n pl* Fernmeldetechnik* *f*, Nachrichtenwesen *n*
communications *n pl* Nachrichten *f pl*; ~ **network** Nachrichtennetz *n*; ~ **satellite** Fernmeldesatellit *m*, Kommunikationssatellit *m*, Nachrichtensatellit *m*
communiqué *n* Kommuniqué *n*
community aerial Gemeinschaftsantenne *f*; ~ **listening** Gemeinschaftsempfang *m*; ~ **television (CTV)** Ortsantennenanlage *f*; ~ **viewing** Gemeinschaftsempfang *m*
commutating frequency Umschaltfrequenz *f*
commutation *n* Umschaltung *f*
commutator *n* Kollektor *m*
company *n* (perf.) Ensemble *n*
comparison amplifier Vergleichsverstärker *m*; ~ **measurement** Vergleichsmessung *f*; ~ **pulse** Vergleichsimpuls *m*; ~ **test** Vergleichstest *m*; ~ **voltage** Vergleichsspannung *f*
compatibility *n* Kompatibilität *f*, Verträglichkeit *f*
compatible *adj* kompatibel *adj*
compendium *n* Auszug *m*; ~ *n* Kompendium *n*
compensate *v* ausgleichen *v*
compensating developer

Ausgleichsentwickler *m*
compensation *n* Ausgleich *m*; ~ *n* (financial) Abfindung *f*
compère *n* Conferencier *m*, Spielleiter *m*
competitive-game programme Wettbewerbssendung *f*
compilation *n* zusammenfassender Filmbericht
compile *v* zusammenstellen *v*
compiler *n* (EDP) Kompilierer *m*, Compiler *m*
compiling programme (EDP) Kompilierer *m*, Compiler *m*
complement gate (EDP) Komplementgatter *n*; ~ **representation** (EDP) Komplementärdarstellung *f*
complementary colour Gegenfarbe *f*, Komplementärfarbe *f*; ~ **gaussian circuit** komplementärer Glockenkreis (Secam)
complete *v* (F) abdrehen *v*; ~ **effects without speaker** Tongemisch *n*; ~ **programme circuit** Programmleitung *f*; ~ **shadow** Kernschatten *m*; ~ **sound** Programmton *m*
completion report (F) Abschlußbericht *m*
component *n* Bauelement *n*, Bauteil *n*; ~ **parts** *n pl* Bestückung *f*; **electronic** ~ elektronisches Bauelement
compose *v* komponieren *v*
composer *n* Komponist *m*; ~ **of film music** Filmkomponist *m*
composite colour signal Farbbildaustastsynchronsignal (FBAS-Signal) *n*, Farbbildsignalgemisch *n*; ~ **colour video signal (comp. sig.)** Farbbildaustastsynchronsignal (FBAS-Signal) *n*, Farbbildsignalgemisch *n*; ~ **picture signal** Bildaustastsynchronsignal (BAS-Signal) *n*; ~ **signal** Bildaustastsynchronsignal (BAS-Signal) *n*, Signalgemisch *n*, Summensignal *n*; ~ **signal with test line** (coll.) Bildaustastsynchronsignal mit Prüfzeile (BASP-Signal); ~ **sound** Tongemisch *n*; ~ **video signal** Bildaustastsynchronsignal (BAS-Signal) *n*; ~ **video signal with insertion test signal** Bildaustastsynchronsignal mit Prüfzeile (BASP-Signal)
composition *n* Komposition *f*
compound *n* (chem.) Verbindung *f*
compressed air Druckluft *f*
compressed-air line Druckluftleitung *f*
compression *n* Kompression *f*; ~ **of dynamic range** Dynamikkompression *f*
compressor *n* Kompressor *m*
compur shutter Compurverschluß *m*
computation *n* Berechnung *f*
compute *v* berechnen *v*
computer *n* Computer *m*, Rechenanlage *f*; ~ **instruction** (EDP) Maschinenbefehl *m*, Maschineninstruktion *f*; ~ **memory** Informationsspeicher *m*
computing speed (EDP) Rechengeschwindigkeit *f*
concave reflector Hohlspiegel *m*
concealed socket Unterputzdose *f*
concentric *adj* konzentrisch *adj*
concert *n* Konzert *n*; ~ **hall** Sendesaal *m*
conclusion *n* Abschluß *m*
condenser *n* Kondensator *m*; ~ *n* (opt.) Kondensor *m*; ~ **lens** Sammellinse *f*, Kondensor *m*; ~ **microphone** Kondensatormikrofon *n*
condensing lens Kondensor *m*
condition *n* Zustand *m*; ~ **of contract** Vertragsbedingung *f*; **latent** ~ latenter Zustand

conductance *n* (DC) Leitwert *m*, Wirkleitwert *m*
conductivity *n* Leitfähigkeit *f*
conductor *n* Dirigent *m*, Kapellmeister *m*; ~ *n* (elec.) Leiter *m*
conduit box Abzweigdose *f*, Abzweigkasten *m*, Anschlußkasten *m*
cone *n* Spotvorsatz *m*; ~ **of light** Lichtkegel *m*; ~ **wheel** Kegelrad *n*
conference circuit Konferenzleitung *f*, Konferenzschaltung *f*; ~ **network** Konferenzleitungsnetz *n*
conjunction *n* (EDP) Konjunktion *f*
connect *v* verbinden *v*, anschließen *v*, schalten *v* (auf); ~ *v* (into a line) einschleifen *v*; ~ **through** *v* durchschleifen *v*; ~ **to** *v* zuschalten *v*; ~ **up** *v* (transmitter) anschließen *v*; **to ~ into circuit** schalten *v*
connected load Anschlußwert *m*
connecting bar Verbindungsleiste *f*; ~ **cable** Verbindungskabel *n*; ~ **clip** Anschlußklemme *f*
connection *n* Verbindung *f*, Anschluß *m*, Schaltung *f*; ~ *n* (tel.) Telefonanschluß *m*, Verbindung *f*; ~ **charge** Anschlußgebühr *f*; ~ **in series** Serienschaltung *f*; ~ **point** Verbindungspunkt *m*; ~ **rose** Anschlußrosette *f*; ~ **to mains** Netzanschluß *m*; **electrical ~** galvanische Verbindung; **parallel ~** rangierbare Verbindung; **physical ~** fliegende Verbindung; **shunt ~** rangierbare Verbindung
connector box Abzweigdose *f*, Abzweigkasten *m*; ~ **plug** Kupplungsstecker *m*; ~ **socket** Kupplungsdose *f*
consequential right Folgerecht *n*
consistency *n* Übereinstimmung *f*
console *n* Bedienungsfeld *n*, Konsole *f*, Pult *n*, Regiepult *n*, Regietisch *m*; ~ *n* (cabinet) Truhe *f*; ~ **typewriter** (EDP) Bedienungsblattschreiber *m*
console-dimmer lever bank Beleuchtungssteuerfeld *n*
consonant articulation Konsonantenverständlichkeit *f*
constancy *n* Konstanz *f*
constant with time zeitkonstant *adj*
constant-circulation lubrication Umlaufschmierung *f*
construction *n* Aufbau *m*; ~ **manager** (set) Bühnenmeister *m*
contact *n* Kontakt *m*; ~ **assembly** Kontaktfedersatz *m*; ~ **loading** Kontaktbelastung *f*; ~ **pin** Kontaktstift *m*; ~ **plug** Kontaktstecker *m*; ~ **print** Kontaktabzug *m*, Kontaktkopie *f*; ~ **printer** Kontaktkopiermaschine *f*; ~ **printing** Kontaktkopieren *n*, Kontaktverfahren *n*; ~ **printing method** Kontaktverfahren *n*; ~ **process** Kontaktverfahren *n*; ~ **resistance** Übergangswiderstand *m*; ~ **spring** Kontaktfeder *f*; ~ **stud** Kontaktstift *m*; ~ **track** Kontaktbahn *f*; **intermittent ~** Wackelkontakt *m*; **loose ~** Wackelkontakt *m*; **protective ~** Schutzkontakt *m*; **scorched ~** verschmorter Kontakt; **to make a ~ print** kontaktkopieren *v*
contactor *n* Schütz *n*
contaminate *v* verunreinigen *v*
contamination *n* Verunreinigung *f*
contents, statement of Inhaltsangabe *f*
contest programme Wettbewerbssendung *f*
contingency insurance Ausfallversicherung *f*
continuation *n* Folge *f*
continuity *n* Kontinuität *f*; ~ *n* (prog.) Übergang *m*, Zwischenverbindung *f*; ~ *n* (script) technisches Drehbuch; ~ *n* (F) Anschluß *m*; ~ *n* (presentation)

Sendekontrolle *f*; ~ **director** Ablaufregisseur *m*; ~ **girl** Ateliersekretärin *f*, Scriptgirl *n*, Script *f*; ~ **list** Schnittliste *f*; ~ **log** Aufzeichnungsprotokoll *n*; ~ **script** Ansagetext *m*, Text *m*; ~ **sheet** (F) Tagesbericht *m*; ~ **shot** Zwischenschnitt *m*; ~ **studio** Ansagestudio *n*, Sprecherstudio *n* ~ **suite** (R) Senderegie *f*, Ablaufregie *f*; ~ **writer** Drehbuchautor *m*

continuous film-printer Durchlaufkopiermaschine *f*; ~ **interference** Dauerstörung *f*; ~ **printer** Durchlaufkopiermaschine *f*; ~ **rotary printer** Durchlaufkopiermaschine *f*; ~ **run** kontinuierlicher Filmlauf

continuously variable transformer Stelltransformator *m*

contour *n* Kontur *f*; ~ **accentuation** Konturverstärkung *f*; ~ **convergence** Konturendeckung *f*; ~ **correction** Konturentzerrung *f*; ~ **correction unit** Bildrandverschärfer *m*; ~ **effect** (VTR) Welligkeit *f*; ~ **impression** Zeichnung *f*; ~ **sharpness** Konturschärfe *f*, Kantenschärfe *f*

contract *n* Vertrag *m*; ~ **on sharing terms** Anteilvertrag *m*; ~ **service** Fremdleistung *f*; **condition of ~** Vertragsbedingung *f*; **duration of ~** Vertragszeit *f*; **length of ~** Vertragszeit *f*; **life of ~** Vertragszeit *f*; **preliminary ~** Vorvertrag *m*; **to put under ~** verpflichten *v*

contracting out of production Produktionsvergabe *f*; ~ **party** Vertragspartner *m*

contrast *n* Kontrast *m*; ~ *n* (F) Steilheit *f*; ~ **balance** Kontrastgleichgewicht *n*; ~ **control** Kontrastregelung *f*; ~ **control knob** Kontrastregler *m*; ~ **effect** Kontrasteffekt *m*; ~ **filter** Kontrastfilter *m*; ~ **range** Helligkeitsumfang *m*, Kontrastbereich *m*, Kontrastumfang *m*, Leuchtdichteumfang *m*; ~ **range of subject** (light) Objektumfang *m* ~ **ratio** Kontrastverhältnis *n*, Kontrastumfang *m*; **acceptable ~ ratio (ACR)** Kontrastumfang *m*

contrasty *adj* kontrastreich *adj*; **too ~** knochig *adj*, zu hart, zu kontrastreich

contre-jour *n* Gegenlicht *n*

contribution *n* Beitrag *m*; ~ *n* (contract) Mitwirkung *f*; ~ **circuit** Einspielleitung *f*, Modulationszubringerleitung *f*, Zuführung *f*, Zuführungsleitung *f*, Zuspielleitung *f*

contributor *n* (journ.) Mitarbeiter *m* ~ *n* (contract) Mitwirkender *m*

control *v* regeln *v*, regulieren *v*, steuern *v*, überwachen *v*; ~ *n* Regelung *f*, Schaltung *f*, Steuerung *f*, Überwachung *f*; ~ *n* (fader) Steller *m*, Regler *m*, Schieber *m* (fam.); ~ **band printer** Blendenbandkopiermaschine *f*; ~ **characteristic** Regelkurve *f*; ~ **circuit** Kontrolleitung *f*, Meldeleitung *f*, Regelschaltung *f*, Steuerstromkreis *m*; ~ **-circuit network** Meldeleitungsnetz *n*; ~ **console** Steuerpult *n*; ~ **cubicle** Abhörbox *f*, Abhörkabine *f*, Regieraum *m*, Regie *f*; ~ **desk** Bedienpult *n*, Kontrollpult *n*, Mischpult *n*, Regiepult *n*, Regietisch *m*, Schaltpult *n*, Stellpult *n*, Überwachungspult *n*; ~ **function** (EDP) Steuerfunktion *f* ~ **-gate** *n* Schütz *n*; ~ **gear** Steuergerät *n*; ~ **grid** Steuergitter *n*; ~ **-grid signal voltage** Gitterwechselspannung *f*; ~ **knob** Bedienungsknopf *m*, Drehknopf *m*, Knopf *m*, Steller *m*, Schieber *m* (fam.), Steuerknopf *m*; ~ **lever** Steuerhebel *m*; ~ **line** Kontrolleitung *f*, Meldeleitung *f*, Mithörkontrolle *f*, Sprechleitung *f*, Steuerleitung *f*; ~ **logic** (EDP) Ansteuerlogik *f*; ~ **loudspeaker** Kontrollautsprecher *m*, Abhörlautsprecher *m*; ~ **of production** Produktionsüberwachung *f*; ~ **panel** Bediengerät *n*, Bedienungsfeld *n*, Konsole *f*, Schalttafel *f*, Schaltbrett *n*, Steuerfeld *n*; ~ **ring** Steuerring *m*; ~ **room** Bedienungsraum *m*, Kontrollraum *m*, Regie *f*, Regiekanzel *f*, Regieraum *m*, Schaltraum *m*, Überwachungsraum *m*; ~ **signal** Steuersignal *n*; ~ **statement** (EDP) Steueranweisung *f*; ~ **station** betriebsführendes Amt; ~ **track** Kontrollspur *f*, Merkspur *f*, Nachsteuerspur *f*, Steuerspur *f*; ~ **-track head** Kontrollspurkopf *m*; ~ **transmitter** Steuersender *m*; ~ **unit** Regeleinheit *f*, Steuerwerk *n*, Steuereinheit *f*; **central** ~ zentralisierte Steuerung; **clamped** ~ getastete Regelung; **linear** ~ linearer Steller; **logarithmic** ~ logarithmischer Steller; **undelayed** ~ verzögerungsfreie Steuerung

controlled condition (EDP) Regelgröße *f*

controller *n* (BBC) (approx.) Programmchef *m*

convergence *n* Deckung *f*, Farbbilddeckung *f*, Konvergenz *f*; ~ **assembly** Konvergenzeinheit *f*; ~ **circuit** Konvergenzplatine *f*; ~ **error** Deckungsfehler *m*; ~ **magnet** Konvergenzmagnet *m*; ~ **panel** Konvergenzplatine *f*; ~ **test pattern** Konvergenztestbild *n*

convergent lens Sammellinse *f*

converging lens Sammellinse *f*

conversion *n* Umsetzung *f*, Umwandlung *f*; ~ **efficiency** Umwandlungswirkungsgrad *m*; ~ **factor** Umrechnungskoeffizient *m*; ~ **filter** Konversionsfilter *m*; ~ **unit** Umrüstteil *n*

convert *v* umsetzen *v*, umwandeln *v*

converter *n* Konverter *m*, Umformer *m*, Umsetzer *m*, Wandler *m*; ~ **current** Mischstrom *m*; ~ **stage** Mischstufe *f*; ~ **tube** Mischröhre *f*

converting *n* (HF) Mischung *f*

convey *v* übermitteln *v*

conveyance *n* Übermittlung *f*

cooling *n* Kühlung *f*; ~ **air** Kühlluft *f*; ~ **blower** Kühlgebläse *n*; ~ **tank** Kühlküvette *f*; ~ **tower** Kühlturm *m*; ~ **vessel** Kühlgefäß *n*; ~ **water** Kühlwasser *n*

cooling-water pump Kühlwasserpumpe *f*

coordinate-setting *n* (EDP) Punktsteuerung *f*

coordination *n* Koordinierung *f*; ~ **centre** Koordinationszentrale *f*; ~ **circuit** Koordinationsleitung *f*; ~ **distance** (sat.) Koordinierungsentfernung *f*

coordinator *n* Koordinator *m*

Copenhagen plan Kopenhagener Wellenplan

coplanar cartridge Coplanarkassette *f*; ~ **cassette** Coplanarkassette *f*

copper bit Lötkolbenspitze *f*; ~ **loss** Kupferverluste *m pl*

co-production *n* Koproduktion *f*, Gemeinschaftsproduktion *f*

copy *v* kopieren *v*; ~ *v* (tape) umspielen *v*; ~ *n* Kopie *f*; ~ *n* (photo) Abzug *m*, Bildkopie *f*; ~ *n* (F) Filmkopie *f*; ~ *n* (journ.) Beitrag *m*; ~ **-taster** Redaktionsassistent *m*; **fresh** ~ frische Kopie

copying *n* Vervielfältigung *f*; ~ *n* (tape) Kopierung *f*, Umschneiden *n*; ~ **equipment** Umspielanlage *f*, Umspielmaschine *f*; ~ **machine** Vervielfältiger *m*; ~ **-machine operator** Vervielfältiger *m*; ~ **work** Reproduktion *f*
copyright *n* Urheberrecht *n*, Copyright *n*, Verlagsrechte *n pl*; ~ **in dramatic character** Urheberpersönlichkeitsrecht *n*; ~ **law** Urheberrechtsgesetz *n*; ~ **protection** Urheberrechtsschutz *m*
cord *n* Kabel *n*; ~ *n* (coll.) Schnur *f*
core *n* Bobby *m*, Filmkern *m*; ~ **array** (EDP) Kernmatrix *f*; ~ **matrix** (EDP) Kernmatrix *f*; ~ **storage** (EDP) Kernspeicher *m*; ~ **storage dump** (EDP) Speicherausdruck *m*; ~ **storage print-out** (EDP) Speicherausdruck *m*
corps de ballet Ballettkorps *n*, Balletttruppe *f*
correct *v* korrigieren *v*, nachsteuern *v*, verbessern *v*; ~ *v* (pict., sound) entzerren *v*
correction *n* Korrektur *f*, Berichtigung *f*, Richtigstellung *f*; ~ *n* (pict., sound) Entzerrung *f*; ~ **filter** Korrekturfilter *m*; ~ **sheet** Änderungsblatt *n*; ~ **signal** Korrektursignal *n*
corrector *n* (pict., sound) Entzerrer *m*
correspondence section Hörerpost* *f*
correspondent *n* Berichterstatter *m*, Korrespondent *m*, Mitarbeiter *m*; **corps of ~s** Korrespondentennetz *n*
corrosion-resistant *adj* korrosionsfest *adj*
cosine *n* Cosinus *m*; ~ **aperture corrector** Cosinus-Entzerrer *m*; ~ **correction** Cosinus-Entzerrung *f*
cosmetics *n pl* Schminkmittel *n pl*
cosmovision *n* Kosmovision *f*
cost accountancy Kalkulation *f*; ~ **accountant** Kalkulator *m*
co-star *n* (F) Partner *m*
cost-sharing *n* Kostenteilung *f*
costume *n* Kostüm *n*; ~ **adviser** Kostümberater *m*; ~ **design** Kostümausstattung *f*, Kostümentwurf *m*; ~ **design unit** Kostümbildnerei *f*; ~ **designer** Kostümbildner *m*, Kostümgestalter *m*; ~ **hire** Kostümverleih *m*; ~ **list** Kostümliste *f*; ~ **plot** Kostümliste *f*; ~ **store** Kostümfundus *m*; ~ **workroom** Kostümwerkstatt *f*; ~ **workshop** Kostümwerkstatt *f*
costumes* *n pl* Kostümbildnerei *f*
costumier *n* Kostümverleiher *m*; *n* (US) Garderobier *m*
cough key Räuspertaste *f*
count-down *n* Startvorlaufzeit *f*, Startzeit *f*
counter *n* Zähler *m*
counterbalance *n* Auswuchtung *f*, Ausgleich *m*; ~ **weight** Kameragewichtsausgleich *m*
countermand *v* widerrufen *v*
counting pulse Zählimpuls *m*
country of destination Bestimmungsland *n*; ~ **of origin** Ursprungsland *n*
couple *v* verkoppeln *v*; ~ **to** *v* ankoppeln *v*
coupler *n* drehbare Steckvorrichtung, Kuppler *m*; **dye** ~ farbige Kupplersubstanz
coupling *n* Ankopplung *f*, Kopplung *f*, Kupplung *f*, Verkopplung *f*; ~ **capacitor** Kopplungskondensator *m*; ~ **diplexer** Koppelweiche *f*; ~ **loop** Koppelschleife *f*; ~ **-out** *n* Auskopplung *f*; ~ **sleeve** Kupplungsbuchse *f*; ~ **transformer** Kopplungsübertrager *m*
course *n* Kursprogramm *n*
court correspondent

Gerichtsreporter *m*; ~ **report** Prozeßbericht *m*; ~ **reporter** Gerichtsreporter *m*

cove *n* Voute *f*

cover *v* berichten *v*, Berichterstattung wahrnehmen; ~ *n* Abdeckung *f*, Schutzdeckel *m*; ~ *n* (mask) Kasch *m*; ~ **plate** Abdeckblech *n*; ~ **sheet** Abdeckblech *n*

coverage *n* (journ.) Berichterstattung *f*; ~ *n* (transmitter) Reichweite *f*, Versorgung *f*; ~ **area** Ausbreitungszone *f*, Sendebereich *m*, Sendegebiet *n*, Anstaltsbereich *m*, Verbreitungsgebiet *n*; ~ **area** (transmitter) Versorgungsbereich *m*, Versorgungsgebiet *n*; ~ **of running story** laufende Berichterstattung; ~ **zone** (sat.) Sichtbarkeitszone *f*; **to ensure full ~ of** abdecken *v*; **wide ~** ausführliche Berichterstattung

covering *n* (cam.) Hülle *f*; ~ *n* (aperture) Abdeckung *f*; **sound-proof ~** schalldichte Hülle

crab *v* (cam.) seitwärts fahren; ~ *n* Parallelfahrt *f*

crabbing *n* seitliche Kamerafahrt

crack *v* knicken *v*; ~ *n* Knick *m*

crackle *v* prasseln *v*; ~ *v* knistern *v*

crackling *n* Prasseln *n*; ~ *n* Knattern *n*; ~ **sound** Knacklaut *m*

craftsman *n* Facharbeiter *m*

crane *n* (F) Kran *m*

craning *n* Schwenk *m*; **lateral ~** seitlicher Schwenk

craning-down *n* Senkrechtschwenk nach unten, senkrechter Schwenk nach unten

craning-up *n* Senkrechtschwenk nach oben, senkrechter Schwenk nach oben

crank *n* Kurbel *f*

credit title Titel *m*

credits *n pl* Titel *m*; **list of ~** Titelliste *f*

creepie-peepie *n* (US) tragbare Fernsehkamera

crest factor Scheitelfaktor *m*; ~ **value** Scheitelwert *m*; ~ **voltage** Scheitelspannung *f*

crew *n* Team *n*

crib card Neger *m* (fam.)

crispening *n* Konturverstärkung *f*

critic *n* Kritiker *m*

critical aperture kritische Blende; ~ **bandwidth** Frequenzgruppe *f*

criticism *n* Kritik *f*

cross *n* (thea. perf.) Gang *m*; **to ~ the line of vision** über die Achse springen

cross arm Traverse *f*

cross-bar *n* Kreuzschiene *f*; ~ *n* (lighting) Kreuzgelenk *n*

cross-colour *n* Leuchtdichte/Chrominanz-Übersprechen *n*, Farbkanalübersprechen *n*

cross connection Querverbindung *f*

cross-connection field Rangierfeld *n*

cross-cutting *n* schnelle Einstellungsfolge; ~ *n* (US) Montage *f*

crossed dipole Kreuzdipol *m*; ~ **spots** *n pl* Kreuzlicht *n*

cross-fade *v* (pict.) überblenden *v*, mischen *v*; ~ *n* Einblendung *f*, Überblendung *f*, Überblenden *n*

cross-fading *n* (pict.) Bildüberblendung *f*

crosshairs *n pl* Fadenkreuz *n*

cross-joint *n* (lighting) Kreuzverschraubung *f*

cross-light *n* Kreuzlicht *n*

cross-line test pattern Kreuzlinientestbild *n*

cross modulation Kreuzmodulation *f*

cross-over frequency Übergangsfrequenz *f*; ~ **network** (acoust.) Frequenzweiche *f*

cross-section of cable

Kabelquerschnitt *m*
crosstalk *v* übersprechen *v*; ~ *n* Tonübersprechen *n*, Übersprechen *n*, Einstreuung *f*; **~ attenuation** Übersprechdämpfung *f*; **~ transmission equivalent** Übersprechdämpfung *f*
crossview *n* Bildintermodulation *f*, Bildübersprechen *n*, Fremdbild *n*, Übersprechen *n*
crowd *n* Komparserie *f*, Statisterie *f* **~ extras** *n pl* Massenkomparserie *f*; **~ scene** Massenszene *f*; **~ shot** Gruppeneinstellung *f*; **~ supers** *n pl* (US) Massenkomparserie *f*
CRT display unit (EDP) Sichtgerät *n*
crush *v* stauchen *v*; ~ *n* Umkehrung *f*; **to ~ the blacks** Schwarzwert stauchen
crushing *n* Stauchung *f*; ~ *n* Umkehrung *f*
crystal *n* Quarz *m*; **~ control** Quarzsteuerung *f*; **~ diode** Richtleiter *m*; **~ microphone** Kristallmikrofon *n*; **~ oscillator** Kristalloszillator *m*, Quarzgenerator *m*, Quarzoszillator *m*; **~ pick-up** Kristalltonabnehmer *m*; **~ reactance** Quarzscheinwiderstand *m*
cubicle *n* Kabine *f*; ~ *n* (R) Kontrollraum *m*, Regie *f*
cue *n* Zeichen *n*, Kommando *n*, Kommandozeichen *n*, Einsatz *m*, Einsatzsignal *n*, Stichwort *n*; ~ *n* (R) Zwischenansage *f*; ~ *n* (F) Marke *f*, Markierung *f*, Schnittmarke *f*; ~ *n* (news) Antext *m*
cue! (F, tape) ab!
cue button Kommandotaste *f*; **~ dot** Überblendzeichen *n*; **~ dots** Koppelzeichen *n pl*, Aktüberblendzeichen *n pl*, Bildüberblendzeichen *n pl*; **~ in** *v* (F) einstarten *v*; **~ light** Kontrollicht *n*, Lichtzeichen *n*, Leuchtzeichen *n*, Signallampe *f*; **~ lights** *n pl* Tannenbaum *m*; **~ line** Kommandoleitung *f*; **~ marks** Bildüberblendzeichen *n pl*; **~ pulse** (TV) Schnittmarke *f*; **~ sheet** Mischplan *m*; **~ track** Kommandospur *f*, Merkspur *f*, Hilfstonspur *f*; **acoustic ~** akustische Markierung; **incoming ~** ankommendes Kommando; **outgoing ~** abgehendes Kommando; **to place ~ marks** einstarten *v*; **to provide with a ~** antexten *v*
cueing *n* (F) Anschluß *m*; **~ circuit** Kommandoleitung *f*; **~ device** (disc) Tonarmlift *m*
cultural affairs *n pl* Kultur* *f*, kulturelles Wort*; **~ affairs editor** Kulturredakteur *m*; **~ documentary** Kulturfilm *m*; **~ editor** Feuilletonredakteur *m*; **~ film** Kulturfilm *m*
curl *v* (F) rollen *v*
current *n* Strom *m*, Saft *m* (fam.); **~ affairs** *n pl* Aktuelles *n*; **~ affairs broadcast** aktuelle Sendung; **~ affairs commentary** Zeitkritik *f*; **~ affairs magazine** (prog.) Umschau *f*; **~ affairs programmes** *n pl* Aktuelles *n*; **~ affairs specials*** *n pl* Dokumentationen* *f pl*; **~ affairs studio** aktuelles Studio; **~ amplification** Stromverstärkung *f*; **~ antinode** Strombauch *m*; **~ consumption** Stromaufnahme *f*; **~ density** Stromdichte *f*; **~ input** Stromaufnahme *f*; **~ intensity** Stromstärke *f*; **~ intersection** Stromknotenpunkt *m*; **~ junction** Stromknotenpunkt *m*; **~ loop** Strombauch *m*; **~ planning** Programmeinplanung *f*; **~ probe** Stromzange *f*, Amperezange *f*; **~ transformer** Stromwandler *m*;

radio talks and ~ affairs programmes *n pl* Zeitfunk *m*
currentless *adj* stromlos *adj*
curriculum *n* Lehrplan *m*, Studienplan *m*
curtain fading shutter Vorhangblende *f*; **~ shutter** Vorhangblende *f*; **~ track** Vorhangschiene *f*; **~ wipe** Vorhangblende *f*; **horizontal ~ shutter** horizontale Vorhangblende; **vertical ~ shutter** vertikale Vorhangblende
curvature *n* Krümmung *f*
curve *n* Kurve *f*; **~ follower** (EDP) Kurvenleser *m*; **~ -plotter** *n* (EDP) Kurvenschreiber *m*, Kurvenzeichner *m*, Plotter *m*; **~ tracer** (EDP) Kurvenleser *m*; **sensitometric ~** sensitometrische Kurve
cut *v* (F, tape) schneiden *v*, cutten *v*, montieren *v*; ~ *v* (pict.) anschneiden *v*; ~ *v* (video) umschneiden *v*, hart überblenden ~ *v* (sound, pict.) wegnehmen *v*; ~ *v* (script) kürzen *v*; ~ *v* (from...to) (sound) überschneiden *v*; ~ *v* (to) umschalten *v* (auf); ~ *n* Schnitt *m*; ~ *n* (R, TV, F, script) Ausschnitt *m*; ~ *n* (F, tape) Cut *m*; ~ *n* (video) harte Aufschaltung, harte Überblendung; ~ *n* (script, tape) Textausschnitt *m*; ~ *n* (pict.) Anschnitt *m*
cut! aus!; ~ (take) Stopp!
cut across *v* überschneiden *v*; **~ away** *v* (US) ausblenden *v* (sich); **~ button** Schnittaste *f*; **~ button** (micr.) Räuspertaste *f*; **~ in** *v* einblenden *v* (sich); **~ into a movement** Anschnitt in der Bewegung; **~ key** Schnittaste *f*, Trenntaste *f*; **~ off** *v* abschneiden *v*, abtrennen *n*; **~ on** harter Schnitt auf; **~ on action** Schnitt in der Bewegung; **~ on move** Schnitt in der Bewegung; **~ out** *v* herausschneiden *v*; **~ out** *v* (elec.) ausschalten *v*; **~ sound !** Ton aus!; **~ to** harter Schnitt zu; **~ together** *v* (F) zusammenschneiden *v*; **electronic ~** elektronischer Schnitt; **in the ~** im Anschnitt; **to ~ identification** Kennung wegnehmen; **to ~ to music** auf Musik schneiden
cut-away *n* Gegenschnitt *m*, Zwischenschnitt *m*; **~ shot** Zwischenschuß *m*
cut-in *n* Schnittbilder *n pl*, Unterschnitt *m*; **~ order** Schnittbildfolge *f*
cut-off area äußerer Kasch, Umfeldbild *n*; **~ frequency** Grenzfrequenz *f*; **~ sensitivity** Grenzempfindlichkeit *f*; **~ voltage** Sperrspannung *f*
cut-out *n* Ausschalter *m*, Schütz *n*, Trennschalter *m*, Unterbrecher *m* **~ diaphragm** Schablonenblende *f*; **~ switch** Pannenschalter *m*, Schutzschalter *m*, Salatschalter *m* (fam.); **magnetic ~ switch** Schutzschalter mit Magnetauslösung; **thermic ~ switch** magnetothermischer Schutzschalter
cuts rack Galgen *m*
cutter *n* Cutter *m*, Cutterin *f*; ~ *n* (F) Filmcutter *m*; ~ *n* (disc) Stichel *m*
cutting *n* Schnittbearbeitung *f*, Schnitt *m*; ~ *n* (pict.) Bildschnitt *m*; ~ *n* (press) Zeitungsausschnitt *m*; **~ bench** Schneidetisch *m*; **~ copy** (F) Schnittkopie *f*; **~ -copy print** Arbeitskopie *f*; **~ machine** Fräsmaschine *f*; **~ mark** Filmeinzeichnung *f*; **~ order** Schnittfolge *f*; **~ -out** *n* Ausschalten *n*, Ausschaltung *f*; **~ pace** Schnittwechsel *m*; **~ point** (F) Schnittmarke *f*; **~ precision** (F) Schnittstabilität *f*; **~ room** Schneideraum *m*; **~ -room log**

Schnittliste *f*; ~ **table** Schneidetisch *m*; ~ **time** Schnittzeit *f*; **final viewing of ~ copy** Schnittabnahme *f*
cybernetics *n* Kybernetik *f*
cycle *n* Schwingungszug *m*; ~ *n* (EDP) Zyklus *m*; ~ **delay unit** (EDP) Impulsspeicher *m*; ~ **time** (EDP) Zykluszeit *f*
cycles per second (cps) Hertz (Hz) *n*
cyclic *adj* (EDP) zyklisch *adj*
cyclorama (cyc) *n* Rundhorizont *m*; ~ **with merging curve** Rundhorizont mit Voute
cylinder *n* (mech.) Trommel *f*
cylindrical *adj* tonnenförmig *adj*

D

dagger operation (EDP) NAND-Funktion *f*
dailies *n pl* (US) Muster *n pl*, Musterkopie *f*
daily allowance Tagegeld *n*; ~ **allowances** Diäten *f pl*; ~ **commentary** Tageskommentar *m*; ~ **fee** Tagesgage *f*; ~ **rate** Tagesgage *f*; ~ **report** (F) Tagesbericht *m*; ~ **selection** (F) Ausmustern *n*
daltonism *n* Farbfehlsichtigkeit *f*
damage *n* Schaden *m*
damp *v* dämpfen *v*; ~ *v* anfeuchten *v*
damping *n* Dämpfung *f*, Bedämpfung *f*
dance music Tanzmusik *f*; ~ **orchestra** Tanzorchester *n*
dark current Dunkelstrom *m*; ~ **period** Dunkelphase *f*; ~ **-picture areas** Tiefen *f pl*; ~ **slide** (photo) Plattenkassette *f*
darken *v* schwärzen *v*
darkroom *n* Dunkelkammer *f*, Dunkelraum *m*; ~ **fog** Entwicklungsschleier *m*; ~ **timer** Belichtungsuhr *f*
dash-board *n* Armaturenbrett *n*
data *n pl* Daten *n pl*; ~ **acquisition** (EDP) Datenaufnahme *f*; ~ **carrier** (EDP) Datenträger *m*; ~ **channel** (EDP) Datenkanal *m*; ~ **collection** (EDP) Datenaufnahme *f*; ~ **display device** (EDP) Datensichtgerät *n*; ~ **file** (EDP) Datei *f*; ~ **flow** (EDP) Datenfluß *m*; ~ **flow chart** (EDP) Datenflußplan *m*; ~ **flow diagram** (EDP) Datenflußplan *m*; ~ **handling** (EDP) Datenbearbeitung *f*; ~ **input** (EDP) Dateneingabe *f*; ~ **medium** (EDP) Datenträger *m*; ~ **processing** (EDP) Datenverarbeitung *f*; ~ **processing system** (EDP) Datenverarbeitungsanlage *f*, Rechenanlage *f*; ~ **set** (EDP) Datei *f*; ~ **sheet** Datenblatt *n*; ~ **sheet** (prod.) Produktionsbericht *m*; ~ **storage** Informationsspeicherung *f*; **electrical ~** elektrische Werte
datum line Bezugslinie *f*
day in the studio Atelierdrehtag *m*; ~ **on location** Außenaufnahmetag *m*; ~ **on the stage** Atelierdrehtag *m*; ~ **range** (transmitter) Tagesreichweite *f*; ~ **working** Tagbetrieb *m*
day-for-night shot Nachteffektaufnahme *f*
daylight *n* Tageslicht *n*; ~ **emulsion** Tageslichtemulsion *f*; ~ **loading spool** Tageslichtspule *f*
daytime service range (transmitter) Tagesreichweite *f*
dazzle *n* Überstrahlung *f*
DC *s.* direct current; ~ **-separating network** Gleichstromweiche *f*
dead *adj* (sound) schalltot *adj*; ~ *adj* (F) abgedreht *adj*; ~ *adj* (news) gestorben *adj*; ~ *adj* (elec.) spannungslos *adj*, stromlos *adj*; ~ **studio** nachhallfreies Studio, schalltotes Studio; ~ **time** (prod.)

Leerlauf *m*
dead-beat *adj* aperiodisch *adj*
deadline *n* Redaktionsschluß *m*
deaf-aid *n* drahtloser Kommandoempfänger; ~ *n* (coll.) Ohrhörer *m*, Schmalzbohrer *m* (fam.), Specknudel *f* (fam.)
debate *n* Diskussion *f*, Gespräch *n*
debugging *n* (EDP) Entstörung *f*, Fehlerbeseitigung *f*, Programmkorrektur *f*
decibel *n* Dezibel *n*; ~ **meter** Dezibelmesser *m*
decimetre waves (DM waves) Dezimeterwellen (UHF) *f pl*
decimetre-wave band Dezimeterwellenbereich *m*
deciphering *n* Entschlüsselung *f*
declutch *v* (mech.) entkuppeln *v*
declutching *n* (mech.) Entkupplung *f*
decoder *n* Dekoder *m*, Farbdekoder *m*; ~ **matrix** Dekodiermatrix *f*, Entschlüsselungsmatrix *f*
decoding *n* Dekodierung *f*
decomposition of spectrum Zerlegung des Spektrums
decor *n* Ausstattung *f*, Bühnenbild *n*, Szenenbild *n*
decoration *n* Dekoration *f*
decorative flat Dekorationswand *f*; ~ **lighting** Effektbeleuchtung *f*; ~ **screen** Dekorationswand *f*
decorator *n* Dekorateur *m*, Deko *m* (fam.)
decouple *v* (meas.) entkoppeln *v*
decoupling *n* (meas.) Entkopplung *f*; ~ **filter** Entkopplungsfilter *m*
decrease *v* abnehmen *v*; ~ *n* Abnahme *f*, Verkleinerung *f*; ~ *n* (level) Pegelabfall *m*
de-emphasis (DE) *n* Deemphasis *f*, Frequenzgangnachentzerrung *f*, Nachentzerrung *f*; ~ *n* (sound) Absenkung *f*
deep shadow Kernschatten *m*
defect *n* Fehler *m*, Schaden *m*
defective *adj* fehlerhaft *adj*, gestört *adj*
defence correspondent Wehrexperte *m*
defer *v* verschieben *v*
deferment *n* Verschiebung *f*
deferred *adj* zeitversetzt *adj*; ~ **relay** zeitversetzte Livesendung, zeitversetzte Übertragung
definition *n* (opt.) Auflösung *f*; ~ *n* (pict.) Kantenschärfe *f*, Schärfe *f*, Scharfzeichnung *f*; ~ **of image** Abbildungsgüte *f*; **good ~** naturgetreue Wiedergabe; **lack of ~** Unschärfe *f*
deflect *v* ablenken *v*
deflecting unit Ablenkeinheit *f*; ~ **voltage** (EDP) Ablenkspannung *f*
deflection *n* Ablenkung *f*, Abweichung *f*, Schwingung *f*; ~ **circuit** Ablenkschaltung *f*; ~ **coil** Ablenkspule *f*; ~ **time** Ablenkzeit *f*
defocus *v* Bild in die Unschärfe ziehen
degausser *n* Entmagnetisierungsdrossel *f*
degaussing *n* Entmagnetisierung *f*
degradation *n* Beeinträchtigung *f*; ~ *n* (tech.) Güteabfall *m*
degree *n* Stufe *f*, Grad *m*; ~ **of acidity** Säuregrad *m*; ~ **of echo** Hallanteil *m*; ~ **of enlargement** Vergrößerungsmaßstab *m*; ~ **of sharpness** Schärfegrad *m*
delay *v* verzögern *v*; ~ *n* Verzögerung *f*; ~ *n* (time) Wartezeit *f*; ~ **demodulation** Laufzeitdemodulation *f*; ~ **distortion** Laufzeitverzerrung *f*; ~ **line** Laufzeitleitung *f*, Verzögerungsleitung *f*, Laufzeitglied *n*, Laufzeitkette *f*; ~ **-line detector** Laufzeitdemodulator *m*; ~ **network** Laufzeitkette *f*; ~ **system** Signalverzögerungssystem *n*;

~ time Laufzeit *f*, Verzögerungszeit *f*; **~ -time difference** Laufzeitdifferenz *f*; **~ unit** Verzögerungskassette *f*; **acoustic ~ line** (EDP) akustische Verzögerungsleitung; **sonic ~ line** (EDP) akustische Verzögerungsleitung; **variable ~ line** einstellbare Verzögerungsleitung
delivery spool Vorratstrommel *f*
delta system Dreiecksystem *n*; **~ voltage** Dreieckspannung *f*
demagnetisation *n* Entmagnetisierung *f*
demagnetiser *n* Entmagnetisierungsdrossel *f*
demagnetising coil Entmagnetisierungsdrossel *f*
demodulator *n* Demodulator *m*
demonstration tape Vorführband *n*
dendriform exposure of film Verblitzung *f*
denial *n* Dementi *n*
densitometer *n* Densitometer *n*
densitometric *adj* densitometrisch *adj*
densitometry *n* Densitometrie *f*
density *n* Dichte *f*, Deckung *f*, Schwärzung *f*; **~ latitude** Schwärzungsumfang *m*; **~ range** Dichtebereich *m*, Schwärzungsbereich *m*, Schwärzungsumfang *m*; **~ scale** Schwärzungsumfang *m*; **~ step** Schwärzungsstufe *f*; **~ value** Helligkeitswert *m*, Schwärzungsstufe *f*; **~ wedge** Keilvorlage *f*; **diffuse ~** diffuse Schwärzung; **fixed ~** gleichbleibende Schwärzung; **maximum ~** maximale Schwärzung; **variable ~** veränderliche Schwärzung
department *n* Abteilung *f*, Hauptabteilung (HA) *f*, Referat *n*, Ressort *n*
dependability *n* Zuverlässigkeit *f*
dependence of attenuation upon frequency frequenzabhängige Dämpfung
dephase *v* aus der Phase bringen
depot *n* Lager *n*, Magazin
depress, to ~ the camera Kamera senken
depth of field Schärfentiefe *f*, Tiefenschärfe *f*; **~ of field chart** Tiefenschärfentabelle *f*; **~ of focus** Fokusdifferenz *f*, Schärfentiefe *f*, Tiefenschärfe *f*; **~ of modulation** Modulationstiefe *f*
deputy *adj* stellvertretend *adj*
desaturate *v* entsättigen *v*, verweißlichen *v*
desaturation *n* Entsättigung *f*, Verweißlichung *f*
description *n* Beschreibung *f*
desensitise *v* desensibilisieren *v*
desensitised *adj* unsensibilisiert *adj*
design *n* Zeichnung *f*, Entwurf *n*, Modell *n*; *n* (set) Dekoration *f*; **~ costs** Ausstattungskosten *plt*; **~ department** Ausstattungsabteilung *f*; **~ planning meeting** Ausstattungsbesprechung *f*, Baubesprechung *f*; **~ team** Ausstattungsstab *m*
designation *n* Benennung *f*, Bezeichnung *f*
designer *n* Bühnenbildner *m*, Szenenbildner *m*, Zeichner *m*; **~** *n* (set) Ausstatter *m*
designer's office Architektenbüro *n*
desk *n* Pult *n*; **~** *n* (editorial) Ressort *n*, Desk *m*; **~ microphone** Tischmikrofon *n*; **~ operator** Tontechniker *m*
detach *v* auseinandernehmen *v*
detachable *adj* abnehmbar *adj*
detail contrast Detailkontrast *m*; **~ drawing** Detailzeichnung *f*
detecting element Meßfühler *m*
detective film Kriminalfilm *m*, Krimi *m* (fam.)
detector *n* Detektor *m*,

Gleichrichter *m*; ~ **amplifier** Anzeigeverstärker *m*; ~ **valve** Gleichrichterröhre *f*
develop *v* entwickeln *v*
developer *n* (FP) Entwickler *m*, Filmentwickler *m*
developing *n* (FP) Entwicklung *f*; ~ **agent** Entwicklungssubstanz *f*; ~ **bath** Entwicklerbad *n*; ~ **equipment** Entwicklungsanlage *f*; ~ **machine** Entwicklungsmaschine *f*; ~ **plant** Entwicklungsanlage *f*; ~ **process** Entwicklungsprozeß *m*; ~ **tank** Entwicklerdose *f*, Entwicklertank *m*, Bädertank *m*
development *n* Entwicklung *f*; ~ **contrast** Entwicklungskontrast *m*; ~ **costs** Entwicklungskosten *plt* ~ **engineer** Entwicklungsingenieur *m*
deviate *v* aussteuern *v*
deviating prism Umlenkprisma *n*
deviation *n* Abweichung *f*; ~ *n* (freq.) Frequenzhub eines Wobblers, Hub *m*; ~ **mirror** Umlenkspiegel *m*; ~ **wedge** Umlenkprisma *n*
device *n* Gerät *n*, Apparat *m*; ~ **request interrupt** (EDP) Unterbrechung *f*
diagonal join Diagonalklebestelle *f*; ~ **of picture** Bilddiagonale *f*; ~ **scratch** Schrägschramme *f*; ~ **splice** Diagonalklebestelle *f*; ~ **wipe** Diagonalblende *f*, Schrägblende *f*
diagonal-cutting pliers *n pl* Seitenschneider *m*
diagram *n* Diagramm *n*, Grafik *f*, grafische Darstellung, Kurve *f*, Schaubild *n*, Schautafel *f*, Zeichnung *f*
dial *n* (rec.) Skala *f*; ~ *n* (tel.) Wähler *m*
dialect broadcast Mundartsendung *f*
dialog system (EDP) Frage/Antwort-System *n*, Dialogsystem *n*
dialogue *n* Dialog *m*; ~ **direction** Dialogregie *f*, Dialogführung *f*; ~ **director** Dialogregisseur *m*; ~ **scene** Dialogszene *f*; ~ **script** Dialogbuch *n*, Dialogliste *f*
dialoguist *n* Dialogautor *m*
diaphragm *n* (opt.) Blende *f*; ~ *n* (tel.) Membran *f*; ~ **ring** Blendenring *m*; ~ **scale** Blendenskala *f*; ~ **setting** Blendeneinstellung *f*; **automatic** ~ Springblende *f*; **semi-automatic** ~ Springblende *f*; **to close** ~ Blende schließen; **to open** ~ Blende öffnen
diapositive *n* Diapositiv *n*, Dia *n*, Lichtbild *n*
diascope *n* (becoming obsolete) Prüfprojektor *m*
die *n* Stanze *f*
dielectric constant Dielektrizitätskonstante *f*
difference frequency Differenzfrequenz *f*, Differenzton *m*; ~ **frequency method** Differenztonverfahren *n*; ~ **signal** Differenzsignal *n*
differential amplifier Differenzverstärker *m*; ~ **gain** differentielle Verstärkung; ~ **gain distortion** differentieller Verstärkungsfaktor; ~ **microphone** Kompensationsmikrofon *n*; ~ **transformer** Differentialübertrager *m*
differentiate *v* differenzieren *v*
differentiating amplifier Differenzierverstärker *m*
diffuse *v* (opt.) zerstreuen *v*, soften *v* ~ *adj* diffus *adj*
diffused *adj* diffus *adj*; ~ **light** Streulicht *n*
diffuser *n* Blende *f*, Softscheibe *f*, Weichstrahler *m*; ~ **lens** Diffuserlinse *f*; ~ **scrim** Weichzeichner *m*

diffusing disc Weichbildscheibe *f*; **~ filter** (opt.) Diffusionsfilter *m*; **~ lens** Diffuserlinse *f*, Softlinse *f*; **~ screen** Streulichtschirm *m*, Streuschirm *m*
diffusion *n* Diffusion *f*, Streuung *f*, Zerstreuung *f*; ~ *n* (F, photo) Weichzeichnung *f*; **~ angle** (lighting) Streuwinkel *m*; **~ factor** Streulichtfaktor *m*
digit emitter (EDP) Impulsgeber *m*
digital *adj* (EDP) digital *adj*; **~ computer** (EDP) Digital-Rechner *m*; **~ counter** Digitalzähler *m*; **~ display** (EDP) digitale Anzeige; **~ meter** Digitalmeßinstrument *n*; **~ reader** Zifferanzeigegerät *n*; **~ read-out** Digitalanzeige *f*
digital-to-analog converter (EDP) Digital-Analog-Umsetzer *m*
digitiser *n* (EDP) Analog-Digital-Umsetzer (ADU) *m*
dilute *v* verdünnen *v*
diluting agent Verdünner *m*
dilution *n* Verdünnung *f*; ~ *n* (col.) Verwässerung *f*
dim *v* (light) abblenden *v*, herunterregeln *v*
dimension *n* Format *n*, Größe *f*, Maß *n*; **~ of picture** Bildformat *n*
dimensions *n pl* Abmessungen *f pl*
diminish *v* abnehmen *v*; ~ *v* verkleinern *v*
diminution *n* Verkleinerung *f*
dimmer *n* Lichtregler *m*, Steller *m*, Schieber *m* (fam.), Verdunkler *m*; **~ bank** Beleuchtungssteuerfeld *n*
dimming *n* (light) Abblende *f*, Abblendung *f*, Ausblende *f*, Abnahme *f*; **~ switch** Verdunkler *m*
diode *n* Diode *f*; **~ rectifier** Diodengleichrichter *m*; **~ terminal** Diodenanschluß *m*
dioptre *n* Dioptrie (dptr) *f*; **~ correction** Dioptrieausgleich *m*
dip soldering Tauchlöten *n*; **to ~ the sound** abblenden *v*
diplexer *n* Trennweiche *f*, Weiche *f*, Multiplexer *m*
diplomatic desk (R, TV) Außenpolitik* *f*, Politik Ausland* *f*; **~ unit*** (R, TV) Außenpolitik* *f*, Politik Ausland* *f*
dipole *n* Dipol *m*; ~ *n* Dipolantenne *f*; **~ aerial** Dipolantenne *f*; **~ array** Dipolgruppe *f*; **~ panel** Dipolfeld *n* **crossed ~** Kreuzdipol *m*; **plain ~** gestreckter Dipol
direct *v* richten *v* (auf); ~ *v* (prod.) inszenieren *v*, Regie führen; ~ *adj* direkt *adj*; **~ broadcast by satellite** direkte Satellitenübertragung; **~ current (DC)** Gleichstrom *m*; **~ current amplifier** Gleichstromverstärker *m*; **~ current component** Gleichstromanteil *m*, Gleichstromkomponente *f*; **~ current motor** Gleichstrommotor *m*; **~ current resistance** Gleichstromwiderstand *m*; **~ current restoration** Schwarzwerthaltung *f*, Schwarzwertwiedergabe *f*, Schwarzwertfesthaltung *f*; **~ current restoration diode** Schwarzwertdiode *f*; **~ current voltage** Gleichspannung *f*; **~ current voltage amplifier** Gleichspannungsverstärker *m*; **~ -detection receiver** Geradeausempfänger *m*; **~ hook-up** (coll.) Direktschaltung *f*; **~ print** Kontaktkopie *f*, Klatschkopie *f*; **~ printing** Abklatschen *n*; **~ reception** Direktempfang *m*; **~ relay** Direktschaltung *f*, Direktübertragung *f*; **~ transmission** Direktübertragung *f*; **~ wave** Bodenwelle *f*; **centrifugally-governed ~ current**

motor fliehkraftgeregelter Gleichstrommotor
directed by ... (credits) Bildführung hatte ..., Regie *f*
directing station betriebsführendes Amt
direction *n* Spielleitung *f*, Regie *f*, Inszenierung *f*; ~ *n* (TV) Bildführung *f*; ~ *n* (instruction) Weisung *f*; **~ of light** Lichtrichtung *f*; **~ of lighting** Lichtführung *f*, Lichtgestaltung *f*; **~ of maximum radiation** Hauptstrahlrichtung *f*; **~ of reception** Empfangsrichtung *f*; **~ of rotation** Drehrichtung *f*; **~ of travel** Laufrichtung *f*; **~ of winding** Wicklungssinn *m*
directional aerial Richtantenne *f*, Richtfunkantenne *f*, Richtstrahlantenne *f*; **~ coupler** Richtkoppler *m*; **~ effect** Richtwirkung *f*; **~ gain** Antennengewinn einer Richtantenne; **~ information** (stereo) Richtungsinformation *f*; **~ link** Richtfunkstrecke *f*, Richtfunkverbindung *f*; **~ pattern** Richtcharakteristik *f*, Richtdiagramm *n*; **~ slip** Gleitrichtung *f*
directive *n* Weisung *f*
directivity *n* Peilwirkung *f*, Richtwirkung *f*
director *n* Direktor *m*; ~ *n* Regisseur *m*, Spielleiter *m*; ~ *n* (TV) Bildregisseur *m*; ~ *n* (F) Realisator *m*; **~ of engineering** technischer Direktor; **~ of finance** Finanzdirektor *m*; **~ of photography** Chefkameramann *m*, erster Kameramann, Lichtgestalter *m*; **~ of programmes** Programmdirektor *m*; **~ of programmes, radio** (BBC) stellvertretender Hörfunkdirektor **~ of programmes, television** (BBC) stellvertretender Fernsehdirektor; **~ of radio programmes** Programmdirektor Hörfunk; **~ of television programmes** Programmdirektor Fernsehen
directorate *n* Direktion *f*
director-cameraman *n* Kameramann und Regisseur in einer Person, Regisseur-Kameramann *m*, Regie-Kameramann *m*
director-general *n* Intendant *m*; **deputy ~** stellvertretender Intendant
director-general's office Intendanz *f*
director's conception Regiekonzeption *f*; **~ finder** Bildausschnittsucher *m*; **~ seat** Regiestuhl *m*; **~ staff** Regiestab *m*
dirt in the gate Negativfussel *m*
disabling signal (EDP) Sperrsignal *n*
disc *n* Schallplatte *f*, Grammofonplatte *f*, Platte *f*; ~ *n* (tape) Teller *m*; **~ drive** (EDP) Platteneinheit *f*; **~ -jockey** *n* Disk-Jockey *m*; **~ library** Plattenarchiv *n*, Schallplattenarchiv *n*; **~ programme** Schallplattenprogramm *n*; **~ recorder** Plattenaufnahmegerät *n*, Plattenschneidegerät *n*; **~ scratch** Schramme *f*; **~ trimmer** Scheibentrimmer *m*; **~ -type trimmer** Scheibentrimmer *m*; **unprocessed ~** ungepreßte Schallplatte
discharge *n* Entladung *f*; **~ resistance** Entladewiderstand *m* **static ~** statische Entladung
discharged lamp Leuchtstoffröhre *f*
discharging resistor Entladewiderstand *m*
disconnect *v* abschalten *v*, abtrennen *v*, ausschalten *v*, entkuppeln *v*
disconnecting switch Ausschalter *m*
disconnection *n* Abschaltung *f*, Ausschalten *n*,

Ausschaltung *f*, Entkupplung *f*, Leitungsunterbrechung *f*
discotheque *n* Diskothek *f*
discriminator *n* Diskriminator *m*
discussion *n* Diskussion *f*, Gespräch *n*; **~ chairman** Diskussionsleiter *m*, Gesprächsleiter *m*, Moderator *m*; **~ programme** Diskussionssendung *f*; **to chair a ~** eine Diskussion leiten
disenchanted, to be ~ with s.th. sich etwas abschminken (fam.)
disengage *v* (elec.) entkuppeln *v*
disengaging *n* (elec.) Entkupplung *f*
dismantle *v* auseinandernehmen *v*; **~** *v* abbauen *v*
dismantling *n* Abbau *m*
dismount *v* auseinandernehmen *v*
dispatch *n* Bericht *m*; **~ rider** Außenbote *m*, Bote *m*; **cabled ~** Kabelbericht *m*
dispersal *n* (opt.) Zerstreuung *f*
disperse *v* (opt.) zerstreuen *v*.
dispersion *n* Dispersion *f*, Streuung *f*, Zerstreuung *f*; **~ of light** Lichtzerlegung *f*; **~ point** Streupunkt *m*; **main ~ point** maximaler Streupunkt
displace *v* verschieben *v*
displacement *n* Verschiebung *f*; **~ in straight line** gradlinige Verschiebung; **axial ~** axiale Verschiebung
display primaries Empfängerprimärvalenzen *f pl*; **~ tube** Schirmbildröhre *f*, Schirmröhre *f*, Wiedergaberöhre *f* **~ unit** (EDP) Sichtgerät *n*
disposal *n* Abwicklung *f*
disruptive voltage Durchschlagspannung *f*
dissipated heat Verlustwärme *f*
dissolution *n* (opt.) Auflösung *f*
dissolve *v* auflösen *v*; **~** *v* (pict.) durchblenden *v*, überblenden *v*; **~** *n* Bildüberblendung *f*, Blende *f*, Durchblendung *f*, Überblendung *f*, Überblenden *n*
dissolving power Auflösungsvermögen *n*
distance *n* Entfernung *f*; **~ scale** Entfernungsskala *f*, Meterskala *f*; **~ setting** Entfernungseinstellung *f* **finite ~** endliche Entfernung; **minimum focusing ~** kürzeste scharf einstellbare Entfernung; **to estimate ~** Entfernung schätzen
distant control Fernschaltung *f*
distorting lens Anamorphot *m*
distortion *n* Verzeichnung *f*, Verzerrung *f*; **~ analyser** Verzerrungsmeßgerät *n*; **~ area** innerer Kasch; **~ measuring set** Verzerrungsmeßgerät *n*; **~ range** Verzerrungsgebiet *n*; **build-up and delay ~** Verzerrung durch Ein- und Ausschwingvorgänge; **geometric ~** geometrische Verzerrung; **harmonic ~** harmonische Verzerrung; **linear ~** lineare Verzerrung; **non-linear ~** nichtlineare Verzerrung; **optical ~** optische Verzeichnung; **transient ~** Verzerrung durch Ein- und Ausschwingvorgänge
distributed reactance verteilte Blindwiderstände
distributing agency Verleihfirma *f*; **~ network** Leitungsnetz *n*; **~ organisation** Verleihorganisation *f*
distribution *n* Verteilung *f*; **~** *n* (F) Verleih *m*; **~ agreement** Verleihvertrag *m*, Verwertungsvertrag *m*; **~ amplifier** Verteilerverstärker *m*; **~ board** Schalttafel *f*, Schaltbrett *n*, Verteiler *m*, Verteilertafel *f*; **~ box** Abzweigdose *f*, Abzweigkasten *m*, Verteilerkasten *m*; **~ circuit** Verteilerkreis *m*, Verteilerleitung *f*; **~ circuit** (tech.) Sendeleitung *f*; **~ company** Verwertungsgesellschaft *f*; **~ conduit** Verteilerleitung *f*;

~ **frame** Rangierverteiler *m*, Verteiler *m*, Verteilertafel *f*; ~ **line** Verteilerleitung *f*; ~ **network** Leitungsnetz *n*, Verteilungsnetz *n*, Verteilnetz *n*; ~ **panel** Verteilertafel *f*, Rangierfeld *n*; ~ **print** Verleihkopie *f*; ~ **right** Verbreitungsrecht *n*; ~ **rights** *n pl* Verwertungsrecht *n*; ~ **rights** (F) Verleihrechte *n pl*; ~ **satellite** Verteilersatellit *m*; ~ **stub** Stichleitungsverteilung *f*; ~ **switchboard** Verteilerschrank *m* ~ **system** Verteilungsnetz *n*, Verteilnetz *n*; **national ~ network** nationales Verteilungsnetz; **spectral ~ of radiation** spektrale Strahlungsverteilung

distributor *n* Verteiler *m*; ~ *n* (F) Verleiher *m*, Verleihfirma *f*

distributors *n pl* Verleih *m*

distributor's film Verleihfilm *m*; ~ **share** Verleihanteil *m*, Verwertungsanteil *m*

disturbance due to interference Interferenzstörung *f*

disturbed *adj* gestört *adj*

disturbing voltage Störspannung *f*, Fremdspannung *f*

diurnal range (transmitter) Tagesreichweite *f*

divergence *n* Divergenz *f*, Abweichung *f*

divergent lens Zerstreuungslinse *f*

diverging lens Zerstreuungslinse *f*

dividing filter Multiplexer *m*; ~ **network** (acoust.) Frequenzweiche *f*

document film Dokumentenfilm *m*

documentary *n* (R, TV) Dokumentarbericht *m*, Dokumentarfeature *n*, Dokumentation *f*, Feature *n*, Tatsachenbericht *m*; ~ *n* (F) Dokumentarfilm *m*, Dokumentation *f*; ~ *n* (bcast.) Dokumentarsendung *f*; ~ **and talks programmes*** Feature* *n*; ~ **feature** Dokumentarbericht *m*, Dokumentarfeature *n*, Dokumentation *f*, Feature *n*, Tatsachenbericht *m*; ~ **film** Dokumentarfilm *m*, Dokumentation *f*; **drama ~** Dokumentarspiel *n*, szenische Dokumentation, Semidokumentation *f*; **dramatised ~** Dokumentarspiel *n*, szenische Dokumentation, Semidokumentation *f*

documentation *n* Dokumentation *f*

document-copying stock Dokumentenfilm *m*

documents scanner Dokumentenabtaster *m*

doll buggy (US) Dolly *m*

dolly *n* Dolly *m*, Kamerafahrgestell *n*, Kamerawagen *m*; ~ **in** *v* Kamera vorwärts fahren, vorwärts fahren, vorfahren *v*; ~ **out** *v* Kamera rückwärts fahren, rückwärts fahren; ~ **shot** Kamerafahrt *f*

domestic programme nationales Programm; ~ **receiver** Heimempfänger *m*; ~ **studio equipment** Heimstudioanlage *f*

door contact Türkontakt *m*

door-keeper *n* Pförtner *m*

dope *n* (coll.) Information *f*

dope-sheet *n* Inhaltsangabe *f*, Begleittext *m*, Dopesheet *n*; ~ *n* (shooting) Aufnahmebericht *m*, Filmbericht *m*, Kamerabericht *m*

doping *n* Lackieren *n*

dosage *n* Dosierung *f*

dosimeter *n* Dosierungsgerät *n*

dosing *n* Dosierung *f*

dot *n* (light) Blende *f*; ~ **grating** Punktgitter *n*

dot-sequential *adj* punktsequent *adj*

double *v* (perf.) doubeln *v*; ~ *n* Doublette *f*; ~ *n* (perf.) Doppelgänger *m*, Doubel *n*; ~ **16** Doppel 16 *n*

double-balanced modulator Ringmodulator *m*
double-beam oscilloscope Zweistrahloszillograf *m*
double-chamber magazine Zweiraumkassette *f*
double-channel *adj* zweikanalig *adj*
double exposure Doppelbelichtung *f*, Zweitbelichtung *f*
double-headed *adj* zweistreifig *adj*; ~ **camera** Bild-Ton-Kamera *f*; ~ **system** Zweistreifenverfahren *n*
double image Geisterbild *n*
double-perforated film doppelt perforierter Film, zweiseitig perforierter Film; ~ **stock** doppelt perforierter Film, zweiseitig perforierter Film
double-play tape Doppelspielband *n*
doubler *n* Verdoppler *m*
double-shoot *v* mit zwei Kameras aufnehmen **double-sideband modulation (DSB modulation)** Doppelseitenbandmodulation *f*, Modulation mit doppeltem Seitenband (DSB)
double-sideband receiver Zweiseitenbandempfänger *m*
double socket Doppeldose *f*
double-speed *adj* mit zweierlei Geschwindigkeit
doublet *n* (US) Dipol *m*; ~ *n* (US) Dipolantenne *f*
double track Doppelspur *f*
double-track printing Zweibandkopierung *f*
douser *n* (F) Feuerschutzklappe *f*; ~ *n* (lighting) Blende *f*
dovetail *n* Schwalbenschwanz *m*
down lead (aerial) Niederführung *f*; ~ **time** (EDP) Ausfallzeit *f*
down-link *n* (sat.) Abwärtsverbindung *f*; ~ **frequency** (sat.) Abwärtsfrequenz *f*
downstream *adj* nachgeschaltet *adj*, stromabwärts *adj*
draft agreement Vertragsentwurf *m* ~ **contract** Vertragsentwurf *m*; ~ **screenplay** Rohdrehbuch *n*; ~ **script** Rohdrehbuch *n*, Treatment *n*
drafting office Zeichenbüro *n*
dragon's-teeth wipe Zerreißblende *f*
drama *n* Drama *n*, Schauspiel *n*
drama* *n* Schauspiel* *n*
drama documentary Dokumentarspiel *n*, szenische Dokumentation, Semidokumentation *f*; ~ **producer** Spielleiter *m*; ~ **studio** Hörspielstudio *n*
dramatic composition of picture Bilddramaturgie *f*
dramatisation *n* Dramatisierung *f*
dramatised documentary Dokumentarspiel *n*, szenische Dokumentation, Semidokumentation *f*
dramatist *n* Dramatiker *m*
dramaturgy *n* Dramaturgie *f*
drapes *n pl* (coll.) Dekorateur *m*, Deko *m* (fam.); ~ **workshop** Dekowerkstatt *f*
draughtsman *n* Bauzeichner *m*, Zeichner *m*; **technical ~** technischer Zeichner
drawing *n* Zeichnung *f*, Skizze *f*; ~ **office** Zeichenbüro *n*; ~ **pattern** Zeichenvorlage *f*
dress, to make ~ patterns Schnittmuster anfertigen
dresser *n* Ankleider *m*, Garderobier *m*, Garderobiere *f*
dressing *n* (set) Ausstattung *f*; ~ **cubicle** Ankleidekabine *f*
dressing-room *n* Ankleideraum *m*, Garderobe *f*
dressmaker *n* Kostümschneider *m*, Schneider *m*, Damenschneiderin *f*, Schneiderin *f*
dressmaking *n* Schneiderei *f*
drift *n* Abweichung *f*; ~ *n* (VTR) Drift *f*; ~ *n* (disc, tape) Schlupf *m*; ~ **error** (EDP) Driftfehler *m*
drive *v* steuern *v*; ~ *v* (transmitter) ansteuern *v*; ~ *n* Antrieb *m*; ~ *n*

(ampl.) Steuerung *f*; ~ **belt** Antriebsriemen *m*; ~ **capstan** (tape) Bandantriebswelle *f*; ~ **capstan** Antriebswelle *f*; ~ **gear** Antriebszahnrad *n*; ~ **mechanism** Laufwerk *n*; ~ **motor** Antriebsmotor *m*; ~ **pinion** Antriebsritzel *n*; ~ **roller** Antriebsrolle *f*; ~ **shaft** (tape) Bandantriebswelle *f*; ~ **shaft** Antriebsachse *f*; ~ **signal** Ansteuerungssignal *n*, Steuersignal *n*

drive-in cinema Autokino *n*

driver *n* Treiberstufe *f*; ~ **stage** Treiberstufe *f*; ~ **transformer** Treibertransformator *m*

driving power Steuerleistung *f*; ~ **stage** Vorstufe *f*

droit de suite Folgerecht *n*

drop *v* (prog.) absetzen *v*; ~ **in level** Pegelabfall *m*

drop-out *n* (tape) Bandfehlstelle *f*; ~ *n* Ausfall *m*; ~ *n* (sound) Drop-out *m*; ~ **suppression** (sound) Drop-out-Unterdrückung *f*

dropped, to be (prog.) ausfallen *v*

drown out *v* (sound) zudecken *v*

drum *n* Trommel *f*; ~ **diaphragm** Trommelblende *f*; ~ **shutter** Trommelblende *f*

dry *v* trocknen *v*; ~ **box** Trockenschrank *m*; ~ **cell battery** Trockenbatterie *f*; ~ **ice** Trockeneis *n*; ~ **joint** fehlerhafte Lötstelle, kalte Lötstelle; ~ **run** Probedurchlauf *m*, Drehprobe *f*; **to ~ out by suction** Feuchtigkeit absaugen

drying *n* Trocknung *f*; ~ **cabinet** Trockenschrank *m*; ~ **chamber** Trockenschrank *m*; ~ **hood** Trockenhaube *f*

drying-out *n* Trocknen *n*

dual beam Zweistrahl *m*

dual-standard *adj* Zweinormen- (in Zus.); ~ **projector** Zweiformatbildprojektor *m*

dual trace Zweistrahl *m*

dual track Zweispur *f*

dual-track recorder Doppelspur-Tonbandgerät *n*; ~ **tape recorder** Zweispurmaschine *f*

dub *v* (F) doubeln *v*, synchronisieren *v*; ~ *v* (tape) kopieren *v*, umspielen *v*; ~ *v*(sync) anlegen *v*; ~ *n* (tape) Kopie *f*; ~ **in** *v* einblenden *v*; **to ~ music** Musik unterlegen, untermalen *v*; **to ~ sound effects** Geräusch unterlegen; **to ~ to script** synchronisieren nach Vorlage; **to ~ to visual tape** synchronisieren nach Textband; **to ~ with music** Musik anlegen

dubbed *adj* synchronisiert *adj*; ~ **effect** Synchrongeräusch *n*

dubbing *n* (tape) Kopie *f*, Kopierung *f*; ~ *n* (F) Doubeln *n*, Synchronisation *f*, Synchronisierung *f*, Synchronisieren *n*; ~ **actor** Synchronsprecher *m*; ~ **company** Synchronfirma *f*; ~ **cue sheet** Synchronliste *f*; ~ **director** Synchronregisseur *m*; ~ **editor** Dialogregisseur *m*; ~ **from disc** Schallplattenumschnitt *m*; ~ **loop** Synchronschleife *f*; ~ **mixer** (F) Mischtonmeister *m*; ~ **of effects** Geräuschsynchronisation *f*; ~ **part** Synchronrolle *f*; ~ **speaker** Synchronsprecher *m*; ~ **studio** Synchronatelier *n*; ~ **theatre** Synchronstudio *n*, Mischstudio *n*; ~ **voice** Synchronstimme *f*, Stimmdoubel *n*; ~ **with visual tape** Textbandverfahren *n*

dull *adj* matt *adj*

dummy *adj* künstlich *adj*; ~ **aerial** künstliche Antenne; ~ **load** künstlicher Lastwiderstand, Vernichtungswiderstand *m*

dump, core storage (EDP) Speicherausdruck *m*

dupe *v* duppen *v*; ~ *n* Duplikat *n*,

Dup *n* (fam.), Bilddup *n*; **~ negative** Duplikatnegativ *n*, Dupnegativ *n*; **~ positive** Duplikatpositiv *n*, Duppositiv *n*; **~ reversal** Duplikatumkehrfilm *m*
duping *n* (FP) Doubeln *n*, Duplikatprozeß *m*; **~ print** Lavendel *n*; **~ process** Duplikatprozeß *m*; **suitable for ~** duplikatfähig *adj*
duplex circuit Duplexleitung *f*, Gegensprechverbindung *f*
duplicate *v* duppen *v*; ~ *n* Duplikat *n*, Dup *n* (fam.), Kopie *f*; **~ negative** (black and white) Zwischennegativ *n*; **~ reversal** Duplikatumkehrfilm *m*; **~ reversal stock** Duplikatumkehrfilm *m*
duplicated film Duplikatfilm *m*; **~ negative** Duplikatnegativ *n*, Dupnegativ *n*; **~ negative** (black and white) Zwischennegativ *n*; **~ positive** Duplikatpositiv *n*, Duppositiv *n*
duplicating *n* (tape) Kopierung *f*; **~ film** Duplikatfilm *m*; **~ negative** Duplikatnegativ *n*; **~ positive** Duplikatpositiv *n*, Duppositiv *n*; **~ process** Duplikatprozeß *m*; **~ stock** Duplikatfilm *m*
duplication *n* Vervielfältigung *f*
duplicator *n* Vervielfältiger *m*
duration *n* Dauer *f*, Laufzeit *f*; ~ *n* (F) Filmlänge *f*; **~ of change-over** Umschaltzeit *f*; **~ of production** Produktionsdauer *f*; **~ of propagation** Übertragungszeit *f*; **~ of tape** Abspieldauer *f*; **~ of transmission** Sendedauer *f*, Übertragungsdauer *f*, Übertragungszeit *f*; **excessive ~** Überlänge *f*; **insufficient ~** Unterlänge *f*
dust *v* abstauben *v*; **~ core** Massekern *m*; **~ cover** Schutzdeckel *m*
duty *n* Dienst *m*; **~ cycle** Tastverhältnis *n*; **~ editor** Redakteur vom Dienst, diensthabender Redakteur, Dienstleiter *m*; **~ engineer** Ingenieur vom Dienst (IvD); **~ office** Hörerauskunft* *f*; **~ officer** Leiter vom Dienst (LvD); **~ planner** (EBU) Planungsingenieur *m*; **~ presentation editor** (TV) diensthabender Sendeleiter; **~ presentation officer** (R) diensthabender Sendeleiter; **~ roster** Dienstplan *m*
dwell time Verweilzeit *f*
dye *n* Farbe *f*, Farbstoff *m*
dynamic *adj* dynamisch *adj*; **~ flow chart** (EDP) Datenflußplan *m*; **~ flow diagram** (EDP) Datenflußplan *m*; **~ range** Dynamikbereich *m*, Dynamikumfang *m*, Lautstärkeumfang *m*
dynamically balanced rotationssymmetrisch *adj*
dynamics *n* Dynamik *f*
dynamotor *n* Umformer *m*
dynode *n* Dynode *f*, Prallanode *f*; **~ spot** Dynodenfleck *m*

E

earpad, foam-rubber Gummimuschel *f*
earphone *n* Ohrhörer *m*, Schmalzbohrer *m* (fam.), Specknudel *f* (fam.)
earphones *n pl* Kopfhörer *m*
earpiece *n* Hörer *m*, Ohrhörer *m*, Schmalzbohrer *m* (fam.), Specknudel *f* (fam.)
ear-plug *n* drahtloser Kommandoempfänger
ear-shot *n* Hörweite *f*
earth *v* erden *v*; ~ *n* Erdanschluß *m*, Erde *f*, Erdung *f*; **~ connection**

Erdanschluß *m*, Erdleitung *f*, Erdungsleitung *f*; ~ **mat** (aerial) Erdfeld *n*; ~ **orbit** Erdumlaufbahn *f*; ~ **rod** Erdspieß *m*; ~ **satellite** Erdtrabant *m*; ~ **spike** Erdspieß *m* ~ **station** Bodenstation *f*, Erdefunkstelle *f*; ~ **wire** Erdleitung *f*, Erdungsleitung *f*; **non-fused** ~ Schutzerde *f*

earthed cathode circuit Kathodenbasis (KB) *f*, Kathodenbasisschaltung *f* (KB); ~ **plug** Schukostecker *m*; ~ **socket** Schukosteckdose *f*

earthing *n* Erdung *f*; ~ **braid** Masseband *n*; ~ **isolator** Erdungstrenner *m*; ~ **strap** Masseband *n*

earth's magnetic field Erdmagnetfeld *n*; ~ **shadow area** Erdschattenzone *f*

easel *n* Staffelei *f*

eaves aerial Dachrinnenantenne *f*

echo *v* nachhallen *v*, hallen *v*; ~ *n* Echo *n*, Hall *m*, Resonanz *f*; ~ *n* (TV) Geisterbild *n*; ~ **chamber** Nachhallraum *m*; ~ **effect** (TV) Doppelkontur *f*; ~ **go** Hallausgang *m*; ~ **microphone** Echomikrofon *n* ~ **plate** Hallplatte *f*, Nachhallplatte *f*; ~ **return** Halleingang *m*; ~ **room** Hallraum *m*, Echoraum *m*, Nachhallraum *m* ~ **source** Hallgenerator *m*; **to add** ~ Hall geben

ECO circuit ECO-Schaltung *f*

economics correspondent, ~ **editor** Wirtschaftsredakteur *m*

eddy current Wirbelstrom *m*

eddy-current loss Wirbelstromverlust *m*

edge *n* Kante *f*; ~ *n* (imp.) Flanke *f*; ~ **correction** Kantenanhebung *f*; ~ **effect** Kanteneffekt *m*; ~ **flare** Störsignal *n*; ~ **fog** Randschleier *m*; ~ **fringing** Randeffekt *m*; ~ **guide** seitliche Andruckkufe; ~ **light** Seitenlicht *n*; ~ **lighting** Randaufhellung *f*; ~ **marking** Randmarkierung *f*; ~ **number** Fußnummer *f*; ~ **numbering** Randnumerierung *f*; ~ **sharpness** Konturschärfe *f*, Kantenschärfe *f*; ~ **steepness** Flankensteilheit *f*; ~ **track** Randspur *f*

edge-number *v* randnumerieren *v*; **to ~ a film** Film randnumerieren

edit *v* bearbeiten *v*, redigieren *v*; ~ *v* (F, tape) schneiden *v*, cutten *v*, montieren *v*; ~ **cue** (TV) Schnittmarke *f*; ~ **down** *v* kürzen *v*, raffen *v*; ~ **down** *v* (tape) in der Länge umschneiden; ~ **down** *v* (script) zusammenstreichen *v*; ~ **out** *v* herausstreichen *v*; ~ **pulse** (VTR) Schneideimpuls *m*, Schnittimpuls *m*, Schnittmarke *f*

editec *n* Editec *f*, elektronische MAZ-Schneideeinrichtung

editing *n* Redaktion *f*; ~ *n* (F, tape) Schnitt *m*, Schnittbearbeitung *f*, Fertigung *f*; ~ **acceptance** Schnittabnahme *f*; ~ **accuracy** (VTR) Schnittstabilität *f*; ~ **check** Schnittkontrolle *f*; ~ **date** Schneidetermin *m*; ~ **list** Schnittliste *f*; ~ **period** Schneidezeit *f*; ~ **room** Schneideraum *m*; ~ **stability** (VTR) Schnittstabilität *f*; ~ **table** Schneidetisch *m*; ~ **time** Schnittzeit *f*; **electronic ~** elektronische Schnittbearbeitung, elektronischer Schnitt; **electronic ~ system** elektronische MAZ-Schneideeinrichtung; **manual ~** mechanische Schnittbearbeitung, mechanischer Schnitt; **physical ~** mechanischer Schnitt; **VT ~ system** MAZ-Schneideeinrichtung *f*

editola *n* (US) Bildbetrachter *m*

editor *n* Redakteur *m*; ~ *n* (chief) Chefredakteur *m*; ~ *n* (F, tape)

Cutter *m*, Cutterin *f*; ~ **for the day** (TV) Chef vom Dienst (CvD); ~ **-in-chief** *n* Chefredakteur *m*
editorial *n* Leitartikel *m*; ~ **assistant** Hilfsredakteur *m*, Redaktionsassistent *m*; ~ **conference** Redaktionsbesprechung *f*, Redaktionskonferenz *f*; ~ **desk** Redaktion *f*, Redaktionsraum *m*; ~ **meeting** Redaktionsbesprechung *f*; ~ **responsibility** Programmverantwortung *f*; ~ **staff** Redaktion *f*; ~ **-writer** *n* (US) Leitartikler *m*
editorialise *v* leitartikeln *v* (fam.)
editorialist *n* (US) Leitartikler *m*
editor's report (ER) Cutterbericht *m*, Cutterzettel *m*
educational broadcast Lehrsendung *f*; ~ **broadcasting*** Bildung* *f*, Erziehung* *f*; ~ **broadcasting** Bildungsfunk *m*; ~ **course** Kursprogramm *n*; ~ **film** Schulfilm *m*, Unterrichtsfilm *m*; ~ **programme** Bildungsprogramm *n*; ~ **radio** Bildungsfunk *m*; ~ **television (ETV)** Bildungsfernsehen *n*, Lehrfernsehen *n*, Schulfernsehen *n*, Unterrichtsfernsehen *n*
effect *n* Effekt *m*; ~ **light** Effektlicht *n*, Effektspitze *n*; ~ **lighting** Effektlicht *n*, Effektspitze *n*; ~ **microphone** Effektmikrofon *n*; ~ **music** Effektmusik *f*; **cartoon** ~ Trickeffekt *m*; **optical** ~ optischer Trick; **special** ~ Trick *m*, Trickeffekt *m*; **stroboscopic** ~ stroboskopischer Effekt; **stunt** ~ Trickeffekt *m*
effective power Wirkleistung *f*; ~ **radiated power (ERP)** effektive Strahlungsleistung (ERP), Sendeleistung *f*; ~ **range** Nutzbereich *m*; ~ **transmission gain** Betriebsverstärkung *f*
effects *n pl* Geräusche *n pl*, Geräuschkulisse *f*; ~ **box** Kompendium *n*; ~ **circuit** IT-Leitung *f*, internationale Tonleitung, Begleittonleitung *f*; ~ **lighting** Effektbeleuchtung *f*; ~ **matte** Blendenschablone *f*, Schablonenblende *f*; ~ **microphone** Geräuschmikrofon *n*; ~ **operator** Geräuschemacher *m*, Geräuschtechniker *m*; ~ **room** Trickstudio *n*; ~ **sound** Raumton *m*; ~ **spot** Effektscheinwerfer *m*; ~ **studio** Geräuschstudio *n*; ~ **tape** Geräuschband *n*; ~ **track** Geräuschband *n*; ~ **with colour lighting** Farbenspiel *n*
EID guide Bärenführer *m* (fam.)
eidophor *n* Eidophor *m*, Fernsehgroßbildprojektor *m*
eigenfrequency *n* (acoust.) Eigenfrequenz *f*
eight-track punched tape (EDP) Achtspur-Lochstreifen *m*
elbow *n* (piping) Winkelstück *n*
electric *adj* elektrisch *adj*; ~ **arc** Lichtbogen *m*; ~ **charge** Ladung *f*; ~ **circuit** Stromkreis *m*; ~ **fire** Heizsonne *f*; ~ **power** Kraftstrom *m*
electrical *adj* elektrisch *adj*; ~ **interference** Nebengeräusch *n*; ~ **power engineer** Starkstromingenieur *m*; ~ **power workshop** Starkstromwerkstatt *f*
electrician *n* Elektriker *m*, Elektromechaniker *m*, Starkstromelektriker *m*
electrician's knife Kabelmesser *n*
electricity *n* Elektrizität *f*
electro-acoustics *n* Elatechnik (Ela) *f*, Elektroakustik (Ela)
electrode *n* Elektrode *f*
electrodynamic *adj* elektrodynamisch *adj*; ~ **loudspeaker** elektrodynamischer Lautsprecher
electrolysis *n* Elektrolyse *f*;

~ **junction** Lokalelement *n*, Übergangselement *n*
electrolytic capacitor Elektrolytkondensator *m*, Elko *m* (fam.)
electromagnet *n* Elektromagnet *m*
electromagnetic *adj* elektromagnetisch *adj*
electron *n* Elektron *n*; ~ **beam** Elektronenstrahl *m*; ~ **beam recording** Elektronenstrahlaufzeichnung *f*; ~ **focusing** Strahlstrombündelung *f*; ~ **gun** Elektronenkanone *f*; ~ **multiplier** Elektronenvervielfacher *m*, Sekundärelektronenvervielfacher *m*; ~ **optics** Elektronenoptik *f*
electronic *adj* elektronisch *adj*; ~ **data processing (EDP)** elektronische Datenverarbeitung (EDV); ~ **film recorder** Filmaufzeichnungsgerät *n*; ~ **film recording (EFR)** Filmaufzeichnung (FAZ) *f*; ~ **inlay** Trickeinblendung *f*; ~ **outline generator** Kaschgeber *m*; ~ **switch unit** Trickmischeinrichtung *f*; ~ **test pattern generator** Universaltestbildgeber *m*; ~ **video recording (EVR)** elektronische Bildaufzeichnung
electronicam *n* Electronic-Cam (E-Cam) *f*
electronics *n* Elektronik *f*
electrostatic loudspeaker elektrostatischer Lautsprecher; ~ **microphone** Kondensatormikrofon *n*
element *n* Bauteil *n*, Glied *n*
elevate, to ~ the camera Kamera heben
elevation angle Erhebungswinkel *m*
eliminate, to ~ jamming entstören *v*
elongation *n* Verlängerung *f*
embargo *n* Nachrichtensperre *f*, Sperrfrist *f*
embargoed news item Sperrfristmeldung *f*; ~ **till ...** Sperrfrist bis ...
emergence lens Austrittslinse *f*; ~ **plane** Austrittsebene *f*
emergency button Notdruckknopf *m*; ~ **exit** Notausgang *m*; ~ **generator** Notstromgenerator *m*; ~ **lighting** Notbeleuchtung *f*; ~ **power plant** Notstromaggregat *n* ~ **repair** Notreparatur *f*
emission *n* Ausstrahlung *f*, Strahlung *f*
emit *v* (tech.) ausstrahlen *v*
emitter *n* Emitter *m*; ~ **follower** Emitterfolger *m*, Emitterverstärker *m*
employee *n* Angestellter *m*
employment contract Dienstvertrag *m*
empty reel Leerspule *f*; ~ **spool** Leerspule *f*
emulsion *n* Emulsion *f*, Schicht *f*; ~ **batch number** Emulsionschargennummer *f*; ~ **carrier** Schichtträger *m*; ~ **coating** Emulsionsschicht *f*; ~ **for artificial light** Kunstlichtemulsion *f*; ~ **layer** Beschichtung *f*, Emulsionsschicht *f*; ~ **scratch** Schichtschramme *f*; ~ **side** Emulsionsebene *f*, Schichtseite *f*, Schichtlage *f*; ~ **speed** (FP) Empfindlichkeit *f*; ~ **stripping** Entschichtung *f*; ~ **support** Schichtträger *m*; **orthochromatic ~** orthochromatische Emulsion; **panchromatic ~** panchromatische Emulsion; **sensitive ~** empfindliche Schicht
enclosure *n* (loudspeaker) Zarge *f*
encode *v* kodieren *v*, verschlüsseln *v*
encoder *n* Koder *m*, Enkoder *m*
encoding *n* Verschlüsselung *f*
encore *n* (thea.) Zugabe *f*
end board (EB) Schlußklappe (SK) *f* ~ **captions** *n pl* Nachspann *m*;

~ **credits** *n pl* Nachspann *m*; ~ **mark** (EDP) Endezeichen *n*; ~ **of job (EOJ)** (EDP) Ende des Ablaufs ~ **of switching sequence** Schaltende *n*; ~ **time** Endzeit *f*; ~ **titles** *n pl* Abspanntitel *m*, Abspann *m* (fam.), Endtitel *m*, Nachspann *m*, Schlußtitel *m*
endless screw Schnecke *f*
energise *v* (elec.) speisen *v*
energising current Erregerstrom *m*
energy distribution Energieverteilung *f*
engage *v* einrasten *v*; ~ *v* (staff) einstellen *v*; ~ *v* (perf.) engagieren *v*, verpflichten *v*
engaged tone Besetztzeichen *n*
engagement *n* (staff) Einstellung *f*; ~ *n* (perf.) Engagement *n*
engineer *n* Techniker *m*; ~ *n* Ingenieur *m*; **all-round** ~ (coll.) Breitbandtechniker *m*; **chief** ~ leitender Ingenieur
engineer-in-charge *n* Aufsichtsingenieur *m*, Oberingenieur *m*
engineering *n* Technik *f*; ~ **directorate** technische Direktion; ~ **equipment*** Technische Ausrüstung*; ~ **operations and maintenance** Betriebstechnik *f*
engraved ring Gravurring *m*
enlarge *v* vergrößern *v*
enlargement *n* Vergrößerung *f*, Vergrößerungskopie *f*
enlarger *n* Vergrößerungsapparat *m*
ensemble *n* Ensemble *n*; ~ *n* (mus.) Musikensemble *n*
enter *v* (perf.) auftreten *v*
entertainment *n* Unterhaltung *f*; ~ **tax** Vergnügungssteuer *f*; **light** ~ leichte Unterhaltung
entry level Eintrittsebene *f*; ~ **plane** Eintrittsebene *f*
envelope *n* (coll.) Bildstartmarke *f*; ~ **curve** Hüllkurve *f*; ~ **delay** Gruppenlaufzeit *f*
epidiascope *n* Epidiaskop *n*
episcope *n* Episkop *n*
equal energy spectrum Gleichenergiespektrum *n*; ~ **energy white** Gleichenergieweiß *n*
equalisation *n* Ausgleich *m*; ~ *n* (pict., sound) Entzerrung *f*
equalise *v* ausgleichen *v*; ~ *v* (pict., sound) entzerren *v*
equaliser *n* (pict., sound) Entzerrer *m*
equalising *n* Ausgleich *m*; ~ **amplifier** Entzerrerverstärker *m* ~ **pulse** Ausgleichsimpuls *m*, Halbzeilenimpuls *m*, Trabant *m*, Hilfssynchronsignal *n*
equatorial orbit Äquatorialbahn *f*
equip *v* bestücken *v*
equipment *n* Ausrüstung *f*, Ausstattung *f*, Bestückung *f*, Anlage *f*, Einrichtung *f*, Geräte *n pl*; ~ *n* Apparat *m*; **mobile** ~ mobile Produktionsmittel; **stationary** ~ stationäre Produktionsmittel
equipotential *adj* äquipotential *adj*.
equivalent circuit diagram Ersatzschaltbild *n*; ~ **resistance** Verlustwiderstand *m*
erase *v* löschen *v*; ~ *v* (EDP) auslochen *v*; ~ **current** Löschstrom *m*; ~ **cut-out key** Löschsperre *f*; ~ **frequency** Löschfrequenz *f*; ~ **head** Löschkopf *m*; ~ **oscillator** Löschgenerator *m*; ~ **voltage** Löschspannung *f*
erasing *n* Löschung *f*; ~ **current** Löschstrom *m*; ~ **head** Löschkopf *m*
erasion *n* Löschung *f*
erasure *n* Auslöschung *f*, Löschung *f*
erecting prism Umkehrprisma *n*
error *n* Fehler *m*; ~ **checking** (EDP) Fehlerprüfung *f*; ~ **correction** Nachsteuerung *f*; ~ **detection**

(EDP) Fehlererkennung *f*; **~ in density** (neg.) Deckungsfehler *m*; **~ message** (EDP) Fehlermeldung *f* **~ probability** (EDP) Fehlerwahrscheinlichkeit *f*; **~ rate** (EDP) Fehlerhäufigkeit *f*; **~ voltage (EV)** Fehlerspannung *f*, Nachsteuerspannung *f*; **~ voltage relay** Fehlerspannungsrelais (FU-Schalter) *n*; **accumulated ~** (EDP) akkumulierter Fehler

establish *v* einrichten *v*

established post Planstelle *f*

establishing shot Gesamtaufnahme *f*

estimate *n* Kostenvoranschlag *m*

Eurovision *n* Eurovision *f*, Euro *f* (fam.); **~ caption** Eurovisionszeichen *n*; **~ control centre (EVC)** Eurovisionskontrollzentrum *n*; **~ exchange** Eurovisionsaustausch *m*; **~ hook-up** Eurovisionssendung *f*; **~ identification** Eurovisionskennung *f*; **~ network** Eurovisionsnetz *n*; **~ news exchange** Eurovisionsnachrichtenaustausch *m*; **~ operations** *n pl* Eurovisionsabwicklung *f*; **~ procedure** Eurovisionsabwicklung *f*; **~ relay** Eurovisionsübertragung *f*; **~ transmission** Eurovisionssendung *f*; **~ tune** Eurovisionsfanfare *f*

evaluate *v* auswerten *v*

evaluated *adj* (tech.) bewertet *adj*

evaluation *n* Auswertung *f*

evening edition Abendausgabe *f*; **~ performance** Abendvorstellung *f* **~ programme** Abendprogramm *n*

even-order harmonic distortion gradzahliger Klirrfaktor

event *n* Veranstaltung *f*

examination *n* Prüfung *f*

excerpt *n* Auszug *m*, Textausschnitt *m*

excess current Überstrom *m*; **~ voltage cut-out** Überspannungssicherung *f*

excessive duration Überlänge *f*; **~ effects** *n pl* Überdeckungseffekt *m*; **~ footage** Überlänge *f*; **~ level of effects** Überdeckungseffekt *m*; **~ voltage** Überspannung *f*

exchange *n* (PO) Vermittlungsstelle *f*, Vermittlung *f*; **~ fault gang** Störtrupp *m*

excise *v* herausschneiden *v*, herausstreichen *v*

excitation *n* (transmitter) Ansteuerung *f*; **~ purity** Farbreinheitsgrad *m*

excite *v* (transmitter) ansteuern *v*

exciter lamp Lichttonlampe *f*, Tonprojektorlampe *f*; **~ lamp assembly** Tonlampengehäuse *n*; **~ lamp housing** Tonlampengehäuse *n*

exciting current Erregerstrom *m*

exclusive *adj* Exklusiv- (in Zus.); **~ rights** *n pl* Ausschließlichkeitsrecht *n*

execution *n* Durchführung *f*

executive instruction (EDP) Organisationsbefehl *m*

exempt from royalties frei von Rechten

exhaust air Abluft *f*

exhauster *n* Entlüfter *m*

exhibit *v* vorführen *v*

exhibition *n* Vorführung *f*; **~ permit** Vorführgenehmigung *f*; **~ rights** *n pl* Ausstellungsrecht *n*; **~ rights** (F) Vorführungsrechte *n pl*

exit *n* Ausgang *m*; **~** *n* (perf.) Abgang *m*; **~ pupil** Austrittslinse *f*

expedient *n* Hilfsquelle *f*

expenses *n pl* Spesen *plt*

experiment *n* Probe *f*

experimental film Experimentalfilm *m*

expert *n* Fachmann *m*, Sachverständiger *m*, Experte *m*

exploit *v* auswerten *v*

exploitation *n* Auswertung *f*, Verwertung *f*
explosion *n* Explosion *f*; ~ **shutter** Explosionsblende *f*
expose *v* belichten *v*; **to ~ thin** anbelichten *v*
exposure *n* Belichtung *f*; ~ *n* (photo) Aufnahme *f*; ~ **chart** Belichtungstabelle *f*; ~ **control band** Blendenband *n*; ~ **control strip** Blendenband *n*; ~ **guide** Belichtungstabelle *f*; ~ **index** Belichtungsindex *m*; ~ **latitude** Belichtungsspielraum *m*; ~ **meter** Belichtungsmesser *m*; ~ **of optical track** Randspurbelichtung *f*; ~ **period** Belichtungszeit *f*; ~ **scale** Belichtungstabelle *f*; ~ **table** Belichtungstabelle *f*; ~ **test** Belichtungsprobe *f*; ~ **time** Belichtungszeit *f*; ~ **timer** Belichtungsuhr *f*; ~ **value** (FP) Lichtwert *m*
expression *n* (EDP) Ausdruck *m*
extended control Nebenbedienung *f* ~ **control panel** Nebenbediengerät *n*; ~ **elevation** (design) Abwicklung *f*
extensible *adj* ausziehbar *adj*
extension *n* Verlängerung *f*; ~ *n* (cam.) Auszug *m*; ~ **cable** Verlängerungskabel *n*; ~ **circuit** Verlängerungsleitung *f*; ~ **factor** Verlängerungsfaktor *m*; ~ **tube** Tubus *m*, Tute *f* (fam.); **double ~** doppelter Auszug
exterior *n* Außenaufnahme *f*; ~ *adj* Außen- (in Zus.), Freilicht- (in Zus.); ~ **set** Außenbau *m*; ~ **shooting** Außenaufnahme *f*; ~ **shot,** Außenaufnahme *f*
external broadcasting* Sendungen für das Ausland*; ~ **broadcasting service** Auslandsdienst *m*; ~ **control** Fremdsteuerung *f*; ~ **excitation** Fremdansteuerung *f*; ~ **modulation** Fremdmodulation *f*; ~ **production** Fremdproduktion *f*; ~ **programme** Fremdprogramm *n*; ~ **signal** Fremdsignal *n*
extinction *n* Auslöschung *f*, Löschung *f*
extra *n* Komparse *m*, Statist *m*
extract *n* Auszug *m*
extra-high frequency (EHF) Millimeterwellenbereich (EHF) *m*
extrapolation *n* Hochrechnung *f*
extras *n pl* Komparserie *f*, Statisterie *f*
extra's fee Komparsengage *f*
extreme close-up (ECU) Makroaufnahme *f*; ~ **long shot (ELS)** Weiteinstellung *f*
eye guard Augenmuschelkissen *n*; ~ **level** Augenhöhe *f*; ~ **light** Augenlicht *n*; ~ **line** Augenhöhe *f*; ~ **piece** Kameralupe *f*, Okular *n*
eye-witness account Augenzeugenbericht *m*; ~ **programme** Reportagesendung *f* ~ **report** Reportage *f*

F

face impression Gesichtsabdruck *m*
facilities *n pl* (prog.) Programmhilfe *f*; **technical ~** *n pl* technische Hilfe
facility *n* Gefälligkeit *f*, Leistung *f*, Sachleistung *f*; ~ *n* (prog.) Programmhilfe *f*; ~ *n* (bcast.) Sendehilfe *f*; ~ **recording** Gefälligkeitsaufnahme *f*
facsimile broadcasting Bildfunk *m*; ~ **receiver** Bildfunkempfänger *m*; ~ **transmission** Bildfunk *m*, Bildtelegrafie *f*; ~ **transmitter** Bildfunksender *m*, Bildgeber *m*, Bildsender *m*
fact film (US) Dokumentarfilm *m*, Dokumentation *f*
fade *v* blenden *v*, überblenden *v*; ~ *v* (col.) ausbleichen *v*; ~ *v* (level)

wegnehmen *v*; ~ *v* (sound) abklingen *v*; ~ **away** *v* verhallen *v*; ~ **down** *v* abblenden *v*, ausblenden *v*; ~ **down** *v* (sound) abklingen lassen; ~ **down** *v* (zoom) zuziehen *v*; ~ **in** *v* (pict., sound) aufblenden *v*, aufziehen *v*, einblenden *v*; ~ **in** *v* (pict.) Bild aufziehen; ~ **out (FO)** *v* ausblenden *v*, abblenden *v*; ~ **out** *v* (sound) abklingen lassen; ~ **out** *v* (zoom) zuziehen *v*; ~ **over** *v* weich überblenden; ~ **to black** Schwarzblende *f*; ~ **up** *v* (pict., sound) aufziehen *v*, aufblenden *v*; ~ **up** *v* (pict.) Bild aufziehen; **chemical** ~ chemische Blende; **to ~ down to black** Schwarz ziehen, Schwarzblende ziehen

fade-in *n* Aufblende *f*, Aufblendung *f*, Einblendung *f*

fade-out *n* Abblende *f*, Abblendung *f*, Ausblende *f*

fade-over *n* Überblendung *f*, Überblenden *n*, weiche Überblendung

fader *n* Steller *m*, Regler *m* (fam.), Schieber *m* (fam.), Überblender *m*, Überblendregler *m*, Überblendvorrichtung *f*, Potentiometer *n*, Pot *m* (fam.), Einmischer *m*, Abschwächer *m*, Bildregler *m*; ~ **desk** Stellpult *n*; **calibrated** ~ geeichter Abschwächer; **linear** ~ linearer Steller; **logarithmic** ~ logarithmischer Steller

fade-up *n* (TV) Aufblende *f*, Aufblendung *f*; ~ *n* (sound) Toneinblendung *f*

fading *n* Überblendung *f*, Überblenden *n*; ~ *n* (recpn.) Fading *n*, Schwund *m*, Wellenschwund *m*; **selective** ~ selektiver Schwund

fading-down *n* Abblende *f*, Abblendung *f*, Ausblende *f*

fading-out *n* Ausblenden *n*, Ausblendung *f*

fading-up *n* (TV) Aufblende *f*, Aufblendung *f*

fail *v* (tech.) ausfallen *v*

failure *n* (tube) Ausfall *m*, Fehler *m*, Panne *f*; ~ **rate** (EDP) Ausfallquote *f*, Ausfallrate *f*

fake *n* Fälschung *f*; **to ~ a scene** Türken bauen

fall-off *n* (level) Pegelabfall *m*; ~ *n* (light) Abnahme *f*

fall time Abfallzeit *f*

family of characteristics Kennlinienschar *f*; ~ **of curves** Kurvenschar *f*; ~ **programme** Familienprogramm *n*; ~ **series** Familienserie *f*

fan *n* Gebläse *n*; ~ *n* Windmaschine *f*; ~ **wipe** Fächerblende *f*

farce *n* Schwank *m*

farmers' programme Landfunksendung *f*

fashion board Titelkarton *m*, Zeichenkarton *m*

fast-break switch Schnellstopschalter *m*

fault *n* Fehler *m*, Störung *f*; ~ **caption** Störungsdia *n*; ~ **clearance** Störungsbeseitigung *f* ~ **current** Fehlerstrom *m*; ~ **current relay** Fehlerstromrelais (FI-Schalter) *n*; ~ **-locating** *n* Fehlersuche *f*; ~ **location** Fehlereingrenzung *f*; ~ **message** (EDP) Fehlermeldung *f*; ~ **report** Fehlermeldung *f*, Störmeldung *f*; ~ **time** (EDP) Ausfallzeit *f*; **technical** ~ technische Störung; **temporary** ~ (bcast.) unbeabsichtigte kurze Unterbrechung; **to clear a** ~ Störung beseitigen, Störung beheben; **to localise a** ~ einen Fehler eingrenzen

faulty *adj* fehlerhaft *adj*, gestört *adj*; ~ **exposure** Fehlbelichtung *f*; ~ **switching** Fehlschaltung *f*

feature *v* (perf.) herausstellen *v*; ~ *n* Feature *n*; ~ *n* (R) Hörbild *n*

~ **film** Spielfilm *m*; ~ **series** Hörfolge *f*; **second ~ film** zweiter Film

fee *n* Gebühr *f*; ~ *n* (perf.) Gage *f*, Honorar *n*; ~ **claim** Gagenanspruch *m*; ~ **demand** Gagenanspruch *m*; ~ **entitlement** Gagenanspruch *m*; ~ **scale** Honorarrahmen *m*; **to pay a ~ for** honorieren *v*; **~s department** Honorarabteilung *f*

feed *v* versorgen *v*; ~ *v* (insert) einspielen *v*, zuspielen *v*; ~ *v* (reel) abwickeln *v*; ~ *v* (elec.) speisen *v*; ~ *n* Zuführung *f*, Vorschub *m*, Speisung *f*; ~ *n* (reel) Abwicklung *f*; ~ *n* (coll.) (line) Modulationszubringung *f*; ~ **back** *v* rückkoppeln *v*; ~ **line** Zuführung *f*, Zuführungsleitung *f*; ~ **magazine** Abwickelkassette *f*; ~ **of tapping point** Anzapfspeisung *f*; ~ **reel** Abwickelspule *f*, Abwickeltrommel *f*; ~ **spool** Abwickelspule *f*, Abwickeltrommel, Vorratstrommel *f*; ~ **sprocket** Filmtransportrolle *f*, Vorwickelrolle *f*

feedback *n* Rückkopplung *f*, Rückwirkung *f*; ~ *n* (information) Rückmeldung *f*; ~ **tendency** Rückkopplungsneigung *f*, Schwingneigung *f*

feeder *n* Antennenkabel *n*, Antennenleitung *f*, Energieleitung *f*, Feeder *m*, Antennenzuleitung *f*; ~ **circuit** Modulationszubringerleitung *f*; ~ **line** Antennenspeiseleitung *f*

feed-forward control (EDP) Vorwärtsregelung *f*

feeding *n* (elec.) Speisung *f*; ~ *n* (reel) Abwicklung *f*; ~ **claw** Transportgreifer *m*

feed-through capacitor Durchführungskondensator *m*; ~ **sleeve** Durchführungsbuchse *f*

felt mat Filzscheibe *f*; ~ **roller** Filzröllchen *n*; ~ **washer** Filzscheibe *f*

female multi-point connector Federleiste *f*; ~ **socket** Anbaudose *f*

ferrite aerial Ferritantenne *f*; ~ **bead** Dämpfungsperle *f*; ~ **core** (EDP) Ferritkern *m*

ferrous coated tape Schichtband *n*

festival *n* Festspiele *n pl*, Festwoche *f*

fibre optics Faseroptik *f*

fidelity curve Wiedergabekurve *f*; ~ **of reproduction** Wiedergabetreue *f*

fiducial mark Bezugspunkt *m*

field *n* Feld *n*; ~ *n* (US) Ressort *n*; ~ *n* (speciality) Fachgebiet *n*; ~ *n* (video) Halbbild *n*, Teilbild *n*; ~ **blanking pulse** Vertikalaustastimpuls *m*; ~ **coil** Feldspule *f*, Feldwicklung *f*, Magnetspule *f*; ~ **duration** Halbbilddauer *f*, Teilbilddauer *f*; ~ **effect transistor (FET)** Feldeffekttransistor (FET) *m*; ~ **flattener** Feldlinse *f*; ~ **frequency** (50 or 60 Hz) Bildfrequenz *f*, Halbbildfrequenz *f*, Rasterwechselfrequenz *f*, Vertikalfrequenz *f* (V-Frequenz); ~ **-frequency square wave** V-frequentes Rechtecksignal; ~ **lens** Feldlinse *f*; ~ **mesh** Feldnetz *n*; ~ **of focus** Tiefenschärfebereich *m* ~ **of view** Blickfeld *n*, Gesichtsfeld *n*; ~ **of vision** Blickfeld *n*, Bildfeld *n*; ~ **of vision** (cam.) Schußfeld *n*; ~ **period** Halbbilddauer *f*; ~ **pick-up** (US) Außenaufnahme *f*, Außenübertragung *f* (AÜ); ~ **pulse** Vertikalimpuls (V-Impuls) *m*, Halbbildimpuls *m*; ~ **rate** Teilbilddauer *f*; ~ **-sequential system** Rasterwechselverfahren *n* ~ **strength** Feldstärke *f*; ~ **-strength measuring** Feldstärkemessung *f*;

~ **synchronising pulse** Vertikalsynchronimpuls *m*; ~ **winding** Feldwicklung *f*; **optical** ~ optisches Feld
figurine *n* Figurine *f*
filament *n* Glühdraht *m*, Heizfaden *m*; ~ *n* (tube) Heizung *f*; ~ **battery** Heizbatterie *f*; ~ **voltage** Heizspannung *f*; **balanced** ~ symmetrierte Heizung
file *v* archivieren *v*; ~ *n* (EDP) Datei *f*; ~ **copy** Archivfilm *m*; ~ **of circuit diagrams** Schaltplanmappe *f*
filing clerk Registrator *m*; ~ **system** Archivierung *f*
fill light Aufhellicht *n*, Aufheller *m*, Füllicht *n*
filler *n* Aufhellicht *n*, Aufheller *m*, Füllicht *n*; ~ *n* (prog.) Pausenfüller *m*, Programmfüller *m*, Füllprogramm *n*; ~ **lighting** Aufhellung *f*
fill-in light Aufhellicht *n*, Aufheller *m*, Füllicht *n*
fill-up *n* Pausenfüller *m*, Programmfüller *m*, Füllprogramm *n*
film *v* filmen *v*, aufnehmen *v*, drehen *v*, Film drehen, kurbeln *v* (fam.); ~ *v* verfilmen *v*; ~ *n* Film *m*; ~ *n* (coll.) Filmband *n*, Filmstreifen *m*, Streifen *m*; ~ (compp.) Film- (in Zus.); ~ **adaptation** Filmbearbeitung *f*; ~ **advance** Filmtransport *m*; ~ **archives** *n pl* Filmarchiv *n*, Filmothek *f*; ~ **author** Filmautor *m*; ~ **backing** Lichthofschutzschicht *f*; ~ **base** Filmträger *m*, Schichtträger *m*, Träger *m*; ~ **bobbin** Filmkern *m*; ~ **business** Filmbranche *f*; ~ **cabinet** Filmschrank *m*; ~ **camera** Filmkamera *f*, Aufnahmekamera *f*; ~ **can** Filmbüchse *f*; ~ **caption** Filmtitel *m*; ~ **carrier** Filmträger *m*; ~ **cassette** Filmkassette *f*, Filmmagazin *n*, Filmladekassette *f*; ~ **cement** Filmkitt *m*, Kleber *m*; ~ **censor** Filmprüfer *m*; ~ **censorship office** Filmprüfstelle *f*; ~ **channel** Filmkanal *m*; ~ **-cleaning** Filmreinigung *f*; ~ **clip** Filmausschnitt *m*; ~ **club** Filmclub *m*; ~ **comedy** Filmkomödie *f*; ~ **consumption** Filmverbrauch *m*; ~ **core** Filmkern *m*; ~ **crew** Aufnahmegruppe *f*, Kamerateam *n*: ~ **critic** Filmkritiker *m*, Filmredakteur *m*; ~ **cutter** Filmcutter *m*; ~ **-cutting** *n* Filmschnitt *m*; ~ **density** Filmdichte *f*; ~ **-developing** *n* Filmentwicklung *f*; ~ **dimension** Filmmaß *n*; ~ **director** Filmregisseur *m*; ~ **distribution** Filmverleih *m*; ~ **distributor** Filmverleiher *m*; ~ **distributors** *n pl* Filmverleih *m*; ~ **drive** Filmtransport *m*; ~ **-edge marker light aperture** Randbelichtungsfenster *n*; ~ **-editing** *n* Filmschnitt *m*; ~ **-editing machine** Filmschneidegerät *n*; ~ **editor** Filmcutter *m*, Cutter *m*, Cutterin *f* ~ **editor** (credits) Schnitt *m*; ~ **editor** (F) Schnittmeister *m*; ~ **editor's report (FER)** Cutterbericht *m*, Cutterzettel *m*; ~ **examination** Filmprüfung *f*; ~ **examiner** Filmprüfer *m*; ~ **excerpt** Filmausschnitt *m*; ~ **feed** Filmvorschub *m*, Filmfortschaltung *f*; ~ **-feed sprocket** Filmtransportrolle *f*; ~ **festival** Filmfestspiele *n pl*; ~ **-footage counter** Meterzähler *m*; ~ **for adults** Film für Erwachsene; ~ **format** Filmformat *n*; ~ **gate** Filmfenster *n*, Bildfenster *n*; ~ **-gate mask** Bildfensterabdeckung *f*, Bildfenstereinsatz *m*, Bildmaske *f*; ~ **gauge** Filmformat *n*; ~ **grader** Kopiermeister *m*; ~ **grain** Filmkorn *n*; ~ **guide**

Filmführung *f*; ~ **image** Filmbild *n*; ~ **industry** Filmindustrie *f*, Filmwirtschaft *f*; ~ **inject** Filmbeitrag *m*, Unterschnitt *m*, ~ **insert** Filmeinspielung *f*, Unterschnitt *m*; ~ **item** Filmbeitrag *m*; ~ **jam** Filmsalat *m* ~ **joiner** Filmklebepresse *f*; ~ **laboratory** Filmlabor *n*, Kopieranstalt *f*, Kopierwerk *n*, Entwicklungsanstalt *f*; ~ **librarian** Filmarchivar *m*; ~ **library** Kinemathek *f*, Filmarchiv *n*, Filmothek *f*; ~ **loop** Filmschlaufe *f*, Filmschleife *f*, ~ **magazine** Filmkassette *f*, Filmmagazin *n*, Filmladekassette *f*; ~ **magazine** (press) Filmmagazin *n*, Filmzeitschrift *f*; ~ **-maker** *n* Filmemacher *m*, Cineast *m*; ~ **manufacture** Rohfilmherstellung *f*; ~ **manufacturer** Rohfilmhersteller *m*; ~ **material** Filmmaterial *n*; ~ **material assistant** Materialassistent *m*; ~ **material report** Materialbericht *m*; ~ **music** Filmmusik *f*; ~ **mutilation** Filmbeschädigung *f*; ~ **narrative** Filmerzählung *f*; ~ **operations** Betriebstechnik Film; ~ **operations and services*** Atelierbetrieb* *m*; ~ **-pack** *n* Filmpack *m*; ~ **path** Filmbahn *f*; ~ **-polishing machine** Filmmattiermaschine *f*, Filmpoliermaschine *f*; ~ **pressure guide** Filmandruckschiene *f*; ~ **-printer** *n* Filmkopienfertiger *m*, Filmkopierer *m*, Filmkopiermaschine *f*; ~ **-printing** *n* Filmkopierung *f*; ~ **-processing** *n* Filmbearbeitung *f*, Filmentwicklung *f*; ~ **-processing department** Entwicklungsabteilung *f*; ~ **-processing laboratory** Kopierwerk *n*; ~ **producer** Filmhersteller *m*; ~ **production** Filmherstellung *f*, Filmproduktion *f*; ~ **projection** Filmvorführung *f*; ~ **projector** Filmprojektor *m*; ~ **pulldown time** Bildfortschaltzeit *f*; ~ **-purchasing** *n* Filmbeschaffung *f*; ~ **-record** *v* FAZ aufzeichnen, Film aufzeichnen, fazen *v* (fam.); ~ **recorder** Filmaufzeichnungsgerät *n*, FAZ-Anlage *f* (FAZ); ~ **report** Filmbericht *m*, Kamerabericht *m*; ~ **review** Filmkritik *f*; ~ **rewind** Filmumroller *m*; ~ **roller** Transportrolle *f*; ~ **run** Filmlauf *m* ~ **run-out** Filmauslauf *m*; ~ **salesman** Akquisiteur *m*, Verleihvertreter *m*; ~ **scanner** Filmabtaster *m*, Filmgeber *m*; ~ **scanning** Filmabtastung *f*; ~ **schedule** Aufnahmeplan *m*; ~ **screening** Filmvorführung *f*; ~ **sequence** Filmbeitrag *m*; ~ **sequencing time** Bildfortschaltzeit *f*; ~ **service** Filmbüro *n*; ~ **shot** Filmaufnahme *f*; ~ **shrinkage** Filmschrumpfung *f* ~ **size** Filmformat *n*; ~ **society** Filmclub *m*; ~ **speed indicator** (F) Tachometer *m*; ~ **splicer** Filmklebepresse *f*; ~ **spool** Filmspule *f*; ~ **stapler** Klammerzange *f*; ~ **-star** *n* Filmstar *m*; ~ **stock** Filmmaterial *n*; ~ **stock** (store) Filmlager *n*; ~ **storage** Filmlagerung *f*; ~ **-storage cabinet** Filmschrank *m*; ~ **story** (US) Filmbericht *m*; ~ **strip** Bildband *n*, Filmband *n*, Filmstreifen *m*, Streifen *m*; ~ **studio** Filmatelier *n*, Filmstudio *n*, Filmaufnahmestudio *n*; ~ **studios** *n pl* Atelierbetrieb *m*; ~ **summary** zusammenfassender Filmbericht; ~ **support** Filmträger *m*; ~ **take** Filmaufnahme *f*; ~ **technician** Filmtechniker *m*; ~ **technology** Filmtechnik *f*; ~ **test strip** Filmprobe *f*; ~ **title** Filmtitel *m*; ~ **title with music** Musiktitel *m* ~ **track** Filmkanal *m*; ~ **-trade press** Filmpresse *f*; ~ **traffic** Filmspedition *f*; ~ **transport** Filmtransport *m*; ~ **travel** Filmlauf *m*, Filmtransport *m*; ~ **treatment** Filmbehandlung *f*; ~ **unit** Aufnahmegruppe *f*; ~ **valuation board** Filmbewertungsstelle *f*; ~ **version** Verfilmung *f*; ~ **-viewer** *n* Filmbetrachter *m*, Bildbetrachter *m*; ~ **width** Filmbreite *f*; ~ **with magnetic edge sound track** Film mit Magnetrandspur; ~ **with magnetic sound track** Film mit Magnetspur; ~ **with magnetic track** Film mit Magnetspur; **banned** ~ nicht freigegebener Film; **blank** ~ Weißfilm *m*; **creased** ~ geknickter Film; **exposed** ~ belichteter Film; **full-length** ~ abendfüllender Film, Spielfilm *m*; **indented** ~ geräderter Film; **lacquered** ~ lackierter Film; **non-flam** ~ Sicherheitsfilm *m*; **scratched** ~ verregneter Film, verschrammter Film; **second** ~ zweiter Film; **to bring out a** ~ Film herausbringen; **to edge-number a** ~ Film randnumerieren; **to release a** ~ Film herausbringen; **to rubber-number a** ~ Film randnumerieren **to screen a** ~ Film ansehen, Film vorführen; **to shoot a** ~ Film drehen; **to take a** ~ Film drehen; **to view a** ~ Film ansehen; **unexposed** ~ unbelichteter Film; **waxed** ~ gewachster Film; **white** ~ Weißfilm *m*

filmed opera Opernfilm *m*

filmic *adj* Film- (in Zus.), filmisch *adj*

filming *n* Dreh *m*, Dreharbeiten *f pl*, Filmaufnahme *f*; ~ **permission** Dreherlaubnis *f*, Aufnahmegenehmigung *f*; ~ **permit** Aufnahmegenehmigung *f*

filmology *n* Filmkunde *f*, Filmologie *f*

filter *v* filtern *v*; ~ *n* Filter *m*; ~ **border** Filterrand *m*; ~ **coefficient** Filterfaktor *m*; ~ **factor** Filterfaktor *m*; ~ **foil** Filterfolie *f*; ~ **frame** Filterrahmen *m*; ~ **holder** Filterhalter *m*, Filterhalterung *n*; ~ **input** Filtereingang *m*; ~ **layer** Filterschicht *f*; ~ **network** Filternetz *n*; ~ **out** *v* aussieben *v*; ~ **pass-band** Durchlaßbandbreite *f*; ~ **section** Siebglied *n*; ~ **slot** (cam.) Filtereingang *m*; ~ **turret** Filterrad *n*, Filterrevolver *m*; ~ **wheel** Filterrad *n*, Filterrevolver *m*

filtering *n* Siebung *f*

final amplifier Endverstärker *m*; ~ **amplifier stage** Endverstärkerstufe *f*; ~ **blanking** Nachaustastung *f*; ~ **-check picture** Kontrollendbild *n*; ~ **control element** (EDP) Regelglied *n*, Stellglied *n*; ~ **cut** Feinschnitt *m*; ~ **picture quality check** Bildendkontrolle *f*; ~ **scene** Schlußszene *f*; ~ **stage** Endstufe *f*; ~ **version** Endfassung *f*; ~ **viewing** Endabnahme *f*, Abnahme *f*; ~ **viewing of cutting copy** Schnittabnahme *f*

finance* *n* Rechnungswesen* *n*

finance department Finanzabteilung *f*; ~ **directorate** Finanzdirektion *f*

financial equalisation Finanzausgleich *m*

fine adjustment Feineinstellung *f*; ~ **control** Feineinstellung *f*; ~ **cut** Feinschnitt *m*; ~ **grain** Feinkorn *n*

fine-grain *adj* feinkörnig *adj*; **~ developer** Feinkornentwickler *m*; **~ film** Feinkornfilm *m*; **~ print** Feinkornkopie *f*, Marronkopie *f*, Zwischenpositiv *n*; **~ stock** Feinkornfilm *m*; **~ stock for duping** Lavendelmaterial *n*
fine groove Mikrorille *f*
fineness of grain Auflösungsvermögen *n*
fine setting Feineinstellung *f*
fine tuning Scharfabstimmung *f*
finish *v* abschließen *v*; **~** *v* (F) abdrehen *v*; **~** *n* Fertigung *f*; **~** *n* (F) Auslauf *m*
finishing *n* Endfertigung *f*, Endkonfektionierung *f*, Fertigung *f*, Konfektionierung *f*; **~ time** Endzeit *f*
fire *v* (flashlight) auslösen *v*; **~ extinguisher** Feuerlöscher *m*
fire-light effect Feuerbeleuchtungseffekt *m*
fireman *n* Feuerwehrmann *m*; **head ~** Brandmeister *m*
fire-proof *adj* feuerfest *adj*; **~ magazine** Feuerschutztrommel *f*
fire-resistant *adj* feuerfest *adj*
fire shutter (F) Feuerschutzklappe *f*
firing circuit Zündkreis *m*
first broadcast Erstsendung *f*, Erstausstrahlung *f*, Ursendung *f*; **~ dynode spot** Dynodenfleck *m*; **~ generation** (tape) erste Kopie; **~ night** Premiere *f*, Erstaufführung *f*, Uraufführung *f*; **~ performance** Uraufführung *f*; **~ reading** Leseprobe *f*; **~ rehearsal** Stellprobe *f*; **~ release** Nullkopie *f*; **~ release print** Korrekturkopie *f*; **~ run** Erstaufführung *f*, Uraufführung *f*; **~ -run theatre** Erstaufführungskino *n*, Erstaufführungstheater *n*; **~ showing** Erstsendung *f*; **~ trial print** (FP) Testkopie *f*; **~ violin** erste Geige, Konzertmeister *m*
fish-eye lens Fischauge *n*
fit *v* anpassen *v*
fitter *n* Schlosser *m*
fitting *n* (elec.) Armatur *f*, Fassung *f*
fittings *n pl* Zubehör *n*
fix *v* fixieren *v*
fixed *adj* feststehend *adj*; **~ angle** (opt.) Festeinstellung *f*; **~ -angle lens** Festobjektiv *n*; **~ focus** Fixfokus *m*; **~ lens** Festobjektiv *n*; **~ pin** Justierstift *m*; **~ price** Festpreis *m*
fixed-satellite service fester Funkdienst mit Satelliten
fixing *n* Fixieren *n*; **~ bath** Fixierbad *n*; **~ chain** Befestigungskette *f*; **~ tank** Fixiertank *m*
flag *n* Blende *f*, Lichtblende *f*, Wattussy *m* (fam.)
flags *n pl* (lighting) Franzose *m* (fam.)
flange *n* Flansch *m*; **~ to** *v* anflanschen *v*
flange-mount *v* anflanschen *v*
flange socket Flanschdose *f*
flange-type plug Flanschdose *f*; **~ socket** Flanschdose *f*
flap up *v* aufklappen *v*
flare *n* Überstrahlung *f*
flash *n* Blitz *m*; **~** *n* (news) Vorrangmeldung *f*; **~ gun** Blitzgerät *n*; **~ news** Blitznachrichten *f pl*; **~ -over** *n* Spannungsüberschlag *m*, Überschlag *m*; **~ -over voltage** Überschlagspannung *f*; **~ programme** Blitzprogramm *n*; **~ unit** Blitzgerät *n*
flashback *n* Rückblende *f*
flashlight *n* Blitzlicht *n*
flat *m* (set) Blende *f*, Kulissenwand *f*, Normblende *f*; **~** *adj* (pict.) kontrastarm *adj*, flau *adj*; **~ clamp** (lighting) Messerschmitt *m* (fam.); **~ clamp** Blendenklammer *f*, Kulissenklammer *f*; **~ pack component** Flachbauelement *n*; **~ rate** Pauschale *f*; **~ -rate payment** Pauschalierung *f*; **~ -top**

aerial Flächenantenne *f*; **to be ~** grau in grau sein; **to pay a ~ rate** pauschalieren *v*
flaw *n* (opt.) Fehler *m*, Linsenfehler *m*
flesh tone Gesichtsfarbe *f*
flex *n* Kabel *n*, Schnur *f*; **twisted ~** gewendeltes Kabel
flexible conduit Metallschlauch *m*; **~ connector** Kupplung *f*; **~ cord** Schnur *f*; **~ cord distribution** Schnurverteilung *f*
flicker *v* flackern *v*; **~** *v* flimmern *v*; **~** *n* Flackern *n*; **~** *n* Flimmern *n*
flickering *n* Flimmern *n*
flicks *n pl* (coll.) Kintopp *m* (fam.)
flip caption Klapptitel *m*; **~ titles** *n pl* Klapptitel *m*
flip-flop *n* Flip-Flop *n*; **~ circuit** (EDP) bistabiler Multivibrator, bistabile Kippschaltung, Flip-Flop-Schaltung *f*; **~ register** (EDP) Flip-Flop-Register *n*
flipper *n* Klappwand *f*
float *n* Beleuchtungsrampe *f*
floater *n* Filmeinblendung *f*, Filminsert *m*
floating *adj* erdfrei *adj*; **~ battery** Pufferbatterie *f*; **~ point** (EDP) Gleitkomma *n*
floating-point operation (EDP) Gleitkomma-Operation *f*
flood *n* (coll.) Fluter *m*, Flutlicht *n*
floodlight *n* Flutlicht *n*; **~ projector** Flutlichtscheinwerfer *m*
floor level Studioebene *f*; **~ manager** Aufnahmeleiter *m*; **~ mixer** (F) Studiotonmeister *m*; **~ plan** Studiogrundriß *m*; **~ stand** Bodenstativ *n*
flop *v* (coll.) nicht ankommen
flow *n* Ablauf *m*; **~ of production** Produktionsablauf *m*; **~ rate** Zulaufmenge *f*
flowmeter *n* Dosierungsgerät *n*, Flüssigkeitsmengenmesser *m*
fluctuation *n* (tech.) Schwankung *f*
fluff *v* stottern *v*, verhaspeln *v* (sich), versprechen *v* (sich); **~** *n* Versprecher *m*
fluid iris Flüssigkeitsblende *f*, Küvette *f*
fluorescence *n* Fluoreszenz *f*
fluorescent lamp Fluoreszenzlampe *f*, Leuchtstofflampe *f*; **~ material** Leuchtstoff *m*; **~ screen** Leuchtschirm *m*, Leuchtstoffschirm *m*; **~ substance** Selbstleuchter *m*; **~ tube** (US) Fluoreszenzlampe *f*
flutter *v* flackern *v*, flattern *v*; **~** *n* Flackern *n*, schnelle Tonhöhenschwankungen **~ and wow** (disc) Gleichlaufschwankung *f*; **~ echo** (US) Mehrfachecho *n*; **no ~ and wow** (disc) Gleichlauf *m*
flux, magnetic Magnetfluß *m*, magnetischer Fluß
flyback *n* Rücklauf *m*, Strahlrücklauf *m*; **~ beam** Rücklaufstrahl *m*; **~ circuit** (US) Rückleitung *f*; **~ signal** Rücklaufsignal *n*; **~ suppression** Rücklaufaustastung *f*
flying-spot scanner Lichtpunktabtaster *m*, Punktlichtabtaster *m*; **~ scanning** Lichtpunktabtastung *f*, Punktlichtabtastung *f*; **~ store** (EDP) Bildröhrenspeicher *m*
flyman *n* Schnürbodentechniker *m*
flywheel *n* Schwungrad *n*, Schwungscheibe *f*; **~ circuit** Schwungradkreis *m*; **~ mass** Schwungmasse *f*; **~ oscillator** Schwungradoszillator *m*; **~ synchronisation** Schwungradsynchronisation *f*
focal distance Brennweite *f*; **~ length** Brennweite *f*; **double ~ length** doppelte Brennweite; **long ~ length** große Brennweite, lange Brennweite; **short ~ length** kurze Brennweite; **to increase ~ length** vergrößern *v*

focal plane Bildebene *f*, Brennpunktebene *f*
focal-plane shutter Schlitzverschluß *m*
focal point Brennpunkt *m*
focus *v* einstellen *v*, fokussieren *v*, scharf einstellen, Schärfe einstellen, Schärfe ziehen, ziehen *v*; ~ *n* Brennpunkt *m*, Fokus *m*; ~ *n* Scharfeinstellung *f*; ~ **calibration tape** Brennweitenband *n*, Schärfenband *n*; ~ **handle** Schärferad *n*; ~ **knob** Schärferad *n*; ~ **of divergence** Zerstreuungspunkt *m*; ~ **operator** zweiter Kameraassistent, Schärfeassistent *m*, Schärfezieher *m*; ~ **puller** Kameraassistent *m*, Schärfeassistent *m*, Schärfezieher *m*; ~ **ring** Brennweitenring *m*, Schärfenring *m*; ~ **setting** Entfernungseinstellung *f*; ~ **up** *v* Bild aus der Unschärfe ziehen; **in** ~ scharf *adj*; **lack of** ~ Unschärfe *f*; **long** ~ große Brennweite, lange Brennweite; **minimum** ~ kürzeste scharf einstellbare Entfernung; **minimum range of** ~ kürzeste scharf einstellbare Entfernung; **out of** ~ unscharf *adj*; **short** ~ kurze Brennweite; **to bring into** ~ scharf einstellen, Schärfe einstellen, Schärfe ziehen; **to bring out of** ~ verstellen *v*
focusing *n* Einstellung *f*, Scharfeinstellung *f*, Fokussierung *f*; ~ *n* Bündelung *f*; ~ **electrode** elektrostatische Linse; ~ **ring** Objektivring *m*; ~ **scale** Entfernungsskala *f*
fog *v* verschleiern *v*; ~ *n* Schleier *m*; ~ **machine** Nebelmaschine *f*
foil *n* (VTR) Klebeband *n*
foldback *n* (prod.) Mithörkontrolle *f*; ~ **circuit** Mithörleitung *f*
folded dipole Faltdipol *m*
folding tripod Klappstativ *n*
folk music Volksmusik *f*
follow focus shot Verfolgungsaufnahme *f*; ~ **shot** Verfolgungsaufnahme *f*; ~ **spot** Verfolgerscheinwerfer *m*, Verfolger *m* (fam.), Verfolgerspot *m*; ~ **spotlight** Verfolgerscheinwerfer *m*, Verfolger *m* (fam.), Verfolgerspot *m*; ~ **up** *v* nachsteuern *v*; ~ **-up** *n* Nachführung *f*
follower *n* Verfolgerscheinwerfer *m*, Verfolger *m* (fam.), Verfolgerspot *m*
following shot Mitschwenk *m*
foot control Fußtaste *f*; ~ **lighting** Rampenbeleuchtung *f*; ~ **switch** Fußtaste *f*
footage *n* Filmlänge *f*, Länge *f*, Meterlänge *f*; ~ **counter** Filmlängenmeßuhr *f*, Fußlängenzähler *m*, Meterzähler *m*; ~ **for printing** Kopierer (K) *m*; ~ **mark** Längenmarkierung *f*; ~ **number** Fußnummer *f*; **excessive** ~ Überlänge *f*; **insufficient** ~ Unterlänge *f*
footlight *n* Rampenlicht *n*, Beleuchtungsrampe *f*
footlights *n pl* Fußrampe *f*, Lichtrampe *f*
forces network Militärsender *m*; ~ **station** Militärsender *m*
foreground *n* Vordergrund *m*; ~ **model** Vorsatzmodell *n*
foreign correspondent Auslandskorrespondent *m*; ~ **coverage** Auslandsberichterstattung *f*; ~ **-language courses by television** Sprachfernsehen *n*; ~ **news** *n pl* Berichterstattung Ausland; ~ **news** *n pl* (US) Außenpolitik* *f*; **premises in** ~ **country** Auslandsstudio *n*
foreman *n* Vorarbeiter *m*; ~ *n* Werkmeister *m*
forked bracket Gabelhalterung *f*

form *v* formieren *v*
format *n* Format *n*, Größe *f*; **~** *n* (prog.) Funkform *f*, Sendeform *f*; **~ error** (EDP) Formatfehler *m*; **scanned ~** abgetastetes Format
formation *n* Formierung *f*
forming *n* Formierung *f*
formula language (EDP) Formelsprache *f*
formulate *v* abfassen *v*
forward-acting regulator Vorwärtsregelung *f*
forward motion Vorlauf *m*, Vorwärtsgang *m*; **~ planning** Vorausplanung *f*; **~ voltage** Durchlaßspannung *f*; **fast ~ run** schneller Vorlauf
forward-to-back ratio Vor-Rückverhältnis *n*
foundation light Grundlicht *n*
four-frame motion Vierergang *m*
four-pole network Vierpol *m*
four-terminal network Vierpol *m*
four track Vierspur *f*
four-track machine Vierspurmaschine *f*
four-wire circuit Vierdrahtleitung *f*; **~ control circuit** Vierdrahtmeldeleitung *f*; **~ line** Vierdrahtleitung *f*
frame *v* Bild einstellen, einstellen *v*, in die Bildmitte setzen, verstellen *v*; **~** *n* Rahmen *m*, Rahmengestell *n*; **~** *n* (pict.) Bild *n*, Bildfeld *n*, Einzelbild *n*, Feld *n*, Filmbild *n*, Kader *m*, Vollbild *n*; **~ aerial** Rahmenantenne *f*; **~ bar** Bildsteg *m*; **~ counter** Bildzähler *m*; **~ duration** Bilddauer *f*; **~ edge** Bildkante *f*; **~ flyback** Bildrücklauf *m*; **~ frequency** Bildfrequenz *f*, Bildwechselfrequenz *f*, Vollbildfrequenz *f*; **~ gauge** Bildschritt *m*; **~ height** Bildhöhe *f* **~ hold** Bildfangregler *m*, Bildfang *m*; **~ joint** Scharnier *n*; **~ -limiting** *n* (TV) Bildbegrenzung *n*; **~ line** Bildstrich *m*, Bildsteg *m*; **~ position** Bildlage *f*; **~ -pulling** *n* Ausfall des Bildgleichlaufs; **~ pulse** (TV) Schnittmarke *f*; **~ repetition rate** Vollbildfrequenz *f*; **~ roll** Bilddurchlauf *m*, Bildkippen *n*; **~ rolling** Ziehen des Bildes; **~ scan** Bildablenkung *f*; **~ -scan transformer** Bildablenktransformator *m*; **~ -sequential** *adj* bildsequent *adj*; **~ size** Bildformat *n*; **~ sweep unit** Bildkippgerät *n*; **~ sync** Bildsynchronimpuls *m*, Bildwechselimpuls *m*; **~ synchronisation** Bildsynchronisation *f*; **~ synchronising pulse** Bildsynchronimpuls *m*, Bildwechselimpuls *m*; **to be in ~** im Blickfeld sein
frame-by-frame display Einergang *m*; **~ exposure** Einzelbildaufnahme *f*
frames per second (fps) Bilder pro Sekunde
framing *n* Bild *n*, Bildbegrenzung *f*, Bildeinstellung *f*, Bildstricheinstellung *f*, Einstellung *f*; **~ control** Bildfangregler *m*, Bildfang *m*; **~ mask** Bildmaske *f*; **bad ~** fehlerhafte Bildeinstellung
free from water wasserfrei *adj*; **~ of charge** gebührenfrei *adj*
free acoustics Freiakustik *f*
freedom of the press Pressefreiheit *f*
free field Freiakustik *f*
free-lance *n* freier Mitarbeiter; **~** *adj* freiberuflich *adj*; **~ producer** freier Produzent
free-running *adj* unverkoppelt *adj*
free space Spielraum *m*
freeze effect Stopptrick *m*; **~ frame** Standbildverlängerung *f*, Standkopie *f*, weiterkopiertes

Einzelbild; ~ **frame effect** Stopptrick *m*; ~ **framing** Standkopieren *n*; **to ~ the action** Standbild fahren

frenchman *n* Lichtblende *f*, Blende *f*

frequencies, to cut off Frequenzen beschneiden

frequency *n* Frequenz *f*; ~ **allocation** Frequenzverteilung *f*; ~ **allocation plan** Wellenplan *m*, Frequenzplan *m*; ~ **band** Frequenzband *n*; ~ **bandwidth** Frequenzbandbreite *f*; ~ **change** Frequenzänderung *f*; ~ **changer** Frequenzumsetzer *m*, Frequenzumwandler *m*; ~ **control** Scharfabstimmung *f*; ~ **-control crystal** Steuerquarz *m*; ~ **converter** Frequenzumwandler *m*; ~ **correction** Scharfabstimmung *f*; ~ **-correction circuit** Frequenznachsteuerkreis *m*; ~ **-dependent** *adj* frequenzabhängig *adj*; ~ **deviation** Frequenzhub *m*; ~ **deviation meter** Frequenzhubmesser *m*; ~ **distortion** Frequenzgangverzerrung *f*, Frequenzverzerrung *f*; ~ **divider** Frequenzteiler *m*; ~ **-division multiplex** (stereo) Frequenzmultiplex *m*; ~ **doubler** Frequenzverdoppler *m*; ~ **drift** Frequenzabweichung *f*, Frequenzdrift *f*; ~ **fall-off** Frequenzabfall *m*; ~ **fluctuation** Frequenzschwankung *f*; ~ **generator** Frequenzgenerator *m* ~ **limit** Frequenzgrenze *f*; ~ **magnetic tape** Frequenzgangtestband *n*; ~ **mark** Frequenzmarke *f*; ~ **marker** Frequenzmarke *f*; ~ **-measuring bridge** Frequenzmeßbrücke *f*; ~ **meter** Frequenzmesser *m*; ~ **modulation (FM)** Frequenzmodulation (FM) *f*; ~ **of lights** Scheinwerferdichte *f*; ~ **offset** Frequenzversatz *m*; ~ **plan** Wellenplan *m*, Frequenzplan *m*; ~ **range** Bandbreite *f*, Empfangsbereich *m*, Empfangsgebiet *n*, Frequenzbereich *m*; ~ **raster** Frequenzraster *m*; ~ **response** Amplituden-Frequenzgang *m*, Amplitudengang *m*, Frequenzgang *m*; ~ **response characteristic** Frequenzcharakteristik *f*; ~ **response correction stage** Klangentzerrerstufe *f*; ~ **response curve** Wiedergabekurve *f*; ~ **response equalisation** Frequenzgangbegradigung *f*, Frequenzgangentzerrung *f*; ~ **run** Tonfolge *f*; ~ **-selective** *adj* frequenzselektiv *adj*; ~ **selector switch** Frequenzumschalter *m*; ~ **separator** Frequenzweiche *f*; ~ **series** Frequenzreihe *f*; ~ **shift** Frequenzverschiebung *f*; ~ **spectral line** Frequenzlinie *f*; ~ **spectrum** Frequenzspektrum *n*; ~ **synchronisation** Frequenzgleichheit *f*; ~ **test pattern** Frequenztestbild *n*; ~ **translator** Frequenzumsetzer *m*; ~ **trimming limits** Nachstimmbereich *m*; ~ **tuning** Frequenzabstimmung *f*; ~ **variation** Frequenzänderung *f*; **as a function of ~** frequenzabhängig *adj*; **automatic ~ control (AFC)** automatische Frequenznachsteuerung, automatische Scharfabstimmung; **dependence of attenuation upon ~** frequenzabhängige Dämpfung; **high ~ (HF)** hohe Frequenz; **low ~ (LF)** tiefe Frequenz; **radio ~ (RF)** Hochfrequenz *f* (HF), Radiofrequenz *f* (RF); **super-high ~ (SHF)** superhohe Frequenz; **ultra-high ~ (UHF)** ultrahohe Frequenz (UHF), Ultrakurzwelle *f*

(UKW); **vertical ~** (US) Vertikalfrequenz (V-Frequenz) *f*; **very high ~ (VHF)** sehr hohe Frequenz, Ultrakurzwelle *f* (UKW) **very low ~ (VLF)** Längstwellenfrequenz *f*
Fresnel lens Fresnelsche Linse, Stufenlinse *f*; **~ lens spotlight** Stufenlinsenscheinwerfer *m*
friction *n* Friktion *f*; **~ clutch** Friktionskupplung *f*; **~ drive** Friktionsantrieb *m*; **~ head** Friktionskopf *m*
fringe *n* Saum *m*; **~ effect** Randeffekt *m*
front credits *n pl* Namensvorspann *m*; **~ element** Frontlinse *f*; **~ face** Vorderflanke *f*; **~ lens** Frontlinse *f* **~ lens element** Eintrittslinse *f*; **~ light** Frontallicht *n*, Vorderlicht *n*; **~ page** erste Seite; **~ panel** Frontplatte *f*; **~ projection** Aufprojektion (Aufpro) *f*; **~ window** Frontfenster *n*
front-to-back ratio Vor-Rückverhältnis *n*
front-to-rear ratio Vor-Rückverhältnis *n*
frozen picture Standbild *n*, Standbildverlängerung *f*, Standkopie *f*, weiterkopiertes Einzelbild
frying *n* Zischen *n*
fuel cell Brennstoffzelle *f*
full-circle panoramic shot Rundschwenk *m*
full coverage ausführliche Berichterstattung; **~ drive** Vollaussteuerung *f*; **~ -format** *adj* formatfüllend *adj*; **~ -frame** *adj* bildfüllend *adj*; **~ house** ausverkauft *adj*; **~ -length film** abendfüllender Film, Spielfilm *m*; **~ -length shot (FLS)** Halbtotale *f*; **~ modulation** Vollaussteuerung *f*, Vollpegel *m*; **~ score** Partitur *f*; **~ synchronisation** Vollsynchronisation *f*; **~ track** Vollspur *f*; **~ -wave rectifier** Doppelweggleichrichter *m*, Zweiweggleichrichter *m*
fullness of tone (mus.) Klangfülle *f*
function *n* (event) Veranstaltung *f*; **~ chart** (EDP) Funktionsdiagramm *n*; **~ part** (EDP) Operationsteil *m*; **~ selection** Betriebsartenwahl *f*; **~ selector switch** Betriebsartenschalter *m*; **~ switch** Funktionswahlschalter *m*; **~ table** (EDP) Funktionstabelle *f*, Wertetabelle *f*, Wahrheitstabelle *f*; **~ test** Funktionsprüfung *f*
functional diagram Funktionsdiagramm *n*, Funktionsschaltplan *m*; **~ diagram** (EDP) Logikschaltbild *n*
fundamental *n* Grundton *m*; **~** *n* Grundwelle *f*; **~ frequency** Grundfrequenz *f*; **~ tone** Grundton *m*; **~ wave** Grundwelle *f*
funds *n pl* Mittel *n pl*
furnisher *n* Ausstatter *m*
furnishing *n* (set) Ausstattung *f*
furnishings store Möbelfundus *m*
furniture restorer Möbelrestaurator *m*; **~ store** Möbelfundus *m*
further education Erwachsenenbildung *f*
fuse *v* durchbrennen *v*; **~** *v* durchschlagen *v*; **~** *n* Sicherung *f*; **~ holder** Sicherungshalter *m*; **~ switch** Sicherungsschalter *m*; **rapid ~** flinke Sicherung; **slow ~** träge Sicherung
fuzziness *n* Unschärfe *f*

G

gag *n* Gag *m*; **~ up** *v* (US) vergagen *v*
gag-man *n* (US) Gagman *m*
gag-writer *n* Gagman *m*

gain *n* Gewinn *m*, Verstärkung *f*; **~ control** Verstärkungsregelung *f*; **~ control** (fader) Verstärkungssteller *m*, Verstärkungsregler *m* (fam.); **~ variation** Verstärkungsänderung *f*; **automatic ~ control (AGC)** automatische Verstärkungsregelung; **differential ~** differentielle Verstärkung; **variable ~** veränderliche Verstärkung
gallery *n* Beleuchtergang *m*, Galerie *f*; ~ *n* (coll.) (control room) Regie *f*, Regiekanzel *f*, Regieraum *m*
gallows arm Scheinwerfergalgen *m*
galvanometer *n* Galvanometer *n*
gamma *n* Gamma *n*, Steilheit *f*; **~ characteristic** Gradationskurve *f*, Gammazeitkurve *f*, Gradationsverlauf *m*; **~ control** Gammaregelung *f*, Gradationsregelung *f*; **~ correction** Gammaentzerrung *f*, Gradationsentzerrung *f*; **~ distortion** Gradationsverzerrung *f*; **~ selector** Gammaschalter *m*; **~ value** Gammawert *m*; **multiple ~** multiplikatives Gamma; **overall ~** über alles Gamma
gang *n* Schicht *f*
ganging *n* Gleichlauf *m*
gantry *n* Beleuchterbrücke *f*, Beleuchterbühne *f*
gap *n* Spalt *m*, Abtastspalt *m*; **~ adjustment** Spalteinstellung *f*; **~ depth** Kopfspalttiefe *f*; **~ length** Spaltbreite *f*; **~ loss** Kopfspaltverlust *m*, Spaltdämpfung *f*; **~ setting** Spalteinstellung *f*; **~ width** Kopfspaltbreite *f*; **effective ~ length** magnetische Kopfspaltlänge; **physical ~ length** Kopfspaltlänge *f*
garage foreman Garagenmeister *m*
garbled *adj* verstümmelt *adj*
gate *v* auftasten *v*, austasten *v*; ~ *n* Schattenraster *m*; ~ *n* Bildfenster *n*; ~ *n* Schwelle *f*; ~ *n* (elec.) Torschaltung *f*; **~ circuit** Auftastschaltung *f*, Gatter *n*, Torschaltung *f*; **~ circuit switch** Torschalter *m*; **~ pressure** (cam.) Kufendruck *m*; **~ pressure plate** (cam.) Kufe *f*; **~ pulse** Auftastimpuls *m*; **~ runner** (proj.) Kufe *f*; **~ runner pressure** (proj.) Kufendruck *m*
gating *n* Auftastung *f*, Austastung *f*
gauge *v* peilen *v*; ~ *n* Format *n*, Größe *f*
gaussian filter circuit Glockenkreis *m* (Secam)
gauze *n* Gaze *f*
gear *v* (mech.) übersetzen *v*; ~ *n* Getriebe *n*; **~ down** *v* untersetzen *v*; **~ drive** Zahnantrieb *m*; **~ ratio** Übersetzungsverhältnis *n*; **~ reduction** Untersetzung *f*; **~ rim** Zahnkranzrolle *f*; **~ ring** Zahnkranzrolle *f*; **~ unit** Getriebe *n*; **~ wheel** Zahnrad *n*
gearing *n* (mech.) Übersetzung *f*
gears *n pl* Getriebe *n*
gelatin *n* Gelatine *f*; **~ filter** Gelatinefilter *m*
general ambient light Gesamtaufhellung *f*; **~ audience programme** Familienprogramm *n* **~ film catalogue** Filmverzeichnis *n*; **~ lighting** Gesamtaufhellung *f*; **~ production insurance** Produktionsversicherung *f*; **~ -purpose test-signal generator** Universaltestbildgeber *m*; **~ retainer** Pauschale *f*; **~ scene lighting** Szenenbeleuchtung *f*; **~ view** Überblick *m*, Übersicht *f*
generating plant Stromaggregat *n*; **~ set** Aggregat *n*; **~ unit** Stromaggregat *n*
generator *n* Generator *m*, Lichtmaschine *f*, Oszillator *m*; **mobile ~** fahrbare Lichtmaschine

Geneva cross Malteserkreuz *n*; **~ movement** Malteserkreuzgetriebe *n*
genre *n* Genre *n*; **~ music** Genremusik *f*
geometric aperture geometrische Blende; **~ error** Geometriefehler *m*
geometrical test pattern Geometrietestbild *n*
German Television ARD Deutsches Fernsehen (DFS); **~ Television ZDF** ZDF *n* (Zweites Deutsches Fernsehen)
get up *v* (part) einstudieren *v*
getter *n* Getterpille *f*
ghost *n* Geisterbild *n*; **~ image** Geisterbild *n*
ghosting *n* Doppelkontur *f*; ~ *n* (opt.) ziehende Blende
girdle *n* Gurt *m*
glamour light Glamourlicht *n*
glancing light Streiflicht *n*
glass plate Glasplatte *f*
glazier *n* Glaser *m*
global fee Pauschalgage *f*, Pauschalhonorar *n*; **~ sum** Pauschale *f*; **payment of ~ fee** Pauschalierung *f*; **to contract at a ~ fee** pauschalieren *v*; **to pay a ~ fee** pauschalieren *v*
glow-discharge *n* Glimm-Entladung *f*; **~ lamp** Glimmlampe *f*; **~ tube** Glimmröhre *f*
glow-lamp *n* Glimmlampe *f*
go ahead! ab! abfahren!; **~ out** *v* über den Sender gehen; **~ over** *v* (to) (bcast.) umschalten *v* (nach), abgeben *v* (an); **to ~ out by mistake** aus Versehen über den Sender gehen
go-ahead signal Fertigmeldung *f*
go-between *n* (coll.) Verbindungsmann *m*
gobo *n* Lichtblende *f*, Blende *f*, Neger *m* (fam.); **~ arm** Scheitelhänger *m*
goniometry *n* Peilung *f*
gonoscope *n* Bildausschnittsucher *m*
goose neck (US) Schwanenhals *m*, Gänsegurgel *f*
govern *v* regulieren *v*
government spokesman Regierungssprecher *m*
governor *n* Regler *m*
gradation *n* Abstufung *f*, Gradation *f*; **~ of printing paper** Gradation eines Fotopapiers; **flat ~** flache Gradation
grade *v* (opt.) abstufen *v*; ~ *v* (FP) entzerren *v*, Licht bestimmen; ~ *n* Stufe *f*
grader *n* (FP) Entzerrer *m*, Lichtbestimmer *m*
grading *n* (FP) Entzerrung *f*, Lichtbestimmung *f*; **~ bench** Lichtbestimmungstisch *m*; **~ chart** Lichtbestimmungsplan *m*, Lichtzettel *m*; **~ copy** Lichtbestimmungskopie *f*, Testkopie *f*; **~ print** Lichtbestimmungskopie *f*; **~ strip** (FP) Bildband *n*
gradual filter Verlaufblende *f*, Verlauffilter *m*
graduate *v* (opt.) abstufen *v*
graduated filter Verlaufblende *f*, Verlauffilter *m*
graduation *n* Abstufung *f*, Skala *f*, Teilung *f*
grain *n* (F) Korn *n*, Körnigkeit *f*
graininess *n* Körnigkeit *f*
gramophone *n* Plattenmaschine *f*, Plattenspieler *m*; **~ amplifier** Schallplattenverstärker *m*; **~ industry** Schallplattenindustrie *f* **~ librarian** Plattenarchivar *m*; **~ library** Plattenarchiv *n*, Schallplattenarchiv *n*, Diskothek *f*; **~ programme** Nummernprogramm *n*; **~ record** Grammofonplatte *f*, Schallplatte *f* **~ turntable** Schallplattenteller *m*, Plattenteller *m*
grams *n pl* (coll.)

Schallplattenmusik *f*, Bandmusik *f*
granularity *n* Körnigkeit *f*
granulation *n* Körnigkeit *f*
granule *n* (TV) Korn *n*
graph *n* Diagramm *n*, Grafik *f*, grafische Darstellung, Kurve *f*, Schaubild *n*, Schautafel *f*; ~ **plotter** (EDP) Kurvenschreiber *m*, Kurvenzeichner *m*, Plotter *m*
graphic *n* Grafik *f*, grafische Darstellung; ~ **artist** Gebrauchsgrafiker *m*, grafischer Zeichner *m*; ~ **design*** Grafik* *f*; ~ **designer** Grafiker *m*; ~ **display unit** (EDP) Kurvenschreiber *m*, Kurvenzeichner *m*, Plotter *m*; ~ **output unit** (EDP) Kurvenschreiber *m*, Kurvenzeichner *m*, Plotter *m*
grass *n* (coll.) (TV) Grieß *m*
grating *n* Gitter *n*, Rost *m*
grease paint Schminke *f*; ~ **pencil** Fettstift *m*
green-room *n* Künstlerfoyer *n*, Künstlerzimmer *n*, Konversationszimmer *n*
grey *adj* grau *adj*; **to be** ~ grau in grau sein
grey scale Graukeil *m*, Grauskala *f*
grey-scale chart Grauwerttafel *f*; ~ **correction** Grauentzerrung *f*; **calibrated** ~ **chart** harmonisch abgestufte Grauwerttafel
grey step Graustufe *f*
grey value Grauwert *m*
grid *n* Gitter *n*, Gitterrostdecke *f*, Rost *m*, Schnürboden *m*, Schutzgitter *n*; ~ *n* (elec.) Netz *n*; ~ **bias supply** Gitterspannungsnetzgerät *n*; ~ **bias voltage** Gittervorspannung *f*; ~ **circuit** Gitterkreis *m*; ~ **-circuit tuning** Gitterkreisabstimmung *f*; ~ **current** Gitterstrom *m*; ~ **leak** (coll.) Gitterwiderstand *m*; ~ **leak resistance** Gitterableitwiderstand *m*; ~ **-plate capacitance** Gitteranodenkapazität *f*; ~ **-plate tube capacity** Gitteranodenkapazität *f*; ~ **rectifier** Gittergleichrichter *m*; ~ **resistance** Gitterwiderstand *m*; ~ **slot** (lighting) Rille *f*; ~ **test pattern** Gittertestbild *n*; ~ **voltage** Gitterspannung *f*; **to join the** ~ sich an das Netz hängen; **to leave the** ~ vom Netz abgehen
grille *n* Gitter *n*; ~ *n* (test chart) Konvergenztestbild *n*
grip *n* Schwenkgriff *m*; ~ *n* (coll.) (cam. crew) Kamerafahrer *m*, Dollyfahrer *m*; ~ *n* (US) (worker) Atelierarbeiter *m*, Bühnenarbeiter *m*
gripper *n* Greifer *m*
groove *n* Nut *f*; ~ *n* (disc) Rille *f*, Schallrille *f*, Tonspur *f*; ~ **angle** Rillenwinkel *m*, Stichelwinkel *m*; ~ **of record** Schallrille *f*; ~ **spacing ratio** Füllgrad *m*
ground *v* nullen *v*; ~ *v* (US) erden *v*; ~ *n* (elec.) Masse *f*; ~ *n* (US) Erde *f*, Erdung *f*; ~ **-collector circuit** Kollektorgrundschaltung *f*, Kollektorschaltung *f*; ~ **conductivity** Bodenleitfähigkeit *f*; ~ **cove** Vorsatzrampe *f*; ~ **-glass plate** Mattscheibe *f*; ~ **-glass screen** Mattscheibe *f*; ~ **noise** Eigenrauschen *n*; ~ **signal station** Erdefunkstelle *f*; ~ **station** Erdefunkstelle *f*; ~ **wave** Bodenwelle *f*; ~ **-wave propagation** Bodenwellenausbreitung *f*; ~ **-wave service area** Nahempfangsgebiet *n*
grounded anode amplifier Anodenbasisschaltung *f*; ~ **cathode circuit** Kathodenbasis (KB) *f*, Kathodenbasisschaltung *f*

(KB)
grounded-base connection Basisgrundschaltung *f*, Basisschaltung *f*
grounded-emitter configuration Emitterbasisschaltung *f*, Emitterschaltung *f*
grounded-grid circuit Gitterbasisschaltung *f*
grounding *n* (US) Erdung *f*
group *n* Band *f*, Ensemble *n*; **~ aerial** Dipolgruppe *f*; **~ amplifier** Summenverstärker *m*; **~ contract** Gruppenvertrag *m*; **~ control** Gruppensteuerung *f*; **~ delay** Gruppenlaufzeit *f*; **~ delay difference** Gruppenlaufzeitdifferenz *f*; **~ delay distortion** Laufzeiteffekt *m*; **~ fader** Summensteller *m*, Summenregler *m* (fam.); **~ mixer** Gruppenmischer *m*; **~ of channels** Kanalgruppe *f*; **~ shot** Gruppeneinstellung *f*
grouping *n* (transmitter) Zusammenschaltung *f*
grub screw Madenschraube *f*, Gewindestift *m*
guard *n* Schutzgrill *m*; **~** *n* (staff) Wachmann *m*; **~ band** (freq.) Sicherheitsband *n*; **~ band** (F) Sicherheitsspur *f*; **~ grid** Schutzgitter *n*; **~ -rail** *n* Brüstung *f*, Schutzgeländer *n*; **~ track** (F) Sicherheitsspur *f*
guest performance Gastspiel *n*
guide *n* Führung *f*; **~ bushing** Führungsbuchse *f*; **~ circuit** Guide-Leitung *f*; **~ pin** Führungsbolzen *m*, Führungsstift *m*; **~ pulley** Führungsrolle *f*; **~ rail** Laufschiene *f*; **~ roller** Führungsrolle *f*, Laufrolle *f*, Umlenkrolle *f*; **~ sleeve** Führungsbuchse *f*; **~ track** Hilfstonspur *f*, Kontrollspur *f*
guy *v* abspannen *v*, verankern *v*, verspannen *v*; **~ rope** Pardune *f*, Abspannseil *n*; **~ wire** Pardune *f*, Abspannseil *n*
gyrating mass Schwungmasse *f*
gyroscopic drive Kreiselantrieb *m*; **~ head** Kreiselkopf *m*; **~ mounting** Kameraschwenkkopf mit Kreiselantrieb, Schwenkkopf mit Kreiselantrieb
gyro-tripod *n* Kreiselstativ *n*

H

hackneyed *adj* abgedroschen *adj*
hair dryer Fön *m*; **~ in printer gate** Kopierfussel *m*; **~ light** Spitze *f*, Spitzenlicht *n*
hairpiece *n* Haarteil *n*
halation *n* Lichthof *m*, Überstrahlung *f*
half-shade *n* Halbschatten *m*
half-shadow *m* Halbschatten *m*
half-tone *n* Halbton *m*, Grauwert *m*; **~ distortion** Grauwertverzerrung *f* **~ rendering** Grauwertwiedergabe *f*; **~ reproduction** Halbtonwiedergabe *f*
half-track *n* Halbspur *f*
half-wave *n* Halbwelle *f*; **~ rectifier** Einweggleichrichter *m*
hall noise Saalgeräusch *n*
halo *n* Haloeffekt *m*, Lichthof *m*, Überstrahlung *f*; **~ effect** Haloeffekt *m*
halogen light Halogenlicht *n*
halt instruction (EDP) Stoppbefehl *m*
halyard *n* Zugseil *n*
ham *n* (coll.) Funkamateur *m*; **~ actor** (coll.) Schmierenkomödiant *m*; **~ up** *v* (perf.) schmieren *v*
hand boom Mikrofonangel *f*; **~ cable** Handkabel *n*; **~ control** Handregelung *f*, Handsteuerung *f* **~ -drawn** *adj* handgezeichnet *adj*;

~ **-held camera** Handkamera *f*; ~ **-held microphone** Handmikrofon *n*; ~ **-held TV camera** tragbare Fernsehkamera; ~ **lamp** Handlampe *f*, Handleuchte *f*; ~ **over** *v* (to) (bcast.) abgeben *v* (an), übergeben *v* (an); ~ **-rail** *n* Brüstung *f*, Schutzgeländer *n*

handle *v* (story) aufziehen *v*; ~ *n* Haltebügel *m*

handover point Übergabepunkt *m*

hang over *v* (sound, pict.) überhängen *v*

hanger *n* (lighting) Hänger *m*

hanging grid (lighting) Hängegitter *n*

Hanover bars (coll.) PAL-Jalousieeffekte *m pl*

hard *adj* (pict.) hart *adj*; ~ **film** kontrastreiches Filmmaterial

hardening of emulsion Härtung der Emulsion, Schichthärtung *f*

hardness *n* (F) Steilheit *f*

hardware *n* Hardware *f*; ~ **operation** (EDP) festverdrahteter Funktionsablauf

harmonic *n* Harmonische *f*, Oberschwingung *f*, Oberton *m*, Oberwelle *f*; ~ **distortion attenuation** Klirrdämpfung *f*; ~ **distortion factor** Klirrfaktor (K) *m*; ~ **distortion meter** Klirrfaktormesser *m*; ~ **filter** Oberwellenfilter *m*; ~ **generator** Verzerrer *m*; ~ **oscillation** Oberschwingung *f*; ~ **trap** Oberwellenfilter *m*; ~ **vibration** Oberschwingung *f*; ~ **wave** Oberwelle *f*; **even-order ~ distortion** gradzahliger Klirrfaktor; **odd-order ~ distortion** ungradzahliger Klirrfaktor; **second-order ~ distortion** quadratischer Klirrfaktor; **third-order ~ distortion** kubischer Klirrfaktor

harmony *n* Übereinstimmung *f*

harsh *adj* (sound) hart *adj*

Hartley circuit Dreipunktoszillatorschaltung *f*; ~ **oscillator** Dreipunktoszillatorschaltung *f*; ~ **oscillator circuit** Hartley-Schaltung *f*

hazy *adj* unscharf *adj*

head *n* (chief) Leiter *m*; ~ **adjustment** Eintaumeln des Kopfes; ~ **assembly** Tonabnehmer *m*, Tonabtaster *m*; ~ **-clogging** *n* Kopfzuschmieren *n*, Kopfzusetzen *n*; ~ **dressmaker** Zuschneider *m*; ~ **electrician** Elektromeister *m*; ~ **electrician** Oberbeleuchter *m*; ~ **gap** Kopfspalt *m*, Luftspalt *m*, Tonspalt *m*; ~ **leader** Filmvorspann *m*, Startband *n*, Startvorspann *m*, Vorspannfilm *m* ~ **of department** Abteilungsleiter *m*, Hauptabteilungsleiter *m*; ~ **of design** Ausstattungsleiter *m*; ~ **of desk** Redaktionsleiter *m*, Ressortleiter *m*, Ressortchef *m*; ~ **of news** Chefredakteur *m*; ~ **of overseas office** (BBC) Auslandsstudioleiter *m*; ~ **of presentation** Sendeleiter *m*; ~ **of publicity** (BBC) Pressechef *m*; ~ **of radio drama** Hörspielleiter *m*; ~ **of scripts** Chefdramaturg *m*; ~ **-support assembly** Kopfträger *m*; ~ **track** Kopfspur *f*; ~ **wear** Kopfabrieb *m*; ~ **wheel** Kopfrad *n*, Magnetkopfrad *n*; ~ **-wheel rotating speed** Kopfradgeschwindigkeit *f*; ~ **winding** Kopfwicklung *f*; **incorrect ~ position** (VTR) Bandführungsfehler *m*

heading *n* Titel *m*

headless screw Madenschraube *f*, Gewindestift *m*

headline *n* Schlagzeile *f*

headphone *n* Kopfhörer *m*

headset *n* Hörer *m*, Kopfgeschirr *n*, Kopfhörsprechgarnitur *f*,

Sprechgeschirr *n*
hearing *n* Gehör *n*; ~ **aid** Hörgerät *n*
heat exchanger Temperaturaustauscher *m*; ~ **filter** Wärmeschutzfilter *m*; ~ **protection filter** Wärmeschutzfilter *m*; ~ **rays** Wärmestrahlen *m pl*; ~ **sink** Kühlkörper *m*
heater *n* Heizfaden *m*; ~ **voltage** Heizspannung *f*
heating *n* Heizung *f*; ~ **engineer** Heizungstechniker *m*
heavy current Starkstrom *m*
height control Bildhöhenregler *m*
helical recording Schrägschriftaufzeichnung *f*; ~ **scan** Schrägschriftaufzeichnung *f*; ~ **scan system** Helicalscanverfahren *n*
helicopter shot Hubschrauberaufnahme *f*
helix *n* Schnecke *f*; ~ **cable** Spiralkabel *n*
helmsman *n* Kamerafahrer *m*, Dollyfahrer *m*
help *n* Hilfeleistung *f*
helper *n* Gehilfe *m*, Assistent *m*
hermaphrodite connector Zwitterstecker *m*
Hertz (Hz) *n* Hertz (Hz) *n*
heterodyne interference Störüberlagerung *f*
heterodyning *n* Überlagerung *f*
hexadecimal *adj* (EDP) sedezimal *adj*, hexadezimal *adj*; ~ **number** (EDP) Sedezimalzahl *f*, Hexadezimalzahl *f*
HI arc-lamp Bogenlampe *f*
hi-fi *n* Hi-Fi *n*
high band Highband *n*
high-band standards *n pl* Highband-Norm *f*
high-contrast *adj* kontrastreich *adj*; ~ **film** kontrastreiches Filmmaterial, Dokumentenfilm *m* **very ~ film stock** Superkontrastmaterial *n*
high-definition lens Hartzeichner *m*
high fidelity (hi-fi) hohe Wiedergabegüte (Hi-Fi)
high-fidelity *adj* klanggetreu *adj*
high frequency (HF) Hochfrequenz (HF) *f*
high-frequency *adj* hochfrequent *adj*, Hochfrequenz- (HF) (in Zus.); ~ **circuit** Hochfrequenzleitung *f*; ~ **emphasis** Höhenanhebung *f*; ~ **loudspeaker** Hochtonlautsprecher *m*; ~ **transmitter** Kurzwellensender *m*
high-impedance *adj* hochohmig *adj* ~ **tap** hochohmige Anzapfung
high intensity (HI) Hochintensität (HI) *f*
high-intensity arc lamp Hochintensitätslampe *f*; ~ **carbon (HI carbon)** Hochintensitätskohle *f*
high key (HK) High-key *n*
highlight *n* Glanzlicht *n*, Spitze *f*, Spitzenlicht *n*; ~ **brightness** Spitzenhelligkeit *f*; **to set a ~** Spitzen setzen
highlights *n pl* Lichter *n pl*
highly directional microphone Richtmikrofon *n*; ~ **reflective screen** Perlleinwand *f*; ~ **resistive** *adj* hochohmig *adj*
high-pass filter Hochpaß *m*, Hochpaßfilter *m*
high pitch Hochton *m*
high-power arc lamp Hochintensitätslampe *f*; ~ **station** Großsender *m*; ~ **transmitter** Großsender *m*
high-precision crystal Präzisionsquarz *m*
high-resistance *adj* hochohmig *adj*
high-speed *adj* (FP) empfindlich *adj* ~ **camera** Zeitdehnerkamera *f*; ~ **camera-work** Zeitdehnung *f*; ~ **effect** Zeitdehnung *f*; ~ **picture** Zeitdehneraufnahme *f*; ~ **printer** (EDP) Schnelldrucker *m*;

~ **shooting** Zeitdehnung *f*; ~ **shot** Zeitdehneraufnahme *f*
high tension (HT) Hochspannung *f*
high-tension battery Anodenbatterie *f*; ~ **power unit** Hochspannungsnetzgerät *n*
high voltage (HV) Hochspannung *f*
high-voltage overhead line Hochspannungsfreileitung *f*; ~ **transformer** Hochspannungstransformator *m*
hinge *n* Scharnier *n*
hinged arm (lighting) Gelenkarm *m* ~ **lid** Klappdeckel *m*
hire *v* mieten *v*; ~ *v* (US) (staff) einstellen *v*; ~ *n* Mieten *n*; ~ **charge** Leihmiete *f*; ~ **fee** Leihgebühr *f*; ~ **service** Verleih *m*
hiss *v* zischen *v*
hissing *n* Zischen *n*
history of broadcasting Rundfunkgeschichte *f*
hit *n* Schlager *m*, Hit *m*, Heuler *m*; ~ *n* (prog.) Knüller *m* (fam.); ~ **parade** Schlagerparade *f*; ~ **song** Schlager *m*; ~ **tune** Schlager *m*; **to be a** ~ einschlagen *v*
hold back *v* (news) zurückhalten *v*; ~ **control** Bildfangregler *m*, Bildfang *m*; ~ **frame** Standbildverlängerung *f*, Standkopie *f*, weiterkopiertes Einzelbild; ~ **framing** Standkopieren *n*; ~ **-in circuit** Wiedereinschaltautomatik *f*; ~ **it!** (take) Stopp!; ~ **range** Synchronisierbereich *m*; ~ **take** Reserveaufnahme *f*
holding contact Selbsthaltekontakt *m*
holiday relief Aushilfskraft *f*; ~ **relief** Hilfskraft *f*
hologram *n* Hologramm *n*
home news Berichterstattung Inland; ~ **political news** Innenpolitik* *f*; ~ **receiver** Heimempfänger *m*; ~ **track** Eigenspur *f*, Home-track *n*
hood *n* Haube *f*
hook up *v* anschließen *v*, zuschalten *v*
hook-up *n* Konferenzschaltung *f*, Schaltkonferenz *f*; ~ *n* (tech.) Kopplung der Kreise; ~ *n* (transmitter) Zuschalten eines Senders, Zusammenschaltung *f*
horizontal (H) *adj* Horizontal- (H-) (in Zus.); ~ **bar** Horizontalbalken *m*; ~ **blanking pulse** Horizontalaustastimpuls *m*; ~ **blanking pulse** (US) Zeilenaustastimpuls *m*; ~ **definition** Horizontalauflösung *f* ~ **deflection** Zeilenablenkung *f*; ~ **flyback** (US) Zeilenrücklauf *m*; ~ **frequency** (US) Zeilenfrequenz *f*; ~ **hold** Zeilenfangregler *m*; ~ **image** Querbild *n*; ~ **jitter** horizontale Bildstandschwankungen; ~ **pan** Horizontalschwenk *m*; ~ **picture** Querbild *n*; ~ **rewind** Horizontalumroller *m*; ~ **saw-tooth** Horizontalsägezahn *m*; ~ **scratch** Querschramme *f*; ~ **sweep** Zeilenablenkung *f*; ~ **synchronising pulse** Horizontalimpuls (H-Impuls) *m*, Horizontal-Synchronimpuls *m*, Zeilensynchronimpuls *m*; ~ **wipe** rollender Schnitt
horn gramophone Trichtergrammofon *n*; ~ **loudspeaker** Trichterlautsprecher *m*; ~ **radiator** Hornstrahler *m*
horse opera (US coll.) Wildwestfilm *m*, Western *m*
hostess *n* Empfangsdame *f*
hot cathode Glühelektrode *f*; ~ **spot** Leuchtfleck *m*
hour-counter *n* Stundenzähler *m*
house foreman Hausmeister *m*; ~ **light** Baulicht *n*, Studiolicht *n*; ~ **manager** Hausverwalter *m*
housing *n* Gehäuse *n*

howl *v* heulen *v*; ~ *n* Jaulen *n*; ~ **round** *v* (acoust.) rückkoppeln *v*
howling *n* Jaulen *n*; ~ *n* (coll.) (acoust.) Rückkopplung *f*
howl-round *n* (acoust.) Rückkopplung *f*
hub *n* Bobby *m*, Filmkern *m*
hue *n* Farbe *f*, Farbton *m*, Farbwert *f*; ~ **error** Farbabweichung *f*
hum *v* brummen *v*, summen *v*; ~ *n* Brumm *m*, Brummton *m*; ~ **amplitude modulation** Brummstör-Amplitudenmodulation *f*; ~ **bar** Brummstreifen *m*; ~ **bars** *n pl* Brummüberlagerung *f*; ~ **buckling** Heizsymmetrierung *f*; ~**-reduction factor** Siebfaktor *m*; ~ **superimposition** Brummüberlagerung *f*; ~ **suppression** Brummunterdrückung *f*; ~ **voltage** Brummspannung *f*
humidity *n* Feuchtigkeit *f*; **relative ~ (RH)** relative Feuchtigkeit
humming noise Brumm *m*, Brummton *m*
hunting *n* Pendelbewegung *f*; ~ *n* (sound) Nachlauf *m*
Hurter and Driffield curve (H a. D curve) Gradationskurve *f*, Gammazeitkurve *f*, Gradationsverlauf *m*, Schwärzungskurve *f*
hybrid *n* (tel.) Gabelschaltung *f*; ~ **amplifier** Gabelverstärker *m*; ~ **circuit** Hybridschaltung *f*; ~ **computer** (EDP) Hybridrechner *m*; ~ **set** (tel.) Gabelschaltung *f*
hydraulic *adj* hydraulisch *adj*; ~ **stand** Pumpstativ *n*; ~ **tripod** (cam.) Teleskopsäule *f*
hypersensitisation *n* Übersensibilisierung *f*
hypo *n* Fixiernatron *n*
hypobath *n* Fixierbad *n*
hypsogram *n* Pegeldiagramm *n*
hysteresis loop Hysteresisschleife *f*; ~ **losses** Hysteresisverluste *m pl*; ~ **motor** Stromverdrängungsmotor *m*

I

IC socket IC-Fassung *f*
iconoscope *n* Ikonoskop *n*, Bildaufnahmeröhre *f*
ideal magnetic medium Normalmagnetband *n*; ~ **reproducing head** Normalhörkopf *m*
ident *n* (coll.) Kennung *f*
identifiable signal Kennung *f*
identification *n* Kennung *f*; ~ **caption** Bildkennung *f*; ~ **generator** Kennungsgeber *m*; ~ **leader** (F) Allonge *f*; ~ **signal** Kennungssignal *n*; ~ **signal** (station) Stationskennung *f*; ~ **source** Kennungsgeber *m*; ~ **tape** Kennungsband *n*; ~ **trailer** Endband *n*; **to cut** ~ Kennung wegnehmen; **to give** ~ Kennung geben; **to take away** ~ Kennung wegnehmen
idiot card (coll.) Neger *m* (fam.)
idler *n* freilaufende Rolle, Laufrolle *f*, Umlenkrolle *f*, Zwischenrad *n*
idling *n* Leerlauf *m*
ignition circuit Zündkreis *m*; ~ **noise** Funkenstörung *f*
illuminate *v* beleuchten *v*
illumination photometer Luxmeter *n*; ~ **zone** (sat.) Sichtbarkeitszone *f*
illustration *n* Illustration *f*
image *n* Bild *n*; ~ **area** Bildausschnitt *m*, Bildfeld *n*; ~ **contrast** Bildkontrast *m*; ~ **converter** Bildwandler *m*; ~ **converter resolution** Schärfe des Bildwandlers; ~ **converter sharpness** Bildwandlerschärfe *f*; ~ **defect** Abbildungsfehler *m*;

~ **definition** Bildschärfe *f*; ~ **detail** Bilddetail *n*, Bildeinzelheit *f*; ~ **distortion** Bildverzerrung *f*; ~ **drop-out** Bildausfall *m*; ~ **erecting prism** Umkehrprisma *n* ~ **field** Bildfeld *n*; ~ **frequency** Spiegelfrequenz *f*; ~ **frequency rejection** Spiegelselektion *f*; ~ **height** Bildhöhe *f*; ~ **iconoscope** Super-Ikonoskop *n*; ~ **lens** Abbildungslinse *f*; ~ **orthicon (IO)** Image-Orthikon (IO) *n*, Bildaufnahmeröhre *f*, Super-Orthikon *n*; ~ **-orthicon tube** Orthikon *n*; ~ **plane** Abbildungsebene *f*, Bildebene *f*; ~ **point** Bildpunkt *m*; ~ **reproduction** Bildwiedergabe *f*; ~ **reversal** Solarisation *f*; ~ **scanning** Bildabtastung *f*; ~ **sharpness** Bildschärfe *f*; ~ **shift** Bildverschiebung *f*; ~ **size** Abbildunggröße *f*, Bildformat *n*; **blurred** ~ verschleiertes Bild; **converted** ~ umgesetztes Bild; **inverted** ~ kopfstehendes Bild; **latent** ~ latentes Bild, unsichtbares Bild; **upside-down** ~ kopfstehendes Bild

immersion printing Feuchtkopierung *f*

immune from interference störfrei *adj*; ~ **to vibration** schwingfest *adj*

immunity to vibration Rüttelsicherheit *f*

impact sound Trittschall *m*

impact-sound filter Trittschallfilter *m*

impairment *n* Beeinträchtigung *f*, Fehler *m*, Güteabfall *m*; **definitely objectionable** ~ deutlich störender Fehler; **definitely perceptible but not disturbing** ~ gut wahrnehmbarer aber nicht störender Fehler; **imperceptible** ~ nicht wahrnehmbarer Fehler; **just perceptible** ~ gerade wahrnehmbarer Fehler; **somewhat objectionable** ~ leicht störender Fehler

impedance *n* Impedanz *f*, Scheinwiderstand *m*; ~ **adapter** Widerstandsanpasser *m*; ~ **matching** Impedanzanpassung *f*; ~ **matching device** Impedanzanpasser *m*; ~ **matching network** Widerstandsanpasser *m*; ~ **matching transformer** Widerstandstransformator *m*; ~ **matrix** Widerstandsmatrix *f*; ~ **measuring bridge** Scheinwiderstandsmeßbrücke *f*; **matched** ~ angepaßter Widerstand

implosion *n* Implosion *f*

implosion-proof *adj* implosionsgeschützt *adj*

impression, visual visueller Eindruck

improve *v* verbessern *v*

improvisation *n* Improvisierung *f*

impulse *n* Impuls *m*; ~ **duration** (EDP) Impulsdauer *f*; ~ **generator** Impulsgeber *m*, Impulsgenerator *m*; ~ **interference** Störspitze *f*; ~ **length** (EDP) Impulsdauer *f*; ~ **recurrence rate** (EDP) Impulsfolgefrequenz *f*; ~ **repetition rate** (EDP) Impulsfolgefrequenz *f*

inaudible *adj* unhörbar *adj*

incandescent lamp Glühlampe *f*, Vakuumlampe *f*; ~ **light** Glühlicht *n*

inching knob Blendennachdrehvorrichtung *f*

incidental advertising Schleichwerbung *f*; ~ **music** Begleitmusik *f*; ~ **music for radio drama** Hörspielmusik *f*

inclusive-OR circuit (EDP) Inklusives-ODER-Schaltung *f*

income *n* Einnahmen *f pl*

incoming *adj* (line) ankommend *adj* ~ **circuit** Empfangsleitung *f*; ~ **frequency** Empfangsfrequenz *f*; ~ **TV circuit** (to a centre)

Fernsehzuführungsleitung *f*
incorrect *adj* fehlerhaft *adj*; **~ head position** (VTR) Bandführungsfehler *m*
incremental switch Schrittschaltwerk *n*
independent of frequency frequenzunabhängig *adj*; **~ of mains** netzunabhängig *adj*; **~ television** (GB) kommerzielles Fernsehen
index tube Indexröhre *f*
indexing *n* (EDP) Indizieren *n*
indicate *v* (tech.) anzeigen *v*
indicated frequency Anzeigefrequenz *f*
indicating element (EDP) Anzeigeeinheit *f*
indication *n* (tech.) Anzeige *f*; **~ on picture** Lichtzeiger im Bildfeld
indicator *n* Anzeigegerät *n*; **~ instrument** Zeigerinstrument *n*; **~ lamp** Signallampe *f*; **~ light** Kontrollicht *n*; **~ panel** (EDP) Anzeigefeld *n*; **~ panel** Leuchtfeld *n*
indirect wave Raumwelle *f*
individual contract Einzelvertrag *m* **~ control** Einzelsteuerung *f*; **~ listening** Einzelempfang *m*; **~ viewing** Einzelempfang *m*
indoor aerial Innenantenne *f*, Zimmerantenne *f*; **~ shot** Innenaufnahme *f*
inductance *n* Induktivität *f*; ~ *n* (coil) Drossel *f*, Drosselspule *f*; **~ bridge** Induktivitätsmeßbrücke *f* **~ coil** Drossel *f*, Drosselspule *f*
induction *n* Induktion *f*; **~ coil** Induktionsspule *f*; **~ current** Erregerstrom *m*; **~ loop** Induktionsschleife *f*; **~ manifold** Verteilerleitung *f*; **~ motor** Drehstrommotor *m*; **static ~** Influenz *f*
inductive *adj* induktiv *adj*
inductivity *n* Induktivität *f*
inductor *n* (elec.) Spule *f*
industrial *adj* (component) kommerziell *adj*; **~ film** Industriefilm *m*; **~ photo** Werkaufnahme *f*
infinity adjustment Unendlicheinstellung *f*; **~ focus** Unendlicheinstellung *f*; **~ focusing** Unendlicheinstellung *f*
informant *n* Informant *m*
information *n* Information *f*; **~ bit** (EDP) Informationsbit *n*; **~ caption** Zwischentitel *m*; **~ carrier** (EDP) Informationsträger *m*; **~ film** Informationsfilm *m*; **~ flow** (EDP) Informationsfluß *m*; **~ office** Presseabteilung *f*, Pressestelle *f*; **~ on road conditions** Straßenzustandsbericht *m*; **~ processing** (EDP) Nachrichtenverarbeitung *f*; **~ source** Nachrichtenquelle *f*; **~ track** (EDP) Informationsspur *f*; **~ unit** (EDP) Informationseinheit *f*; **to release ~** Information freigeben
informational programme Informationsprogramm *n*
infrared *adj* infrarot *adj*; **~ filter** Infrarotfilter *m*
infrasonic *adj* Infraschall- (in Zus.)
infrasound *n* Infraschall *m*
inherent distortion Eigenverzerrung *f*; **~ film noise** Eigengeräusch *n*; **~ instability** Schwingneigung *f*; **~ noise** Eigengeräusch *n*
inhibit impulse (EDP) Inhibitimpuls *m*
inhibiting signal (EDP) Sperrsignal *n*
initial transient Einschwingvorgang *m*
initial-velocity current Anlaufstrom *m*
inject *v* einspielen *v*, zuspielen *v*; ~ *v* einblocken *v* (fam.); ~ *n* Einblendung *f*, Einspielung *f*; ~ *n*

(item) Kurzbeitrag *m*
injury *n* Schaden *m*
inky *n* Glühlichtscheinwerfer *m*; **~ dinky** *n* Inky Dinky *n*
inlay *v* eintasten *v*; ~ *v* (pict.) überblenden *v*; ~ *n* Eintastung *f*, Inlay *n*, Überblendung *f*, Überblenden *n*
input *n* (tech.) Eingang *m*; ~ *n* (EDP) Eingabe *f*; **~ capacitance** Eingangskapazität *f*; **~ circuit** Eingangsschaltung *f*; **~ device** (EDP) Eingabegerät *n*; **~ energy** Eingangsenergie *f*; **~ equipment** (EDP) Eingabegerät *n*; **~ impedance** Eingangsimpedanz *f* **~ level** Eingangspegel *m*; **~ loading** Eingangsbelastung *f*; **~ offset voltage** Eingangsfehlspannung *f*; **~ -output statement** (EDP) Ein-Ausgabebefehl *m*; **~ picture** Eingangsbild *n*; **~ power** Eingangsenergie *f*; **~ resistance** Eingangswiderstand *m*; **~ selector** Eingangskreuzschiene *f*; **~ sensitivity** Eingangsempfindlichkeit *f*; **~ signal** Eingangssignal *n*; **~ stage** Eingangsstufe *f*, Vorstufe *f*; **~ switching matrix** Eingangskreuzschiene *f*; **~ transformer** Eingangsübertrager *m*; **~ voltage** Eingangsspannung *f*; **balanced ~** symmetrischer Eingang
inquiry *n* (EDP) Anfrage *f*
insert *v* einfügen *v*, einschieben *v*, einblocken *v* (fam.); ~ *v* (network) einschleifen *v*; ~ *v* (progr.) einsetzen *v*, einspielen *v*, zuspielen *v*; ~ *n* Einblendung *f*, Einschaltung *f*, Einspielung *f*, Insert *n*, Zwischenschnitt *m*; ~ *n* (item) Kurzbeitrag *m*; **~ tape** Zuspielband *n*; **to ~ into programme** ins Programm einsetzen
insertion *n* Zuschaltung *f*, Zwischenschaltung *f*; **~ gain** Zwischenschaltleistungs-verstärkung *f*; **~ loss** Einfügungsdämpfung *f*, Grunddämpfung *f*, Zwischenschaltleistungsverlust *m* **~ signal** Prüfsignal *n*; **~ signal generator** Prüfzeilengenerator *m*; **~ test signal** Prüfzeile *f*; **national ~ test signal** Prüfzeile für Sendestraße; **network ~ test signal** Prüfzeile für Sendestraße
inspect *v* überwachen *v*
inspection *n* Überwachung *f*; ~ *n* Prüfung *f*; **~ lamp** Handlampe *f*, Handleuchte *f*
inspired news item Zweckmeldung *f*
installation *n* Anlage *f*, Einrichtung *f*; ~ *n* (tel.) Telefonanschluß *m*; **~ engineer** Ausstattungsingenieur *m*
instalment *n* Folge *f*
instantaneous value Augenblickswert *m*, Momentanwert *m*
instantaneously-operating *adj* unverzögert *adj*
instruction *n* Weisung *f*; ~ *n* (EDP) Befehl *m*; **~ code** (EDP) Befehlscode *m*; **~ word** (EDP) Befehlswort *n*; **branch ~** (EDP) Sprungbefehl *m*; **branching ~** (EDP) Sprungbefehl *m*; **control transfer ~** (EDP) Sprungbefehl *m*; **jump ~** (EDP) Sprungbefehl *m*
instructional film Lehrfilm *m*, Erziehungsfilm *m*
instructor *n* Lehrlingsausbilder *m*
instrument *n* Gerät *n*; **~ panel** Armaturenbrett *n*; **optical ~** optisches Mittel
insufficient duration Unterlänge *f*; **~ footage** Unterlänge *f*
insulating layer Sperrschicht *f*; **~ sleeve** Isolierschlauch *m*; **~ tape** Isolierband *n*; **~ tubing**

Isolierschlauch *m*
insulation *n* Isolierung *f*; **~ resistance** Isolationswiderstand *m*; **~ test** Isolationsprüfung *f*
insurance, general production Produktionsversicherung *f*
integrated circuit (IC) integrierter Schaltkreis, integrierte Schaltung, integrierter Baustein
intelligibility *n* Verständlichkeit *f*
intensification *n* (photo) Verstärkung *f*; **photographic ~** fotografische Verstärkung; **variable ~** veränderliche Verstärkung
intensifier *n* (FP) Verstärker *m*
intensify *v* (light) verstärken *v*
intensity *n* Intensität *f*; **~** *n* (video) Helligkeit *f*; **~ and phase stereophony** Intensitäts- und Phasenstereofonie *f*; **~ control** (lighting) Lichtwertregler *m*; **~ -difference stereo** Intensitätsstereofonie *f*; **~ modulation** Helligkeitssteuerung *f*; **~ stereophony** Intensitätsstereofonie *f*
intercarrier *n* Differenzträger *m*; **~ hum** Intercarrierbrumm *m*; **~ sound system** Intercarrierverfahren *n*, Zwischenträgerverfahren *n*; **~ system** Differenzträgerverfahren *n*
interchangeable *adj* auswechselbar *adj*; **~ filter** (elec.) Aufsteckfilter *m* **~ lens** Wechselobjektiv *n*
intercom *n* (coll.) Gegensprechanlage *f*, Sprechanlage *f*, wechselseitiger Sprechverkehr, Wechselsprechanlage *f*
intercommunication *n* wechselseitiger Sprechverkehr; **~ circuit** Wechselsprechverbindung *f*; **~ system** Sprechanlage *f*, Wechselsprechanlage *f*
interconnect *v* zusammenschalten *v*
interconnection *n* Zusammenschaltung *f*, Zwischenschaltung *f*, Vermaschung *f*, Querverbindung *f*
intercut *v* (sound) unterschneiden *v*
interdot flicker Zwischenpunktflimmern *n*
interface *n* (EDP) Nahtstelle *f*, Schnittstelle *f*
interfere *v* stören *v*
interfered with gestört *adj*
interference *n* Interferenz *f*, Störung *f*; **~** *n* (parasitic) Nebengeräusch *n*; **~ caused by switching** Schaltstörung *f*; **~ compensation** Störkompensation *f*; **~ elimination** Entstörung *f*; **~ filter** Funkentstörfilter *m*, Interferenzfilter *m*; **~ -free** *adj* störfrei *adj*; **~ pattern** Störmuster *n*; **~ peak** Störspitze *f*; **~ pulse** Störimpuls *m*; **~ signal** Störsignal *n*; **~ suppression** Entstörung *f*; **~ suppressor** Entstörfilter *m*; **~ voltage** Störspannung *f*, Fremdspannung *f*; **disturbance due to ~** Interferenzstörung *f*
interfering field (elec.) Fremdfeld *n*; **~ signal** Störsignal *n*
interior *n* (F) Innenaufnahme *f*; **~ shooting** Innenaufnahme *f*; **~ shot** Innenaufnahme *f*
interiors, to begin the ins Atelier gehen
interlace *n* (TV) Zwischensprung *m*, Zwischenzeile *f*; **~ sequence** Teilbildfolgezahl *f*, Teilbildzahl *f*; **bad ~** schlechte Zwischenzeile
interlaced fields ineinandergeschriebene Halbbilder; **~ picture** Zwischenzeilenbild *n*; **~ scanning** Zeilensprung *m*, zeilensprungartige Abtastung, Zwischenzeilenabtastung *f*;

~ scanning (method) Zwischenzeilenverfahren *n*
interlacing *n* Zwischenzeilenverfahren *n*
interleaving *n* Verschachtelung *f*
interline *n* Zwischenzeile *f*; **~ flicker** Zwischenzeilenflimmern *n*
interlock *n* Interlock *n*
interlocking circuit Verriegelung *f*
interlocutor *n* Gesprächspartner *m*
interlude music Zwischenmusik *f*; **~ slide** Pausenbild *n*
intermediate amplifier Zwischenverstärker *m*; **~ announcement** Zwischenansage *f*; **~ dupe** Zwischenduplikat *n*; **~ frequency (IF)** Zwischenfrequenz (ZF) *f*; **~-frequency method** Zwischenfrequenzverfahren *n*; **~-frequency transposition** Zwischenfrequenzumsetzung *f*; **~ image-forming lens** Zwischenabbildungsobjektiv *n*; **~ layer** Zwischenschicht *f*; **~ negative** Intermed-Negativ *n*, Internegativ *n*, Zwischennegativ *n*; **~ plate** Zwischenplatte *f*; **~-point feed** Zwischenpunkteinspeisung *f*; **~ positive** Intermed-Positiv *n*, Interpositiv *n*; **~ ring** Zwischenring *m*
intermission *n* (US) (thea.) Pause *f*
intermittent contact Wackelkontakt *m*; **~ mechanism** Filmfortschaltung *f*; **~ movement** Filmfortschaltung *f*, Schrittschaltwerk *n*; **~ printer** Schrittkopiermaschine *f*; **~ scratch** Sprungschramme *f*
intermodulation *n* Intermodulation *f*, Zwischenmodulation *f*
internal aerial Innenantenne *f*; **~ auditor*** (BBC) Revision* *f*; **~ noise** (ampl.) Eigenrauschen *n*; **~ resistance** Innenwiderstand *m*; **~ telephone** Betriebstelefon *n*
international sound (coll.) internationales Tonband *n* (IT-Band); **~ sound circuit** IT-Leitung *f*, internationale Tonleitung, Begleittonleitung *f*; **~ sound track** internationales Tonband *n* (IT-Band); **~ standard** internationale Norm
interneg *n* (coll.) Intermed-Negativ *n*, Internegativ *n*
internegative *n* (interneg) Intermed-Negativ *n*, Internegativ *n*; **~** *n* (col.) Zwischennegativ *n*, Farbduplikatnegativ *n*
inter-office slip Laufzettel *m*
interpolation *n* Zwischenschaltung *f*
interpos *n* (coll.) Intermed-Positiv *n*, Interpositiv *n*
interpose *v* einschieben *v*
interposition *n* Zwischenschaltung *f*
interpositive *n* Intermed-Positiv *n*, Interpositiv *n*
interpret *v* (tech.) auswerten *v*
interpretation *n* Darstellung *f*; **~** *n* (tech.) Auswertung *f*
interrogate *v* abfragen *v*
interrupt *v* unterbrechen *v*; **~** *n* (EDP) Programmunterbrechung *f*
interrupted, to be (oscillator) abreißen *v*
interrupter *n* (elec.) Unterbrecher *m*, Zerhacker *m*
interruption *n* Unterbrechung *f*
inter-satellite service Intersatellitenfunkdienst *m*
inter-scene transition Szenenübergang *m*
intersynchronisation *n* wechselseitige Taktverkopplung *f*
interval *n* (thea.) Pause *f*; **~ caption** Pausenbild *n*; **~ music** Zwischenmusik *f*; **~ signal** Pausenzeichen *n*; **~ slide** Pausenbild *n*
interview *v* interviewen *v*; **~** *n*

Interview *n*; ~ **by telephone** Telefoninterview *n*
interviewee *n* Interviewpartner *m*
interviewer *n* Interviewer *m*
Intervision *n* Intervision *f*
intro *n* (coll.) Einführung *f*, Einleitung *f*; ~ *n* (coll) (news) Antext *m* (fam.)
introduce *v* einführen *v*, einleiten *v*
introduction *n* Einführung *f*, Einleitung *f*; ~ *n* (news) Antext *m* (fam.)
introductory presentation Kopfansage *f*
inventory audit* Inventarverwaltung* *f*
inverse of amplification factor Durchgriff *m*
inversion *n* Umtastung *f*; ~ *n* (EDP) Inversion *f*
inverting prism Umkehrprisma *n*
iodine lamp Jodlampe *f*
ion burn Ionenfleck *m*; ~ **spot** Einbrennfleck *m*, Ionenfleck *m*; ~ **trap** Einbrennschutz *f*, Ionenfalle *f*
ionospheric wave Raumwelle *f*
iris *n* Blende *f*, Iris *f*; ~ **adjustment** Blendenregulierung *f*; ~ **aperture** Blendenöffnung *f*; ~ **diaphragm** Irisblende *f*, Kreisblende *f*; ~ **fade** Irisblende *f*; ~ **in** *v* zukreisen *v*; ~ **out** *v* abblenden *v*, aufblenden *v*, aufkreisen *v*; ~ **setting** Blendeneinstellung *f*; ~ **wipe** Irisblende *f*
iron loss Eisenverlust *m*
irradiate *v* überstrahlen *v*
irradiated area Einstrahlungsgebiet *n*; ~ **point** Strahlauftreffpunkt *m*
irradiation *n* Überstrahlung *f*
irregular rotational movement (disc) Gleichlaufschwankung *f*
isolate *v* (elec.) entkoppeln *v*
isolated *adj* spannungslos *adj*
isolating choke Pufferdrossel *f*; ~ **loop** Trennschleife *f*; ~ **section** Trennschleife *f*; ~ **switch** Trennschalter *m*; ~ **transformer** Trenntransformator *m*
isolation *n* (elec.) Entkopplung *f*; ~ **amplifier** Trennverstärker *m*; ~ **network** Trennschaltung *f*
isolator *n* Trennschalter *m*
item *n* (news) Beitrag *m*, Meldung *f*, Nachrichtenbeitrag *m*, Stück *n* (fam.); ~ **of information** Information *f*; ~ **of test equipment** Servicegerät *n*; ~ **with newsreader in vision** Wortmeldung *f*; ~ **with newsreader on camera** Wortmeldung *f*
iterative network Kettenleiter *m*

J

jack *n* Buchse *f*, Klinke *f*; ~ **panel** Klinkenfeld *n*
jackfield *n* Steckfeld *n*; ~ **distribution** Schnurverteilung *f*
jam *v* stören *v*; ~ *v* (mech.) klemmen *v*
jammed *adj* gestört *adj*
jamming *n* Störgeräusch *n*, Störung *f*; ~ *n* (mech.) Klemmung *f*; ~ **noise** Störgeräusch *n*
jazz *n* Jazz *m*; ~ **programme** Jazzsendung *f*; ~ **up** *v* vergagen *v*
jellies *n pl* (coll.) Gelatinefilter *m*
jib *n* Ausleger *m*; ~ **arm** Ausleger *m* ~ **swing** Schwenkbereich *m*
jibbing *n* seitlicher Schwenk
jingle *n* (coll.) (prog.) Kennung *f*
jitter *v* flackern *v*; ~ *n* Flackern *n*, Jitter *n*, Störung *f*; **horizontal ~** horizontale Bildstandschwankungen
jitters *n pl* Mäusezähnchen *n pl*
job *n* (journ.) Auftrag *m*
jockey roller Spannrolle *f*
Johnson noise (pict.) Grieß *m*
join *v* anschließen *v*, anschließen *v* (sich), verkoppeln *v*; ~ *v* (F, tape)

kleben *v*, zusammenschneiden *v*; ~ *n* Klebestelle *f*; **bad ~** fehlerhafte Klebestelle; **faulty ~** fehlerhafte Klebestelle; **noisy ~** Tonblitz *m*

joiner *n* Tischler *m*; ~ *n* (F, tape) Klebelade *f*, Klebepresse *f*, Schneidelehre *f*; **~ tape** Unterkleber *m*

joiner's shop Tischlerei *f*

joining *n* Kleben *n*; **~ cement** Filmkitt *m*; **~ tape** (F, sound) Klebeband *n*

joint broadcast by ... angeschlossen waren ...; **~ media** *n pl* Medienverbund *m*; **~ production** Gemeinschaftsproduktion *f*; **~ programme** Gemeinschaftsprogramm *n*, Gemeinschaftssendung *f*, gemeinsames Programm

jointer *n* Klebelade *f*, Klebepresse *f*, Schneidelehre *f*

joist *n* (set) Träger *m*

journal *n* Zeitung *f*

journalism *n* Journalismus *m*, Publizistik *f*

journalist *n* Journalist *m*

journalists *n pl* Zeitungsleute *plt*

juice *n* (coll.) Elektrizität *f*, Strom *m*, Saft *m* (fam.); **to put on the ~** (coll.) besaften *v* (fam.)

jump cut (editing) Bildsprung *m*; Sprung *m*; **~ -cut** *v* auf Sprung kleben; **~ on** *v* (caption) einspringen *v*

jumper panel (US) Steckfeld *n*

junction *n* Anschluß *m*, Übergang *m*, Verbindung *f*, Verbindungsstelle *f*; ~ *n* (prog.) Zwischenverbindung *f*; **~ amplifier** Knotenpunktverstärker *m*; **~ box** Abzweigdose *f*, Anschlußdose *f*, Abzweigkasten *m*, Kabelkasten *m*, Verteilerkasten *m*; **~ cable** Verbindungskabel *n*; **~ circuit** Anschlußleitung *f*, Verbindungsleitung *f*; **~ diode** Flächendiode *f*; **~ point** Anschlußpunkt *m*, Knotenpunkt *m*, Verbindungspunkt *m*, Verzweigungspunkt *m*; **~ resistance** Knotenpunktwiderstand *m*; **international ~** internationale Verbindung

junk *n* Abfall *m*, Ausschuß *m*

jury *n* Jury *f*

K

Kelvin degrees (K) Kelvin-Grade *m pl*; **~ meter** Farbtemperaturmesser *m*, Lichtfarbmeßgerät *n*

key *n* Taste *f*; ~ *n* (lighting) Hauptlicht *n*; **~ animation** Hauptphase *f*; **~ animator** Hauptphasenzeichner *m*; **~ in** *v* eintasten *v*; **~ light** Hauptlicht *n*, Führungslicht *n*, Führung *f*; **~ lighting** Hauptbeleuchtung *f*, Führungslicht *n*, Führung *f*; **~ number** Fußnummer *f*

keyboard *n* Tastatur *f*

keyed *adj* getastet *adj*

keying *n* Eintastung *f*, Tastung *f*; **~ frequency** Umtastfrequenz *f*; **~ impulse** Tastimpuls *m*; **~ pulse** Tastimpuls *m*; **~ ratio** Tastverhältnis *n*; **~ signal** Tastsignal *n*; **~ tube** Taströhre *f*; **~ valve** Taströhre *f*

keynote *n* Grundton *m*

keys *n pl* Tastatur *f*

keystone distortion Trapezverzerrung *f*

kick-back pulse Rückschlagimpuls *m*

kicker light Gegenstreiflicht *n*

kill, to ~ a set (US) abbauen *v*

kilometric waves *n pl* Langwelle

(LW) *f*
kine *v* (coll.) FAZ aufzeichnen, Film aufzeichnen, fazen *v* (fam.)
kinescope *n* (US) Bildröhre *f*, Bildwiedergaberöhre *f*, Fernsehröhre *f*, Wiedergaberöhre *f*; ~ *n* (US) (EFR) Filmaufzeichnungsgerät *n*, FAZ-Anlage *f* (FAZ); ~ **recording** (US) Filmaufzeichnung (FAZ) *f*
kink *v* knicken *v*; ~ *n* Knick *m*
Klystron *n* Klystron *n*
knee *n* Knick *m*
knife-edge contact Messerkontakt *m*
knife switch Hebelschaltung *f*
knob *n* Drehknopf *m*, Knopf *m*
knob-twist fader Drehsteller *m*, Drehregler *m*
knurled knob Rändelknopf *m*; ~ **wheel** Rändelscheibe *f*

L

lab *n* (coll.) Labor *n*, Laboratorium *n*
label *n* Etikett *n*, Beschriftungsbild *n*; **non-standard** ~ (EDP) nichtstandardisiertes Etikett
laboratory *n* Labor *n*, Laboratorium *n*; ~ **assistant** Laborant *m*; ~ **chemist** Kopierwerkchemiker *m* ~ **engineer** Laboringenieur *m*; ~ **technician** Kopierwerktechniker;m.; Labortechniker;m. *m*; ~ **work** Kopieranstaltsarbeiten *f pl*
labour court Arbeitsgericht *n*
labs *n pl* (coll.) Labor *n*, Laboratorium *n*
lace up *v* einlegen *v*, Film einlegen, einfädeln *v*
lacing-up *n* Filmeinlegen *n*, Filmeinfädelung *f*
lack of contrast Kontrastlosigkeit *f*; ~ **of definition** Unschärfe *f*; ~ **of focus** Unschärfe *f*
lacking contrast kontrastlos *adj*
lacquering *n* Lackieren *n*; ~ **of emulsion** Schichtlackierung *f*
laminating process Bespurung *f*
lamp *n* Lampe *f*, Leuchte *f*, Scheinwerfer *m*; ~ **blackening** Lampenschwärzung *f*, Lichterschwärzung *f*; ~ **cable** Lampenkabel *n*; ~ **complement** Scheinwerferbestückung *f*; ~ **current** Lichtstrom *m*; ~ **cut-out** Lampenschere *f*; ~ **filament** Lampenwendel *f*; ~ **fixture** Lampenhalter *m*; ~ **gallows arm** Lampengalgen *m*; ~ **holder** Glühlampenfassung *f*, Lampenfassung *f*; ~ **housing** Lampenhaus *n*; ~ **offset arm** Lampengalgen *m*; ~ **socket** Lampenfassung *f*, Glühlampenfassung *f*, Lampensockel *m*; ~ **stand** Scheinwerferstand *m*, Scheinwerferstativ *n*; ~ **suspension** Scheinwerferaufhängung *f*; ~ **trolley** Beleuchterfahrzeug *n*; ~ **trunnion** Scheinwerferschwenk *m*; **discharged** ~ Leuchtstoffröhre *f*; **reflector** ~ verspiegelte Lampe
land line Überlandleitung *f*; ~ **-line connection** Bodenleitungsverbindung *f*; ~ **mobile service** öffentlicher beweglicher Landfunk (ÖBL)
language course Sprachkursus *m*; ~ **tuition** Sprachunterricht *m*
lantern *n* Blende *f*
lanyard microphone Lavalliermikrofon *n*
lap dissolve Bildüberblendung *f*, Durchblendung *f*, Überblendung *f*, Überblenden *n*
lapel microphone Ansteckmikrofon *n*, Knopflochmikrofon *n*
lap-fade *v* (pict.) überblenden *v*

large-screen projection Großbildprojektion *f*; ~ **television projection** Fernsehgroßbildprojektion *f*
Larsen effect Larseneffekt *m*
laser *n* Laser *m*
late news *n pl* (TV) Spätausgabe *f*
late-night edition (TV) Spätausgabe *f*; ~ **performance** Nachtvorstellung *f*
lateral dolly shot Parallelfahrt *f*
lath *n* Latte *f*
latitude *n* Spielraum *m*
lattice *n* Gitter *n*; ~ **mast** Gittermast *m*; ~ **section** Kreuzglied *n*
launch *v* (F) herausbringen *v*
lavalier microphone Lavalliermikrofon *n*
lavender *n* Lavendel *n*; ~ **print** Lavendelkopie *f*, Zwischenpositiv *n*
layer *n* Schicht *f*, Überzug *m*; **light-sensitive** ~ lichtempfindliche Schicht; **sensitive** ~ empfindliche Schicht
laying *n* (coll.) (cable) Verlegung *f* (fam.)
lay-on roller Andruckrolle *f*
layout *n* (journ.) Aufbau *m*; ~ **plan** Lageplan *m*
lazyboy *n* Scherenarm *m*
LC circuit LC-Glied *n*
lead *n* (story) Aufmacher *m*; ~ *n* (elec.) Leitung *f*; ~ *n* (tip-off) Tip *m*, Aizes *n pl* (fam.); ~ **role** Titelrolle *f*; ~ **story** Aufmacher *m*; ~ **with** *v* (bcast.) anfangen *v* (mit), aufmachen *v* (mit)
leader *n* (press) Leitartikel *m*; ~ *n* (mus.) Konzertmeister *m*; ~ *n* (tape) Vorlaufband *n*, Startband *n* ~ *n* (F) Filmvorspann *m*, Startvorspann *m*, Vorspann *m*; ~ **duration** Vorlaufzeit *f*; ~ **film** Vorspannfilm *m*; ~ **film** (FP) Zugfilm *m*; ~ **length** Vorlauflänge *f*; ~ **tape** Vorspannband *n*; ~ **with frame bars** Startband mit Bildstrich; **black** ~ Vorspannschwarzfilm *m*; **framed** ~ Vorspann mit Bildstrich; **head** ~ Filmvorspann *m*, Startband *n*, Startvorspann *m*, Vorspannfilm *m* **mag** ~ (coll.) Startband für Cord; **magnetic film** ~ Startband für Cord; **white** ~ Weißfilm *m*
leader-writer *n* Leitartikler *m*
lead-in *n* Einführung *f*, Einleitung *f* ~ *n* (news) Antext *m* (fam.); ~ **groove** Einlaufrille *f*; **to write the** ~ antexten *v*
leading article Leitartikel *m*; ~ **edge** Vorderflanke *f*; ~ **part** Hauptrolle *f*
lead-out groove Auslaufrille *f*
leakage current Leckstrom *m*, Fehlerstrom *m*, Reststrom *m*; ~ **current relay** Fehlerstromrelais (FI-Schalter) *n*
lease *n* (line) Vermietung *f*
leased circuit Mietleitung *f*; ~ **line** Mietleitung *f*
Lecher wire Lecherleitung *f*
left signal Linkssignal (L-Signal) *n*
legal adviser Justitiar *m*; ~ **adviser's department** Justitiariat *n*; ~ **department** Rechtsabteilung *f*
length *n* Länge *f*, Meterlänge *f*; ~ *n* (time) Laufzeit *f*; ~ **of cable** Kabelstrecke *f*
lengthening *n* Verlängerung *f*
lens *n* Linse *f*, Objektiv *n*; ~ **aberration** Linsenfehler *m*; ~ **adapter** Objektivring *m*; ~ **aerial** Linsenantenne *f*; ~ **angle** Aufnahmewinkel *m*; ~ **aperture** Blendenöffnung *f*; ~ **barrel** Objektivfassung *f*; ~ **brush** Abstaubpinsel *m*; ~ **cap** Objektivdeckel *m*, Schutzkappe *f*; ~ **carrier** Standarte *f*; ~ **correction** Vergütung *f*; ~ **cover** Objektivdeckel *m*, Schutzkappe *f*; ~ **diameter** Linsendurchmesser *m* ~ **error** Linsenfehler *m*;

~ **-fastening ring** Objektivfassungsring *m*; ~ **flare** Linseneffekt *m*, Überstrahlung *f*; ~ **guard** Schutzkappe *f*; ~ **hood** Gegenlichtblende *f*, Sonnenblende *f*, Sonnentubus *m*; ~ **impairment** Linsenfehler *m*; ~ **indicator** Objektivanzeiger *m*; ~ **locking lever** Objektivverriegelungsgriff *m*; ~ **mount** Objektivfassung *f*, Objektivhalterung *f*, Standarte *f*; ~ **plate** Objektivstütze *f*; ~ **port** Kabinenfenster *n*; ~ **ring** Objektivring *m*; ~ **set** Objektivsatz *m*; ~ **shade** Gegenlichtblende *f*, Sonnenblende *f*; ~ **speed** Lichtstärke *f*; ~ **standard** Standarte *f*; ~ **stop** (opt.) Blende *f*; ~ **strength** Stärke einer Linse; ~ **system** Optik *f*; ~ **tube** Vorsatztubus *m*; ~ **turret** Objektivrevolver *m*, Revolverkopf *m*; **acoustic** ~ akustische Linse; **additional** ~ Vorsatzlinse *f*; **attachment** ~ Vorsatzlinse *f*; **cemented** ~ gekittete Linse; **clear** ~ klare Linse; **convergent** ~ Sammellinse *f*; **converging** ~ Sammellinse *f*; **electromagnetic** ~ elektromagnetische Linse; **electronic** ~ elektronische Linse; **electrostatic** ~ elektrostatische Linse; **Fresnel** ~ Fresnelsche Linse, Stufenlinse *f*; **hammered** ~ gehämmerte Linse; **interchangeable** ~ Wechselobjektiv *n*; **matt** ~ matte Linse; **supplementary** ~ Vorsatzlinse *f*; **supplementary close-up** ~ Vorsatzlinse für Nahaufnahme

lenticulated film Farbrasterfilm *m*

lessen *v* abnehmen *v*

lettered title Schreibtitel *m*

lettering artist Schriftgrafiker *m*

level *n* Pegel *m*; ~ **adjustment** Einpegeln *n*, Pegeln *n*; ~ **breakdown** Pegeleinbruch *m*; ~ **check** Pegelkontrolle *f*; ~ **check** (speaker) Textprobe *f*, Verständigungsprobe *f*; ~ **-checking set** Pegelkontrollgerät *n* ~ **control** Pegelaussteuerung *f*; ~ **deviation** Pegelabweichung *f*; ~ **diagram** Pegeldiagramm *n*; ~ **difference** Pegelunterschied *m*; ~ **generator** Pegelgeber *m*; ~ **indication** Pegelanzeige *f*; ~ **indicator** Pegelanzeiger *m*, Aussteuerungsmesser *m*; ~ **magnetic tape** Pegeltestband *n*; ~ **-measuring set** Pegelmesser *m*; ~ **meter** Pegelmesser *m*; ~ **reading** Pegelanzeige *f*; ~ **sense** (EDP) Spannungsabfrage *f*; ~ **up** *v* eintaumeln *v*; **to adjust** ~ pegeln *v*

levelling plate Nivellierplatte *f*

lever *n* Fühlhebel *m*; ~ **bank** (lighting) Beleuchtungssteuerfeld *n*; ~ **switch** Hebelschaltung *f*

liaison office Verbindungsreferat *n*, Verbindungsstelle *f*; ~ **officer** Verbindungsmann *m*

librarian *n* Bibliothekar *m*, Archivar *m*

library *n* Bibliothek *f*, Archiv *n*; ~ **assistant** Archivgehilfe *m*; ~ **film** Archivfilm *m*, Archivaufnahme *f*; ~ **material** Archivmaterial *n*, Fremdfilmmaterial *n*; ~ **picture** Archivaufnahme *f*; ~ **shot** Archivaufnahme *f*; ~ **still** Archivaufnahme *f*; **to put in the** ~ archivieren *v*

libretto *n* Textbuch *n*

licence *n* Lizenz *f*; ~ **exemption** Kostenbefreiung *f*; ~ **fee** Lizenzgebühr *f*, Lizenzbetrag *m*; ~ **fee** (R, TV) Gebühr *f*; ~ **-fee collection area** Gebühreneinzugsgebiet *n*, Einzugsgebiet *n*; ~ **-fee collection office** Gebühreneinzugsstelle *f*; ~ **-free** *adj* frei von Rechten; ~ **-holder** *n* Rundfunkteilnehmer *m*,

Gebührenzahler *m*; ~ **period** Lizenzdauer *f*; ~ **revenue** Gebührenaufkommen *n*
licensee *n* Lizenzinhaber *m*, Lizenznehmer *m*
licenser *n* Lizenzgeber *m*
licensing authority Lizenzgeber *m*; ~ **department** Lizenzabteilung *f*
lift *v* (video) abheben *v*; ~ *n* (video) Abhebung *f*; ~ **in frequency response** Frequenzganganhebung *f*
lifting device Hebevorrichtung *f*
light *v* ausleuchten *v*, beleuchten *v*; ~ *n* Licht *n*; ~ **barrier** Lichtschranke *f*; ~ **beam** Lichtstrahl *m*; ~ **box** Lichtkasten *m*, Lichtfeld *n*; ~ **-bulb** *n* Birne *f*; ~ **cell** Lichtempfänger *m*; ~ **-change control** (FP) Lichtwertregler *m*; ~ **-change point** (FP) Lichtwertzahl *f*; ~ **comedy** Boulevardstück *n*; ~ **-control tape** Lichtsteuerband *n*, Lichtband *n*; ~ **correction filter** Lichtausgleichfilter *m*; ~ **cross-over** Lichtübergang *m*; ~ **curtain** Lichtvorhang *m*; ~ **direction** Lichtführung *f*, Lichtgestaltung *f*; ~ **display panel** Leuchtfeld *n*; ~ **distribution** Lichtverteilung *f*; ~ **distribution curve** Lichtverteilungskurve *f*; ~ **entertainment** leichte Unterhaltung; ~ **entertainment film** Unterhaltungsfilm *m*; ~ **entertainment programme** Unterhaltungsprogramm *n*, Unterhaltungssendung *f*; ~ **flux** Lichtstrom *m*; ~ **flux compensation** Lichtflußkompensation *f*; ~ **fog** Lichtschleier *m*; ~ **fogging** Lichtschleier *m*; ~ **gap** Lichtspalt *m*; ~ **indication** Lichtanzeige *f*; ~ **indicator** Leuchtzeichen *n*; ~ **intensity** Lichtintensität *f*, Lichtstärke *f*; ~ **interference** Störlicht *n*; ~ **loss** Lichtverlust *m*; ~ **meter** Lichtmeßgerät *n*, Belichtungsmesser *m*; ~ **modulation** Lichtmodulation *f*; ~ **music** leichte Musik, Unterhaltungsmusik *f* (U-Musik); ~ **orchestra** Unterhaltungsorchester *n*; ~ **output** Lichtausbeute *f*, Lichtleistung *f*; ~ **pen** Lichtschreibgerät *n*, Lichtstrahlschreiber *m*; ~ **pen** (EDP) Leuchtstift *m*; ~ **period** (cam.) Hellphase *f*; ~ **-proof** *adj* lichtundurchlässig *adj*; ~ **radiation** Lichtstrahlung *f*; ~ **ray** Lichtstrahl *m*; ~ **reading** Lichtanzeige *f*; ~ **-sensitive** *adj* lichtempfindlich *adj*; ~ **sensitivity** Lichtempfindlichkeit *f*; ~ **signal** Lichtzeichen *n*; ~ **slit** Lichtspalt *m* ~ **source** Lichtquelle *f*; ~ **spot** Lichtfleck *m*, Lichtmarke *f*, Lichtpunkt *m*; ~ **-tight** *adj* lichtdicht *adj*, lichtundurchlässig *adj*; ~ **trap** Lichtschleuse *f*; ~ **value** (FP) Lichtwert *m*; ~ **-value level** Lichtwert *m*; ~ **-value number** Lichtwertzahl *f*; ~ **valve** Spaltoptik *f*; ~ **yield** Lichtausbeute *f*; **cold** ~ Kaltlicht *n* **diffuse** ~ diffuses Licht, weiches Licht; **diffused** ~ diffuses Licht; **dimmed** ~ gedämpftes Licht; **flat** ~ flaches Licht; **hard** ~ hartes Licht; **incident** ~ einfallendes Licht; **parallel** ~ **rays** gerichtetes Licht; **reflected** ~ reflektiertes Licht; **scattered** ~ diffuses Licht; **soft** ~ weiches Licht; **steep** ~ steiles Licht; **subdued** ~ gedämpftes Licht; **sudden** ~ **change** Lichtsprung *m*; **to dim the** ~ Licht abblenden; **to fade down the** ~ Licht abblenden; **to fade up the** ~ Licht aufblenden; **to set the** ~ **level** Licht bestimmen; **to step down the** ~ Licht abstufen; **to**

take down the ~ Licht abblenden; **ultraviolet ~** ultraviolettes Licht

lighting *n* Ausleuchtung *f*, Beleuchtung *f*, Beleuchtungswesen *n*; **~ barrels** *n pl* Scheinwerfergestänge *n*; **~ bridge** Beleuchterbrücke *f*, Beleuchterbühne *f*; **~ cameraman** Chefkameramann *m*, erster Kameramann, Lichtgestalter *m*; **~ circuit** Beleuchtungsstromkreis *m*; **~ console** Lichtorgel *f*, Lichtstellanlage *f*, Lichtregelanlage *f*; **~ contrast** Beleuchtungskontrast *m*; **~ contrast ratio** Beleuchtungsverhältnis *n*; **~ control** Beleuchtungssteuerung *f*, Lichtsteuerung *f*, Lichtregie *f*; **~-control console** Beleuchtungspult *n*, Lichtstellanlage *f*, Lichtregelanlage *f*, Stellwerk *n*; **~-control desk** Lichtsteuerpult *n*; **~-control equipment** Lichtstellanlage *f*, Lichtregelanlage *f*; **~-control panel** Lichtsteuerpult *n*; **~ control room** Beleuchtungsraum *m*, Lichtsteuerraum *m*; **~-control unit** Lichtregeleinheit *f*; **~ crew** Beleuchtertrupp *m*; **~ department** Beleuchtungsdienst *m*; **~ director** Lichtgestalter *m*; **~ effect** Lichteffekt *m*; **~ electrician** Beleuchter *m*; **~ equipment** Beleuchtungsanlage *f*, Beleuchtungseinrichtung *f*, Beleuchtungsgeräte *n pl*, Beleuchtungsmaterial *n*; **~ float** Lichtwanne *f*; **~ gallery** Beleuchtergalerie *f*; **~ grid** Gitterdecke *f*, Gitterrostdecke *f*, Lichtgitter *n*; **~ installation** Beleuchtungsanlage *f*, Beleuchtungseinrichtung *f*; **~ level** Beleuchtungsstärke *f*; **~-level range** Beleuchtungsumfang *m*; **~ man** Beleuchter *m*; **~ nest** Nest *n* (fam.); **~ plot** Lichtplan *m*; **~ pole** Stange *f*; **~ power circuit** Lichtnetz *n*; **~ rail** Lichtleiste *f*, Lichtzeile *f*; **~ rectifier unit** Lichtregeleinheit *f*; **~ rigging time** Lichtbauzeit *f*; **~ setting** Einleuchtung *f*, Lichtsetzung *f*; **~ setting time** Einleuchtzeit *f*; **~ set-up** Lichtsetzung *f*; **~ stand-in** Lichtdoubel *n*; **~ supervisor** Beleuchtungsmeister *m*, Lichtingenieur *m*; **~ suspension grid** Gitterrostdecke *f*; **~ trolley** Lichtwagen *m*; **~ trough** Lichtwanne *f*, Wanne *f*; **~ truck** (OB) Lichtwagen *m*; **~ unit** Beleuchtungskörper *m*; **~ -up** *n* Ausleuchten *n*; **~ van** (OB) Lichtwagen *m*; **~ vehicle** (OB) Lichtwagen *m*; **~ with hard-shadow effect** Ausleuchtung mit Schlagschatteneffekt, Beleuchtung mit Schlagschatteneffekt; **~ workshop** Beleuchtungswerkstatt *f*; **flat ~** flache Ausleuchtung, flache Beleuchtung; **indirect ~** indirekte Beleuchtung; **to correct ~** nachleuchten *v*; **to increase ~ level** Licht aufblenden; **to reduce ~ level** Licht abblenden; **to set the ~** einleuchten *v*

lightning arrester Überspannungssicherung *f*; **~ protection** Blitzschutz *m*; **~ stick** Blitzzange *f*

lights *n pl* (pict.) Lichter *n pl*; **~ !** Licht ein!; **~ on!** Licht ein!; **~ out!** Licht aus!; **~ up!** alles Licht!; **kill the ~ !** Licht aus!; **to set the ~** Licht einrichten, Licht setzen

limit frequency Grenzfrequenz *f*; **~ of resolution** Auflösungsgrenze *f*; **~ of sensitivity** Empfindlichkeitsgrenze *f*

limiter *n* Begrenzer *m*

limiting *n* Begrenzung *f*, Abschneiden *n*;

~ **height** Bauhöhe *f*; ~ **sensitivity** Grenzempfindlichkeit *f*

linage *n* Zeilenhonorar *n*

line *n* Leitung *f*, Strecke *f*, Strippe *f* (fam.); ~ *n* (tel.) Telefonanschluß *m* ~ *n* (video) Zeile *f*; ~ *n* (US) (elec.) Netz *n*; ~ *n* (perf.) Fach *n*; ~ **amplifier** Leitungsverstärker *m*; ~ **amplitude** Zeilenamplitude *f*; ~ **attenuation** Leitungsdämpfung *f* ~ **balance** Leitungsnachbildung *f*; ~ **blanking** Zeilenabtastung *f*; ~ **blanking pulse** Zeilenaustastimpuls *m*; ~ **booking** Leitungsbestellung *f*; ~ **bookings section** Leitungsbüro *n*; ~ **check** Leitungsprüfung *f*; ~ **connection** (US) Netzanschluß *m*; ~ **deflection coil** Horizontalablenkspule *f*; ~ **duration** Zeilendauer *f*; ~ **equaliser** Leitungsentzerrer *m*; ~ **fault** Leitungsfehler *m*; ~ **feed** (elec.) Leitungsüberspielung *f*; ~ **feed** (EDP) Zeilenvorschub *m*; ~ **flyback** Zeilenrücklauf *m*; ~ **flyback period** Zeilenrücklaufzeit *f*; ~ **-free** *adj* zeilenfrei *adj*; ~ **frequency** Horizontalfrequenz *f*, Zeilenfrequenz *f*; ~ **-frequency adjustment** Einstellen der Zeilenfrequenz; ~ **-frequency setting** Einstellen der Zeilenfrequenz; ~ **-frequency square wave** H-frequentes Rechtecksignal; ~ **grating** Liniengitter *n*; ~ **hum** Leitungsbrumm *m*; ~ **input** Leitungseingang *m*; ~ **interlace** Zeilensprung *m*; ~ **jitter** Zeilenspratzer *m*; ~ **loss** Leitungsverlust *m*, Leitungsdämpfung *f*; ~ **matching transformer** Leitungsanpaßtransformator *m*; ~ **noise** Zeilenrauschen *n*; ~ **of loudspeakers** Schallzeile *f*; ~ **of vision** (opt.) Achse *f*; ~ **offset** Zeilenoffset *n*; ~ **output** Leitungsausgang *m*; ~ **output transformer (LOPT)** Zeilenablenktransformator *m*; ~ **pairing** schlechte Zwischenzeile; ~ **period** Zeilendauer *f*, Zeilenzeit *f*; ~ **posting** Zeileneinstellung *f*; ~ **printer** (EDP) Zeilendrucker *m*; ~ **-pulling** *n* Zeilenversatz *m*, Ausfall des Zeilengleichlaufs, Bildauskippen *n*; ~ **pulse** Horizontalimpuls (H-Impuls) *m*, Horizontal-Synchronimpuls *m*, Zeilensynchronimpuls *m*; ~ **scanning** Zeilenablenkung *f*, Zeilenabtastung *f*; ~ **-scanning pattern** Zeilenraster *m*; ~ **-sequential** *adj* zeilensequent *adj*; ~ **source loudspeaker** Tonwanne *f*, Wanne *f*; ~ **source unit** Tonwanne *f*, Wanne *f*; ~ **spectrum** Linearitätsspektrum *n*; ~ **standard** Zeilennorm *f*; ~ **-sync separator** S-Separator *m*; ~ **synchronisation signal** Zeilengleichlaufsignal *n*; ~ **synchronising pulse** Horizontalimpuls (H-Impuls) *m*, Horizontal-Synchronimpuls *m*, Zeilensynchronimpuls *m*; ~ **-synchronous** *adj* zeilensynchron *adj*; ~ **-tearing** *n* Ausfall des Zeilengleichlaufs, Bildauskippen *n*, Zeilenreißen *n*; ~ **terminal** Leitungsendpunkt *m*; ~ **termination** Leitungsabschluß *m*; ~ **transformer** Leitungsübertrager *m*; ~ **traversal** Zeilendurchlauf *m*; ~ **up** *v* einpegeln *v*, pegeln *v*; ~ **-up tape** Bezugsband *n*; **closed** ~ abgeschlossene Leitung; **homogeneous** ~ homogene Leitung; **incoming** ~ ankommende Leitung; **open-ended** ~ offene Leitung; **outgoing**

~ abgehende Leitung; **recording from ~** Aufzeichnung über Strecke; **simulated ~** nachgebildete Leitung; **terminated ~** abgeschlossene Leitung; **to be on the ~** in der Leitung sein; **to cross the ~ of vision** über die Achse springen; **to have on the ~** in der Leitung haben; **to record down the ~** über Leitung aufnehmen, über Leitung aufzeichnen; **uniform ~** homogene Leitung;
line's dead! Leitung ist tot!

linearity *n* Linearität *f*; **~ defect** Linearitätsfehler *m*; **~ error** Linearitätsfehler *m*; **~ test pattern** Linearitätstestbild *n*, Geometrietestbild *n*

line-at-a-time printer (EDP) Zeilendrucker *m*

line-of-sight path quasioptische Lichtlinie

line-up *n* Einpegeln *n*, Pegeln *n*; **~ instructions** *n pl* Abgleichanweisung *f*; **~ period** (transmission) Einregelzeit *f*; **~ time** Vorbereitungszeit *f*, Vorschaltzeit *f*, Vorlaufzeit *f*; **~ tone** Abstimmton *m*, Meßton *m*

lining-up *n* Motivsuche *f*

link *v* verbinden *v*; **~** *n* (chain) Glied *n*; **~** *n* (line) Verbindung *f*; **~ coupling** Linkstrecke *f*; **~ line** Linkstrecke *f*; **~ receiver** Richtfunkempfänger *m*; **~ transmitter** Richtfunksender *m*; **reversible ~** richtungsumschaltbare Verbindung; **unidirectional ~** gerichtete Verbindung

linkage *n* (EDP) Verknüpfung *f*

linked *adj* (with) (transmitter) angeschlossen *adj*

lip microphone Lippenmikrofon *n*, Nahbesprechungsmikrofon *n*

lip-sync *v* Bildband und Tonband auf gleiche Länge ziehen, hinziehen *v*; **~** *adj* lippensynchron *adj*; **to bring into ~** Bildband und Tonband auf gleiche Länge ziehen, hinziehen *v*

liquid meter Flüssigkeitsmengenmesser *m*

liquidation *n* Abrechnung *f*, Abwicklung *f*

list of credits Titelliste *f*; **~ of cut-ins** Schnittbildfolge *f*

listen *v* (tape) abhören *v*; **~ in** *v* Radio hören

listener *n* Hörer *m*, Zuhörer *m*; **~** *n* (R) Hörfunkhörer *m*, Rundfunkhörer *m*; **~ research** Hörerforschung *f*

listeners' letters *n pl* Hörerpost *f*; **~ requests** Hörerwünsche *m pl*

listening cubicle Abhörbox *f*, Abhörkabine *f*; **~ report** Abhörbericht *m*; **~ room** Abhörraum *m*

lit area Ausleuchtungszone *f*, Szenenbeleuchtungsumfang *m*

litz wire Litze *f*, Hochfrequenzlitze *f*

live *adj* direkt *adj*, Live- (in Zus.); **~** *adj* (echo) hallig *adj*; **~** *adv* live *adv*; **~ animation** Sachtrick *m*; **~ broadcast** Direktsendung *f*, Direktübertragung *f*, Livesendung *f*, Liveübertragung *f*, Originalübertragung *f*; **~ commentary** Livereportage *f*; **~ from ...** eine Direktsendung aus ...; **~ inject** Livebeitrag *m*; **~ insert** Livebeitrag *m*; **~ production** Liveproduktion *f*; **~ programme** Liveprogramm *n*; **~ radio broadcast** Hörfunklivesendung *f*; **~ relay** Direktübertragung *f*, Liveübertragung *f*, Livereportage *f*; **~ relay by satellite** direkte Satellitenübertragung; **~ show** Liveproduktion *f*; **~ studio** Livestudio *n*; **~ studio** (echo) Studio mit Nachhall; **~ television**

broadcast Fernsehdirektübertragung *f*; **~ television relay** Fernsehdirektübertragung *f*; **~ television relay by satellite** direkte Fernsehübertragung vom Satelliten; **~ television transmission** Fernsehlivesendung *f*; **~ transmission** Direktsendung *f*, Direktübertragung *f*, Livesendung *f*, Liveübertragung *f*, Originalübertragung *f*; **to broadcast ~** direkt senden, live senden

liven up *v* aufmöbeln *v*

liveness *n* Halligkeit *f*

load *v* (cam.) einlegen *v*; ~ *n* (elec.) Beanspruchung *f*, Belastung *f*; **~ impedance** Belastungsimpedanz *f*; **~ instruction** (EDP) Ladebefehl *m*; **~ resistance** Belastungswiderstand *m*; **~ resistance** (transmitter) Auskoppelwiderstand *m*; **maximum ~** maximale Beanspruchung; **to ~ a camera** Film einlegen

loader *n* Ladekassette *f*

loading *n* (elec.) Beanspruchung *f*, Belastung *f*; ~ *n* (cam.) Filmeinlegen *n*; **resistive ~** ohmsche Belastung

lobe *n* Keule *f*; **~ width** (aerial) Halbwertsbreite *f*

local battery (LB) Ortsbatterie (OB) *f*; **~ -battery circuit** OB-Leitung *f*; **~ -battery connection** Ortsbatterieanschluß *m*; **~ -battery exchange** Ortsbatterievermittlung *f*; **~ -battery line** OB-Leitung *f*; **~ -battery telephone (LB telephone)** OB-Telefon *n*; **~ broadcast** (US) Regionalsendung *f*; **~ broadcasting** (US) Regionalprogramm *n*; **~ circuit** Ortsleitung *f*; **~ end** Ortsleitung *f*, Zubringerleitung *f*, Zubringer *m* (fam.); **~ fading** Nahschwund *m*; **~ line** Ortsleitung *f*; **~ news** Lokalnachrichten *f pl*; **~ news** (US) regionale Berichterstattung, Regionalnachrichten *f pl*; **~ program** (US) Regionalsendung *f*; **~ sound** internationaler Ton; **~ station** (US) Regionalanstalt *f*; **~ supply** Eigenversorgung *f*, Selbstversorgung *f*; **~ television** (US) Regionalfernsehen *n*; **~ time** Ortszeit *f*; **~ transmitter** Ortssender *m*

localise, to ~ a fault einen Fehler eingrenzen

location *n* Aufnahmegelände *n*, Aufnahmeort *m*, Drehort *m*, Schauplatz *m*, Standort *m*, Motiv *n*, Originalmotiv *n*; **~ film** Originalfilm *m*; **~ hunt** Motivsuche *f*; **~ set** Außenbau *m*; **~ shooting** Außenaufnahme *f*; **~ shot** Außenaufnahme *f*; **~ survey** Motivbesichtigung *f*, Vorbesichtigung *f*; **original ~** realer Außendekor; **outdoor ~** realer Außendekor; **to film on ~** am Originalmotiv drehen

lock *v* einrasten *v*; ~ *v* (video) synchronisieren *v*; ~ *v* (cam.) feststellen *v* ; ~ *n* (sound, light) Schleuse *f*; **~ in** *v* (oscillator) einspringen *v*, locken *v* **to ~ on to** (electron.) sich aufschalten auf

lockable oscillator Nachführungsoszillator *m*

locked *adj* eingelassen *adj*; ~ *adj* (video) synchron *adj*, synchronisiert *adj*; **~ colour carrier** verkoppelter Farbträger *m*

locked-phase, in ~ relation phasenstarr *adj*

lock-in range Einspringbereich *m*, Fangbereich *m*, Mitnahmebereich *m*, Ziehbereich *m*

locking *n* Blockierung *f*, Verriegelung *f*; ~ *n* (video)

Synchronisieren *n*; ~ **bar** Sperriegel *m*; ~ **circuit** Nachführungskreis *m*, Synchronisierleitung *f*; ~ **contact** Selbsthaltekontakt *m*; ~ **device** Arretierung *f*; ~ **lever** Verriegelungsgriff *m*; ~ **mechanism** Verriegelung *f*; ~ **pin** Sperrstift *m*; ~ **pulse** Verriegelungsimpuls *m*; ~ **range** Haltebereich *m*, Nachziehbereich *m*, Synchronisierbereich *m*; ~ **ring** Feststellring *m*, Verriegelungsring *m*

locksmith *n* Schlosser *m*

log *n* Stundenbericht *m*

log-book *n* Schnittliste *f*

logic diagram (EDP) Logikschaltbild *n*; ~ **unit** (EDP) Digital-Baustein *m*, Logik-Baustein *m*; **internal** ~ (EDP) interne Logik

logical AND circuit (EDP) UND-Gatter *n*, Koinzidenzgatter *n*; ~ **product** (EDP) Konjunktion *f*

log-masking *n* (US) Gammaentzerrung *f*

log-periodic aerial logarithmische Antenne

long-distance circuit Fernleitung *f*; ~ **line** Fernleitung *f*; ~ **network** Fernleitungsnetz *n*; ~ **shot** Fernaufnahme *f*

longitudinal magnetisation Längsmagnetisierung *f*; ~ **recording** Gegentakt-Längsaufzeichnung *f*, Längsschriftaufzeichnung *f*; ~ **wave** Longitudinalwelle *f*

long persistence tube Speicherröhre

long-playing disc Langspielplatte (LP) *f*; ~ **record (LP)** Langspielplatte (LP) *f*; ~ **tape (LP tape)** Langspielband *n*

long shot (LS) Fernaufnahme *f*, Gesamtaufnahme *f*, Totale *f*

long-term *adj* langfristig *adj*; ~ **stability** Langzeitstabilität *f*

long wave (LW) Langwelle (LW) *f*

long-wave band Langwellenbereich *m*; ~ **transmitter** Langwellensender *m*

loop *v* (line) schleifen *v*; ~ *n* (F) Filmschleife *f*, Schleife *f*; ~ **aerial** Rahmenantenne *f*; ~ **cabinet** Schleifendurchziehkasten *m*, Schleifenkasten *m*; ~ **frame** Schleifenrahmen *m*; ~ **stand** Schleifenständer *m*; ~ **through** *v* (cable) durchschleifen *v*; **closed** ~ (EDP) geschlossene Schleife; **open** ~ (EDP) offener Regelkreis; **to run a** ~ Schleife fahren

loose contact Wackelkontakt *m*; **too** ~ (pict.) zuviel Luft

loss *n* (sig.) Abnahme *f*; ~ **by reflection** Reflexionsverlust *m*; ~ **factor** Verlustfaktor *m*; ~ **of level** Pegelverlust *m*; ~ **of loops** Schleifenschwund *m*; ~ **of picture lock** Bildkippen *n*; ~ **of quality** Güteabfall *m*; ~ **of signal** Signalausfall *m*; ~ **of sound** Tonausfall *m*; ~ **of synchronism** Phasenausfall *m*; ~ **of voltage** Spannungsausfall *m*; ~ **resistance** Verlustwiderstand *m*, Dämpfungswiderstand *m*

lot *n* Aufnahmegelände *n*, Aufnahmeort *m*, Ateliergelände *n*, Filmgelände *n*, Gelände *n*

loud *adj* (col.) knallig *adj*

loudness *n* Lautheit *f*, Tonstärke *f*; ~ **level** Lautstärkepegel *m*; ~ **level meter** Lautstärkemesser *m*; ~ **meter** Lautheitmesser *m*; ~ **range** Lautstärkeumfang *m*

loudspeaker *n* Lautsprecher *m*, Strahler *m*; ~ **baffle** Lautsprecherschallwand *f*; ~ **case** Lautsprecherbox *f*, Lautsprecherschrank *m*; ~ **chassis** Lautsprecherchassis *n*; ~ **layout** Lautsprecheranordnung *f*; ~ **system** Lautsprechersystem *n*; **coil-driven** ~ elektrodynamischer Lautsprecher; **electrodynamic** ~

elektrodynamischer Lautsprecher **electrostatic ~** elektrostatischer Lautsprecher; **moving-coil ~** elektrodynamischer Lautsprecher
low band Low-band *n*
low-band standards *n pl* Low-band-Norm *f*
low-contrast *adj* (pict.) kontrastarm *adj*, flau *adj*, soßig *adj*
low-current installation Schwachstromanlage *f*; **~ workshop** Schwachstromwerkstatt *f*
low frequencies Tiefen *f pl*
low frequency (LF) Langwelle (LW) *f*, Niederfrequenz *f* (NF), Tiefton *m*
low-frequency amplifier Niederfrequenzverstärker *m*; **~ band** Langwellenbereich *m*; **~ generator** Tieftongenerator *m*; **~ loudspeaker unit** Baßlautsprecher *m*; **~ noise** Zeilenrauschen *n*; **~ parameter** Niederfrequenzparameter *m*; **~ rejection filter** Tiefensperre *f*; **~ transmitter (LF transmitter)** Langwellensender *m*
low-gamma *adj* soßig *adj*
low-impedance tap niederohmige Anzapfung
low key Low-key *n*
low-noise *adj* geräuscharm *adj*, rauscharm *adj*
low-pass filter Tiefpaßfilter *m*, Tiefpaß *m*
low-pitched notes Tiefen *f pl*
low-power transmitter Füllsender *m*, Kleinsender *m*, Ortssender *m*
low tension Niederspannung *f*
low-tension battery Heizbatterie *f*; **~ lamp** Niederspannungslampe *f*, Niedervoltlampe *f*
low voltage Niederspannung *f*
low-voltage current Schwachstrom *m*; **~ lamp** Niederspannungslampe *f*, Niedervoltlampe *f*; **~ mains** *n pl* Niederspannungsnetz *n*; **~ switchboard** Niederspannungszentrale *f*
lubrication *n* Schmierung *f*
lumen meter Leuchtdichtemesser *m*
luminance *n* Leuchtdichte *f*, Luminanz *f*; **~ chart** Lichtzettel *m* **~ flicker** Helligkeitsflimmern *n*; **~ level** Leuchtdichtepegel *m*; **~ range** Luminanzspektrum *n*; **~ signal** Helligkeitssignal *n*, Leuchtdichtesignal *n*, Luminanzsignal *n*, Y-Signal *n*; **~ spectrum** Luminanzspektrum *n*
luminescence *n* Lumineszenz *f*
luminescent material Leuchtstoff *m*; **~ screen** Leuchtschirm *m*, Leuchtstoffschirm *m*
luminosity *n* Helligkeit *f*; **relative ~ factor** spektrale Hellempfindlichkeitskurve
luminous coating Leuchtschicht *f*; **~ density** Leuchtdichte *f*; **~ digital indicator** Leuchtzifferanzeige *f*; **~ efficiency** Lichtleistung *f*; **~ flux** Lichtstrom *m*; **~ -flux measurement** Lichtstrommessung *f*; **~ intensity** Lichtstärke *f*; **~ push button** Leuchtdrucktaste *f*; **~ source** Lichtquelle *f*; **~ texture** Leuchtdichtestruktur *f*
lump sum Pauschale *f*
luxmeter *n* Luxmeter *n*

M

M. and E. version IT-Fassung *f*
machine instruction (EDP) Maschinenbefehl *m*, Maschineninstruktion *f*; **~ language** (EDP) Maschinensprache *f*; **available ~ time** (EDP) verfügbare Benutzerzeit

machine-oriented language (EDP) maschinennahe Programmiersprache, maschinenorientierte Programmiersprache
macro definition (EDP) Makrodefinition *f*; **~ -filming** *n* Detailaufnahme *f*; **~ instruction** (EDP) Makroaufruf *m*; **~ shot** Makroaufnahme *f*
macrophotography *n* Detailaufnahme *f*
mag leader (coll.) Startband für Cord
magazine *n* Magazin *n*, Kassette *f*; **~** *n* (press, type of prog.) Magazin *n*; **~ card** Klappenliste *f*; **~ lid** Kassettendeckel *m*; **~ programme** Magazinsendung *f*; **cultural ~** literarisches Magazin; **literary ~** literarisches Magazin; **topical ~** aktuelles Magazin
magnesium flare Magnesiumfackel *f*
magnet, annular Ringmagnet *m*
magnetic *adj* magnetisch *adj*; **~ amplifier** Magnetverstärker *m*, Transduktor *m*; **~ balance track** Magnetausgleichsspur *f*; **~ biasing** Vormagnetisierung *f*; **~ button** Magnettaste *f*; **~ card** (EDP) Magnetkarte *f*; **~ centre track** Magnetmittenspur *f*; **~ circuit-breaker** Magnetschutzschalter *m*; **~ coil** Magnetspule *f*; **~ core** (EDP) Magnetkern *m*; **~ disc** Magnetplatte *f*; **~ disc store** (EDP) Magnetplattenspeicher *m*; **~ drum store** (EDP) Magnettrommelspeicher *m*; **~ field** Magnetfeld *n*; **~ film** Cordband *n*, Cord *n*, Magnetperfoband *n*, Magnetsplitfilm *m*, Perfoband *n*, Perfomagnetband *n*, Split *m* (17,5 Cord); **~ film deformation** Magnetfilmverformung *f*; **~ film leader** Startband für Cord; **~ film mechanism** Magnetfilmlaufwerk *n*; **~ film recording machine** Cordmaschine *f*, Cordspieler *m*; **~ flux** Magnetfluß *m*, magnetischer Fluß; **~ gap** Kopfspalt *m*, Luftspalt *m*; **~ head** Magnetkopf *m*, Magnettonkopf *m*; **~ laminating tape** Kaschierband *n* **~ lamination** Magnetrandbespuren *n*, Magnetrandbeschichten *n*; **~ picture** Magnetbild *n*; **~ recorder** magnetische Aufzeichnungsanlage, Magnettongerät *n*, Magnetofon *n*, Magnetofongerät *n*; **~ recording** Magnetaufzeichnung *f*; **~ recording medium** Magnetschriftträger *m*, Magnettonmaterial *n*; **~ sound** Magnetton *m*; **~ sound film** Magnetfilm *m*; **~ sound head** Magnettonkopf *m*; **~ sound recording** Magnettonaufnahme *f*; **~ sound reproduction** Magnettonwiedergabe *f*; **~ sound stripe** Film mit Magnetspur; **~ sound tape** Magnettonband *n*; **~ stripe** Laminierband *n*; **~ striping** Magnetrandbespuren *n*, Magnetrandbeschichten *n*; **~ tape** Magnetband *n*, Magnettonband *n*; **~ tape cartridge** (EDP) Magnetbandkassette *f*; **~ tape drive** (EDP) Magnetbandlaufwerk *n*; **~ tape recorder** Magnettongerät *n*, Magnetofon *n*, Magnetofongerät *n*; **~ tape store** (EDP) Magnetbandspeicher *m*, Bandspeicher *m*; **~ tape unit** (EDP) Magnetbandgerät *n*; **~ track** Magnetrandspur *f*, Magnetspur *f*; **~ transfer** Überspielung von Licht- auf Magnetton; **~ transfer** (tape) Kopiereffekt *m*; **~ wire** Magnetdraht *m*, Magnettondraht *m*; **combined ~ sound (Commag)** kombinierter Magnetton

(COMMAG); **remanent ~ flux** remanenter Magnetfluß; **residual ~ flux** remanenter Magnetfluß; **separate ~ sound (Sepmag)** separater Magnetton (SEPMAG); **two separate ~ sound tracks (Sepdumag)** separater Magnetton auf zwei Spuren (SEPDUMAG)

magnetically recorded image Magnetbild *n*

magnetisation *n* Magnetisierung *f*

magnetism *n* Magnetismus *m*; **remanent ~** remanenter Magnetismus; **residual ~** remanenter Magnetismus

magnifier *n* Lupe *f*

magnify *v* vergrößern *v*

magnifying glass Lupe *f*; **~ lens** Lupe *f*

magoptical copy Magoptical-Kopie *f*; **~ print** Magoptical-Kopie *f*

main *adj* Haupt- (in Zus.); **~ carrier** Hauptträger *m*; **~ control (MC)** Endkontrolle *f*; **~ control room (MCR)** Endkontrolle *f*; **~ distributing frame (MDF)** Hauptverteiler *m*; **~ distribution cable** (aerial) Stammleitung *f*; **~ distribution frame (MDF)** Lötigel *m*; **~ feature film** Hauptfilm *m*; **~ isolating switch** Haupttrennschalter *m*; **~ light** Hauptlicht *n*, Führungslicht *n*, Führung *f*; **~ lighting** Hauptbeleuchtung *f*; **~ memory** (EDP) Arbeitsspeicher *m*, Hauptspeicher *m*, Primärspeicher *m*; **~ -memory capacity** (EDP) Arbeitsspeicherkapazität *f*; **~ news transmission** Hauptnachrichten *f pl*; **~ reference library** Zentralarchiv *n*; **~ station** (transmitter) Großflächensender *m*; **~ studio** Hauptstudio *n*; **~ switch** Hauptschalter *m*; **~ title** Haupttitel *m*

mains *n pl* (elec.) Hauptleitung *f*, Netz *n*, Starkstromnetz *n*; **~ circuit connection** Netzanschluß *m*; **~ current** Netzstrom *m*; **~ failure** Netzausfall *m*, Netzstörung *f*; **~ frequency** Netzfrequenz *f*; **~ hum** Netzbrumm *m*; **~ lead** Anschluß *m*, Anschlußkabel *n*; **~ lighting supply** Lichtnetz *n*; **~ motor** Netzmotor *m*; **~ noise** Netzgeräusch *n*; **~ -operated** *adj* netzabhängig *adj*; **~ operation** Netzbetrieb *m*; **~ power unit** Netzteil *m*, Netzanschlußgerät *n*, Netzgerät *n*; **~ rectifier** Netzgleichrichter *m*; **~ set** Netzgerät *n*; **~ supply** Netz *n*, Netzanschluß *m*, Netzspeisung *f*, Netzversorgung *f*; **~ supply operation** Netzspeisung *f*; **~ supply panel** Netzeinschub *m*; **~ switch** Netzschalter *m*; **~ transformer** Netztransformator *m*; **~ voltage** Anschlußspannung *f*, Netzspannung *f*; **interconnecting ~** *n pl* vermaschtes Netz; **regulated ~ supply** geregeltes Netz; **single-phase ~ supply** Lichtnetz *n*; **stabilised ~** *n pl* geregeltes Netz; **three-phase ~ supply** Kraftnetz *n*; **unregulated ~ supply** ungeregeltes Netz; **unstabilised ~** *n pl* ungeregeltes Netz

maintain *v* (tech.) warten *v*

maintenance *n* Wartung *f*, Betriebswartung *f*, Reparatur *f*, Bedienung *f*; **~ area** Bedienungsraum *m*; **~ engineer** Meßingenieur *m*; **~ of development standard** Entwicklungskonstanz *f*; **~ room** Meßraum *m*; **~ service** Wartungsdienst *m*, Meßdienst *m*; **~ technician** Meßtechniker *m*

make *v* (profit) einspielen *v*; **~ up** *v* Maske machen, schminken *v*; **to ~**

start marks Film einstarten, einstarten *v*, Startmarkierungen anbringen
make-up *n* Maske *f*; ~ *n* (material) Schminke *f*; ~ **artist** Maskenbildner *m*, Maske *f* (fam.), Schminkmeister *m*; ~ **chart** Schminkvorlage *f*, Schminkzettel *m*; ~ **department** Maskenbildnerei *f*; ~ **example** Schminkvorlage *f*, Schminkzettel *m*; ~ **materials** *n pl* Schminkmaterial *n*; ~ **media** Schminkmittel *n pl*; ~ **reference** Maskenvorlage *f*; ~ **room** Maskenbildnerwerkstatt *f*, Maske *f* (fam.), Schminkraum *m*; ~ **supervisor** Schminkmeister *m*; ~ **table** Schminktisch *m*; ~ **treatment** Schminken *n*
maltese cross Malteserkreuz *n*; ~ **cross assembly** Malteserkreuzgetriebe *n*; ~ **cross transmission** Malteserkreuzwelle *f*
management *n* Leitung *f*; ~ **accountancy** Kalkulation *f*; ~ **accountant** Kalkulator *m*
manager *n* Leiter *m*
managing director (BBC) Programmdirektor *m*; ~ **director of radio** (BBC) Hörfunkdirektor *m*, Programmdirektor Hörfunk; ~ **director of television** (BBC) Fernsehdirektor *m*, Programmdirektor Fernsehen
manganin *n* Manganin *n*
manifold *n* Verteiler *m*
manual *adj* manuell *adj*; ~ **control** Handregelung *f*, Handsteuerung *f* ~ **exchange** Handvermittlungsanlage *f*; ~ **operation** Handregelung *f*, Handsteuerung *f*; ~ **telephone system** Handvermittlung *f*
manually controlled motor Handregelmotor *m*
manufacture *n* Herstellung *f*
manuscript (MS) *n* Manuskript *n* (MS)
margin of image Bildrand *m*
marginal comment Glosse *f*; ~ **definition** (pict.) Randschärfe *f*
marionette player Marionettenspieler *m*
mark *n* Marke *f*, Markierung *f*, Zeichen *n*
marker *n* Marke *f*, Markierung *f*, Sichtzeichen *n*; ~ *n* (device) Markiervorrichtung *f*
marking *n* Markierung *f*; ~ **device** Markiervorrichtung *f*
mark-to-space ratio Impulstastverhältnis *n*
mask *v* (FP) maskieren *v*; ~ *v* (EDP) ausblenden *v*; ~ *n* Kasch *m*, Maske *f*, Vignette *f*; ~ *n* (make-up) Maske *f*; ~ **generator** Rahmengeber *m*
masking *n* (aperture) Abdeckung *f*; ~ **frame** Abdeckrahmen *m*
mass media Massenmedien *n pl*; **instrument of ~ communication** Massenkommunikationsmittel *n*
mast *n* Mast *m*; ~ **diplexer** (Aerial) Mastweiche *f*; ~ **-head amplifier** Antennenmastverstärker *m*, Mastverstärker *m*; ~ **height** Masthöhe *f*; ~ **inclinometer** Mastneigungsmesser *m*; ~ **lead-through** (aerial) Mastdurchführung *f*; ~ **radiator** Antennenmast *m*; ~ **warning lights** *n pl* Mastbefeuerung *f*
master *n* (F, tape) Original *n*; ~ *n* (disc) Negativ *n*; ~ **amplifier** Summenverstärker *m*; ~ **control (MC)** Endkontrolle *f*; ~ **control room (MCR)** Endkontrolle *f*, Regiezentrale *f*, Sendezentrale *f*; ~ **copy** Mutterband *n*; ~ **file** (EDP) Stammdatei *f*; ~ **frequency** Mutterfrequenz *f*; ~ **generator** Muttergenerator *m*; ~ **oscillator (MO)** Mutteroszillator *m*, Steueroszillator *m*, Steuersender *m*; ~ **print** Originalkopie *f*; ~ **shot**

Gesamtaufnahme *f*; ~ **station** Muttersender *m*, Primärstrahler *m*; ~ **switch** (EDP) Hauptschalter *m*; ~ **tape** Aufnahmetonband *n*, Mutterband *n*, Originalaufzeichnung *f*; ~ **transmitter** Muttersender *m*

match *v* abgleichen *v*, angleichen *v*, anpassen *v*

matching *n* Angleichung *f*, Anpassung *f*; ~ **circuit** Anpassungskreis *m*; ~ **device** Anpassungsvorrichtung *f*, Anpassungsglied *n*; ~ **element** Anpassungselement *n*; ~ **impedance** Anpassungsimpedanz *f*; ~ **network** Anpassungsnetzwerk *n*; ~ **resistance** Anpassungswiderstand *m*; ~ **resistor** Anpassungswiderstand *m*; ~ **section** Anpaßglied *n*; ~ **transformer** Anpassungsübertrager *m*, Zwischenübertrager *m*; ~ **unit** Meßadapter *m*

material *n* Material *n*, Stoff *m*; **recorded** ~ aufgezeichnetes Material

matrix *v* matrizieren *v*; ~ *n* Matrix *f*, Matrize *f*, Kreuzschiene *f*; ~ **circuit** Matrixschaltung *f*; ~ **distribution panel** Kreuzschienenverteiler *m*; ~ **jackfield** Kreuzschienensteckfeld *n*; ~ **printer** (EDP) Matrixdrucker *m*; ~ **selector** Kreuzschienenwähler *m*; ~ **stage** Matrixstufe *f*; ~ **switching point** Schaltstelle mit Kreuzschiene; **linear** ~ lineare Matrix

matt *adj* matt *adj*

matte *n* Kasch *m*, Schablone *f*, Maske *f*, Vignette *f*; ~ **box** Kaschhalter *m*, Kompendium *n*; ~ **holder** Kaschhalter *m*; **to print with ~ effect** mit Maske kopieren

maximum amplitude Maximalamplitude *f*; ~ **density** Endschwärzung *f*; ~ **field angle** Maximalfeldwinkel *m*; ~ **field of view** Maximalbildfeld *n*; ~ **level** Vollpegel *m*, Vollaussteuerung *f*; ~ **permissible load** Höchstbeanspruchung *f*; ~ **value of signal** Signalhöchstwert *m*; ~ **-voltage relay** Überspannungsrelais *n*; ~ **volume** (sound) Vollaussteuerung *f*

mean value Mittelwert *m*

means *n* Mittel *n*; **audio-visual** ~ audiovisuelle Mittel

measure *n* Maß *n*

measurement *n* Maß *n*, Messung *f*; ~ **by substitution** Substitutionsmessung *f*; ~ **of colour coordinates** Farbortmessung *f*; ~ **of exposure** Belichtungsmessung *f*; ~ **of light level** Beleuchtungsstärkemessung *f*; ~ **output** Meßausgang *m*; ~ **range** Meßbereich *m*; ~ **-range extension** Meßbereichserweiterung *f*; ~ **techniques** *n pl* Meßtechnik *f*; **densitometric** ~ densitometrische Messung

measurements* *n pl* Meßdienst* *m*, Meßtechnik* *f*

measuring *n* Messung *f*; ~ **adapter** Meßadapter *m*; ~ **amplifier** Meßverstärker *m*; ~ **apparatus** Meßgerät *n*; ~ **bridge** Meßbrücke *f*, Brückenmeßgerät *n*; ~ **circuit** Meßschaltung *f*; ~ **demodulator** Meßdemodulator *m*; ~ **desk** Meßplatz *m*; ~ **head** Meßkopf *m*; ~ **instrument** Meßgerät *n*; ~ **line** Meßleitung *f*; ~ **point** (EDP) Meßstelle *f*; ~ **position** Meßplatz *m*; ~ **sensitivity** Meßempfindlichkeit *f*; ~ **station** Meßstation *f*; ~ **transformer** Meßwandler *m*; ~ **voltage** Meßspannung *f*

mechanic *n* Schlosser *m*
mechanical *adj* mechanisch *adj*; **~ animation** Schiebetrick *m*; **~ recording** mechanische Aufzeichnung
mechanised book-keeping Maschinenbuchhaltung *f*
media *n pl* Kommunikationsmittel *n pl*; **joint ~** *n pl* Medienverbund *m*
medical unit betriebsärztliche Dienststelle
medium close-up (MCU) Halbnahe *f*; **~ frequency (MF)** Mittelwelle *f*; **~ -frequency band (MF band)** Mittelwellenbereich *m*; **~ -frequency transmitter** Mittelwellensender *m*; **~ long shot (MLS)** Halbtotale *f*; **~ of information** Informationsübermittler *m*; **~ shot (MS)** Halbnahe *f*; **~ wave** Mittelwelle (MW) *f*; **~ -wave band** Mittelwellenbereich *m*; **~ -wave transmitter** Mittelwellensender *m*
member of a chorus Chorist *m*, Chorsänger *m*; **~ of cast** Mitwirkender *m*; **~ of staff** Angestellter *m*; **~ of unestablished staff** Zeitvertragsinhaber *m*
membrane *n* Membran *f*
memorisation of data Informationsspeicherung *f*
memory *n* (EDP) Speicher *m*; **~ address** (EDP) Speicheradresse *f*; **~ capacity** (EDP) Speicherkapazität *f*; **~ cycle** (EDP) Speicherzyklus *m*; **~ location** (EDP) Speicherplatz *m*; **~ size** (EDP) Speicherkapazität *f*; **~ system** (EDP) Speichersystem *n*; **bulk ~** (EDP) Großraumspeicher *m*; **delay-line ~** (EDP) Laufzeitspeicher *m*; **disc ~** (EDP) Plattenspeicher *m*; **external ~** (EDP) externer Speicher; **fast ~** (EDP) Speicher mit schnellem Zugriff; **high-speed ~** (EDP) Speicher mit schnellem Zugriff; **main ~** (EDP) Arbeitsspeicher *m*, Hauptspeicher *m*, Primärspeicher *m*; **permanent ~** (EDP) permanenter Speicher; **random-access ~** (EDP) Speicher mit direktem Zugriff, Speicher mit wahlfreiem Zugriff; **rapid ~** (EDP) Speicher mit schnellem Zugriff; **read-only ~** (EDP) Festwertspeicher *m*; **scratchpad ~ (SPM)** (EDP) Zwischenspeicher *m* **thin-film ~** (EDP) Dünnfilmspeicher *m*; **working ~** (EDP) Arbeitsspeicher *m*, Hauptspeicher *m*, Primärspeicher *m*
mend *v* reparieren *v*
menu caption (coll.) Programmtafel *f*
mercury vapour lamp Quecksilberdampflampe *f*
merging curve Voute *f*
mesh *n* (orthicon) Gitter *n*; **~ effect** Gitterstruktur *f*; **~ voltage** Dreieckspannung *f*
message *n* Mitteilung *f*; **~** *n* (R, TV) Durchsage *f*; **~** *n* (agency) Meldung *f*, Bericht *m*
messenger *n* Bote *m*; **~ service** Botenmeisterei *f*; **~ supervisor** Botenmeister *m*
metal foil Metallfolie *f*; **~ framework** Metallgerüst *n*; **~ negative** (disc) Negativ *n*; **~ rack** Metallgerüst *n*; **~ scaffolding** Metallgerüst *n*
metallised resistor Schichtwiderstand *m*
meteorological report Wetterbericht *m*
meter *n* Anzeigegerät *n*; **~ cupboard** Zählerschrank *m*; **~ pulse** Zählimpuls *m*; **~ reading** Meßanzeige *f*
method *n* System *n*, Verfahren *n*
metronome *n* Taktgeber *m*
micro- (compp.) Mikro- (in Zus.)

microcinematography *n* Mikrokinematographie *f*
micro-circuitry *n* Mikrotechnik *f*
microfilm *n* Mikrofilm *m*
microgroove *n* Mikrorille *f*; **~ system** Füllschriftverfahren *n*
microinstruction *n* (EDP) Mikrobefehl *m*
microphone *n* Mikrofon *n*, Mikro *n* (fam.), Tüte *f* (fam.); **~ boom** Mikrofongalgen *m*, Tongalgen *m*, Galgen *m*; **~ capsule** Mikrofonkapsel *f*; **~ cut key** Räuspertaste *f*; **~ hiss** Mikrofonrauschen *n*; **~ noise** Mikrofonrauschen *n*; **~ power supply** Mikrofonspeisung *f*; **~ pre-amplifier** Mikrofonverstärker *m*; **~ socket** Mikrofonanschlußkasten *m*; **~ storeman** Mikrofonwart *m*; **beam ~** stark gebündeltes Mikrofon; **bidirectional ~** Achtermikrofon *n*, Mikrofon mit Achtercharakteristik, Achter *m* (fam.); **differential ~** Kompensationsmikrofon *n*; **directional ~** gerichtetes Mikrofon **dynamic ~** dynamisches Mikrofon **electrostatic ~** Kondensatormikrofon *n*; **figure-of-eight ~** Achtermikrofon *n*, Mikrofon mit Achtercharakteristik, Achter *m* (fam.); **highly directional ~** Richtmikrofon *n*; **hyperdirectional ~** stark gebündeltes Mikrofon; **lip ~** Lippenmikrofon *n*, Nahbesprechungsmikrofon *n*; **necklace ~** Umhängemikrofon *n*; **noise-cancelling ~** Nahbesprechungsmikrofon *n*; **omnidirectional ~** richtungsunempfindliches Mikrofon, ungerichtetes Mikrofon, Kugelmikrofon *n*, Kugel *f* (fam.); **portable ~** tragbares Mikrofon; **pressure-gradient ~** Gradientenmikrofon *n*; **radio ~** drahtloses Mikrofon; **static ~** Standmikrofon *n*; **unidirectional ~** einseitig gerichtetes Mikrofon, Richtmikrofon *n*
microphony *n* Mikrofonie *f*, Ton im Bild, Larseneffekt *m*, Klingneigung *f*
microphotography *n* Mikrofotografie *f*
microprogramme *n* (EDP) Mikroprogramm *n*
microscope projection Mikroprojektion *f*
microswitch *n* Mikroschalter *m*, Miniaturschalter *m*
microwave contribution circuit Richtfunkzubringerlinie *f*; **~ link** Richtfunkstrecke *f*, Richtfunkverbindung *f*, Dezistrecke *f*; **~ link system** Richtfunk (RiFu) *m*; **~ network** Richtfunknetz *n*; **~ radio station** Richtfunkstelle *f*; **~ receiver** Richtfunkempfänger *m* **~ repeater point** Mikrowellenverstärkerstelle *f*; **~ transmission service*** Richtfunkübertragungsdienst* *m*; **~ transmitter** Richtfunksender *m*
middle distance Mittelgrund *m*
midget amplifier Miniaturverstärker *m*
mid-shot (MS) *n* Halbnahe *f*
mike *n* (coll.) Mikrofon *n*, Mikro *n* (fam.), Tüte *f* (fam.); **to fondle the ~** ins Mikrofon kriechen (fam.); **to hog the ~** (coll.) am Mikrofon kleben, mikrogeil sein (fam.); **to hug the ~** ins Mikrofon kriechen (fam.)
military affairs specialist Wehrexperte *m*
milkiness *n* (FP) Trübung *f*
milky *adj* soßig *adj*

milled knob Rändelknopf *m*; **~ wheel** Rändelscheibe *f*
miller *n* Fräsmaschine *f*
milling machine Fräsmaschine *f*
mimic diagram Lichtmodell *n*
miniature *n* (set) Modell *n*
minimum capacitance Anfangskapazität *f*; **~ operating value** Ansprechschwelle *f*
minority programme Minderheitenprogramm *n*
mirror *n* Spiegel *m*; **~ drum** Spiegelzylinder *m*; **~ lamp** Spiegellampe *f*; **~ lens** Spiegellinse *f*; **~ reflex camera** Spiegelreflexkamera *f*; **~ reflex system** Spiegelreflexsystem *n*; **~ shutter** Spiegelblende *f*, Blendenflügel *m*; **dichroic ~** dichroitischer Spiegel, farbzerlegender Spiegel; **semi-reflecting ~** halbdurchlässiger Spiegel; **semi-silvered ~** halbdurchlässiger Spiegel
miscasting *n* Fehlbesetzung *f*
miscellaneous news *n pl* Vermischtes *n*
mismatch *v* fehlanpassen *v*; ~ *n* Fehlanpassung *f*
mismatching *n* Fehlanpassung *f*
mistake *n* Fehler *m*
mistuning *n* (TV set) fehlerhafte Bildeinstellung
mix *v* durchblenden *v*, mischen *v*; ~ *v* (pict.) überblenden *v*; ~ *n* Mischung *f*, Überblendung *f*, Überblenden *n*; ~ *n* (pict.) Bildüberblendung *f*, Durchblendung *f*; **~ in** *v* überblenden *v*; **~ on focus pull** Unschärfeblende *f*
mixed blanking pulses Austastgemisch *n*; **~ blanking signal** Austastgemisch *n*; **~ colour** Mischfarbe *f*; **~ crystal** Mischkristall *m*; **~ light** Mischlicht *n*; **~ signal** Summensignal *n*; **~ sync signals** *n pl* Synchronsignalgemisch *n*; **~ syncs** *n pl* (coll.) Synchronsignalgemisch *n*
mixer *n* Mischpult *n*; ~ *n* (operator, appar.) Mischer *m*; **~ amplifier** Mischverstärker *m*; **~ current** Mischstrom *m*; **~ diode** Mischdiode *f*; **~ stage** Mischstufe *f* **~ tube** Mischröhre *f*; **~ valve** Mischröhre *f*; **mobile ~** bewegliches Mischpult
mixing *n* Mischung *f*; **~ conditions** Mischbedingungen *f pl*; **~ console** Mischpult *n*, Tonmischpult *n*; **~ desk** Mischpult *n*, Mischtisch *m*, Regiepult *n*, Regietisch *m*; **~ head** Mischkopf *m*; **~ room** Mischatelier *n*; **~ studio** Mischstudio *n*; **~ suite** Mischstudio *n*; **~ tape** Zuspielband *n*; **~ transformer** Mischübertrager *m*
mix-through *n* Bildüberblendung *f*
mixture *n* Mischung *f*
mnemonic *adj* mnemotechnisch *adj* **~ code** (EDP) Buchstabencode *m*
mobile *adj* beweglich *adj*, fahrbar *adj*; **~ camera** fahrbare Kamera; **~ cinema van** Kinomobil *n*; **~ control room (MCR)** Bildaufnahmewagen *m*, Fernsehübertragungswagen *m*, Regiewagen *m*; **~ front light dimmer** Vorderlichtwagen *m*; **~ hoist** Laufkran *m*; **~ OB unit** Fernsehübertragungszug *m*, Übertragungszug *m*; **~ studio** fahrbares Studio; **~ telecine** Filmgeberwagen *m*; **~ unit** (TV) Fernsehübertragungszug *m*; **~ video tape recorder (MVTR)** MAZ-Wagen *m*, Fernsehaufnahmewagen *m*; **~ VTR (MVTR)** Aufzeichnungswagen *m*
mock-up *n* naturgetreues Modell
mode *n* (EDP) Betriebsart *f*; **~ of operation** Arbeitsweise *f*,

Betriebsart *f*; ~ **selector** Betriebsartenschalter *m*
model *n* Modell *n*; ~ **for model shot** Trickmodell *n*
model-maker *n* Modellbauer *m*, Modellschreiner *m*
moderator *n* (US) Diskussionsleiter *m*, Gesprächsleiter *m*, Moderator *m*
modular construction Bausteintechnik *f*; ~ **system** Modultechnik *f*
modulate *v* modulieren *v*, aussteuern *v*
modulation *n* Modulation *f*, Aussteuerung *f*; ~ **characteristics** Modulationseigenschaften *f pl*; ~ **circuit** Modulationsleitung *f*, Modulationssendeleitung *f*; ~ **depth** Modulationsgrad *m*; ~ **distortion** Modulationsklirrfaktor *m*; ~ **factor** Modulationsgrad *m*; ~ **feed** Modulationszubringung *f*; ~ **feeder circuit** Modulationszubringerleitung *f*; ~ **frequency (MF)** Modulationsfrequenz (MF) *f*; ~ **index** Modulationsindex *m*; ~ **indicator** Modulationspegelanzeiger *m*, Modulationsanzeiger *m*; ~ **input** Modulationszubringung *f*; ~ **input circuit** Modulationszubringerleitung *f*; ~ **level meter** Modulationsaussteuerungsmesser *m*; ~ **meter** Modulationspegelanzeiger *m*, Modulationsanzeiger *m*; ~ **monitoring** Modulationsüberwachung *f*; ~ **noise** Modulationsrauschen *n*; ~ **output** Modulationsausgang *m*; ~ **range** Aussteuerungsbereich *m*; ~ **ratio** Modulationsgrad *m*; ~ **signal** Modulationssignal *n*, Bildsignal *n* (B-Signal); ~ **transfer curve** Modulationsübertragungsfunktion (MÜF) *f*; ~ **valve** Modulationsröhre *f*; **double-sideband ~ (DSB modulation)** Doppelseitenbandmodulation *f*, Modulation mit doppeltem Seitenband (DSB); **subliminal ~** unterschwellige Modulation; **suppressed-carrier ~** Modulation mit unterdrücktem Träger
modulation-to-interference ratio Störmodulationsverhältnis *n*
modulator *n* Modulator *m*; ~ **valve** Modulationsröhre *f*; **symmetrical ~** symmetrischer Modulator
module *n* Baustein *m*, Modul
moiré *n* Riffelmuster *n*, Moiré *n*; ~ **pattern** Riffelmuster *n*, Moiré *n*
moisten *v* anfeuchten *v*
monitor *v* abhören *v*, überwachen *v*; ~ *n* (sound) Abhörer *m*; ~ *n* (pict.) Bildkontrollempfänger *m*, Bildmonitor *m*, Monitor *m*; ~ **calibration level** Eichpegel für Monitor (PEM); ~ **picture** Vorschaubild *n*; ~ **programme** (EDP) Monitor *m*; ~ **screen** Kontrollschirm *m*; **preview ~** Vorschaumonitor *m*
monitoring *n* Überwachung *f*, Betriebsaufsicht *f*; ~ *n* (sound) Abhören *n*, Abhörkontrolle *f*; ~ **amplifier** Abhörverstärker *m*; ~ **area** Kontrollraum *m*; ~ **bay** Kontrollgestell *n*; ~ **desk** Überwachungspult *n*; ~ **line** Überwachungsleitung *f*, Kontrollschiene *f*; ~ **loudspeaker** Kontrollautsprecher *m*, Abhörlautsprecher *m*, Abhörer *m*; ~ **of operations** Betriebsüberwachung *f*; ~ **of outgoing sound signal** Mithörkontrolle der Sendemodulation; ~ **of transmitted sound signal** Mithörkontrolle der HF-

Modulation; ~ **output** Kontrollausgang *m*; ~ **receiver** Überwachungsempfänger *m*; ~ **report** Abhörbericht *m*; ~ **room** Abhörraum *m*; ~ **service** Abhördienst *m*; ~ **station** Funkmeßdienst* *m*
monkey wrench Franzose *m*
mono *adj* (coll.) monaural *adj*, monophon *adj*, einkanalig *adj*; ~ **receiver** Monoempfänger *m*
monochromatic *adj* monochromatisch *adj*
monochrome *adj* einfarbig *adj*, monochromatisch *adj*, schwarzweiß *adj*; ~ **copy** Einfarbenkopie *f*; ~ **print** Einfarbenkopie *f*; ~ **production** Schwarzweißproduktion *f*; ~ **transmitter** Schwarzweißsender *m*
monopack *n* Monopack *n*
monophonic *adj* monaural *adj*, monophon *adj*, einkanalig *adj*; ~ **signal** Monosignal *n*
monoscope *n* Monoskop *n*
monostable circuit (EDP) monostabiles Flip-Flop, monostabile Kippschaltung; ~ **flip-flop** (EDP) monostabiles Flip-Flop, monostabile Kippschaltung; ~ **multivibrator** (EDP) monostabiles Flip-Flop, monostabile Kippschaltung; ~ **trigger circuit** (EDP) monostabiles Flip-Flop, monostabile Kippschaltung
montage *n* Montage *f*
mood music Stimmungsmusik *f*, Effektmusik *f*
morning programme Vormittagsprogramm *n*
Morse character Morsezeichen *n*; ~ **signal** Morsezeichen *n*; **copying of ~ signals** Aufnehmen von Morsezeichen
mosaic printer (EDP) Matrixdrucker *m*; ~ **screen film** Farbrasterfilm *m*
motif *n* (mus.) Motiv *n*
motion *n* Bewegung *f*, Lauf *m*
motion-picture *n* Film *m*; ~ **camera** Filmkamera *f*
motion unsharpness Bewegungsunschärfe *f*
motor armature Motoranker *m*; ~ **board** Laufwerkplatte *f*; ~ **drive** Motorantrieb *m*; ~ **pool*** Fahrbereitschaft* *f*; ~ **protection switch** Motorschutzschalter *m*
motor-boating *n* (tech.) Blubbern *n*, Tonblubbern *n*, Knattern *n*
mount *v* (paste up) aufziehen *v*; ~ *v* (editing) montieren *v*, zusammenschneiden *v*
mounting *n* Armatur *f*, Halterung *f*; **mobile ~ unit** fahrbarer Untersatz **swivel ~** schwenkbare Halterung
mouse's teeth Mäusezähnchen *n pl*
movable *adj* beweglich *adj*
move *n* (F perf.) Gang *m*
movement *n* Bewegung *f*
movie *n* (US) Film *m*; ~ **camera** Aufnahmekamera *f*; ~ **theater** (US) Filmtheater *n*, Lichtspieltheater *n*, Kino *n*
moviegoer *n* (US) Zuschauer *m*
moving coil Drehspule *f*; ~ **coil** (micr.) Tauchspule *f*; ~ **-coil instrument** Drehspulinstrument *n* ~ **-coil loudspeaker** elektrodynamischer Lautsprecher ~ **pin** Greifer *m*
muddled, to get verhaspeln *v* (sich)
multi *n* (coll.) Multivibrator *m*
multi-band amplifier Mehrbereichverstärker *m*
multi-channel *adj* Mehrkanal- (in Zus.); ~ **aerial** Mehrbereichantenne *f*; ~ **amplifier** Mehrkanalverstärker *m*; ~ **modulation** Mehrfachmodulation *f*; ~ **modulation link** Mehrfachmodulationsweg *m*; ~ **telephone cable**

Vielfachkanalfernsprechleitung *f*
multi-coloured *adj* mehrfarbig *adj*
multi-contact plug Vielfachstecker *m*; ~ **socket** Vielfachgegenstecker *m*; ~ **strip** Steckerleiste *f*, Mehrfachkontaktleiste *f*
multi-flap shutter Jalousieblende *f*
multi-focus lens Multifokusobjektiv *n*
multi-grid tube Mehrgitterröhre *f*; ~ **valve** Mehrgitterröhre *f*
multilateral *n* multilaterale Sendung; ~ *adj* multilateral *adj*; ~ **programme** Gemeinschaftssendung *f*; ~ **sound track** Mehrzackenschrift *f*
multi-layer colour film Mehrschichtenfarbfilm *m*
multi-level *adj* Mehrebenen- (in Zus.)
multi-media system Medienverbundsystem *n*
multimeter *n* Mehrfachmeßgerät *n*, Vielfachmeßgerät *n*, Multimeter *n*
multi-modulation system Mehrfachmodulationssystem *n*
multi-path effect Geisterbild *n*
multiple cable Mehrfachkabel *n*; ~ **echo** Mehrfachecho *n*; ~ **ghosting** Mehrfachkontur *f*; ~ **input transformer** Mischübertrager *m*; ~ **plug** Vielfachstecker *m*; ~ **-pole** *adj* mehrpolig *adj*; ~ **socket** Mehrfachbuchse *f*; ~ **talkback system** Mehrfachgegensprechanlage *f*
multiplex *n* Konferenzschaltung *f*; ~ **broadcast** Ringsendung *f*; ~ **modulation** Mehrfachmodulation *f*; ~ **signal** Multiplexsignal *n*; ~ **speech channel** multiplexe Sprechverbindung; ~ **speech connection** multiplexe Sprechverbindung; ~ **transmission** Konferenzsendung *f*
multiplier *n* Multiplier *m*, Vervielfacher *m*
multi-point connection Mehrfachstecker *m*
multipolar *adj* mehrpolig *adj*
multi-range *adj* Mehrbereich- (in Zus.); ~ **battery-charger** Mehrbereichladegerät *n*
multi-satellite link Satellitenverbindung mit mehreren Satelliten
multi-socket strip Steckerleiste *f*, Mehrfachkontaktleiste *f*
multitester *n* Vielfachmeßgerät *n*
multi-track *adj* Mehrspur- (in Zus.); ~ **recording system** Schallaufnahmeverfahren mit mehreren Tonspuren; ~ **tape recorder** Mehrspurbandmaschine *f*, Mehrfachbandspieler *m*
multivibrator *n* Multivibrator *m*, Kippschaltung *f*; **astable** ~ astabiler Multivibrator; **bistable** ~ bistabiler Multivibrator; **gating** ~ getriggerter Multivibrator; **monostable** ~ monostabiler Multivibrator
multi-way connector Vielfachgegenstecker *m*
mumble *v* nuscheln *v* (fam.)
mush area Frequenzauslöschung *f*
music *n* Musik *f*; ~ **and effects track (M and E track)** internationales Tonband *n* (IT-Band); ~ **archives** *n pl* Musikarchiv *n*; ~ **arranger** Notenbearbeiter *m*; ~ **broadcast** Musiksendung *f*; ~ **carpet** Musikteppich *m*; ~ **cassette** Musikkassette *f*; ~ **copyist** Notenschreiber *m*; ~ **critic** Musikkritiker *m*; ~ **ensemble** Klangkörper *m* ~ **library** Musikbücherei *f*; ~ **library** (scores) Notenarchiv *n*; ~ **line** Modulationsleitung *f*, Modulationssendeleitung *f*; ~ **magazine** Musikmagazin *n*; ~ **mixer** (F) Musiktonmeister *m*; ~ **programme** Musikprogramm *n*;

~ proof-reader Notenkorrektor *m*; **~ publisher** Musikverleger *m*; **~ recording** Musikaufnahme *f*; **~ score** Partitur *f*; **~ studio** Musikstudio *n*, Musikaufnahmeatelier *n*; **~ tape** Musikband *n*; **~ track** Musikband *n*; **contemporary ~** zeitgenössische Musik; **incidental ~** untermalende Musik; **light ~** leichte Musik, Unterhaltungsmusik *f* (U-Musik); **pre-classical ~** Altes Werk*; **serious ~** ernste Musik (E-Musik); **setting to ~** Vertonung *f*; **sheet of ~** Notenblatt *n*; **solemn ~** getragene Musik; **symphonic ~** sinfonische Musik; **to dub with ~** Musik anlegen; **to set to ~** vertonen *v*; **to sync up with ~** Musik unterlegen

musical *n* Musical *n*; **~ arrangement** Musikarrangement *n*; **~ caption** Kennung *f*; **~ director** Kapellmeister *m*; **~ material** Musikmaterial *n*; **~ title** Musiktitel *m*

musician on contract Vertragsmusiker *m*

mute *adj* stumm *adj*

mutual conductance (tube) Steilheit *f*

muzak *n* (coll.) Musikberieselung *f*

mystery play Kriminalspiel *n*

N

nadir *n* Fußpunkt *m*

name part Titelrolle *f*

NAND operation (EDP) NAND-Funktion *f*

narration *n* Sprechertext *m*, Begleittext *m*

narrative *n* Filmtext *m*

narrator *n* Erzähler *m*; **~** *n* (F) Filmsprecher *m*, Sprecher *m*

narrow band Schmalband *n*; **~ gauge** Schmalfilmformat *n*

narrow-gauge film Schmalfilm *m*; **~ spool** Schmalfilmspule *f*

narrow tape Schmalband *n*

national news (US) Berichterstattung Inland; **~ programme** Gemeinschaftsprogramm *n*

natural frequency (acoust.) Eigenfrequenz *f*; **~ interior** reales Dekor; **~ oscillation** Eigenschwingung (LC) *f*; **~ resonance** Eigenresonanz *f*

neck strap Tragriemen *m*

necklace microphone Umhängemikrofon *n*

needle pulse Nadelimpuls *m*; **~ time** vertraglich festgelegte Sendezeit für Schallplatten

neg cutter *n* (coll.) Filmkleber *m*, Kleber *m*

negation *n* (EDP) Inversion *f*

negative *n* Negativ *n*, Negativmaterial *n*; **to cut a ~** Negativ abziehen

negative colour film Negativfarbfilm *m*; **~ current feedback** Stromgegenkopplung *f*; **~ -cutter** *n* Filmkleber *m*, Kleber *m*, Negativabzieher *m*, Negativcutter *m*; **~ cutting** Negativschnitt *m*, Nachschneiden *n*; **~ -cutting bench** Negativabziehtisch *m*, Negativsynchronabziehtisch *m*; **~ -cutting room** Negativabziehraum *m*; **~ developing** Negativentwicklung *f*; **~ development** Negativentwicklung *f*; **~ dirt** Negativstaub *m*; **~ distortion** Kissenverzerrung *f*; **~ feedback** Gegenkopplung *f*; **~ film** Negativfilm *m*; **~ image** Negativbild *n*; **~ lens** Zerstreuungslinse *f*; **~ light box**

Negativlichtkasten *m*; **~ material** Negativmaterial *n*; **~ picture** Negativbild *n*; **~ -positive process** Negativ-Positiv-Verfahren *n*; **~ report** Negativbericht *m*, Bildnegativbericht *m*; **~ scratch** Negativschramme *f*, Primärschramme *f*; **~ sparkle** Negativschmutz *m*; **~ stock** eingelagertes Negativ, Negativfilm *m*, Negativmaterial *n*; **~ synchroniser** Negativabziehtisch *m*, Negativsynchronabziehtisch *m*; **~ temperature coefficient resistor (NTC resistor)** NTC-Widerstand *m*, Warmleiter *m*, Heißleiter *m*

nemo *n* (US) Außenaufnahme *f*, Außenübertragung (AÜ)

neon tester Spannungsprüfer *m*

net *n* (lighting) Softscheibe *f*; **~ cost** Selbstkosten *plt*

network *n* Netz *n*, Leitungsnetz *n*, Netzwerk *n*, vermaschtes Netz; **~ analog** (EDP) Netzmodell *n*; **~ director** Ablaufregisseur *m*; **~ hook-up** Netzzusammenschaltung *f*; **~ planning** Netzplanung *f*; **~ programme** nationales Programm; **~ switching** Netzschaltung *f*; **interconnected ~** vermaschtes Leitungsnetz

neutral *n* Nullerde *f*; **~ density filter** Neutralgraufilter *m*, Dichtefilter *m*; **~ density fluctuation** Dichteschwankungen *f pl*; **~ filter** Dichtefilter *m*; **~ wedge** Graukeil *m*, Grauskala *f*

neutralisation *n* Neutralisation *f*

new production Neuproduktion *f*; **~ talent** Nachwuchs *m*; **~ tape** Frischband *n*

news *n pl* Nachrichten *f pl*; **~ agency** Nachrichtenagentur *f*; **~ analysis** Kommentar *m*; **~ analyst** Kommentator *m*; **~ and current affairs** *n pl* Aktuelles *n*; **~ and current affairs*** *n pl* Politik und Zeitgeschehen*, Nachrichtenabteilung *f*; **~ and current affairs programme** Informationsprogramm *n*; **~ blackout** *n* Nachrichtensperre *f*; **~ broadcast** Nachrichtensendung *f*, Informationssendung *f*; **~ broadcasting** (R,TV) Nachrichtengebung *f*; **~ bulletin** Nachrichtensendung *f*; **~ bulletin** (R) Hörfunknachrichten *f pl*; **~ coverage** aktuelle Berichte, Reportage *f*; **~ desk** Redaktion *f*, Redaktionsraum *m*; **~ director** (US) Chefredakteur *m*; **~ exchange** Nachrichtenaustausch *m*; **~ flash** Kurznachricht *f*, Blitzmeldung *f*; **~ headlines** Kurznachrichten *f pl*; **~ intake** Meldungsanfall *m*; **~ item** Meldung *f*, Nachricht *f*, Nachrichtenbeitrag *m*; **~ material** Nachrichtenmaterial *n*, Information *f*; **~ offer** Nachrichtenangebot *n*; **~ peg** Aufhänger *m*; **~ picture** Pressefoto *n*; **~ programme** Nachrichtensendung *f*; **~ prospects** *n pl* Themenliste *f*; **~ release** Nachrichtengebung *f*; **~ report** Meldung *f*, Reportage *f*; **~ research** Recherche *f*; **~ round-up** Vermischtes *n*; **~ service** Nachrichtendienst *m*; **~ show** (US) Nachrichtensendung *f*, News-Show *f*; **~ source** Nachrichtenquelle *f*; **~ story** Meldung *f*; **~ studio** Nachrichtenstudio *n*; **~ summary** Kurznachrichten *f pl*; **~ transmission** *f* Nachrichtenübermittlung *f*, Nachrichtenübertragung *f*, Nachrichtensendung *f*; **in the ~** aktuell *adj*; **inspired ~ item** Zweckmeldung *f*

newscast *n* Nachrichten *f pl*, Nachrichtensendung *f*
newscaster *n* Nachrichtensprecher *m*, Sprecher *m*
newsfilm *n* aktueller Filmbericht, Nachrichtenfilm *m*, Filmnachrichten *f pl*
newsletter *n* Informationsdienst *m*, Pressedienst *m*
newsman *n* (US) Berichterstatter *m*, Journalist *m*, Reporter *m*
newspaper *n* Zeitung *f*
newspapermen *n pl* (US) Zeitungsleute *plt*
newsreader *n* Nachrichtensprecher *m*, Sprecher *m*; **~ in vision** Nachrichtensprecher im On
newsreel *n* Reportagefilm *m*; ~ *n* (cinema) Wochenschau *f*, Filmnachrichten *f pl*
newsroom *n* Nachrichtenredaktion *f*, Redaktion *f*, Redaktionsraum *m*
newswriter *n* (US) Nachrichtenredakteur *m*
NG *n* (coll.) Nichtkopierer (NK) *m*, schlechte Aufnahme; ~ *adj* (coll.) (take) wertlos *adj*; **~ take** (coll.) Nichtkopierer (NK) *m*, schlechte Aufnahme
nickel-iron-alkaline accumulator Stahlakkumulator *m*
Ni-Fe accumulator Stahlakkumulator *m*
nigger *n* Lichtblende *f*, Blende *f*, Neger *m* (fam.)
night programme Nachtprogramm *n*; **~ range** (transmitter) Nachtreichweite *f*; **~ shot** Nachtaufnahme *f*
nitrate film Nitrofilm *m*
nitrocellulose film Nitrofilm *m*; **~ stock** Zellhornfilm *m*
no-current relay Stromausfallrelais *n*
noise *n* Geräusch *n*, Rauschen *n*, Rauschton *m*; **~ blanking** Störaustastung *f*; **~ -cancelling microphone** Nahbesprechungsmikrofon *n*; **~ current** Rauschstrom *m*; **~ factor** Rauschzahl *f*; **~ figure** Rauschmaß *n*, Rauschzahl *f*; **~ interference** Störgeräusch *n*; **~ level** Geräuschpegel *m*, Rauschpegel *m*, Störpegel *m*; **~ limiter** Rauschbegrenzer *m*, Störbegrenzer *m*; **~ limiting** Rauschbegrenzung *f*, Störbegrenzung *f*; **~ meter** Geräuschspannungsmesser *m*, Störspannungsmesser *m*; **~ peaks** Rauschspitzen *f pl*; **~ potential** Rauschspannung *f*; **~ resistance** Rauschwiderstand *m*; **~ source** Störquelle *f*; **~ suppression** Geräuschunterdrückung *f*, Entstörung *f*; **~ suppressor** Geräuschabschwächer *m*; **~ track** Rauschspur *f*; **~ value** Geräuschwert *m*; **~ voltage** Geräuschspannung *f*, Rauschspannung *f*, Störspannung *f*, Fremdspannung *f*; **continuous ~** kontinuierliches Rauschen; **impulsive ~** impulsförmiges Rauschen; **periodic ~** periodisches Rauschen; **pink ~** farbiges Rauschen; **static ~** statisches Rauschen; **to be degraded by high ~ level** verrauschen *v*; **weighted ~ voltage** bewertete Geräuschspannung; **white ~** Weißton *m*, weißes Rauschen
noiseless *adj* geräuschlos *adj*
noisy *adj* verrauscht *adj*; **~ join** Tonblitz *m*; **to be ~** rauschen *v*
no-load current Leerlaufstrom *m*; **~ operation** Leerlauf *m*; **~ voltage** Leerlaufspannung *f*
nominal frequency Nennfrequenz *f*, Sollfrequenz *f*, Betriebsfrequenz *f* **~ power** Nennleistung *f*; **~ speed** Sollgeschwindigkeit *f*; **~ value** Sollwert *m*; **~ voltage** Nennspannung *f*
non-conjunction *n* (EDP) NAND-

Funktion *f*
non-directional aerial ungerichtete Antenne
non-flam film Sicherheitsfilm *m*
non-fused earth Schutzerde *f*
non-halating *adj* lichthoffrei *adj*
non-linear *adj* unlinear *adj*
non-linearity *n* Unlinearität *f*
non-original material Fremdfilmmaterial *n*
non-profit-making organisation gemeinnützige Organisation
non-reactive resistance Verlustwiderstand *m*
non-reverberant *adj* schalltot *adj*
non-stop background music Musikberieselung *f*
non-synchronous *adj* asynchron *adj*
non-transparent *adj* undurchsichtig *adj*
NOR-function *n* (EDP) NOR-Funktion *f*
norm *n* Norm *f*
normal colour sight Farbnormalsichtigkeit *f*
NOT operation (EDP) Inversion *f*
notch *n* Nut *f*; **~ filter** Lochfilter *m*, Fallenfilter *m*
notch-filter circuit Fallenkreis *m*
note *n* Ton *m*
notice *n* (press) Kritik *f*; **at long ~** langfristig *adj*
no-volt release relay Spannungsausfallrelais *n*
NTC resistor Heißleiter *m*
null drift (EDP) Nullpunktverschiebung *f*
number of frames Bildzahl *f*; **~ of frames per second** Bildfolgefrequenz *f*; **~ of lines** Zeilenzahl *f*; **~ of switching operations in given period** Schalthäufigkeit *f*
nut, annular Ringmutter *f*
nuvistor *n* Nuvistor *m*
Nyquist receiver Nyquistempfänger *m*

O

OB commentary Außenreportage *f*; **~ line** Übertragungsleitung *f*; **~ location** Außenübertragungsort *m*; **~ point** Außenübertragungsort *m*, Übertragungsort *m*; **~ production** Außenproduktion *f*; **~ recording** Außenaufzeichnung *f*, Außenaufnahme *f*; **~ scanner** (coll.) Bildaufnahmewagen *m*; **~ unit** Aufnahmegruppe *f*; **~ van** Übertragungswagen *m*, Ü-Wagen *m*; **~ vehicle** Übertragungswagen *m*, Ü-Wagen *m*
obits *n pl* (coll.) Nekrolog *m*, Nachrufe *m pl*, Heldenfriedhof *m* (fam.), Leichenmappe *f* (fam.)
obituaries *n pl* Nekrolog *m*, Nachrufe *m pl*, Heldenfriedhof *m* (fam.), Leichenmappe *f* (fam.)
object time (EDP) Programmlaufzeit *f*
objective *n* Linse *f*, Objektiv *n*; **~ lens** Objektiv *n*, Abbildungslinse *f*; **~ mount** Objektivfassung *f*
oblique magnetisation Schrägmagnetisierung *f*
ocular *n* Okular *n*
odd-order harmonic distortion ungradzahliger Klirrfaktor
off *n* Off *n*
off (switch) aus
off-centre, to ~ the picture aus der Bildmitte setzen; **to compose ~** aus der Bildmitte setzen
offcuts *n pl* (F) Schnittmaterial *n*
offer *v* (elec.) aufschalten *v*
office *n* Dienststelle *f*; **~ head** Dienststellenleiter *m*; **~ printing** Vervielfältigung *f*
office-printing machine Vervielfältiger *m*
official journey Dienstreise *f*; **~ statement** Kommuniqué *n*;

~ **telephone call** Dienstgespräch *n*
off-line mode (EDP) Off-Line-Betrieb *m*; ~ **operation** (EDP) Off-Line-Betrieb *m*
off-prompt side bühnenrechts *adv*
off-screen narration Off-Kommentar *m*; ~ **narration script** Off-Text *m*; ~ **narrator** Off-Sprecher *m*; ~ **voice (OSV)** Off-Stimme *f*; **to speak** ~ aus dem Off sprechen
offset *n* Offset *n*; ~ **operation** Offsetbetrieb *m*; ~ **zero** Nullpunktunterdrückung *f*
off-tube commentary Kommentar am Monitor
ohmic resistance Gleichstromwiderstand *m*, Verlustwiderstand *m*, Wirkwiderstand *m*
oil bath Ölbad *n*
oil-filled friction head Friktionsschwenkkopf *m*; ~ **transformer** Öltransformator *m*
old *adj* (coll.) (news) überholt *adj*
omnibus cue circuit Kommando-Ringnetz *n*
omnidirectional aerial Rundempfangsantenne *f*, Rundstrahlantenne *f*, ungerichtete Antenne; ~ **microphone** richtungsunempfindliches Mikrofon, ungerichtetes Mikrofon, Kugelmikrofon *n*, Kugel *f* (fam.); ~ **radiation** Rundstrahlung *f*, Rundumstrahlung *f*
on *n* On *n*; ~ *adv* ein *adv*; **to be ~ -camera** im On sprechen; **you're ~**! Auftritt!
one-light print Einlichtkopie *f*; ~ **printing** Einlichtkopierung *f*
one-man operation Ein-Mann-Bedienung *f*
one-shot multivibrator (EDP) monostabiles Flip-Flop, monostabile Kippschaltung
one-way speech channel gerichtete Sprechverbindung
on-line mode (EDP) On-Line-Betrieb *m*; ~ **operation** (EDP) On-Line-Betrieb *m*
opaque *adj* lichtundurchlässig *adj*, undurchsichtig *adj*
open *v* aufklappen *v*; ~ *v* (F) anlaufen *v*; ~ **out** *v* (zoom) aufziehen *v* (Zoom); ~ **up** *v* (lens) Blende öffnen; ~ **with** *v* (journ.) anfangen *v* (mit), aufmachen *v* (mit); **to ~ diaphragm** aufblenden *v*
open-air *adj* Freilicht- (in Zus.); ~ **cinema** Freilichtkino *n*; ~ **performance** Freilichtvorführung *f*
open-circuit Leerlauf *m*; ~ **-circuit voltage** Leerlaufspannung *f*
opening announcement Ansage *f*; ~ **captions** *n pl* Filmvorspann *m*; ~ **credits** *n pl* Filmvorspann *m*, Namensvorspann *m*, Titelvorspann *m*, Vorspann *m*, Vorspanntitel *m*; ~ **of aperture** Aufblende *f*, Aufblendung *f*; ~ **of diaphragm** Aufblende *f*, Aufblendung *f*; ~ **titles** *n pl* Anfangstitel *m*, Filmvorspann *m*, Titelvorspann *m*, Vorspann *m*, Vorspanntitel *m*; ~ **titles** *n pl* (TV news) Nachrichtenindikativ *n*
open-wire line Freileitung *f*, Luftleitung *f*
opera *n* Oper *f*; **filmed ~** Opernfilm *m*
operand *n* (EDP) Operand *m*
operate *v* betätigen *v*, schalten *v*, betreiben *v*; **to ~ by remote control** fernbedienen *v*, fernsteuern *v*
operating expenses Betriebskosten *plt*; ~ **frequency** Betriebsfrequenz *f*; ~ **instruction** Bedienungsanleitung *f*, Bedienungsvorschrift *f*, Betriebsanleitung *f*,

Betriebsanweisung *f*; ~ **lever** Steuerhebel *m*; ~ **point** Arbeitspunkt *m*; ~ **procedure** Betriebsabwicklung *f*; ~ **system (OS)** (EDP) Betriebssystem (BS) *n*; ~ **time** Betriebszeit *f*; ~ **time** (reaction) Ansprechzeit *f*; ~ **voltage** Betriebsspannung *f*

operation *n* Betrieb *m*, Bedienung *f*, Abwicklung *f*, Lauf *m*; ~ *n* (EDP) Programmablauf *m*; ~ **by time switch** Betrieb mit Zeitschaltuhr; ~ **by timing switch** Betrieb mit Schaltuhr; ~ **checkout** (EDP) Funktionsprüfung *f*; ~ **-completed indication** Rückmeldung *f*; ~ **cycle** (EDP) Arbeitszyklus *m*; ~ **part** (EDP) Operationsteil *m*; ~ **speed** Laufgeschwindigkeit *f*; **external** ~ Betrieb *m* (fremd); **in** ~ in Betrieb; **independent** ~ autarker Betrieb; **internal** ~ Betrieb *m* (eigen); **local** ~ örtliche Bedienung; **stable** ~ stabiler Betrieb; **to put into** ~ in Betrieb nehmen, in Betrieb setzen

operational earth Betriebserde *f*; ~ **key** Auslösetaste *f*; ~ **reliability** Betriebssicherheit *f*; ~ **supervision** Betriebsüberwachung *f*

operations area Bedienungsraum *m* ~ **centre** Kommandozentrale *f*; ~ **engineer** Betriebsingenieur *m*; ~ **room** Betriebsraum *m*

operator *n* Techniker *m*; ~ *n* (proj.) Vorführer *m*; ~ *n* (cam.) Kameramann *m*; ~ *n* (tel.) Telefonist *m*; ~ **console typewriter** (EDP) Bedienungsblattschreiber *m*; ~ **part** (EDP) Operationsteil *m*

operator's console (EDP) Bedienungsfeld *n*, Konsole *f*; ~ **position** Bedienungsplatz *m*

operetta *n* Operette *f*

opposite phase Gegenphase *f*

opt in *v* anschließen *v* (sich), zuschalten *v* (sich); ~ **out** *v* ausblenden *v* (sich)

optical *n* (animation) optischer Trick *m*, Trickblende *f*, Blende *f*; ~ *adj* optisch *adj*; ~ **bench** optische Bank; ~ **character reader** (EDP) Klarschriftleser *m*; ~ **effects printer** Trickkopiermaschine *f*; ~ **mark reader** (EDP) Markierungsleser *m*; ~ **printer** Truca *f*; ~ **printing** optisches Kopieren; ~ **scratch** Schramme *f*; ~ **sound** Lichtton *m*; ~ **-sound head** Lichttonabtaster *m*; ~ **-sound lamp** Lichttonlampe *f*; ~ **-sound negative** Lichttonnegativ *n* ~ **-sound print** Lichttonkopie *f*; ~ **-sound recorder** Lichttonkamera *f*; ~ **-sound track** Lichttonspur *f*; ~ **-sound transfer** Lichttonumspielung *f*; ~ **system** Optik *f*; ~ **system of projector** Beleuchtungsoptik *f*; ~ **transfer** Überspielung von Magnet- auf Lichtton; ~ **transmission density** Schwärzung *f*; ~ **viewfinder** Direktsucher *m*; ~ **wedge** (FP) Keil *m*; **coated** ~ **system** vergütete Optik; **combined** ~ **sound (Comopt)** kombinierter Lichtton (COMOPT); **separate** ~ **sound (Sepopt)** separater Lichtton (SEPOPT)

optics *n* Optik *f*

optimisation *n* Optimierung *f*

optimise *v* optimieren *v*

optimum colour Optimalfarbe *f*

opting-out *n* Ausblenden *n*, Ausblendung *f*, Programmabschaltung *f*

opt-out *n* Ausblenden *n*, Ausblendung *f*

oral report Referat *n*

oratorio *n* Oratorium *n*

orbit *n* Satellitenbahn *f*, Umlaufbahn *f*; **parking** ~ Wartebahn *f*

orchestra *n* Orchester *n*,

Klangkörper *m*; ~ **attendant** Orchesterwart *m*
orchestral management office Orchesterbüro *n*; ~ **material** Musikmaterial *n*; ~ **musician** Orchestermusiker *m*; ~ **supervisor** Orchesterinspektor *m*
OR-circuit *n* (EDP) ODER-Schaltung *f*
order *v* bestellen *v*; ~ *n* Auftrag *f*, Weisung *f*; **out of ~ (o.o.o.)** gestört *adj*
organ *n* Presseorgan *n*; ~ **music** Orgelmusik *f*
organisation *n* Anstalt *f*, Organisation *f*; ~ **chart** Organisationsplan *m*; ~ **in charge** federführende Anstalt; **non-profit-making ~** gemeinnützige Organisation
organiser *n* (prod.) Disponent *m*
OR-gate *n* (EDP) ODER-Schaltung *f*
origin *n* Quelle *f*, Ursprungspunkt *m*
original *n* (sound tape) Aufnahmetonband *n*; ~ **broadcast** Originalsendung *f*; ~ **commentary** Originalbeitrag *m*; ~ **location** realer Außendekor; ~ **music** Originalmusik *f*; ~ **negative** Originalnegativ *n*; ~ **picture negative** Originalbildnegativ *n*; ~ **radio drama** Originalhörspiel *n*; ~ **radio play** Originalhörspiel *n*; ~ **recording** Originalaufzeichnung *f*; ~ **script** Originaltext *m*; ~ **sound** Originalton (O-Ton) *m*; ~ **sound negative** Originaltonnegativ *n*; ~ **tape** Originalband *n*; ~ **television drama** Originalfernsehspiel *n*; ~ **television play** Originalfernsehspiel *n*; ~ **version** Originalfassung *f*; ~ **work** Originalwerk *n*
originating station abspielende Anstalt, federführende Anstalt; ~ **station** (tech.) Ursprungsdienst *m*
originator *n* Urheber *m*
orthicon *n* Orthikon *n*, Bildaufnahmeröhre *f*
orthochromatic *adj* orthochromatisch *adj*
orthophonic *adj* klanggetreu *adj*
oscillate *v* schwingen *v*
oscillating circuit Schwingkreis *m*
oscillation *n* Schwingung *f*, Schwankung *f*; ~ **frequency** Schwingungszahl *f*; **free ~** freilaufende Schwingung; **partial ~** Partialschwingung *f*
oscillator *n* Oszillator *m*; ~ **crystal** Steuerquarz *m*; **flywheel ~** angestoßener Oszillator; **locked ~** synchronisierter Oszillator; **synchronised ~** synchronisierter Oszillator; **triggered ~** angestoßener Oszillator
oscillogram *n* Oszillogramm *n*
oscillograph *n* Oszillograf *m*
oscilloscope *n* Oszillograf *m*; ~ **screen** Betrachtungsschirm *m*
out of date (news) überholt *adj*; ~ **of focus** unscharf *adj*; ~ **of order (o.o.o.)** gestört *adj*; ~ **of vision (OOV)** im Off
outage *n* (EDP) Ausfall *m*
outdoor *adj* Freilicht- (in Zus.), Außen- (in Zus.); ~ **aerial** Außenantenne *f*; ~ **location** realer Außendekor; ~ **shooting** Außenaufnahme *f*; ~ **shot** Außenaufnahme *f*
outer field Umfeld *n*
outgoing channel (tech.) Sendeleitung *f*; ~ **circuit** Ausgangsleitung *f*, Sendeleitung *f* ~ **modulation** Studioausgangsmodulation *f*; ~ **picture** Endbild *n*, Sendebild *n*; ~ **signal** Studioausgangsbild *n*; ~ **sound** Studioausgangston *m*
outlet *n* Ausgang *m*; ~ *n* (prog.) Termin *m*; ~ **box** Anschluß-

kasten *m*
outline *n* Kontur *f*, Umriß *m*; ~ *n* (dispatch) Aufbau *m*; ~ **picture** Umrißbild *n*
out-of-frame area Umfeldbild *n*
out-of-sync *adj* asynchron *adj*
out-of-vision commentary Off-Kommentar *m*
output *n* (elec.) Ausgang *m*; ~ *n* (EDP) Ausgabe *f*; ~ **amplifier** Ausgangsverstärker *m*, Endverstärker *m*; ~ **amplifier stage** Endverstärkerstufe *f*; ~ **connection** Ausgangsleitung *f*; ~ **coupling** Auskopplung *f*; ~ **frequency** Sendefrequenz *f*; ~ **impedance** Ausgangsimpedanz *f* ~ **level** Ausgangspegel *m*; ~ **matching** Ausgangsanpassung *f*; ~ **monitor** Ausgangsmonitor *m*; ~ **monitoring** Endabhörkontrolle *f* ~ **picture** Ausgangsbild *n*; ~ **power** Ausgangsleistung *f*; ~ **pulse** Ausgangsimpuls *m*; ~ **resistance** Ausgangswiderstand *m*; ~ **selector** Ausgangskreuzschiene *f*; ~ **signal** Ausgangssignal *n*; ~ **stage** Endstufe *f*; ~ **switching matrix** Ausgangskreuzschiene *f*; ~ **transformer** Ausgangstransformator *m*, Ausgangsübertrager *m*
outside *adj* Außen- (in Zus.); ~ **broadcast (OB)** Außenaufnahme *f*, Außenübertragung *f* (AÜ), Übertragung *f*; ~ **broadcast operations** *n pl* Außenbetriebstechnik *f*, Übertragungsdienst *m* (Ü-Dienst); ~ **broadcasting** Übertragungstechnik *f*; ~ **broadcasts* (OB)** Außenbetriebstechnik* *f*, Außenübertragungsdienst* *m*, Übertragungstechnik* *f*; **to be on an ~ job** (coll.) Außendienst haben
out-takes *n pl* Schnittreste *m pl*
out time Endzeit *f*
oven control Heizautomatik *f*
over all ... über alles ...
overall ambient light Gesamtaufhellung *f*; ~ **lighting** Gesamtaufhellung *f*
overcompensate *v* überkompensieren *v*
overcompensation *n* Überkompensation *f*, Überkompensierung *f*
overcurrent *n* Überstrom *m*; ~ **protection** Überstromsicherung *f*; ~ **relay** Überstromrelais *n*
overdamp *v* unterschwingen *v*
overdeveloped *adj* überentwickelt *adj*
overdeveloping *n* Überentwicklung *f*
overdevelopment *n* Überentwicklung *f*
overdrive *v* übersteuern *v*
overdriving *n* Übersteuerung *f*
overexpose *v* überbelichten *v*
overexposure *n* Überbelichtung *f*
overhaul *v* (tech.) überholen *v*
overhauling *n* (tech.) Überholung *f*
overhead crane Laufkran *m*; ~ **line** Luftleitung *f*, Oberleitung *f*; ~ **line** (tel.) Telefonfreileitung *f*; ~ **power line** Starkstromfreileitung *f*
overlap *v* überlappen *v*, überschneiden *v*, mischen *v*; ~ *n* Überlappung *f*
overlapping *n* Überlappung *f*; ~ **area** Überlappungsbereich *m*; ~ **frequency bands** *n pl* Frequenzbandverschachtelung *f*; ~ **region** Überlappungsbereich *m*
overlay *v* (sound) unterschneiden *v*; ~ *v* (pict.) überblenden *v*; ~ *n* Überblendung *f*, Überblenden *n*, Unterschnitt *m*, Schablonentrick *m*; ~ *n* (EDP) Überlagerung *f*; ~ **insertion** Schabloneneinblendung *f*
overlength *n* Überlänge *f*
overload *v* übersteuern *v*; ~ **voltage**

relay Überspannungsrelais *n*
overloading *n* Übersteuerung *f*
overmodulate *v* übermodulieren *v*, übersteuern *v*
overmodulation *n* Übermodulierung *f*, Übersteuerung *f*; **~ of white level** Weißwertübersteuerung *f*
overnight expenses Übernachtungskosten *plt*; **~ programme operations** Nachtbetrieb *m*
overprint *v* einkopieren *v*
overprinting *n* Einkopierung *f*
overrun *v* Sendezeit überschreiten, Sendezeit überziehen, überziehen *v*; **~** *n* Zeitüberschreitung *f*, Überziehen *n*
overscript *v* Text überziehen
overscripted *adj* zuwenig Luft
overseam *v* (video) überschreiben *v*
overseas and foreign relations* (BBC) Auslandsreferat *n*. Auslandsabteilung *f*; **~ office** (BBC) Auslandsstudio *n*; **~ representative** (BBC) Auslandsstudioleiter *m*
overshoot *v* überschwingen *v*; **~** *n* Überschwingen *n*, Überschwingung *f*, Überschwinger *m*; **~ amplitude** Überschwingamplitude *f*; **~ distortion** Überstrahlung *f*
overthrow distortion Überstrahlung *f*
overtime *n* Überstunden *f pl*
overtone *n* Oberton *m*, Oberschwingung *f*
overvoltage *n* Überspannung *f*; **~ lamp** Überspannungslampe *f*; **~ protection** Überspannungsschutz *m*; **~ relay** Überspannungsrelais *n*
overwind *v* (mech.) überdrehen *v*
oxide coating Oxydschicht *f*
oxide-shedding *n* Schichtablösung *f*

P

PA system Beschallungsanlage *f*
Pacco switch Paccoschalter *m*
pack *n* Rucksack *m* (fam.)
packing case Transportkoffer *m*
pack-shot lens Makrokilar *m*
pad *n* (elec.) nachgebildete Leitung, Verlängerungskabel *n*; **to ~ out a story** Zeilen schinden (fam.)
padding *n* Padding *n*
paging device Funkrufdienst *m*
paint *n* Farbe *f*; **~ box** (coll.) Farbkorrektureinrichtung *f*; **~ spraying** Spritzarbeit *f*
painter *n* Maler *m*
pairing *n* Paarigkeit *f*
PAL colour subcarrier PAL-Farbträger *m*; **~ -ident pulse** Koder-Kennimpuls *m*; **~ record** unverkoppeltes PAL; **~ transmit** verkoppeltes PAL; **~ venetian-blind effect** PAL-Jalousieeffekte *m pl*; **delay-line ~** Standard PAL; **recording ~** unverkoppeltes PAL; **simple ~** Simple PAL; **transmission ~** verkoppeltes PAL
pale out *v* entsättigen *v*
paling-out *n* Entsättigung *f*
pan *v* schwenken *v*; **~** *n* Schwenk *m*; **~ -and-tilt arm** Schwenkarm *m*; **~ -and-tilt head** Schwenk- und Neigekopf *m*; **~ bar** Kameraarm *m*; **~ control** Panoramaregelung *f*; **~ filter** Panglas *n*, Panscheibe *f*; **~ head** Kameraschwenkkopf *m*, Schwenkkopf *m*; **~ head with counterbalance weights** Schwenkkopf mit Schwerpunktausgleich; **~ head with gyroscopic drive** Kameraschwenkkopf mit Kreiselantrieb, Schwenkkopf mit Kreiselantrieb; **~ head with**

panning handle Schwenkkopf mit Schwenkarm; ~ **head with vernier control** Schwenkkopf mit Feinantrieb; ~ **-round** *n* Rundschwenk *m*; ~ **shot** Kameraschwenk *m*, Panoramaschwenk *m*
panchromatic *adj* panchromatisch *adj*
panel *n* (set) Wand *f*, Platte *f*; ~ *n* (console) Regiepult *n*, Regietisch *m*; ~ *n* (panellists) Forum *n*; ~ **discussion** Podiumsdiskussion *f*, Podiumsgespräch *n*; **reflecting ~** reflektierende Wand
panellist *n* Diskussionsteilnehmer *m*
panning *n* Schwenk *m*; ~ **handle** Schwenkarm *m*; ~ **head** Kameraschwenkkopf *m*, Schwenkkopf *m*, Panoramakopf *m*; ~ **shot** Schwenk *m*, Panoramaschwenk *m*
panoramic effect Panoramaeffekt *m*; ~ **head** Panoramakopf *m*; ~ **movement** Panoramaschwenk *m*; ~ **receiver** Panoramaempfänger *m*; ~ **screen** Panoramabreitwand *f*
pantograph *n* Scherenarm *m*
paper *n* Zeitung *f*; ~ **print** Bildabzug *m*, Papierabzug *m*; ~ **tape** (EDP) Lochstreifen *m*; ~ **tape code** (EDP) Lochstreifencode *m*; ~ **tape device** (EDP) Lochstreifengerät *n*; ~ **tape punch** (EDP) Lochstreifenlocher *m*; ~ **tape reader** (EDP) Lochstreifenleser *m*; ~ **tape unit** (EDP) Lochstreifengerät *n*; ~ **up** *v* abklammern *v*
papered, to print ~ section Klammerteile fahren, Klammerteile kopieren
paper-to-paper (FP) Klammerteil *n*; **to print ~** Klammerteile fahren, Klammerteile kopieren
parabolic aerial Antennenspiegel *m* ~ **mirror** Parabolspiegel *m*; ~ **radiator** Parabolstrahler *m*; ~ **reflector** Parabolspiegel *m*; ~ **signal** Parabolsignal *n*
paraboloid *n* Parabolstrahler *m*
parallax *n* Parallaxe *f*; ~ **compensation** Parallaxenausgleich *m*; ~ **correction** Parallaxenausgleich *m*; ~ **-free** *adj* parallaxenfrei *adj*; ~ **viewfinder** Parallaxensucher *m*; **free from ~** parallaxenfrei *adj*
parallel adder (EDP) Parallel-Addierwerk *n*; ~ **circuit** Parallelkreis *m*, Nebenschlußleitung *f*; ~ **connection** Parallelschaltung *f*; ~ **element** Querglied *n*; ~ **line** Nebenschlußleitung *f*; ~ **sound system** Paralleltonverfahren *n*
parallel-resonant circuit Parallelschwingkreis *m*
parallel-serial converter (EDP) Parallel-Serien-Umsetzer *m*
parameter *n* Parameter *m*
parapet *n* Brüstung *f*
parasitic element Sekundärstrahler *m*
parent station Muttersender *m*
parity bit (EDP) Paritybit *n*; ~ **check** (EDP) Paritätsprüfung *f*, Parity-Prüfung *f*; ~ **error** (EDP) Paritätsfehler *m*; **vertical ~ check** (EDP) Quer-Paritykontrolle *f*
parking orbit Wartebahn *f*
parliamentary desk Politik Inland*; ~ **unit*** Politik Inland*
part *n* (perf.) Rolle *f*; **bit ~** kleine Rolle; **small ~** kleine Rolle
partial coincident picture kongruentes Teilbild; ~ **exposure** Teilbelichtung *f*; ~ **image** Teilbild *n*; ~ **oscillation** Partialschwingung *f*
participant *n* Teilnehmer *m*, Gesprächspartner *m*, Diskussionsteilnehmer *m*
partitioning *n* Unterteilung *f*

partner *n* Partner *m*
partnership *n* Partnerschaft *f*; **~ contract** Teilhabervertrag *m*
pass-band *n* Durchlässigkeitsbereich *m*; **~ attenuation** Grunddämpfung *f*
paste (on) *v* aufziehen *v*
pastel *n* Pastellfarbe *f*; **~ shade** Pastellton *m*; **~ tone** Pastellton *m*
patching panel Steckfeld *n*
paternoster *n* Schleifenfahrstuhl *m*
pattern *n* Modell *n*
pattern interference (pict.) Störung *f*; **~ -maker** *n* Modellschreiner *m*; **~ tube** Sichtröhre *f*
patterning *n* Farbträgermoiré *n*
pause *n* (sound tape) Kurzstopp *m*
pay *n* Lohn *m*; **~ out** *v* (cable) abwickeln *v*; **~ scale** Vergütungsordnung *f*; **~ television** Münzfernsehen *n*
payment of licence fee Gebührenentrichtung *f*
pay-off fee Ausfallgage *f*
PBX operator Telefonist *m*
peak *n* Spitze *f*; **~** *n* Scheitel *m*; **~ current** Spitzenstrom *m*, Stromspitze *f*; **~ deviation** Spitzenhub *m*; **~ factor** Scheitelfaktor *m*; **~ indicator** Spitzenwertmesser *m*, Spitzenmesser *m*; **~ level** Scheitelpegel *m*, Spitzenwert *m*; **~ level clamping** Spitzenpegelfesthaltung *f*; **~ listening time** Hauptsendezeit *f*; **~ load** Höchstbeanspruchung *f*; **~ meter** Spitzenwertmesser *m*, Spitzenmesser *m*; **~ power** Spitzenleistung *f*; **~ programme meter (PPM)** Spitzenaussteuerungsmesser *m*; **~ rectification** Spitzengleichrichtung *f*; **~ rectifier** Spitzengleichrichter *m*; **~ signal level** Maximalsignalpegel *m*; **~ value** Spitzenwert *m*, Scheitelwert *m*; **~ viewing time** Hauptsendezeit *f*; **~ voltage** Spitzenspannung *f*, Scheitelspannung *f*; **~ voltmeter** Spitzenspannungsmesser *m*; **~ white** Weißspitze *f*; **~ white level** Scheitelpegel für Weiß; **~ white signal** Weißspitzensignal *n*
peak-to-peak voltage Spitze-Spitze-Spannung *f*
pearl screen Perlwand *f*
pedestal *n* Sockel *m*; **~** *n* (cam.) Kamerafahrgestell *n*; **~** *n* (video) Schwarzabhebung *f*, Schwarzabsetzung *f*
peeling-off *n* Schichtablösung *f*
peg *n* (news) Aufhänger *m*
Peirce-function *n* (EDP) NOR-Funktion *f*
pencil microphone Füllhaltermikrofon *n*
pendulum motion Pendelbewegung *f*; **~ saw** Pendelsäge *f*
penumbra *n* Halbschatten *m*
pep up *v* aufmöbeln *v*
percentage tilt prozentuale Dachschräge
perfect pitch absolutes Gehör
perforate *v* (EDP) lochen *v*
perforated *adj* perforiert *adj*; **~ edge** Perforationsseite *f*; **~ magnetic film** Cordband *n*, Cord *n*, Perfoband *n*, Perfomagnetband *n*, Magnetperfoband *n*, Magnetsplitfilm *m*, Split *m* (17,5 Cord); **~ magnetic tape** Cordband *n*, Cord *n*, Perfoband *n*, Perfomagnetband *n*, Magnetperfoband *n*, Magnetsplitfilm *m*, Split *m* (17,5 Cord); **~ scotch tape** Tonunterkleber *m*; **~ tape** (EDP) Lochstreifen *m*; **~ transparent tape** Bildunterkleber *m*
perforating machine Perforiermaschine *f*
perforation *n* Perforation *f*; **~ hole** Perforationsloch *n*; **~ scratch** Perforationsschramme *f*; **damaged ~** ausgezackte Perforation; **picked ~**

angeschlagene Perforation; **torn ~** eingerissene Perforation
perforator *n* Stanzzange *f*; ~ *n* (operator) Locher *m*; ~ *n* (EDP) Lochstreifenstanzer *m*
perform *v* spielen *v*; **to ~ on-camera** vor der Kamera auftreten
performance *n* Aufführung *f*, Darbietung *f*, Darstellung *f*, Durchführung *f*, Spiel *n*, Vorführung *f*, Vorstellung *f*; **~ check** Funktionsprüfung *f*; **~ test** Funktionsprüfung *f*; **private ~** geschlossene Vorstellung
performer *n* Darsteller *m*, Künstler *m*, Ausführender *m*
performers' fees Darstellergagen *f pl*
performing licence Aufführungslizenz *f*; **~ rights** *n pl* Aufführungsrecht *n*
perigee *n* Nahpunkt *m*, Perigäum *n*
period *n* Periode *f*; **~ of use** Einsatzzeit *f*; **~ picture** Kostümfilm *m*; **~ play** Zeitstück *n*
periodical *n* Magazin *n*
peripheral control instruction (EDP) Ein-Ausgabebefehl *m*; **~ station** Randzonensender *m*; **~ unit** (EDP) periphere Einheit
periwig *n* Perücke *f*
permanent circuit Dauerleitung *f*; **~ connection** Festanschluß *m*; **~ magnet** Dauermagnet *m*; **~ network** Dauerleitungsnetz *n*; **~ sound network** Tondauerleitungsnetz *n*, Tonleitungsdauernetz *n*; **~ staff** Festangestellte *pl*; **~ vision network** Bilddauerleitungsnetz *n*
permeability to light Lichtdurchlässigkeit *f*
permissible variation Toleranzbereich *m*
permittivity *n* Dielektrizitätskonstante *f*
perpendicular magnetisation Quermagnetisierung *f*
persistence *n* Nachleuchten *n*, Nachleuchtdauer *f*
personal assistant (PA) persönlicher Referent
personnel *n* Personal *n*
petits droits kleine Rechte
phase *n* Phase *f*; **~ adjustment** Phaseneinstellung *f*; **~ advancer** Phasenschieber *m*; **~ angle** Phasenwinkel *m*; **~ -angle rotation** Phasendrehung *f*; **~ change** Phasenänderung *f*; **~ comparator stage** Phasenvergleichsstufe *f*; **~ comparison** Phasenvergleich *m*; **~ compensation** Phasenentzerrung *f*; **~ control** Phasenregelung *f*; **~ correction** Phasenentzerrung *f*; **~ corrector** Phasengangentzerrer *m*; **~ coupling** Phasenverkopplung *f*; **~ delay** Phasenlaufzeit *f*, Laufzeit *f*; **~ -delay distortion** Laufzeitverzerrung *f*; **~ -delay error** Laufzeitfehler *m*; **~ demodulation** Phasendemodulation *f*; **~ diagram** Phasenbild *n*; **~ displacement** Phasenverschiebung *f*; **~ distortion** Phasenverzerrung *f*, Laufzeitverzerrung *f*; **~ equalisation** Phasenentzerrung *f*; **~ equaliser** Phasengangentzerrer *m*; **~ error** Phasenfehler *m*; **~ failure** Phasenausfall *m*; **~ indicator** Phasenmesser *m*; **~ inverter** Phasenumkehrstufe *f*; **~ inverter stage** Phasenumkehrstufe *f*; **~ lag** Phasennacheilung *f*; **~ lead** Phasenvoreilung *f*; **~ -locked** *adj* phasenstarr *adj*; **~ modulation (PM)** Phasenmodulation (PM) *f*; **~ monitoring** Phasenüberwachung *f*; **~ plane** Abstrahlebene *f*; **~ position** Phasenlage *f*; **~ pre-correction** Phasenvorentzerrung *f*;

~ **relationship** Phasenverhältnis *n*, Phasenlage *f*; ~ **response** Phasenfrequenzgang *m*, Phasengang *m*; ~ **reversal** Phasenumkehrung *f*; ~ **selectivity** Phasenselektivität *f*; ~ **shift** Phasenverschiebung *f*, Phasenänderung *f*, Phasendrehung *f*; ~ **-shift control** Anschnittsteuerung *f*; ~ **shifter** Drehtransformator *m*, Phasenschieber *m*, Phasendrehvorrichtung *f*; ~ **splitter** Phasenumkehrstufe *f*; ~ **synchronisation** Phasensynchronisierung *f*; ~ **synchroniser** Phasensynchronisator *m*; ~ **variation meter** Phasenschwankungsmesser *m*; ~ **variations** *n pl* Phasenschwankung *f*; ~ **voltage** Phasenspannung *f*; **automatic ~ control (APC)** automatische Phasenregelung; **differential ~** differentielle Phase; **differential ~** (coll.) differentieller Phasenfehler; **differential ~ error** differentieller Phasenfehler; **opposite ~** komplementäre Phase

phase/frequency characteristic Phasenfrequenzgang *m*, Phasengang *m*

phasemeter *n* Phasenmesser *m*

phasing *n* Phaseneinstellung *f*

phonogram *n* (legal) Tonträger *m*

phonograph *n* (US) Plattenmaschine *f*, Plattenspieler *m*; ~ **amplifier** (US) Schallplattenverstärker *m*; ~ **record** (US) Schallplatte *f*

phonographic industry Schallplattenindustrie *f*; ~ **recording** Schallplattenaufnahme *f*

phosphor *n* (pict. tube) Leuchtphosphor *m*; ~ **cathode-ray screen** Leuchtschirm *m*, Leuchtstoffschirm *m*

phosphorescent *adj* selbststrahlend *adj*; ~ **material** Leuchtstoff *m*

photo *n* Foto *n*, Fotografie *f*, Lichtbild *n*, Aufnahme *f*; ~ **blow-up (PBU)** Arbeitsfoto *n*

photocathode *n* Fotokathode *f*

photocell *n* Fotozelle *f*, Lichtempfänger *m*; ~ **multiplier** Elektronenvervielfacher *m*; ~ **power supply unit** Fotozellennetzgerät *n*

photoconductive effect innerer Fotoeffekt

photoconductivity *n* Fotoleitfähigkeit *f*

photodiode *n* Fotodiode *f*

photoelectric *adj* fotoelektrisch *adj*; ~ **cell (PEC)** fotoelektrische Zelle, Fotoelement *n*, Fotozelle *f*; ~ **emission** äußerer Fotoeffekt; ~ **reader** (EDP) optischer Abtaster

photoelectron *n* Fotoelektron *n*

photoemission *n* Fotoemission *f*

photogenic *adj* fotogen *adj*

photograph *v* aufnehmen *v*; ~ *n* Foto *n*, Fotografie *f*, Lichtbild *n*, Aufnahme *f*

photographer *n* Fotograf *m*

photographic laboratory Fotolabor *n*; ~ **plate** Platte *f*; ~ **studio** Fotoatelier *n*; ~ **subject** Aufnahmegegenstand *m*; ~ **title** Fototitel *m*; ~ **transmission density** Schwärzung *f*

photography *n* Kameraführung *f*

photometer *n* Lichtmeßgerät *n*, Belichtungsmesser *m*

photometric *adj* fotometrisch *adj*; ~ **aperture** fotometrische Blende

photometry *n* Lichtmessung *f*

photomontage *n* Fotomontage *f*

photomultiplier *n* Fotoelektronenvervielfacher *m*, Fotozellenvervielfacher *m*

photoresistance *n* Fotowiderstand *m*

photosensitive *adj* lichtempfindlich *adj*
photosensitivity *n* Lichtempfindlichkeit *f*
photovoltaic cell Fotoelement *n*
picketing cable Longe *f*
pick up *v* (wireless message) auffangen *v*; ~ **up** *v* (filming) Pick-up machen
pick-up *n* Plattenmaschine *f*, Plattenspieler *m*; ~ *n* (head) Schallplattenabtaster *m*, Tonabnehmer *m*, Abtastdose *f*; ~ *n* (relay) Ansprechen *n*; ~ **amplifier** Schallplattenverstärker *m*; ~ **arm** Tonarm *m*; ~ **arm lowering device** Tonarmlift *m*; ~ **cartridge** Abtastdose *f*, Tonabtastdose *f*, Tondose *f*; ~ **head** Abtastkopf *m*, Hörkopf *m*, Tonabtastkopf *m*, Tonabtastdose *f*, Tondose *f*; ~ **time** (relay) Ansprechzeit *f*; ~ **truck** (US) Fernsehaufnahmewagen *m*; ~ **tube** Aufnahmeröhre *f*, Bildaufnahmeröhre *f*, Bildwiedergaberöhre *f*; ~ **value** (relay) Ansprechwert *m*; **electrodynamic ~** elektrodynamische Abtastdose; **electromagnetic ~** elektromagnetische Abtastdose
pictorial composition Bildgestaltung *f*, Bildkomposition *f*
picture *n* Bild *n*, Aufnahme *f*; ~ *n* (cinema) Film *m*; ~ *n* (frame) Vollbild *n*; ~ **amplitude** Bildamplitude *f*; ~ **and blanking signal** Bildaustastsignal (BA-Signal) *n*, Bildsignal mit Austastung; ~ **and waveform monitor** Bildkontrollgerät *n*; ~ **angle** Bildwinkel *m*; ~ **area** Bildausschnitt *m*, Bildfeld *n*, Schußfeld *n*; ~ **aspect ratio** Bildseitenverhältnis *n*; ~ **background** Bildhintergrund *m*; ~ **bandwidth** Bildbandbreite *f*; ~ **black** Bildschwarz *n*; ~ **breakdown** Bildstörung *f*; ~ **break-up** Bildausreißen *n*; ~ **brightness** Bildhelligkeit *f*; ~ **composition** Bildaufbau *m*, Bildgestaltung *f*, Bildkomposition *f*; ~ **content** Bildinhalt *m*; ~ **contour** Bildkontur *f*; ~ **contrast** Bildkontrast *m*; ~ **control** Bildaussteuerung *f*, Bildkontrolle *f*, Bildüberwachung *f*; ~ **definition** Bildauflösung *f*, Bildschärfe *f*; ~ **detail** Bilddetail *n*, Bildeinzelheit *f*; ~ **displacement** Bildverdrängung *f*; ~ **distortion** Bildverzerrung *f*; ~ **duration** Bilddauer *f*; ~ **edge** Bildkante *f*; ~ **editing** Bildschnitt *m*; ~ **element** (TV) Bildpunkt *m*; ~ **fault** Abbildungsfehler *m*; ~ **feature** Bildreportage *f*; ~ **film** Bildfilm *m*; ~ **flyback** Bildrücklauf *m*; ~ **framing** (proj.) Bildverstellung *f*; ~ **frequency** (25 or 30 Hz) Bildfrequenz *f*, Bildwechselfrequenz *f*, Bildwechsel *m*, Bildzahl *f*, Vollbildfrequenz *f*; ~ **-frequency adjustment** Einstellen der Bildfrequenz; ~ **-frequency setting** Einstellen der Bildfrequenz; ~ **gate** Bildfenster *n*; ~ **geometry** Bildgeometrie *f*; ~ **grain** Bildstruktur *f*; ~ **height** Bildhöhe *f*; ~ **house** Filmtheater *n*, Lichtspieltheater *n*, Kino *n*; ~ **hum** Bildbrumm *m*; ~ **identification** Bildkennung *f*; ~ **information** Bildinformation *f*; ~ **instability** Bildstandfehler *m*; ~ **interference** Bildstörung *f*; ~ **jitter** Bildstandschwankung *f*; ~ **level** Bildpegel *m*; **change of ~ level** Bildpegeländerung *f*; **fluctuation of ~ level** Bildpegelschwankung *f*;

sudden ~ -level change Bildpegelsprung *m*; **~ librarian** *n* Bildarchivar *m*; **~ library** Bildarchiv *n*; **~ line** Bildzeile *f*; **~ matching monitor** Bildanpaßmonitor *m*; **~ material** Bildmaterial *n*; **~ monitor** Bildkontrollempfänger *m*, Bildmonitor *m*, Kontrollmonitor *m*, Signalbildmonitor *m*; **~ monitoring** Bildüberwachung *f*; **~ monitoring receiver** Bildkontrollempfänger *m*, Bildmonitor *m*, Monitor *m*; **~ negative** Bildnegativ *n*, Negativbild *n*; **~ noise** Bildrauschen *n*, Schnee *m*; **~ original** Bildoriginal *n*; **~ output signal** Bildausgangssignal *n*; **~ period** Bildperiode *f*; **~ -phased** *adj* bildsynchron *adj*; **~ position** Bildlage *f*; **~ positive** Bildpositiv *n* **~ quality** Bildgüte *f*, Bildqualität *f*, Abbildungsgüte *f*; **~ raster** Bildraster *m*; **~ ratio** Bildformat *n* **~ receiver** Bildfunkempfänger *m*; **~ recording** Bildaufnahme *f*, Bildaufzeichnung *f*; **~ repetition frequency** Bildfolgefrequenz *f*; **~ reproduction** Bildwiedergabe *f*; **~ resolution** Bildauflösung *f*; **~ roll** Bilddurchlauf *m*, Bildkippen *n*; **~ rushes** Bildmuster *n pl*; **~ scan** Bildablenkung *f*; **~ scanning** Bildabtastung *f*; **~ screen** Bildschirm *m*; **~ shape** Bildformat *n*; **~ sharpness** Bildschärfe *f*; **~ signal** Bildsignal *n* (B-Signal), Videosignal *n*; **~ signal gain** Bildsignalverstärkung *f*; **~ size** Bildformat *n*; **~ slip** Bilddurchlauf *m*, Ziehen des Bildes; **~ start** Bildstart *m*; **~ start mark** Bildstartmarke *f*; **~ steadiness** Bildstand *m*; **~ structure** Bildstruktur *f*; **~ switching error** Bildfehlschaltung *f*; **~ synchronisation** Bildsynchronisation *f*; **~ synchronising pulse** Bildgleichlaufimpuls *m*, Bildimpuls *m*; **~ synthesis** Bildaufbau *m*; **~ -tearing** *n* Zerreißen des Bildes; **~ telegraphy** Bildtelegrafie *f*, Bildfunk *m*; **~ telephone** Bildtelefon *n*; **~ telephony** Bildtelefonie *f*; **~ transmission** Bildtelegrafie *f*, Bildfunk *m*; **~ transmission** (TV) Bildübertragung *f*; **~ transmitter** Bildfunksender *m*, Bildgeber *m*, Bildsender *m*; **~ tube** Bildröhre *f*, Bildwiedergaberöhre *f*, Fernsehröhre *f*, Wiedergaberöhre *f*; **~ white** Bildweiß *n*; **~ window** Filmfenster *n*; **~ without contrast** flaches Bild; **black-and-white ~** einfarbiges Bild, monochromes Bild; **blanked ~ signal** Bildaustastsignal (BA-Signal) *n*, Bildsignal mit Austastung; **build-up of ~** Bildaufbau *m*; **burnt-out ~** kalkiges Bild; **distorted ~** verzerrtes Bild; **extraneous object in ~** Fremdkörper im Bild; **flat ~** flaches Bild; **fogged ~** verschleiertes Bild; **hazy ~** verschleiertes Bild; **misty ~** matschiges Bild; **monochrome ~** einfarbiges Bild, monochromes Bild; **negative ~** negatives Bild; **polychrome ~** mehrfarbiges Bild, polychromes Bild; **rolling ~** rollendes Bild; **soft ~** weiches Bild, verschleiertes Bild; **sooty ~** Bild grau in grau; **synchronous ~** synchrones Bild; **to hold the ~** Bild halten; **to write against the ~** gegen das Bild texten; **uncontrasty ~** weiches Bild; **unstable ~** verwackeltes Bild; **unusable ~** unbrauchbares Bild

picture-and-sound (compp.) Bild-Ton- (in Zus.); **~ disc** Bild-Ton-Platte *f*

pictures *n pl* (coll.) Filmtheater *n*, Lichtspieltheater *n*, Kino *n*; ~ **per second (pps)** Bilder pro Sekunde
picture/sound offset unit Bild-Ton-Versatzvorrichtung *f*
piece *n* (set) Dekorationsteil *n*, Bauelement *n*; ~ *n* (journ.) Artikel *m*, Aufsatz *m*, Beitrag *m*, Bericht *m*, Stück *n* (fam.); ~ *n* (drama) Stück *n*
piezo-electric microphone Kristallmikrofon *n*
pigment *n* Farbstoff *m*; ~ **colour** Pigmentfarbe *f*; ~ **dye** Pigmentfarbe *f*
pile-up *n* (coll.) Filmsalat *m*
pilot *n* (prog.) Testsendung *f*; ~ *n* (coll.) (elec.) Pilotschwingung *f*, Pilotsignal *n*, Pilot *m* (fam.); ~ **broadcast** Pilotsendung *f*, Modellsendung *f*; ~ **film** Pilotfilm *m*; ~ **frequency generator** Steuergenerator *m*; ~ **pin** Greifer *m*; ~ **programme** Pilotprogramm *n*, Testsendung *f*, Versuchssendung *f*; ~ **reference tone** Pilotschwingung *f*; ~ **series** Nullserie *f*; ~ **signal** Pilotsignal *n*, Pilot *m* (fam.); ~ **terminal** Pilottonanschluß *m*; ~ **tone** Pilotton *m*; ~ **-tone equipment** Pilottoneinrichtung *f*; ~ **-tone frequency** Pilottonfrequenz *f*; ~ **-tone generator** Pilottongeber *m*; ~ **-tone process** Pilottonverfahren *n*; ~ **-tone system** Pilottonsystem *n*; ~ **tone track** Hilfstonspur *f*; ~ **transmission** Pilotsendung *f*
pin *n* Sperrstift *m*
pincer *n* Klemmlampe *f*, Pinza *f*
pinch roller Andruckrolle *f*
pin-cushion distortion Kissenverzerrung *f*; ~ **equaliser** Kissenentzerrung *f*
ping-pong shot (coll.) Schuß-Gegenschuß *m*
pin-sharp *adj* gestochen *adj*
pip *n* Marke *f*; ~ *n* (sound) Piep(s)er *m* (fam.)
piped music Musikberieselung *f*
pirate listener Schwarzhörer *m*; ~ **-listener detection** Schwarzhörerfanndung *f*; ~ **station** Piratensender *m*; ~ **transmitter** Schwarzsender *m*; ~ **viewer** Schwarzseher *m*; ~ **-viewer detection** Schwarzseherfahndung *f*
pistol grip Kamerahaltegriff *m*, Revolvergriff *m*
pitch *n* Tonhöhe *f*; ~ **variation** Tonhöhenschwankung *f*; **angle of** ~ Gewindesteigung *f*
place *v* (prog.) terminieren *v*, unterbringen *v*
plan *n* Zeichnung *f*
plane *n* Ebene *f*; **horizontal** ~ horizontale Ebene; **vertical** ~ senkrechte Ebene
plank *n* Bohle *f*, Brett *n*
planning *n* Planung *f*, Disposition *f*, Programmplanung *f*; ~ **and building maintenance*** Liegenschaften* *f pl*; ~ **and installation*** Ausstattungstechnik* *f*; ~ **engineer** Planungsingenieur *m*; ~ **manager** Leiter der Disposition; ~ **meeting** Produktionsbesprechung *f*; **current** ~ laufende Programmplanung; **forward** ~ Vorausplanung *f*; **technical** ~ technische Disposition, technische Planung
plant *n* Anlage *f*, Betriebseinrichtung *f*
plaster *n* Gips *m*
plasterer *n* Kascheur *m*, Stukkateur *m*
plastic effect Bildplastik *f*; ~ **face-piece** Gesichtsplastik *f*
plate *n* (photo) Platte *f*; ~ *n* (tape) Teller *m*; ~ *n* (US) Anode *f*; ~ **camera** Plattenkamera *f*; ~ **holder** (photo) Plattenkassette *f*

platform *n* Podest *n*, Tribüne *f*
play *v* (part) darstellen *v*, spielen *v*; (disc, tape) abspielen *v*; ~ *n* (thea.) Schauspiel *n*, Stück *n*; ~ *n* (tech.) Spielraum *m*; ~ **back** *v* abspielen *v*, wiedergeben *v*; ~ **in** *v* einspielen *v*, zuspielen *v*; ~ **up** *v* (news) Nachricht anheizen, Nachricht hochspielen; **to produce a** ~ ein Stück herausbringen; **to put on a** ~ ein Stück herausbringen
playback *n* Playback *n*, Abspielung *f*, Tonwiedergabe *f*, Wiedergabe *f*, Tonabtastung *f*; ~ **amplifier** Wiedergabeverstärker *m*; ~ **chain** Wiedergabekette *f*; ~ **characteristics** *n pl* Wiedergabecharakteristik *f*; ~ **circuit** Rückspielleitung *f*; ~ **data** Wiedergabedaten *n pl*; ~ **desk** Wiedergabepult *n*; ~ **device** Wiedergabevorrichtung *f*; ~ **duration** Abspieldauer *f*; ~ **equalisation** Wiedergabeentzerrung *f*; ~ **head** Wiedergabekopf *m*, Tonabtastkopf *m*, Hörkopf *m*; ~ **level** Wiedergabepegel *m*; ~ **loss** Wiedergabeverluste *m pl*, Abspielfehler *m*; ~ **unit** Wiedergabegerät *n*; **permissible ~ level** zulässiger Wiedergabepegel
player *n* Schauspieler *m*, Darsteller *m*, Ausführender *m*, Mitwirkender *m*
playing time (tape) Durchlaufzeit *f*
playwright *n* Dramatiker *m*, Stückeschreiber *m* (fam.)
plinth *n* (record-player) Zarge *f*
plop *n* Tonblitz *m*; ~ *n* Piep(s)er *m* (fam.)
plot *n* Handlungsablauf *m*
plotter *n* (EDP) Kurvenschreiber *m*, Kurvenzeichner *m*, Plotter *m*
plotting board (EDP) Kurvenschreiber *m*, Kurvenzeichner *m*, Plotter *m*; ~ **table** (EDP) Kurvenschreiber *m*, Kurvenzeichner *m*, Plotter *m*
plug *n* Kontaktstecker *m*, Stecker *m*, Steckkontakt *m*, Stöpsel *m*; ~ *n* (advert.) Schleichwerbung *f*; ~ **and socket** Steckvorrichtung *f*; ~ **assembly** Kabelsteckvorrichtung *f*; ~ **connection** Steckverbindung *f*; ~ **contact** Steckkontakt *m*; ~ **cord** Rangierkabel *n*; ~ **in** *v* einstecken *v*, stöpseln *v*; ~ **pin** Steckerstift *m*; ~ **socket** Steckdose *f*; ~ **strip** Stiftleiste *f*; ~ **up** *v* stöpseln *v*; **switched ~ socket** schaltbare Steckdose
plug-in *adj* steckbar *adj*; ~ **amplifier** Kassettenverstärker *m*; ~ **card** Steckkarte *f*; ~ **cassette** Steckkassette *f*; ~ **coil** Steckspule *f*; ~ **matrix** Steckkreuzfeld *n*; ~ **panel** Einsteckleiterplatte *f*; ~ **unit** Einschub *m*
Plumbicon *n* Bildaufnahmeröhre *f*
plywood *n* Sperrholz *n*
pneumatic fast-pulldown mechanism Schnellschaltwerk *n*
pocket transistor Taschenempfänger *m*
point *v* (cam.) einstellen *v*, richten *v* (auf); ~ *n* Spitze *f*; ~ **of connection** Verbindungsstelle *f*; ~ **of divergence** Zerstreuungspunkt *m*; ~ **of origin** Ursprungspunkt *m*; ~ **on colour triangle** Farbort *m*
pointer *n* Hinweis *m*, Tip *m*, Wink *m*; ~ **reading** Zeigeranzeige *f*
point-to-point circuit Direktverbindung zwischen zwei Punkten; ~ **radio station** Richtfunkstelle *f*; ~ **radio system** Richtfunk (RiFu) *m*; ~ **transmitter** Richtfunksender *m*; ~ **voice connection** gerichtete Sprechverbindung
polar diagram Richtcharakteristik *f*, Richtdiagramm *n*; ~ **orbit**

Polarbahn *f*
polar-coordinate system Polarkoordinatensystem *n*
polarisation *n* Polarisation *f*, Polarisierung *f*
polarise *v* polarisieren *v*
polarised, horizontally horizontal polarisiert; **vertically** ~ vertikal polarisiert
polarising filter Polarisationsfilter *m*
polarity *n* Polarität *f*; ~ **reversal** Umpolung *f*; **to reverse** ~ umpolen *v*
polaroid *n* Polaroid-Kamera *f*; ~ **camera** Polaroid-Kamera *f*
pole *n* Pol *m*; ~ **-changer** *n* Umpoler *m*; ~ **shoe** Polschuh *m*
polish *v* (F) polieren *v*, blankieren *v*
polishing *n* Polieren *n*; ~ **machine** Blankiermaschine *f*
political desk Politik Inland*
pollute *v* verunreinigen *v*
pollution *n* Verunreinigung *f*
polychromatic *adj* mehrfarbig *adj*; ~ *adj* (appar.) farbtüchtig *adj*; ~ **process** Mehrfarbenverfahren *n*
polychrome *adj* mehrfarbig *adj*; ~ **system** Mehrfarbenverfahren *n*
polyester film Dünnschichtfilm *m*
polyphase current Drehstrom *m*
pop *adj* (coll.) volkstümlich *adj*; ~ **music** Schlagermusik *f*; ~ **programme** Schlagersendung *f*
popular *adj* volkstümlich *adj*; ~ **play** Volksstück *n*; ~ **song** Chanson *n*
porcelain insulator Lüsterklemme *f*
porch *n* Schwarzschulter *f*; **back** ~ hintere Schwarzschulter; **front** ~ vordere Schwarzschulter
pore *n* Pore *f*
porous *adj* porös *adj*
portable *n* (coll.) Kofferradio *n*, Reiseempfänger *m*; ~ *adj* tragbar *adj*; ~ **camera** Handkamera *f*; ~ **charger** Ladekassette *f*; ~ **equipment** Kofferapparatur *f*; ~ **radio** Kofferradio *n*; ~ **receiver** Reiseempfänger *m*; ~ **set** Koffergerät *n*; ~ **tape recorder** Reisetonbandgerät *n*; ~ **TV receiver** Fernsehkofferempfänger *m*; ~ **unit** Koffereinheit *f*
porter *n* Pförtner *m*
portrait attachment Vorsatzlinse für Nahaufnahme
position *n* Einstellung *f*; ~ **indicator** Bandzählwerk *n*
positional hum Geometriebrumm *m*; ~ **information** (stereo) Richtungsinformation *f*
positive *n* Positiv *n*, Positivkopie *f*; ~ **drive** formschlüssiger Antrieb; ~ **film** Positivfilm *m*; ~ **picture** Bildpositiv *n*, Positiv *n*; ~ **print** Positivabzug *m*, Positivkopie *f*; ~ **rush print** Positivmuster *n*; ~ **stock** Positivfilmmaterial *n*; ~ **work print** Positivmuster *n*; **high-contrast** ~ steiles Positivfilmmaterial; **high-contrast** ~ **stock** steiles Positivfilmmaterial **low-contrast** ~ flaches Positivfilmmaterial; **low-contrast** ~ **stock** flaches Positivfilmmaterial
post-acceleration *n* Nachbeschleunigung *f*
post-blanking *n* Nachaustastung *f*
post-censorship *n* Nachzensur *f*
post-correction *n* Nachkorrektur *f*
post-equalisation *n* Nachentzerrung (NE) *f*
post-equalising pulse Nachtrabant *m*
poster *n* Plakat *n*; ~ **title** Plakattitel *m*
postiche section (BBC) Perückenwerkstatt *f*
postpone *v* verschieben *v*
postponement *n* Verschiebung *f*
post room Poststelle *f*
post-sync *v* nachsynchronisieren *v*; ~ **loop** Synchronschleife *f*; ~ **studio** Nachsynchronisationsstudio *n*

post-synching *n* Doubeln *n*, Nachsynchronisation *f*
post-synchronisation *n* Nachsynchronisation *f*
post-synchronise *v* nachsynchronisieren *v*
pot *n* (coll.) Potentiometer *n*, Pot *m* (fam.)
potentiometer *n* Potentiometer *n*, Pot *m* (fam.); **noisy ~** kratzendes Potentiometer; **scratching ~** kratzendes Potentiometer
power *v* Spannung geben; ~ *n* (elec.) Leistung *f*; **~ amplifier** Leistungsverstärker *m*; **~ cable** Netzkabel *n*; **~ consumption** Leistungsaufnahme *f*, Stromaufnahme *f*; **~ current** Kraftstrom *m*; **~ dissipation** Verlustleistung *f*; **~ distribution bay** Netzverteilergestell *n*; **~ failure** Netzausfall *m*, Stromunterbrechung *f*; **~ failure relay** Stromausfallrelais *n*; **~ flux intensity** Feldstärke *f*; **~ line noise** Netzgeräusch *n*; **~ loss** Verlustleistung *f*; **~ of chromatic resolution** Farbauflösungsvermögen *n*; **~ of selection** Unterscheidungsvermögen *n*; **~ pack** Netzteil *m*, Netzanschlußgerät *n*, Netzgerät *n*; **~ panel** Netzschalttafel *f*; **~ plant** Kraftzentrale *f*, Starkstromanlage *f*, Aggregat *n*; **~ plug** Kraftstecker *m*; **~ plug adapter** Kraftsteckkupplung *f*; **~ rectifier** Netzgleichrichter *m*; **~ source** Stromquelle *f*; **~ supply** Energieversorgung *f*, Stromversorgung *f*, Netzversorgung *f*, Spannungsversorgung *f*, Speisung *f*; **~ supply cable** Netzkabel *n*; **~ supply chassis** Netzeinschub *m*; **~ supply system** Starkstromnetz *n* **~ supply unit** Netzteil *m*, Netzanschlußgerät *n*, Netzgerät *n*; **~ supply variation** Stromversorgungsschwankung *f*; **~ switchboard** Netzschalttafel *f*; **~ transformer** Netztransformator *m*; **~ unit** Aggregat *n*, Netzeinschub *m*
pre-accentuation *n* Vorverzerrung *f*
pre-amplifier *n* Vorverstärker *m*, Vorstufe *f*; **~ stage** Vorverstärkerstufe *f*; **tunnel-diode ~** Vorverstärker mit Tunneldiode
pre-assemble *v* vorbauen *v*
pre-assembly *n* Vorbau *m*; **~ shop** Vorbaubühne *f*; **~ studio** Vorbauhalle *f*
pre-bath *n* Vorbad *n*
pre-censorship *n* Vorzensur *f*
precision *n* Präzision *f*; **~ demodulator** Meßmischer *m*; **~ modulator** Meßmischer *m*; **~ offset** Präzisionsoffset *n*; **~ tool maker** Feinmechaniker *m*; **~ tool worker** Feinmechaniker *m*
pre-classical music Altes Werk*
pre-correct *v* vorentzerren *v*
pre-correction *n* Vorentzerrung *f*
pre-detector volume control Rückwärtsregelung *f*
predominance of one colour kippender Farbstich
pre-dubbing *n* Vorsynchronisation *f*
pre-emphasis *n* Anhebung *f*, Frequenzgangvorverzerrung *f*, Preemphasis *f*, Voranhebung *f*, Vorentzerrung *f*, Vorverzerrung *f*
pre-emphasise *v* anheben *v*, vorentzerren *v*
pre-equalisation *n* Vorentzerrung *f*
pre-equalising pulse Vortrabant *m*
pre-expose *v* vorbelichten *v*
pre-exposure *n* Vorbelichtung *f*
pre-film *v* vorabaufnehmen *v*
pre-hear *v* vorhören *v*
pre-hearing *n* Vorhören *n*
prejudice *n* Schaden *m*
preliminary shooting script

Rohdrehbuch *n*
pre-listen *v* vorhören *v*
pre-listening *n* Vorhören *n*, Abhören vor Band
premagnetising *n* Vormagnetisierung *f*
première *n* Premiere *f*, Erstaufführung *f*, Uraufführung *f*
pre-mixing *n* Vormischung *f*
preparation time Vorbereitungszeit *f*
prepare *v* (F) ansetzen *v*
pre-produce *v* vorproduzieren *v*
pre-production *n* Vorproduktion *f*; **~ meeting** Produktionsbesprechung *f*, Regiebesprechung *f*
pre-record *v* vorabaufnehmen *v*; **~ listening** Abhören vor Band
pre-recorded broadcast Bandsendung *f*; **~ programme** Bandsendung *f*
pre-release *n* (F) Interessentenvorführung *f*
pre-roll time Startvorlaufzeit *f*, Vorlaufzeit *f*, Startzeit *f*
pre-school broadcasting Vorschulprogramm *n*
preselect *v* vorwählen *v*
preselection *n* Vorwahl *f*
preselector *n* Vorwähler *m*; **~ matrix** Vorwahlkreuzschiene *f*; **~ setting** Vorwahlstellung *f*
presence filter Präsenzfilter *m*
present *v* (play) herausbringen *v*; ~ *v* (prog.) einführen *v*, moderieren *v*
presentation *n* (announcer) Ansage *f*; ~ *n* (suite) Programmregie *f*
presentation* *n* Sendeleitung* *f*
presentation announcement Programmansage *f*; **~ continuity** Ablauf *m*; **~ director** Ablaufregisseur *m*; **~ editor's log** Sendenachweis *m*; **~ log** Sendeablaufprotokoll *n*; **~ preview of evening programmes** (TV) Generalansage *f*, Hauptansage *f*; **~ schedule** Sendeablaufplan *m*; **~ studio** Ansagestudio *n*, Sprecherstudio *n*; **~ suite** Sendebüro *n*, Senderegie *f*, Ablaufregie *f*; **introductory ~** Kopfansage *f*
presenter *n* Ansager *m*; ~ *n* (anchor man) Moderator *m*
presenter's position Ansageplatz *m*
presenting editor (news) Studioredakteur *m*
preset *v* voreinstellen *v*, vorabstimmen *v*; **switchable ~ tuning** (rec.) schaltbare Festeinstellung
presetting studio Montagehalle *f*, Vorbauhalle *f*
press *v* (key) auslösen *v*; ~ *n* Presse *f*; **~ agency** Pressedienst *m*; **~ and public relations chief** Pressechef *m*; **~ and public relations officer** Pressereferent *m*; **~ conference** Pressekonferenz *f*; **~ law** Pressegesetz *n*; **~ officer** (US) Pressechef *m*; **~ photographer** Bildberichterstatter *m*, Bildreporter *m*, Pressefotograf *m*; **~ reception** Presseempfang *m*; **~ release** Presseverlautbarung *f*, Verlautbarung *f*; **~ review** Presseschau *f*, Pressespiegel *m*, Pressestimmen *f pl*; **~ review editor** Presseschauredakteur *m*; **~ service** Pressedienst *m*; **~ stenographer** Pressestenograf *m* **freedom of the ~** Pressefreiheit *f*
pressmen *n pl* Zeitungsleute *plt*
pressure-air duct Druckluftleitung *f*
pressure-gradient microphone Druckgradientenmikrofon *n*
pressure microphone Druckmikrofon *n*; **~ pad** Andruckkufe *f*; **~ plate** Andruckplatte *f*; **~ roller** Andruckrolle *f*; **~ solenoid** Andruckmagnet *m*
pre-start *n* fliegender Start
pre-transmission test

Vorübertragungsversuch *m*
pretune *v* vorabstimmen *v*
preview *v* vorschauen *v*; ~ *v* (for approval) abnehmen *v*; ~ *n* Vorschau *f*; ~ *n* (F, thea.) Vorpremiere *f*; ~ *n* (for approval) Abnahme *f*, Abnahmevorführung *f*; ~ **date** Vorführtermin *m*; ~ **line** Kontrollschiene *f*; ~ **monitor** Vorschaumonitor *m*; ~ **screening** Abnahmevorführung *f*
primary *n* Primärfarbe *f*; ~ **colour** Primärfarbe *f*, Primärvalenz *f*; ~ **colour component** Primärfarbauszug *m*; ~ **colour image** Farbauszugsbild *n*; ~ **colour raster** Farbauszugsraster *m*; ~ **colour signal** Farbauszugssignal *n*; ~ **current** Primärstrom *m*; ~ **development** Erstentwicklung *f*; ~ **element** Meßfühler *m*; ~ **frequency** Primärträger *m*; ~ **radiator** Primärstrahler *m*; ~ **ray** Primärstrahler *m*; ~ **service area** Nahempfangsgebiet *n*; ~ **tone** Primärton *m*; **virtual** ~ virtuelle Primärvalenz
primer *n* (col.) Grundierfarbe *f*
print *v* (F, photo) Kopie ziehen, kopieren *v*, abziehen *v*, ziehen *v*, umkopieren *v*; ~ *n* (F) Filmkopie *f*, Kopie *f*; ~ *n* (photo) Abzug *m*, Bildkopie *f*; **combined** ~ kombinierte Kopie; **graded** ~ lichtbestimmte Kopie; **married** ~ kombinierte Kopie; **only existing** ~ Unikat *n*; **scratched** ~ verregnete Kopie; **subtitled** ~ Kopie mit Untertiteln; **to ~ with matte effect** mit Maske kopieren; **to clean a** ~ Kopie putzen; **to make a** ~ Kopie ziehen; **to regenerate a** ~ Kopie regenerieren; **to strike a** ~ Kopie ziehen
printable *adj* kopierfähig *adj*
printed circuit gedruckter Schaltkreis, gedruckte Schaltung, Steckleiterplatte *f*; ~ **circuit board (PCB)** Leiterplatte *f*, gedruckte Schaltplatte; ~ **material** Positivfilmmaterial *n*
printer *n* (F) Kopieranlage *f*, Kopiermaschine *f*; ~ *n* (EDP) Drucker *m*; ~ **charge-band** Filterband *n*; ~ **light** Kopierlicht *n* ~ **-light control** Lichtzwischenschaltung *f*; ~ **-light dimming** Kopierdämpfung *f*; ~ **-light setting** Kopierlichtschaltung *f*; ~ **-light strength** Kopierwert *m*; ~ **-light value** Kopierwert *m*; ~ **point** (FP) Lichtwertzahl *f*; ~ **stock** Kopierfilm *m*; **additive** ~ additive Kopiermaschine; **optical** ~ optische Kopiermaschine; **subtractive** ~ subtraktive Kopiermaschine
printing *n* (F) Kopieren *n*, Kopierung *f*; ~ **apparatus** Kopiergerät *n*; ~ **card punch** (EDP) Schreiblocher *m*; ~ **contrast** Kopierkontrast *m*; ~ **control band** Blendenband *n*; ~ **control strip** Blendenband *n*; ~ **department** Kopierabteilung *f*; ~ **fault** Kopierfehler *m*; ~ **-house** *n* Druckerei *f*; ~ **laboratory** Kopieranstalt *f*, Kopierwerk *n*; ~ **length** Kopierlänge *f*; ~ **machine** Kopiermaschine *f*; ~ **-office** *n* Druckerei *f*; ~ **office** Vervielfältigungsstelle *f*; ~ **process** Kopierverfahren *n*; ~ **stock** Kopierfilm *m*; **office** ~ Vervielfältigung *f*; **optical** ~ optisches Kopieren
printout *n* (EDP) Protokoll *n*
print-through *n* Durchklatschen *n*
priority *n* Vorrang *m*; ~ **item** (news) Vorrangmeldung *f*; ~ **processing** (EDP) Prioritätsverarbeitung *f*
prism *n* Prisma *n*; ~ **viewfinder** Prismensucher *m*, Umkehrsucher *m*

prismatic viewfinder Prismensucher *m*, Umkehrsucher *m*
privacy, protection against invasion of Persönlichkeitsschutz *m*
private branch exchange (PBX) Telefonzentrale *f*; ~ **dressing-room** Einzelgarderobe *f*
probe *n* Sonde *f*, Tastkopf *m*
problem-oriented language (EDP) problemnahe Programmiersprache, problemorientierte Programmiersprache
problem play Problemstück *n*
procedure *n* Verfahren *n*
procedure-oriented language (EDP) verfahrensorientierte Programmiersprache
process *v* (tech.) bearbeiten *v*; ~ *v* (F) entwickeln *v*; ~ *n* Verfahren *n*; ~ **automation** (EDP) Prozeßautomatisierung *f*; ~ **communication system** (EDP) Prozeßdaten-Übertragungssystem *n*; ~ **control** (EDP) Prozeßsteuerung *f*; ~ **control computer** (EDP) Prozeßrechner *m* ~ **control system** (EDP) Prozeßsteuersystem *n*, Prozeßdatenverarbeitungssystem *n*; ~ **guiding system** (EDP) Prozeßleitsystem *n*; ~ **interrupt** (EDP) Programmunterbrechung *f*; ~ **shot** Trucaaufnahme *f*; ~ **-shot system** Trucaverfahren *n*; **additive** ~ additives Verfahren; **subtractive** ~ subtraktives Verfahren
processing *n* (sig.) Aufbereitung *f*; ~ *n* (tech.) Verarbeitung *f*, Bearbeitung *f*; ~ **amplifier** Regenerierverstärker *m*; ~ **channel** Umschneideraum *m*, Umspielraum *m*; ~ **laboratory** Kopierabteilung *f*; ~ **machine** Entwicklungsmaschine *f*; ~ **stop** (FP) Haltestelle *f* (fam.); ~ **tank** Bädertank *m*; ~ **unit** (EDP) Zentraleinheit *f*, Prozessor *m*
processor *n* (EDP) Zentraleinheit *f*, Prozessor *m*
produce *v* herstellen *v*; ~ *v* (bcast.) Sendung machen; ~ *v* (direct) inszenieren *v*, Regie führen
producer *n* Produzent *m*; ~ *n* (TV, R) Redakteur *m*, Realisator *m*; ~ *n* (director) Regisseur *m*, Spielleiter *m*; **free-lance** ~ freier Produzent
producer's estimate Produktionsanforderung *f*
producer/scriptwriter *n* Filmredakteur *m*
producing team Aufnahmestab *m*, Aufnahmeteam *n*
product demodulator *s.* product detector; ~ **detector** Produktdetektor *m*
product-group advertising Branchenwerbung *f*
production *n* Produktion *f*, Herstellung *f*; ~ *n* (directing) Spielleitung *f*, Regie *f*, Inszenierung *f*; ~ **assistance** Produktionsbeistellung *f*, Produktionshilfe *f*; ~ **assistant** Produktionsassistent *m*; ~ **budget** Produktionsetat *m*; ~ **capacity** Produktionskapazität *f*; ~ **centre** Produktionskomplex *m*, Produktionszentrum *n*, Studiokomplex *m*; ~ **chart** Produktionsspiegel *m*; ~ **commitment** Produktionsauftrag *m*; ~ **company** Produktionsfirma *f*, Produktionsgesellschaft *f*; ~ **conference** Produktionsbesprechung *f*; ~ **contract** Herstellungsvertrag *m*; ~ **control room** Regie *f*, Regieraum *m*; ~ **costs** Produktionskosten *plt*, Herstellungskosten *plt*; ~ **cubicle** Regie *f*, Regieraum *m*; ~ **dates** *n pl* Produktionstermin *m*; ~ **day**

Produktionstag *m*; **~ department** Produktionsabteilung *f*; **~ facilities** Produktionsanlagen *f pl*, technische Produktionsmittel; **~ lighting** Gesamtszenenbeleuchtung *f*; **~ list** Drehstabliste *f*, Stabliste *f*; **~ manager** Produktionschef *m*, Produktionsleiter *m* (PL); **~ meeting** Produktionsbesprechung *f*; **~ mixer** (F) Studiotonmeister *m*; **~ office** Produktionsbüro *n*; **~ outline** Produktionsablaufplan *m*, vorläufiger Ablaufplan; **~ premises** Produktionsstätten *f pl*; **~ requirements** Dispositionswünsche *m pl*; **~ resources** Produktionsmittel *n pl*; **~ running time** Produktionsdauer *f*; **~ schedule** Produktionsplan *m*, Herstellungsplan *m*; **~ secretary** Produktionssekretärin *f*; **~ site** Produktionsstätte *f*; **~ staff** Produktionsstab *m*; **~ studio** Produktionsstudio *n*; **~ team** Aufnahmestab *m*, Aufnahmeteam *n*, Drehstab *m*; **~ time** Produktionszeit *f*, Herstellungszeit *f*, Fertigungszeit *f*; **~ unit** Produktionseinheit *f*; **approval of ~ budget** Produktionsbewilligung *f*; **own ~** Eigenproduktion *f*

productive capacity Produktionskapazität *f*

professional *n* Profi *m* (fam.); ~ *adj* berufsmäßig *adj*; **~ machine** Studiomaschine *f*

profile spot Effektscheinwerfer *m*

programme *v* programmieren *v*; ~ *n* Programm *n*; ~ *n* (bcast.) Sendung *f*; ~ *n* (thea.) Spielplan *m*; ~ *n* (coll.) (sig.) Modulationssignal *n*; **~ advisory council** Programmbeirat *m* (ARD); **~ band** Programmleiste *f*; **~ cable** Übertragungskabel *n*; **~ circuit** Programmleitung *f*, Modulationsleitung *f*, Modulationssendeleitung *f*; **~ committee** Programmausschuß *m*, Programmkommission *f*; **~ content** Programminhalt *m*; **~ contracts*** Honorarabteilung *f*; **~ contribution** Programmbeitrag *m*; **~ -controlled** *adj* (EDP) programmgesteuert *adj*; **~ coordination** Programmkoordination *f*; **~ coordination circuit** Programmkoordinationsleitung *f*; **~ costs** Programmkosten *plt*; **~ exchange** Programmaustausch *m*; **~ field** Programmsparte *f*; **~ filler** Beiprogramm *n*; **~ flow** Programmablauf *m*; **~ flow chart** Programmablaufplan *m*; **~ flow diagram** Programmablaufplan *m*; **~ for young listeners** Jugendfunk* *m*; **~ for young people** Jugendsendung *f*; **~ gap** Programmlücke *f*; **~ information** Programmhinweise *m pl*; **~ inquiries*** *n pl* Zuschauerauskunft* *f*; **~ insert** Programmeinblendung *f*, Programmbeitrag *m*; **~ inserted at short notice** kurzfristig angesetztes Programm; **~ item** Programmbeitrag *m*; **~ journal** Programmzeitschrift *f*; **~ length** Sendezeit *f*; **~ line** Hörfunkleitung *f*, Modulationsleitung *f*, Modulationssendeleitung *f*, Übertragungskabel *n*, Zubringerleitung *f*, Zubringer *m* (fam.); **~ link** Programmverbindung *f*; **~ maker** Programmgestalter *m*, Programmacher *m*; **~ meter** Aussteuerungsmesser *m*, Modulationsaussteuerungsmesser *m*; **~ music** Programmusik *f*; **~ news** Programmhinweise *m pl*;

~ **notes** *n pl* Ansagetext *m*; ~ **offer** Programmangebot *n*; ~ **on the air!** Sendung läuft!; ~ **operations*** *n pl* Programmabwicklung* *f*; ~ **operations assistant (POA)** Aufnahmeleiter *m*, Tontechniker *m*; ~ **output** Programmleistung *f*; ~ **pattern** Programmschema *n*; ~ **period** Programmzeit *f*; ~ **planning*** Programmdisposition* *f*; ~ **plug** Programmhinweis *m*; ~ **policy** Programmgestaltung *f*; ~ **pool** Programmpool *m*; ~ **preview** Programmvorschau *f*; ~ **production** Programmproduktion *f*; ~ **promotion** Programmhinweis *m* ~ **rating** Programmauswertung *f*; ~ **recording** Programmspeicherung *f*; ~ **relay** Programmübernahme *f*; ~ **schedule** Programmfahne *f*; ~ **schedules** *n pl* Programmplan *m*; ~ **sector** Programmsparte *f*; ~ **segment** (BBC 25 minutes) Programmeinheit *f* (15 Minuten); ~ **selector** Programmwahlanlage (PWA) *f*; ~ **sequence** Programmblock *m*; ~ **servicing department** Produktionsbetrieb* *m*; ~ **sheet** Programmfahne *f*; ~ **signal** Modulationssignal *n*; ~ **sound** Sendeton *m*; ~ **staff** Programmpersonal *n*; ~ **standards** Programmgrundsätze *m pl*, Programmrichtlinien *f pl*; ~ **storage** Programmspeicherung *f* ~ **store** Programmspeicher *m*; ~ **strand** Programmleiste *f*; ~ **structure** Programmstruktur *f*; ~ **supervisor** (EDP) Monitor *m*; ~ **supply** Programmzulieferung *f*, Programmbeistellung *f*, Programmversorgung *f*; ~ **trailer** Programmhinweis *m*; ~ **transition** Programmverbindung *f*; ~ **transmission** Programmübertragung *f*; ~ ~**-volume indicator** Modulationspegelanzeiger *m*, Modulationsanzeiger *m*, Aussteuerungsmesser *m*; **artistic** ~ Nummernprogramm *n*; **canned** ~ Programmkonserve *f*; **commercial** ~ kommerzielle Sendung; **domestic** ~ nationales Programm; **experimental** ~ Versuchsprogramm *n*; **foreground** ~ (EDP) Vordergrundprogramm *n*; **international** ~ **exchange** Internationaler Programmaustausch; **joint** ~ Gemeinschaftsprogramm *n*, Gemeinschaftssendung *f*, gemeinsames Programm; **last-minute** ~ **change** kurzfristige Programmänderung; **main** ~ (EDP) Hauptprogramm *n*; **master** ~ (EDP) Hauptprogramm *n*; **network** ~ nationales Programm; **own** ~ Eigenprogramm *n*; **pilot** ~ Pilotprogramm *n*, Testsendung *f*, Versuchssendung *f*; **pre-produced** ~ vorproduzierte Sendung; **pre-recorded** ~ vorproduzierte Sendung; **recorded** ~ aufgezeichnete Sendung, gespeicherte Sendung; **running** ~ laufendes Programm; **stored** ~ (EDP) gespeichertes Programm; **symbolic** ~ (EDP) symbolisches Programm; **to insert into** ~ ins Programm einsetzen; **to present the** ~ durch die Sendung führen; **topical** ~ aktuelle Sendung; **transcribed** ~ aufgezeichnete Sendung; **trial** ~ Testsendung *f*; **wired** ~ (EDP) festverdrahtetes Programm

programmed instruction (PI) (EDP) programmierte Unterweisung (PU)

programmer *n* Programmgestalter *m*, Programmacher *m*;

~ *n* (EDP) Programmierer *m*
programmes for women Frauenfunk* *m*; ~ **preview** (TV) Programmtafel *f*; **to return to scheduled** ~ Programm fortsetzen, Programm übernehmen
programming *n* Programmplanung *f*, Programmgestaltung *f*; ~ *n* (EDP) Programmierung *f*; ~ **language** (EDP) Programmiersprache *f*
project *v* (F) vorführen *v*, projizieren *v*, wiedergeben *v*; ~ **manager** Projektleiter *m*; ~ **request** Produktionsanmeldung *f*, Projektanmeldung *f*
projecting lens Projektionsoptik *f*
projection *n* Projektion *f*, Vorführung *f*; ~ **angle** Projektionswinkel *m*; ~ **aperture** Bildfenster *n*, Filmfenster *n*; ~ **booth** Filmvorführraum *m*, Vorführkabine *f*; ~ **cut-out** Schablonenmuster für Scheinwerfer; ~ **distance** Projektionsentfernung *f*; ~ **gate** Bildfenster *n*, Projektorbildfenster *n*, Projektorfenster *n*; ~ **opening** Projektorbildfenster *n*, Projektorfenster *n*; ~ **optics** Projektionsoptik *f*; ~ **permit** Vorführgenehmigung *f*, Freigabebescheid *m*; ~ **port** Kabinenfenster *n*; ~ **receiver** Projektionsempfänger *m*; ~ **room** Vorführkabine *f*; ~ **screen** Filmleinwand *f*, Bildwand *f*; ~ **theatre** Vorführkino *n*
projectionist *n* Filmvorführer *m*, Vorführer *m*
projector *n* Projektionsapparat *m*, Projektor *m*; ~ **lamp** (spotlight) Scheinwerferlampe *f*; ~ **lamp** (proj.) Projektionslampe *f*, Lichtwurflampe *f*; **dual-standard** ~ Zweiformatbildprojektor *m*
prolongation *n* Verlängerung *f*; ~ **factor** Verlängerungsfaktor *m*
promote *v* ankündigen *v*
promotion *n* (prog.) Programmankündigung *f*; ~ *n* (advert.) Werbung *f*; ~ **campaign** Werbekampagne *f*
prompt side bühnenlinks *adv*
prompter *n* Teleprompter *m*
prop *n* (coll.) Requisit *n*, Spielrequisit *n*; ~ **room** (coll.) Requisitenraum *m*, Requisite *f* (fam.)
propagation *n* Ausbreitung *f*; ~ **beyond horizon** Überreichweite *f*; **anomalous** ~ Überreichweite *f*
properties *n pl* Requisiten *n pl*, Atelierfundus *m*; ~ **in stock** Fundusbestand *m*
property *n* Requisit *n*, Spielrequisit *n*; ~ **buyer** Außenrequisiteur *m*; ~ **department** Atelierfundus *m*; ~ **list** Requisitenliste *f*; ~ **man** Requisiteur *m*, Innenrequisiteur *m*; ~ **master** Requisiteur *m*; ~ **plot** Requisitenliste *f*; ~ **room** Requisitenraum *m*, Requisite *f* (fam.); ~ **store** Requisitenfundus *m*, Requisitenkammer *f*
props *n pl* (coll.) Requisiten *n pl*, Atelierfundus *m*
propsman *n* (coll.) Requisiteur *m*
protagonist *n* Hauptdarsteller *m*
protected switchgear Schutzschalter *m*
protection against invasion of privacy Persönlichkeitsschutz *m*; ~ **leader** (F) Allonge *f*; ~ **ratio** Schutzverhältnis *n*; ~ **screen** Schutzgitter *n*
protective circuit-breaker Schutzschalter *m*; ~ **clothing** Schutzkleidung *f*; ~ **coating** Schutzschicht *f*; ~ **cover** Schutzdeckel *m*; ~ **earth** Schutzerde *f*; ~ **earthing** Erdungsschutz *m*; ~ **envelope** Schutzhülle *f*; ~ **gelatin layer**

Gelatineschutzschicht *f*; ~ **ground** Schutzerde *f*; ~ **treatment** Filmkonservierung *f*

province *n* (speciality) Ressort *n*

proving circuit Leitungsprüfung *f*

psophometer *n* Psophometer *n*, Geräuschspannungsmesser *m*

psophometric filter Ohrfilter *m*, Ohrkurvenfilter *m*

PTC resistor PTC-Widerstand *m*, Kaltleiter *m*

public *n* Publikum *n*; ~ *adj* öffentlich *adj*; ~ **address (PA)** Beschallung *f*; ~ **address system (PAS)** Beschallungsanlage *f*, Lautsprecherübertragungsanlage *f*, Übertragungsanlage *f*, Publikumslautsprecher *m pl*; ~ **relations** *n pl* Öffentlichkeitsarbeit *f*; **to equip with ~ address** beschallen *v*; **under ~ law** öffentlich-rechtlich *adj*

publication *n* Veröffentlichung *f*; **for ~** zur Veröffentlichung; **not for ~** nicht zur Veröffentlichung

publicity *n* Reklame *f*, Werbung *f*; ~ **department** Presseabteilung *f*, Pressestelle *f*; ~ **film** Werbefilm *m*

publishing rights Veröffentlichungsrechte *n pl*

pull down *v* (set) abbauen *v*; ~ **out** *v* (filming) Luft geben

pulldown *n* Filmtransport *m*; ~ **movement** Filmfortschaltung *f*; ~ **period** Bildfortschaltzeit *f*; ~ **time** Filmfortschaltzeit *f*, Filmschaltzeit *f*

pulley *n* (mech.) Rolle *f*

pull-in range Fangbereich *m*, Mitnahmebereich *m*, Ziehbereich *m*

pulling on whites Blooming *n*

pulling-in circuit Ziehkreis *m*

pull-out *adj* ausziehbar *adj*

pulse *n* Impuls *m*, Takt *m*; ~ **amplitude** Impulsamplitude *f*; ~ **clipper** Impulsabtrennstufe *f*, Impulstrennstufe *f*; ~ **clipping** Impulsabtrennung *f*; ~ **decay time** Impulsabfallzeit *f*; ~ **delay** Impulsverzögerung *f*; ~ **distortion** Impulsverformung *f*; ~ **distributor** Impulsverteiler *m*; ~ **duration** Impulsdauer *f*; ~ **duty factor** Impulstastverhältnis *n*, Tastverhältnis *n*; ~ **edge** Impulsflanke *f*; ~ **fall time** Impulsabfallzeit *f*; ~ **filtration** Impulssiebung *f*; ~ **forming** Impulsformierung *f*; ~ **frequency modulation (PFM)** Impulsfrequenzmodulation (IFM) *f*; ~ **generation and distribution system** Takthaushalt *m*; ~ **generator (PG)** Taktgeber *m*, Impulsgeber *m*, Impulsgenerator *m*; ~ **interference** Impulsstörung *f* ~ **length** Impulsbreite *f*; ~ **modulation** Impulsmodulation *f*; ~ **monitoring** Kamerasignalüberwachung *f*; ~ **operation** Impulsverfahren *n*; ~ **peak power** Impulsspitzenleistung *f*; ~ **position** Impulslage *f*; ~ **rectifier** Impulsgleichrichter *m*; ~ **recurrence frequency (PRF)** Impulsfolgefrequenz *f*; ~ **regeneration** Impulserneuerung *f*; ~ **regenerator** Impulsregenerator *m*; ~ **repetition frequency (PRF)** Impulsfolgefrequenz *f*; ~ **repetition period** Impulsperiodendauer *f*; ~ **restoration** Impulsverbesserung *f*; ~ **rise time** Impulsanstiegzeit *f*; ~ **separation** Impulstrennung *f*, Impulssiebung *f*; ~ **shape** Impulsform *f*; ~ **shaper** Impulsformer *m*; ~ **shaping** Impulsformierung *f*; ~ **switch-on transient** Impulseinschaltvorgang *m*; ~ **synchronisation** Taktsynchronisierung *f*; ~ **tilt**

(imp.) Dachschräge *f*; ~ **train** Impulsserie *f*; ~ **width** Impulsbreite *f*; **complete ~ chain** Impulshaushalt *m*; **field ~** Vertikalimpuls (V-Impuls) *m*, Halbbildimpuls *m*; **vertical ~** (US) Vertikalimpuls (V-Impuls) *m*, Halbbildimpuls *m*
pulse-and-bar test signal 2T-20T-Impuls *m*
pulser *n* Impulsgeber *m*, Impulsgenerator *m*
pump *v* pumpen *v*
punch *v* (EDP) lochen *v*; ~ *n* (appar.) Locher *m*, Stanze *f*; ~ **card** (EDP) Lochkarte *f*; ~ **combination** (EDP) Lochkombination *f*; ~ **up** *v* eintasten *v*
punched card (EDP) Lochkarte *f*; ~ **tape** Belichtungsschablone *f*; ~ **tape** (EDP) Lochstreifen *m*; ~ **tape reader** (EDP) Lochstreifenleser *m*
puncher *n* (operator) Locher *m*
punching machine Lochstanze *f*, Stanze *f*
pup *n* Babyspot *m*, Klemmlampe *f*, Pinza *f*; ~ **stand** Babystativ *n*; **750 Watt ~** Dreiviertel-KW *n*; **500 Watt ~** Halb-KW *n*
Pupin line bespulte Leitung
puppet animation Puppentrick *m*; ~ **film** Puppenfilm *m*
puppeteer *n* Handpuppenspieler *m*, Marionettenspieler *m*
purchased programmes* *n pl* Filmbeschaffung* *f*, Filmredaktion* *f*
pure resistance Wirkwiderstand *m*
purity correction magnet Farbreinheitsmagnet *m*
push *v* (cough key) abdrücken *v*; ~ **button** Drucktaste *f*, Taste *f*; ~ **on** *v* aufstecken *v*
push-on filter Aufsteckfilter *m*
push-over wipe Schiebeblende *f*, seitliche Überblendung
push-pull circuit Gegentaktschaltung *f*; ~ **recording** Gegentaktaufzeichnung *f*; ~ **stage** Gegentaktstufe *f*
push switch Druckschalter *m*
put on *v* ansetzen *v*; ~ **out** *v* (news) absetzen *v*, rausbringen *v* (fam.); ~ **right** *v* verbessern *v*; ~ **through** *v* (to) (tel.) verbinden *v* (mit); ~ **together** *v* zusammenstellen *v*; **to ~ in sync** anlegen *v*; **to ~ on 1000 Hz** 1000 Hz-Ton aufschalten; **to ~ on the air** *v* ausstrahlen *v*; **to ~ to bed** (coll.) Redaktionsschluß machen
putting in circuit Zuschaltung *f*; ~ **into operation** Inbetriebnahme *f* ~ **into service** Inbetriebnahme *f*
pylon *n* Mast *m*
pyrotechnician *n* Pyrotechniker *m*
pyroxylin lacquer Nitrolack *m*

Q

quadrature error (VTR) Quadraturfehler *m*; ~ **fault** (modulation) Quadraturfehler *m*; ~ **modulation** Quadraturmodulation *f*
quadripole *n* Vierpol *m*
quality check Bildendkontrolle *f*, Programmüberwachung *f*
quantiser *n* (EDP) Analog-Digital-Umsetzer (ADU) *m*
quarter-inch tape Schnürsenkel *m* (fam.)
quarter track Viertelspur *f*; ~ **wave** Viertelwelle *f*
quartz iodine lamp Jodquarzlampe *f*; ~ **lamp** Quarzlampe *f*
query *v* (EDP) abfragen *v*; ~ *n* (EDP) Anfrage *f*
quick change magazine Schnellwechselkassette *f*; ~ **motion** Zeitraffer *m*
quick-motion apparatus Zeitraffer

m; ~ **camera** Zeitraffer *m*; ~ **effect** Zeitraffung *f*
quiet, please! Ruhe bitte!
quiz *n* Quiz *n*, Ratespiel *n*; ~ **programme** Quizsendung *f*
quizmaster *n* Spielleiter *m*

R

racing news Pferdesportnachrichten *f pl*
rack *n* Gestell *n*, Rahmengestell *n*; ~ **base** Rahmenträgeruntergestell *n*; ~ **footing** Rahmenträgeruntergestell *n*; ~ **line** (F) Bildsteg *m*
racked blanking Vorspann mit Bildstrich; ~ **spacing** Vorspann mit Bildstrich
racks *n pl* (coll.) Kamerasignalüberwachung *f*; ~ **engineer** (TV) Kameratechniker *m*
radiant energy Strahlungsenergie *f*
radiate *v* (tech.) ausstrahlen *v*; ~ *v* (aerial) abstrahlen *v*
radiated energy Strahlungsenergie *f*; ~ **interference** Fremdeinstrahlung *f*; ~ **power** Strahlungsleistung *f*; **effective ~ power (ERP)** effektive Strahlungsleistung (ERP), Sendeleistung *f*
radiating element (aerial) Primärstrahler *m*; ~ **element of aerial** Antennenstrahler *m*; ~ **surface** Abstrahlebene *f*
radiation *n* (tech.) Ausstrahlung *f*, Strahlung *f*; ~ *n* (aerial) Abstrahlung *f*; ~ **characteristic** Strahlungscharakteristik *f*, Strahlungsdiagramm *n*; ~ **diagram** Strahlungscharakteristik *f*, Strahlungsdiagramm *n*; ~ **pattern** Richtcharakteristik *f*, Richtdiagramm *n*, Strahlungscharakteristik *f*, Strahlungsdiagramm *n*; ~ **resistance** Strahlungswiderstand *m*; ~ **-responsive pick-up** Strahlungsempfänger *m*; ~ **-sensitive pick-up** Strahlungsempfänger *m*; **coloured ~** farbige Strahlung
radiator *n* Strahler *m*
radio *v* funken *v*, senden *v*; ~ *n* Funk *m*, Hörfunk *m*, Hörrundfunk *m*, Radio *n*, Rundfunk *m*, Tonrundfunk *m*; ~ *n* (set) Rundfunkapparat *m*, Rundfunkempfänger *m*, Rundfunkgerät *n*, Radio *n*; ~ *adj* funkisch *adj*, Hörfunk- (in Zus.); ~ **adaptation** Funkbearbeitung *f*; ~ **advertising** Funkwerbung *f*; ~ **amateur** Funkamateur *m*; ~ **and television engineering** Sendebetriebstechnik *f*, Sendetechnik *f*; ~ **and television exhibition** Funkausstellung *f*; ~ **and television operations** *n pl* Sendebetrieb *m*; ~ **beacon** Peilsender *m*, Funkbake *f*, Funkfeuer *n*; ~ **beam** Funkstrahl *m*, Richtfunkstrahl *m*: ~ **bearing** Peilung *f*; ~ **broadcast** Hörfunksendung *f*, Rundfunkübertragung *f*; ~ **broadcasting** Hörfunk *m*; ~ **camera** drahtlose Kamera; ~ **car** Funkwagen *m*, HF-Wagen *m*, drahtloser Ü-Wagen; ~ **centre** Hörfunkkomplex *m*; ~ **channel** Rundfunkkanal *m*; ~ **choir** Rundfunkchor *m*; ~ **chorus** Rundfunkchor *m*; ~ **circuit** Hörfunkleitung *f*; ~ **communication** Funkverbindung *f*, Funkverkehr *m*; ~ **-communication service**

Funkdienst *m*; ~ **-control** *v* fernleiten *v*; ~ **control** Funksteuerung *f*; ~ **control receiver** drahtloser Kommandoempfänger; ~ **corporation** (US) Rundfunkgesellschaft *f*, Rundfunksendegesellschaft *f*, Sendegesellschaft *f*; ~ **direction-finding** Peilung *f*; ~ **directorate** Programmdirektion Hörfunk, Hörfunkdirektion *f*, Hörfunkleitung *f*; ~ **drama** Hörspiel *n*; ~ **drama*** Hörspielabteilung *f*, Hörspiel* *n*; ~ **drama library** Hörspielarchiv *n*; ~ **drama producer** Hörfunkspielleiter *m*, Hörspielregisseur *m*; ~ **drama production** Hörspielinszenierung *f*, Hörspielproduktion *f*; ~ **drama script** Hörspielmanuskript *n*; ~ **engineer** Rundfunktechniker *m*; ~ **engineering** Rundfunktechnik *f*; ~ **financed from licence fees** Gebührenrundfunk *m*; ~ **franchise** Hörfunklizenz *f*; ~ **-frequency** *adj* hochfrequent *adj*, Hochfrequenz- (HF) (in Zus.); ~ **frequency (RF)** Hochfrequenz *f* (HF), Radiofrequenz *f* (RF); ~ **-frequency amplifier** Hochfrequenzverstärker *m*; ~ **-frequency choke** Hochfrequenzdrossel *f*, ~ **-frequency choke coil** Hochfrequenzdrossel *f*; ~ **-frequency circuit** Hochfrequenzleitung *f*; ~ **-frequency coil** Hochfrequenzspule *f*; ~ **frequency filter** Funkentstörfilter *m*; ~ **-frequency generator** Hochfrequenzgenerator *m*; ~ **-frequency protection ratio** Hochfrequenzschutzabstand *m*; ~ **-frequency-wanted/interfering-** Hochfrequenzstörabstand *m*; ~ **interference** Störstrahlung *f*; ~ **interference filter** Funkentstörfilter *m*, Störschutzfilter *m*; ~ **interference group** Störungsannahme* *f*; ~ **interference service** Funkstörmeßdienst* *m*; ~ **journalist** Rundfunkjournalist *m*; ~ **licence** Hörfunkgenehmigung *f*; ~ **licence fee** Hörfunkgebühr *f*; ~ **licence-holder** Hörfunkteilnehmer *m*; ~ **link** Richtfunkstrecke *f*, Richtfunkverbindung *f*; ~ **link hop** Funkfeld *n*, ~ **-link network** Richtfunknetz *n*; ~ **-link system** Richtfunk (RiFu) *m*; ~ **magazine** Hörfunkmagazin *n*; ~ **message** Funkspruch *m*; ~ **microphone** drahtloses Mikrofon; ~ **network** Hörfunknetz *n*; ~ **news** Hörfunknachrichten *f pl*, Nachrichten *f pl*; ~ **news*** Hörfunknachrichten* *f pl*; ~ **OB** Tonreportage *f*; ~ **OB van** Übertragungswagen *m*, Ü-Wagen *m*; ~ **opera** Funkoper *f*; ~ **operator** Funker *m*; ~ **orchestra** Rundfunkorchester *n*; ~ **-photogram** *n* Funkbild *n*, Funkfoto *n*; ~ **picture** Funkbild *n*, Funkfoto *n*; ~ **play** Hörspiel *n*; ~ **playwright** Hörspielautor *m*; ~ **producer** Spielleiter *m*; ~ **production** Hörfunkinszenierung *f*, Hörfunkproduktion *f*; ~ **programme** Hörfunkprogramm *n*, Hörfunksendung *f*, Rundfunksendung *f*; ~ **programme circuit** Hörfunkleitung *f*; ~ **receiver** Rundfunkapparat *m*, Rundfunkempfänger *m*, Rundfunkgerät *n*, Radio *n*; ~ **receiver** (WT) Funkempfänger *m*; ~ **recording** Hörfunkaufnahme *f*; ~ **relay** Hörfunkübertragung *f*,

Rundfunkübertragung *f*; ~ **relay** (WT) Funkrelais *n*; ~ **relay exchange** (PO) Rundfunkvermittlung *f*; ~ **-relay network** Richtfunknetz *n*; ~ **-relay transmission service*** Richtfunkübertragungsdienst* *m*; ~ **serial** Hörfunkreihe *f*; ~ **series** Hörfolge *f*; ~ **service** Hörfunkdienst *m*, Rundfunkdienst *m*; ~ **service** (WT) Funkdienst *m*; ~ **set** Rundfunkapparat *m*, Rundfunkempfänger *m*, Rundfunkgerät *n*, Radio *n*; ~ **station** Rundfunkanstalt *f*, Rundfunkstation *f*, Sendestation *f* ~ **stereophony** Rundfunkstereofonie *f*; ~ **studio** Hörfunkstudio *n*; ~ **switching centre** Tonsternpunkt *m*, Tonstern *m*; ~ **talks and current affairs programmes** *n pl* Zeitfunk *m*; ~ **telephone** Funksprechgerät *n*, Sprechfunkgerät *n*; ~ **-telephone traffic** Sprechfunkverkehr *m*; ~ **tower** Sendeturm *m*; ~ **traffic** Funkverkehr *m*; ~ **transmission** Hörfunkübertragung *f*, Rundfunkübertragung *f*, Funksendung *f*; ~ **transmission** (WT) drahtlose Übertragung; ~ **transmitter** Rundfunksender *m*; ~ **wave** Funkwelle *f*; ~ **writer** Funkautor *m*; **commercial** ~ Werbefunk *m*; **reversible** ~ **link** umzündbares Funkfeld; **steerable** ~ **link** drehbares Funkfeld; **terrestrial** ~ **communication** terrestrischer Funkverkehr; **wired** ~ Drahtfunk *m*

radiogram *n* Musiktruhe *f*

radiophonic *adj* funkisch *adj*, radiofonisch *adj*

radiotelephonic traffic (RT traffic) Funksprechverkehr *m*

radiotelephony (RT) *n* Sprechfunk *m*

rail *n* Schiene *f*; **bent** ~ gebogene Schiene; **curved** ~ gebogene Schiene; **straight** ~ gerade Schiene

railing *n* Brüstung *f*

rainbow test pattern Regenbogentestbild *n*; ~ **test pattern generator** Regenbogengenerator *m*

rain shield Regenschutz *m*

random-access programming (EDP) Random-Access-Programmierung

random noise (pict.) Grieß *m*

range *n* Bereich *m*, Reichweite *f*, Umfang *m*; ~ **of exposure** Belichtungsspielraum *m*; ~ **of focus** Brennweitenbereich *m*; ~ **of light level** Beleuchtungsstärkeumfang *m*; ~ **of luminance** Leuchtdichteumfang *m*; ~ **of tolerance** Toleranzbereich *m*

range extender Brennweitenverlängerer *m*

range-finder *n* Entfernungsmesser *m*; **coupled** ~ gekoppelter Entfernungsmesser

rapid stop Schnellstopp *m*; ~ **stop key** Schnellstopptaste *f*

raster *n* Raster *m*, Bildraster *m*; ~ **definition** Rasterauflösung *f*, Rasterschärfe *f*

ratchet pawl Sperriegel *m*

rate *n* (pulse) Takt *m*; ~ **card** Gebührenordnung *f*, Preisliste *f*

rated output Nennleistung *f*; ~ **power** Nennleistung *f*; ~ **voltage** Nennspannung *f*

ratio control (EDP) Verhältnisregelung *f*, Verhältnissteuerung *f*; ~ **detector** Ratiodetektor *m*, Verhältnisgleichrichter *m*

raw film Rohfilm *m*, Rohfilmmaterial *n*; ~ **stock** Filmmaterial *n*, Rohfilm *m*, Rohfilmmaterial *n*, Aufnahmematerial *n*; ~ **stock**

bobbin Rohfilmkern *m*; ~ **stock centre** Rohfilmkern *m*; ~ **stock core** Rohfilmkern *m*; ~ **stock dimension** Rohfilmmaß *n*; ~ **stock manufacture** Rohfilmherstellung *f*; ~ **stock manufacturer** Rohfilmhersteller *m*; ~ **stock store** Rohfilmlager *n*; ~ **tape** Frischband *n*

ray *n* Strahl *m*; ~ **path** Strahlengang *m*

RBW system RBW-Verfahren *n*

RC coupling RC-Kopplung *f*; ~ **network** RC-Glied *n*; ~ **section** RC-Glied *n*

reactance *n* Blindwiderstand *m*; ~ **coil** Drossel *f*, Drosselspule *f*; ~ **valve** Blindröhre *f*, Reaktanzröhre *f*; **distributed** ~ verteilte Blindwiderstände

reacting time Ansprechzeit *f*

reaction *n* Rückwirkung *f*; ~ **index** Urteilsindex *m*; ~ **shot** Gegeneinstellung *f*, Gegenschuß *m*

reactivation *n* Regenerierung *f*

reactive component Blindanteil *m*; ~ **impedance** Blindwiderstand *m*; ~ **power** Blindleistung *f*

read *v* (meas.) ablesen *v*; ~ *v* (R, TV news) sprechen *v*; ~ **again** *v* wiederholen *v*; ~ **head** (EDP) Lesekopf *m*; ~ **off** *v* ablesen *v*; ~ **out** *v* (EDP) auslesen *v*; ~ **statement** (EDP) Lesebefehl *m*; ~ **-through** *n* Leseprobe *f*

readability *n* Verständlichkeit *f*; ~ *n* (RT) Verständigung *f*

readiness *n* Bereitschaft *f*; ~ **for operation** Betriebsbereitschaft *f*

reading *n* Lesung *f*; ~ *n* (meas.) Anzeige *f*, Meßanzeige *f*; ~ **head** (EDP) Lesekopf *m*

readjust *v* nachstellen *v*

readjustment *n* Nachjustierung *f*; ~ **of black level** Schwarzwertwiederherstellung *f*

ready for operation betriebsbereit *adj*; ~ **for preview** abnahmefertig *adj*; ~ **for release** (F) einsatzbereit *adj*; ~ **for scrutiny** abnahmefertig *adj*, abnahmeklar *adj*; ~ **for transmission** sendefertig *adj*

realignment *n* Nachjustierung *f*

realisation, scenic szenische Auflösung

real-time *adj* (EDP) Echtzeit- (in Zus.), Realzeit- (in Zus.); ~ **clock** (EDP) Realzeituhr *f*, Uhrzeitgeber *m*; ~ **control** (EDP) Realzeitsteuerung *f*; ~ **operation** (EDP) Echtzeitbetrieb *m*, Realzeitbetrieb *m*; ~ **processing** (EDP) Echtzeit-Datenverarbeitung *f*, Sofortverarbeitung *f*; ~ **working** (EDP) Echtzeitbetrieb *m*, Realzeitbetrieb *m*

rear aerial (vehicle) Heckantenne *f*; ~ **element** Austrittsebene *f*; ~ **panel** Rückwand *f*; ~ **projection (RP)** Rückprojektion *f*, Rückpro *f* (fam.), Durchprojektion *f*; ~ **projection screen** Rückproschirm *m*; ~ **wall** Rückwand *f*

reasonableness check (EDP) Plausibilitätsprüfung *f*

rebroadcast *n* (prog.) Wiederholung *f*, Übernahme *f*; ~ (RBR) *n* Ballempfang *m*; ~ **of ...** Übernahme von ...; ~ **receiver** Ballempfänger *m*; ~ **transmitter** Relaissender *m*

rebroadcasting reception (RBR) Ballempfang *m*

re-cable *v* umkabeln *v*

recalibrate *v* nacheichen *v*

recall signal Rückrufzeichen *n*

recasting *n* Umbesetzung *f*

recce *n* (coll.) Lokaltermin *m*, Motivbesichtigung *f*, Motivsuche *f*, Vorbesichtigung *f*

receive *v* empfangen *v*

received frequency

Empfangsfrequenz *f*; ~ **voltage** Empfangsspannung *f*
receiver *n* Empfänger *m*, Empfangsgerät *n*; ~ *n* (tel.) Hörer *m*; ~ **diplexer** Empfängerweiche *f*; ~ **licence fee** Rundfunkgebühr *f*; ~ **primaries** Empfängerprimärvalenzen *f pl*
receiving aerial Empfangsantenne *f* ~ **and measuring station (CEM)** Meß- und Empfangsstation *f*, Frequenzüberwachungszentrale *f*; ~ **circuit** Empfangskreis *m*; ~ **diplexer** Rundfunkempfängerweiche *f*; ~ **end** Empfängerseite *f*; ~ **service** empfangender Dienst; ~ **set** Empfänger *m*, Empfangsgerät *n*; ~ **station** Empfangsstation *f*; ~ **valve** Empfängerröhre *f*
reception *n* Empfang *m*; ~ **conditions** Empfangsverhältnisse *n pl*; ~ **quality** Empfangsgüte *f*, Verständigung *f*; **individual** ~ (sat.) individueller Empfang
receptionist *n* Empfangsdame *f*
reciprocal of amplification factor Durchgriff *m*
reciprocally *adv* wechselweise *adv*
recirculation *n* Flüssigkeitsumwälzung *f*
reclamation *n* Rückgewinnung *f*
recondition *v* (tech.) überholen *v*
reconditioning *n* Instandsetzung *f*, Überholung *f*
reconstruct, to ~ a scene Szene nachstellen
re-cooling plant Rückkühlanlage *f*
record *v* aufnehmen *v*, aufzeichnen *v*, bespielen *v*; ~ *v* (disc, tape) einspielen *v*; ~ *v* (bcast.) mitschneiden *v*, Mitschnitt machen; ~ *n* Platte *f*, Schallplatte *f*; ~ **album** Plattenkassette *f*; ~ **changer** Plattenwechsler *m*; **automatic ~ changer** automatischer Plattenwechsler ~ **library** Plattenarchiv *n*, Schallplattenarchiv *n*; ~ **player** Plattenspieler *m*, Phonogerät *n*, Plattenmaschine *f*; ~ **-playing deck** Platine mit Plattenmaschine, Plattenspielerchassis *n*; ~ **programme** Schallplattenprogramm *n*; ~ **-~ -replay equipment** Aufnahme-Wiedergabegerät *n*, Aufnahme-Wiedergabemaschine *f*; ~ **-replay head** kombinierter Aufnahme-Wiedergabekopf, Kombikopf *m* (fam.); ~ **reproducer** Plattenmaschine *f*, Plattenspieler *m*; ~ **requests** Hörerwünsche *m pl* ~ **turntable** Schallplattenteller *m*, Plattenteller *m*; **to ~ a theatre production** abfotografieren *v*; **to ~ off air** (bcast.) mitschneiden *v*, Mitschnitt machen; **to ~ on film** FAZ aufzeichnen, Film aufzeichnen, fazen *v* (fam.); **to ~ over a circuit** über Leitung aufnehmen, über Leitung aufzeichnen
recorded report Bandreportage *f*
recorder *n* Aufnahmegerät *n*, Aufnahmemaschine *f*, Recorder *m*; ~ *n* (meas.) Schreiber *m*; **magnetic ~** magnetische Aufzeichnungsanlage
recording *n* Aufnahme *f*, Aufzeichnung *f*; ~ *n* (disc, tape) Einspielung *f*; ~ *n* (TV) Kameraaufnahme *f*; ~ *n* (electronics) Speicherung *f*; ~ **apparatus** Schreiber *m*; ~ **car** Aufnahmewagen *m*, Aufzeichnungswagen *m*, Reportagefahrzeug *n*, Reportagewagen *m*, Schnellreportagewagen *m*, Tonaufnahmewagen *m*, Tonwagen *m* (fam.); ~ **chain** Aufnahmekette *f*, Aufzeichnungskette *f*; ~ **channel**

Aufnahmekanal *m*; **~ channel** (room) Magnetofonraum *m*, Regie-Tonträger *m*, Schallaufzeichnungsraum *m*, Tonaufnahmeraum *m*, Tonaufzeichnungsraum *m*, Tonträger *m*, Tonträgerraum *m*; **~ current** Aufsprechstrom *m*, Aufzeichnungsstrom *m*, Kopfstrom *m* (fam.); **~ engineer** Tonmeister *m*; **~ equipment** Aufnahmegerät *n*, Aufzeichnungsanlage *f*; **~ from line** Aufzeichnung über Strecke; **~ head** Aufnahmekopf *m*, Aufzeichnungskopf *m*; **~ head** (EDP) Schreibkopf *m*; **~ key with safety-lock** Aufnahmetaste mit Sperre; **~ level indicator** Aufzeichnungspegelanzeiger *m*; **~ loss** Aufzeichnungsverluste *m pl* **~ material** Aufnahmematerial *n*; **~ medium** Signalschriftträger *m*; **~ mode** (EDP) Aufzeichnungsverfahren *n*; **~ off air** Mitschnitt *m*; **~ room** Aufnahmeraum *m*; **~ speed** Aufnahmegeschwindigkeit *f*, Aufzeichnungsgeschwindigkeit *f*; **~ studio** Tonatelier *n*, Tonaufnahmestudio *n*, Tonstudio *n*, Schallaufzeichnungsraum *m*; **~ system** Aufnahmesystem *n*, Aufzeichnungsanlage *f*, Speichersystem *n*; **~ technique** (EDP) Aufzeichnungsverfahren *n*; **~ theatre** Aufnahmeraum *m*; **~ unit** Aufnahmeeinheit *f*; **~ van** Aufnahmewagen *m*, Aufzeichnungswagen *m*, Reportagefahrzeug *n*, Reportagewagen *m*, Tonaufnahmewagen *m*, Tonwagen *m* (fam.); **~ wire** Magnettondraht *m*; **magnetic ~** magnetische Aufzeichnung; **maximum ~ level** maximaler Aufnahmepegel; **mechanical ~** mechanische Aufzeichnung; **on-the-spot ~** Aufzeichnung an Ort und Stelle; **simultaneous ~** Mitschnitt *m*

recording/reproducing über alles; **~ frequency response** Frequenzgang über alles; **~ magnetic head** kombinierter Magnetkopf; **~ unit** Aufnahme-Wiedergabegerät *n*, Aufnahme-Wiedergabemaschine *f*

recover *v* rückgewinnen *v*

recovery *n* Rückgewinnung *f*

rectangular pulse Rechteckimpuls *m*; **~ pulse train** Rechteckimpulsfolge *f*

rectification *n* Richtigstellung *f*

rectified current Richtstrom *m*; **~ voltage** Richtspannung *f*

rectifier *n* Gleichrichter *m*; **~ valve** Gleichrichterröhre *f*

recuperation *n* (elec.) Rückgewinnung *f*

recurrent network Kettenleiter *m*

red,to give the abläuten *v* **~ -green blind** farbfehlsichtig *adj*; **~ -green blindness** Farbfehlsichtigkeit *f*; **~ light** Rotlicht *n*; **~ master** Marron *n*

redevelopment *n* fotografische Verstärkung

redistribution *n* Wiederverteilung *f*

reduce *v* verkleinern *v*; **~** *v* (pict.) abschwächen *v*; **~** *v* (mech.) untersetzen *v*

reducer *n* (pict.) Abschwächer *m*

reduction *n* Abnahme *f*, Verkleinerung *f*, Reduktion *f*; **~** *n* (level) frequenzabhängiger Pegelabfall; **~** *n* (mech.) Untersetzung *f*; **~** *n* (pict.) Abschwächung *f*; **~ material** Mischband *n*; **~ of reflection** Entspiegeln *n*; **~ print** Verkleinerungskopie *f*; **~ printer** Verkleinerungsmaschine *f*; **~ room** Mischatelier *n*

redundancy *n* Redundanz *f*, informative Überbestimmtheit
reed *n* (freq. meter) Zunge *f*
re-edit *v* umschneiden *v*
reel *v* spulen *v*; ~ *n* Spule *f*, Rolle *f*, Filmrolle *f*, Akt *m*, Aktrolle *f*; ~ **off** *v* abspulen *v*; ~ **(up)** *v* aufspulen *v*, aufwickeln *v*, auftrommeln *v*
re-emission *n* Remission *f*
re-emissive power Remissionsumfang *m*
re-exposure *n* Zweitbelichtung *f*
reference *n* Bezug *m*; ~ **audio level** Tonbezugspegel *m*; ~ **audio tape** Tonbezugsband *n*; ~ **axis** Bezugslinie *f*; ~ **black** Bezugsschwarz *n*; ~ **edge** Anlagekante *f*, Bezugskante *f*; ~ **frequency** Normalfrequenz *f*; ~ **generator** Bezugsgenerator *m*; ~ **level** Bezugspegel *m*; ~ **library** Zeitungsarchiv *n*; ~ **line** Bezugslinie *f*; ~ **luminosity** Bezugshelligkeit *f*; ~ **oscillation** Pilotschwingung *f*; ~ **oscillator** Bezugsoszillator *m*; ~ **phase** Bezugsphase *f*, Vergleichsphase *f*; ~ **point** Bezugspunkt *m*; ~ **pulse** Bezugsimpuls *m*, Vergleichsimpuls *m*; ~ **tape** Bezugsband *n*, Magnetbezugsband *n*, Normband *n*, Normbezugsband *n*; ~ **value** Bezugswert *m*; ~ **voltage** Bezugsspannung *f*, Vergleichsspannung *f*; ~ **white** Bezugsweiß *n*; **to send ~ tone** Meßton aufschalten
reflect out *v* ausspiegeln *v*
reflectance *n* Remission *f*
reflected light measurement Objektmessung *f*; ~ **lighting** Reflexbeleuchtung *f*
reflecting power Reflexionsvermögen *n*, Remissionsumfang *m*
reflection *n* Reflexion *f*, Spiegelung *f*; ~ **coefficient** Reflexionsgrad *m*, Reflexionskoeffizient *m*; ~ **factor** Reflexionsgrad *m*, Reflexionskoeffizient *m*; ~ **filter** Fallenfilter *m*; ~ **loss** Reflexionsverlust *m*; ~ **screen** Sonnenblende *f*
reflectometer *n* (aerial) Vorwärts-Rückwärts-Meßgerät *n*
reflector *n* Reflektor *m*, Spiegel *m*, Hohlspiegel *m*; ~ *n* (spotlight) Scheinwerfer *m*; ~ *n* (lighting) Aufhellschirm *m*; ~ **grid** (aerial) Gitterreflektor *m*; ~ **lamp** verspiegelte Lampe; ~ **lamp** (spotlight) Scheinwerferlampe *f*; ~ **mirror** Reflektorspiegel *m*; ~ **mount** Spiegelfassung *f*; ~ **screen** Aufhellschirm *m*, Reflexionswand *f*; ~ **viewfinder** Brillantsucher *m*; **concave ~** Hohlspiegel *m*
reflex camera Reflexkamera *f*, Spiegelreflexkamera *f*; ~ **finder** Reflexsucher *m*; ~ **mirror shutter** Spiegelreflexblende *f*; ~ **system** Spiegelreflexsystem *n*; ~ **viewfinder** Reflexsucher *m*
refocus *v* Bild aus der Unschärfe ziehen
refraction *n* Brechung *f*
refresher course Fortbildungskurs *m*
refrigeration *n* Kühlung *f*
regenerate *v* regenerieren *v*; ~ *v* (feedback) rückkoppeln *v*
regenerating equipment Regenerationsgerät *n*
regeneration *n* Regeneration *f*, Regenerierung *f*; ~ *n* (feedback) Rückkopplung *f*
regenerative feedback Rückkopplung *f*
regenerator *n* Regenerator *m*
region *n* Bereich *m*; **achromatic ~** achromatischer Bereich
regional broadcast Regionalsendung *f*; ~ **broadcasting act**

Landesrundfunkgesetz *n*; **~ broadcasting station** Landesrundfunkanstalt *f*; **~ centre** Regionalstudio *n*, Regionalanstalt *f*; **~ news** Regionalnachrichten *f pl*, regionale Berichterstattung; **~ play** Volksstück *n*; **~ programme** Regionalprogramm *n*; **~ station** Landesstudio *n*; **~ studio** Außenstudio *n*, Landesstudio *n*; **~ television programmes** *n pl* Regionalfernsehen *n*

register *n* (EDP) Register *n*; **~ of film titles** Filmtitelregister *n*; **~ of titles** Titelregister *n*; **~ pin** Greifer *m*, Sperrgreifer *m*

registration *n* Farbdeckung *f*, Deckung *f*; **~ error** Deckungsfehler *m*; **~ of film title** Filmtitelanmeldung *f*

registry *n* Registratur *f*

regular rotational movement (disc) Gleichlauf *m*

regulate *v* einstellen *v*, regeln *v*, regulieren *v*, steuern *v*

regulation *n* Regelung *f*

regulator *n* Regler *m*

rehearsal *n* Probe *f*, Probeablauf *m*; **~ on stage** Probe in der Dekoration; **~ room** Probenraum *m*; **~ studio** Probenstudio *n*; **~ studios** *n pl* Probenhaus *n*; **~ time** Probenzeit *f*; **~ with cameras** heiße Probe; **~ without recording** kalte Probe

rehearse *v* (scene) einstudieren *v*

reimbursement *n* Kostenerstattung *f*; **~ of expenses** Reisekostenvergütung *f*

reinforce *v* (FP) verstärken *v*

re-issue *v* (F, thea.) wiederherausgeben *v*; ~ *n* (F, thea.) Reprise *f*

reject *v* ausmustern *v*

rejection circuit Sperrschaltung *f*; **~ filter** Sperrfilter *m*

rejector circuit Sperrkreis *m*

relative humidity (RH) relative Feuchtigkeit; **~ luminosity factor** spektrale Hellempfindlichkeitskurve; **~ sensitivity curve** Augenempfindlichkeitskurve *f*

relaxation generator Kippgerät *n*; **~ oscillator** Kippspannungserzeuger *m*, Sägezahngenerator *m*

relay *v* übertragen *v*; ~ *v* (prog.) übernehmen *v*; ~ *n* Relais *n*; ~ *n* (prog.) Übertragung *f*, Übernahme *f*, Ringsendung *f*; ~ *n* (contactor) Schütz *n*; **~ box** Relaisschrank *m*; **~ by loudspeaker** Lautsprecherübertragung *f*; **~ frame** Relaisschrank *m*; **~ lens** Relaisoptik *f*; **~ matrix** Relaiskreuzschaltfeld *n*; **~ of ...** Übernahme von ...; **~ optics** Relaisoptik *f*; **~ receiver** Richtfunkempfänger *m*; **~ room** Schützraum *m*; **~ spring** Relaisschiene *f*; **~ station** Relaisstation *f*, Relaissender *m*; **~ transmitter** Relaissender *m*; **deferred ~** zeitversetzte Livesendung, zeitversetzte Übertragung; **polarised ~** gepoltes Relais, polarisiertes Relais; **slugged ~** ausfallverzögertes Relais

relayed *adj* (transmitter) angeschlossen *adj*; **~ from ...** übertragen aus ...

relaying station übernehmende Anstalt

release *v* (F) herausbringen *v*; ~ *v* (mech) auslösen *v*, ausrasten *v*; ~ *v* (news) freigeben *v*; ~ *n* Auslöser *m*; ~ *n* (F) Einsatz *m*; **~ button** Auslöseknopf *m*; **~ gear** Auslöser *m*; **~ print** (F) Serienkopie *f*, Theaterkopie *f*, Vorführkopie *f*; **~ signal** Auslösezeichen *n*; **to ~ a film** Film herausbringen; **to ~ information** Information freigeben

released, to be herauskommen *v*

reliability *n* Zuverlässigkeit *f*
relief *n* (staff) Hilfskraft *f*; ~ **effect** Bildplastik *f*
religious broadcasting* Kirchenfunk* *m*
remake *n* (F) Neuproduktion *f*, Neuverfilmung *f*, Remake *n*, Wiederverfilmung *f*
remanence *n* remanenter Magnetismus
remit *v* remittieren *v*
remoisten *v* wiederanfeuchten *v*
remote batch processing (EDP) Stapelfernverarbeitung *f*; ~ **broadcast** (US) Außenaufnahme *f*, Außenübertragung *f* (AÜ); ~ **contribution inject** Zuspielung *f* ~ **contribution insert** Zuspielung *f* ~ **control** Fernbedienung *f*, Fernbetätigung *f*, Fernsteuerung *f*, Fernschaltung *f*; ~ **-control equipment** Fernbediengerät *n*; ~ **-control system** Fernwirkeinrichtung *f*, Fernwirksystem *n*; ~ **-control unit** Fernbediengerät *n*; ~ **-controlled** *adj* ferngesteuert *adj*; ~ **-controlled switching** Fernschaltung *f*; ~ **indication** (EDP) Fernanzeige *f*; ~ **monitoring** Fernüberwachung *f*; ~ **release** Fernauslöser *m*; ~ **replay machine** Zuspielmaschine *f*; ~ **start** Fernstart *m*; ~ **switching** Fernschaltung *f*; **to operate by ~ control** fernbedienen *v*, fernsteuern *v*
removable *adj* abnehmbar *adj*, ausziehbar *adj*
removal of mass by flywheel-drilling Auswuchten *n*
remunerate *v* honorieren *v*
remuneration *n* Vergütung *f*; **claim for** ~ Vergütungsanspruch *m*
rendering *n* Reproduktion *f*
rent *v* mieten *v*
rental fee Leihmiete *f*
repair *v* reparieren *v*; ~ *n* Reparatur *f*, Instandsetzung *f*; ~ **shop** Reparaturwerkstatt *f*
repeat *v* wiederholen *v*; ~ *n* Wiederholung *f*; ~ *n* (bcast.) Zweitsendung *f*; ~ **broadcast** Zweitsendung *f*; ~ **fee** Wiederholungshonorar *n*
repeater *n* Kabelverstärker *m*, Verstärker *m*, Zwischenverstärker *m*; ~ **bay** Verstärkergestell *n*; ~ **receiver** Ballempfänger *m*; ~ **station** (PO) Verstärkeramt *n*
repeating accuracy Wiederkehrgenauigkeit *f*; ~ **coil** Übertrager *m*
repertoire *n* Repertoire *n*, Spielplan *m*
repertory *n* Repertoire *n*
repetiteur *n* Korrepetitor *m*
repetition frequency Folgefrequenz *f*
replaceable *adj* auswechselbar *adj*
replacement *n* Ersatzteil *n*; ~ **battery** Ersatzbatterie *f*
replay *n* Wiederholung *f*, Wiedergabe *f*, Abspielung *f*; ~ **chain** Wiedergabekette *f*; ~ **machine** Abspielgerät *n*; ~ **speed** Abspielgeschwindigkeit *f*
replenisher *n* Regenerierflüssigkeit *f*
replenishment *n* Entwicklerregenerierung *f*
reply *n* Gegendarstellung *f*; **to exercise right of** ~ von dem Recht auf Gegendarstellung Gebrauch machen
report *v* berichten *v*, Berichterstattung wahrnehmen; ~ *n* Bericht *m*, Beitrag *m*; **on-the-spot** ~ Augenzeugenbericht *m*
reportage *n* Reportage *f*
reporter *n* Reporter *m*, Berichterstatter *m*; ~ *n* (TV) Realisator *m*
reporting *n* Berichterstattung *f*

representative in foreign country Auslandsstudioleiter *m*
reprint *v* abdrucken *v*; ~ *n* Abdruck *m*
repro *n* (coll.) Wiedergabe *f*
reproduce *v* wiedergeben *v*
reproducer *n* Abspielgerät *n*, Wiedergabegerät *n*
reproducing amplifier Wiedergabeverstärker *m*; ~ **chain** Wiedergabekette *f*; ~ **channel** Wiedergabekanal *m*; ~ **characteristics** *n pl* Wiedergabecharakteristik *f*; ~ **frequency response** Wiedergabecharakteristik *f*; ~ **gap** Wiedergabespalt *m*; ~ **head** Hörkopf *m*, Wiedergabekopf *m*; ~ **loss** Abspielfehler *m*; ~ **stylus** Abspielnadel *f*; ~ **stylus tip** Abtastnadel *f*
reproduction *n* Reproduktion *f*; ~ *n* Wiedergabe *f*; ~ *n* Abspielung *f*; ~ *n* Kopie *f*; ~ **curve** Wiedergabekurve *f*; ~ **equipment** Wiedergabegerät *n*; ~ **fee** Wiederholungshonorar *n*; ~ **fidelity** Wiedergabetreue *f*; ~ **level** Wiedergabepegel *m*; ~ **right** Vervielfältigungsrecht *n*, Wiedergaberecht *n*; **faithful ~** naturgetreue Wiedergabe; **high fidelity ~** naturgetreue Wiedergabe; **mechanical ~ rights** mechanische Wiedergaberechte; **orthophonic ~** naturgetreue Wiedergabe; **quality of ~** Wiedergabegüte *f*, Wiedergabequalität *f*
re-publish *v* wiederherausgeben *v*
requests programme Hörerwünsche *m pl*
re-radiate *v* wiederausstrahlen *v*
re-radiation *n* Wiederausstrahlung *f*, Remission *f*
re-record *v* Aufnahme wiederholen, wiederaufzeichnen *v*, nachproduzieren *v*; ~ *v* (transfer) überspielen *v*, umkopieren *v*, umschneiden *v*, umspielen *v*; ~ *v* (tape) nachproduzieren *v*
re-recording *n* Überspielung *f*, Umschneiden *m*, Umschnitt *m*, Umspielung *f*, Kopie *f*
re-run *v* (teleprinter) wiederholen *v*; ~ *v* (US) (prog.) (bcast.) wiederholen *v*; ~ *n* Reprise *f*; ~ *n* (US) (prog.) Wiederholung *f*
research and development* Forschung und Entwicklung*; ~ **assistant** Rechercheur *m*; ~ **department** Entwicklungsabteilung *f*; ~ **engineer** Entwicklungsingenieur *m*; ~ **specialist** Rechercheur *m*
reservation, with unter Vorbehalt
reserve channel (transmission) Schutzkanal *m*; ~ **circuit** Ersatzleitung *f*, Reserveleitung *f*; ~ **service** Reservebetrieb *m*
reset *v* nachstellen *v*; ~ *n* Rückstellung *f*
reshoot *v* Aufnahme wiederholen, nachdrehen *v*
resident pianist Hauspianist *m*
residual current Reststrom *m*, Anlaufstrom *m*; ~ **interference voltage** Reststörspannung *f*; ~ **noise** Eigengeräusch *n*; ~ **ripple** Restwelligkeit *f*; ~ **voltage** Restspannung *f*, Grundrestspannung *f*
resistance *n* Widerstand *m*; ~ **network** Widerstandsnetzwerk *n* ~ **to short-circuiting** Kurzschlußfestigkeit *f*; **variable ~** veränderlicher Widerstand
resistive loading ohmsche Belastung
resistor *n* Widerstand *m*; **burnt-out ~** verbrannter Widerstand, abgerauchter Widerstand; **variable ~** veränderlicher Widerstand; **voltage-dependent ~ (VDR)** spannungsabhängiger

Widerstand, VDR-Widerstand *m*
resolution *n* (opt.) Auflösung *f*, Auflösungsvermögen *n*; ~ **wedge** Auflösungskeil *m*, Besenkeil *m*
resolve *v* (opt.) auflösen *v*
resolving power (opt.) Auflösungsvermögen *n*
resonance *n* Resonanz *f*; ~ **indication** Resonanzanzeige *f*; ~ **peak** Resonanzspitze *f*
resonant circuit Resonanzkreis *m*, Schwingkreis *m*; ~ **curve** Resonanzkurve *f*; ~ **impedance** Resonanzwiderstand *m*; ~ **voltage** Resonanzspannung *f*
resound *v* hallen *v*
resource *n* Hilfsquelle *f*
response *n* (elec.) Ansprechen *n*; ~ **characteristic** Wiedergabecharakteristik *f*; ~ **sensitivity** Ansprechempfindlichkeit *f*; ~ **threshold** Ansprechschwelle *f*
respool *v* umrollen *v*, umspulen *v*
rest of the news Vermischtes *n*
restoration *n* Instandsetzung *f*
retainer *n* Pauschale *f*
retake *v* Aufnahme wiederholen, nachdrehen *v*, nachaufnehmen *v*, wiederholen *v*; ~ *n* Nachaufnahme *f*, Nacheinstellung *f*, Retake *n*, Wiederaufnahme *f*, Wiederholung *f*; **to do a** ~ Aufnahme wiederholen, nachdrehen *v*, nachaufnehmen *v*, wiederholen *v*
retard *v* verzögern *v*, zurückhalten *v*; ~ **coil** Drossel *f*, Drosselspule *f*
retarding field Bremsfeld *n*
retardment *n* Verzögerung *f*
retention time Speicherzeit *f*
reticule *n* Fadenkreuz *n*
retouch *v* retuschieren *v*
retouching knife Schabemesser *n*
return *n* Rücklauf *m*; ~ **circuit** Rückleitung *f*; ~ **loss** Rückflußdämpfung *f*; ~ **movement** Rücklauf *m*, Rückwärtsgang *m*; ~ **programme circuit** Programmrückspielleitung *f*
revenue *n* Einnahmen *f pl*
reverberant *adj* hallig *adj*
reverberate *v* nachhallen *v*, hallen *v*
reverberation *n* Hall *m*, Nachhall *m*, Halligkeit *f*; ~ **chamber** Hallraum *m*, Echoraum *m*, Nachhallraum *m* ~ **generator** Hallgenerator *m*; ~ **input** Halleingang *m*; ~ **output** Hallausgang *m*; ~ **plate** Hallplatte *f*, Nachhallplatte *f*; ~ **room** Hallraum *m*, Echoraum *m*, Nachhallraum *m*; ~ **time (RT)** Nachhallzeit *f*; **added** ~ überlagerter Hall; **superimposed** ~ überlagerter Hall; **to add** ~ Hall geben
reversal *n* (FP) Umkehr *f*, Umkehrung *f*; ~ **development** Umkehrentwicklung *f*; ~ **duplicate** Umkehrduplikat *n*; ~ **emulsion** Umkehremulsion *f*; ~ **film** Umkehrfilm *m*; ~ **process** Umkehrverfahren *n*; ~ **processing** Umkehrentwicklung *f*
reversal-type colour film Umkehrfarbfilm *m*
reverse *v* (FP) umkehren *v*; ~ *n* (mech.) Rückwärtsgang *m*; ~ **action** Rückwärtsgang *m*; ~ **angle** Gegeneinstellung *f*, Gegenschuß *m*, Achsensprung *m*; ~ **compatibility** Rekompatibilität *f* ~ **feedback** Gegenkopplung *f*; ~ **lighting** Gegenlicht *n*; ~ **mask** Gegenmaske *f*; ~ **motion** Rücklauf *m*, Rückwärtsgang *m*; ~ **-motion effect** Rücklauftrick *m*; ~ **programme circuit** Zuspielleitung *f*; ~ **-running effect** Rücklauftrick *m*; ~ **shot** Gegeneinstellung *f*, Gegenschuß *m*; **to** ~ **polarity** umpolen *v*
reversed-charge call R-Gespräch *n*
reversible *adj* (mech.) umschaltbar *adj*; ~ **radio link** umzündbares Funkfeld
reversing bath Umkehrbad *n*;

~ **prism** Umkehrprisma *n*
review *n* Rundschau *f*, Kritik *f*
reviewer *n* Kritiker *m*
revise *v* überarbeiten *v*
revoke *v* widerrufen *v*
revolution *n* Umwälzung *f*
revolve *v* rundlaufen *v*
revolving colour disc rotierendes Farbenspiel; ~ **stage** Drehbühne *f*
rewind *v* wiederaufspulen *v*, wiederaufwickeln *v*, umspulen *v*, umrollen *v*; ~ *n* Rücklauf *m*, Rückspulung *f*; ~ **bench** Umrolltisch *m*; **fast** ~ schneller Rücklauf; **synchronous** ~ synchroner Rücklauf
rewinder *n* Umroller *m*, Umspuler *m*; **mobile** ~ fahrbarer Umroller; **power** ~ elektrischer Umroller
rewinding *n* Rückspulung *f*, Wiederaufrollen *n*; ~ **machine** Umspuler *m*
rewrite *v* umschreiben *v*, überarbeiten *v*, rewriten *v*
RF heterodyne Hochfrequenzüberlagerung *f*; ~ **resistance** Skineffektwiderstand *m*
RGB levels RGB-Pegel *m pl*; ~ **monitor** RGB-Monitor *m*; ~ **system** RGB-Prinzip *n*, RGB-Verfahren *n*; ~ **waveform monitor** Farbwertkontrollgerät *n*, Farbwertoszillograf *m*, Farbwertoszilloskop *n*; ~ **with separate luminance** RGB+Y-Verfahren *n*
rheostat *n* Stellwiderstand *m*, Regelwiderstand *m*
rhythm *n* Rhythmus *m*, Takt *m*; ~ **carrier** Rhythmusträger *m*; ~ **tape** Rhythmusträger *m*
ribbon feeder Bandleitung *f*, Flachkabel *n*; ~ **microphone** Bändchenmikrofon *n*
richness of tone (mus.) Klangfülle *f*
ridge *n* Einfädelschlitz *m*
rigger *n* Antennenwart *m*
rigging tender Rüstwagen *m*
right of exploitation Auswertungsrecht *n*; ~ **of inspection** (documents, accounts) Einsichtsrecht *n*; ~ **of personal access** Vortragsrecht *n*; ~ **of reply** Recht auf Gegendarstellung; ~ **of usufruct** Nutzungsrecht *n*; ~ **of withdrawal** Rückrufrecht *n*; ~ **of withdrawal because of non-exercise** Rückrufrecht wegen Nichtausübung; ~ **to revoke** Rückrufrecht *n*; **to exercise** ~ **of reply** von dem Recht auf Gegendarstellung Gebrauch machen
right-hand signal Rechtssignal (R-Signal) *n*
rights *n pl* Rechte *n pl*; **all** ~ sämtliche Rechte; **exclusive** ~ ausschließliche Rechte; **full** ~ sämtliche Rechte; **grand** ~ große Rechte; **inclusive** ~ sämtliche Rechte; **limited** ~ beschränkte Rechte; **neighbouring** ~ Leistungsschutzrecht *n*, verwandte Rechte; **related** ~ verwandte Rechte; **restricted** ~ beschränkte Rechte; **single** ~ einfache Rechte; **small** ~ kleine Rechte; **to give up** ~ Rechte abtreten; **to surrender** ~ Rechte abtreten; **total** ~ sämtliche Rechte
rigid in phase phasenstarr *adj*
rim light Gloriole *f*, Kante *f*, Kantenlicht *n*, Streiflicht *n*; ~ **lighting** Randaufhellung *f*
ring *v* (filter) überschwingen *v*; ~ **circuit** Ringleitung *f*; ~ **counter** Ringteiler *m*, Ringzähler *m*; ~ **magnet** Ringmagnet *m*; ~ **main** Ringleitung *f*; ~ **modulator** Ringmodulator *m*; ~ **transformer** Ringübertrager *m*
ringing *n* (filter) Überschwingen *n*, Überschwingung *f*, Einschwingvorgang *m*; ~ **frequency** (filter)

Überschwingfrequenz *f*; **~ frequency** (tel.) Ruffrequenz *f*; **~ key** Ruftaste *f*; **~ signal** Rufsignal *n*
rinse *v* (photo) wässern *v*; **~ fog** Wässerungsschleier *m*
ripple *n* Brumm *m*, Brummton *m*, Brummspannung *f*, Restwelligkeit *f*, Welligkeit *f*; **~ voltage** Brummspannung *f*
rip-up *n* (coll.) Filmsalat *m*, Salat *m* (fam.)
riser *n* Steigleitung *f*
rise time Anstiegzeit *f*, Einschwingzeit *f*
rising main Steigleitung *f*
road cinema Wanderkino *n*; **~ news** *n pl* Straßenzustandsbericht *m*
rod *n* Stange *f*; **~ aerial** Stabantenne *f*
role *n* (perf.) Rolle *f*
roll *v* (pict.) durchlaufen *v*; ~ *v* (start) abfahren *v*; ~ *n* Rolle *f*; ~ *n* (cam.) Filmrolle *f*; **~ !** (order) ab!, abfahren!; **~ out** *v* (EDP) auslesen *v*; **~ VTR!** MAZ ab!
roller *n* Walze *f*; **~ caption** Rolltitel *m*, rollender Ttiel; **~ caption equipment** Rolltitelgerät *n*, Rolltitelmaschine *f*; **~ titles** *n pl* rollender Titel
roll-in time Startvorlaufzeit *f*, Startzeit *f*
rolling cut rollender Schnitt; **~ tripod** Fahrstativ *n*, Rollstativ *n*, Kamerafahrgestell *n*
roll-off *n* (level) frequenzabhängiger Pegelabfall
rollover *n* (tech.) Bildsprung *m*
roll titles *n pl* Rolltitel *m*
romanticiser *n* (opt.) Diffusionsfilter *m*, Softscheibe *f*
roof aerial Dachantenne *f*
room *n* Raum *m*; **~ acoustics** *n pl* Raumakustik *f*, Raumklang *m*, Raumkulisse *f*; **~ aerial** Zimmerantenne *f*; **~ noise** Saalgeräusch *n*; **~ temperature** Raumtemperatur *f*; **dead ~** schalltoter Raum; **screened ~** elektromagnetisch toter Raum
root-mean-square value (RMS value) Effektivwert *m*
rosette *n* Rosette *f*
rostrum *n* Platte *f*, Tribüne *f*; ~ *n* (set) Praktikabel *n*; ~ *n* (appar.) Titelbank *f*; **~ bench** Tricktisch *m*, Trickbank *f*; **~ camera** Trickkamera *f*; **~ camera operator** Trickkameramann *m*; **~ caption shot** Tricktitelaufnahme *f*; **~ film** Trickfilm *m*; **~ shot** Trickaufnahme *f*
rotary capacitor Drehkondensator *m*; **~ converter** Umformer *m*; **~ disc shutter** Flügelblende *f*, Sektorenblende *f*, Umlaufblende *f* **~ potentiometer** Drehpotentiometer *n*; **~ shutter** Umlaufblende *f*; **rear ~ shutter** hintere Umlaufblende **~ switch** Drehschalter *m*, Drehwähler *m*
rotatable *adj* drehbar *adj*
rotate *v* rundlaufen *v*
rotating shutter Flügelblende *f*; **~ wedge range-finder** Drehkeil-Entfernungsmesser *m*
rotation *n* Umwälzung *f*; **~ speed** (disc) Plattendrehzahl *f*
rotor *n* Läufer *m*
rough adjustment Grobeinstellung *f* **~ -cut** *v* Muster zusammenstellen; **~ cut** Rohschnitt *m*; **~ focusing** Grobeinstellung *f*; **~ translation** Rohübersetzung *f*
round table Forum *n*
round-table discussion Podiumsdiskussion *f*, Podiumsgespräch *n*
round-up *n* kurzer Überblick, Rundschau *f*
route *n* Leitweg *m*
routine office Produktionsbüro *n*
routing switch Zuschalter *m*

roving eye Wagen mit drahtloser Kameraanlage
row *n* (EDP) Lochkartenzeile *f*; **~ of lights** Lichtzeile *f*; **~ of loudspeakers** Tonzeile *f*
royalties *n pl* Lizenzgebühr *f*; **exempt from ~** frei von Rechten
royalty *n* Lizenzgebühr *f*, Tantieme *f*
RT apparatus Funksprechgerät *n*, Sprechfunkgerät *n*
rubber foot Gummifuß *m*; **~ gasket** Gummidichtung *f*; **~ -number** *v* randnumerieren *v*; **~ numbering** Randnumerierung *f*; **~ packing** Gummidichtung *f*; **~ washer** Gummidichtung *f*
rumble *n* (disc) Rumpeln *n*
run *v* (F, tape) abfahren *v*; **~** *v* (news) absetzen *v*, rausbringen *v* (fam.); **~** *v* (telex) senden *v*, absetzen *v*; **~** *n* Lauf *m*, Ablauf *m*; **~** *n* (EDP) Programmdurchlauf *m*; **~** *n* (FP) Durchlauf *m*
run ! Bild ab!; **~ of programme** Programmablauf *m*; **~ telecine!** Film ab!; **~ through** *v* (scene) durchspielen *v*; **~ TK!** Film ab!; **~ up** *v* hochlaufen *v*; **~ up** *v* (motor) anlaufen *v*; **to ~ late** (sound) nachhängen *v*
run...! (tape) ab!
runaway *n* Ton läuft weg
run-in groove Einlaufrille *f*
running *n* Lauf *m*
running! läuft! (fam.)
running commentary Reportage *f*, Hörbericht *m*, Augenzeugenbericht *m*; **~ costs** Betriebskosten *plt*; **~ -down time** Nachlaufzeit *f*; **~ order** Ablaufplan *m*, Programmablauf *m*, Programmablaufplan *m*, Fahrplan *m*; **~ speed** Laufgeschwindigkeit *f*; **~ speed of film** Aufnahmegeschwindigkeit *f*; **~ time** Laufzeit *f*; **~ time** (F) Vorführdauer *f*, Filmlänge *f*; **~ -up time** Einlaufzeit *f*; **provisional ~ order** vorläufiger Ablaufplan; **to fix the ~ order** Ablaufplan machen, Ablauf machen; **to make the ~ order** Ablaufplan machen, Ablauf machen; **to remain ~** (F, thea.) auf dem Spielplan bleiben
run-out *n* (F) Nachlauf *m*; **~ groove** Auslaufrille *f*; **~ length** Nachlauflänge *f*
run-through *n* (rehearsal) Drehprobe *f*, Durchlauf *m*, Probedurchlauf *m*; **~** *n* (video) vertikale Synchronisationsstörung
run-up period (script) Buchentwicklung *f*; **~ time** Hochlaufzeit *f*, Startvorlaufzeit *f*, Startzeit *f*; **synchronous ~** synchroner Hochlauf
rush copy, to assemble abklammern *v*
rushes *n pl* Bildmuster *n pl*, Muster *n pl*; **~ log** Klappenliste *f*; **~ roll** Musterrolle *f*; **to assemble ~** Muster zusammenstellen; **to break down ~** Muster trennen; **to sync up ~** Muster anlegen; **to view ~** Muster ansehen
rush print Arbeitskopie *f*, erste Kopie, Testkopie *f*, Musterkopie *f*
rustle *v* knistern *v*

S

safe-area generator mixer Rahmeneinblender *m*
safety belt Sicherheitsgurt *m*; **~ chain** Sicherheitskette *f*; **~ contact** Sicherheitskontakt *m*; **~ copy** Sicherheitskopie *f*; **~ cord** Sicherungsleine *f*; **~ coupling** Schukokupplung *f*; **~ factor** Sicherheitsfaktor *m*; **~ film**

Sicherheitsfilm *m*; ~ **glass** Linsenschutzglas *n*; ~ **harness** Sicherheitsgurt *m*; ~ **magazine** Feuerschutztrommel *f*; ~ **mesh** (lighting) Schutzkappe *f*; ~ **plug** Schutzstecker *m*, Schukostecker *m*; ~ **rail** Schutzgeländer *n*; ~ **regulations** Sicherheitsvorschriften *f pl*; ~ **screen** (F) Feuerschutzklappe *f*; ~ **shutter** (proj.) Feuerschutzklappe *f*; ~ **socket** Schukosteckdose *f*; ~ **stock** Sicherheitsfilm *m*; ~ **track** (F) Sicherheitsspur *f*

salaried employee Gehaltsempfänger *m*

salaries-and-wages office Gehalts- und Lohnstelle *f*

salaries department Gehaltsbüro *n*; ~ **office** Gehalts- und Lohnstelle *f*

salary *n* Gehalt *n*; ~ *n* (perf.) Gage *f*; ~ **scale** Vergütungsordnung *f*

salary-earner *n* Gehaltsempfänger *m*

sample *v* (video) abtasten *v*; ~ *n* Bemusterung *f*, Probe *f*

sampling *n* Bemusterung *f*; ~ **frequency** Schaltfrequenz *f*

satellite *n* Satellit *m*, Trabant *m*; ~ **aerial** Satellitenantenne *f*; ~ **circuit** Satellitenfunkstrecke *f*, Satellitenstrecke *f*, Satellitenleitung *f*, Satellitenverbindung *f*; ~ **-earth link** Satellitenerdverbindung *f*; ~ **link** Satellitenfunkstrecke *f*, Satellitenstrecke *f*, Satellitenleitung *f*, Satellitenverbindung *f*; ~ **network** Satellitennetz *n*; ~ **television** Satellitenfernsehen *n*; ~ **television programme** Satellitenfernsehprogramm *n*; ~ **television transmission** Fernsehübertragung über Satelliten; ~ **transmission** Satellitenübertragung *f*; ~ **-transmitted** *adj* über Satelliten übertragen; ~ **transmitter** Satellitensender *m*; ~ **with multiple access** Satellit für vielfachen Zugang; **active** ~ aktiver Satellit; **artificial** ~ künstlicher Satellit; **direct broadcast** ~ Satellit für direkte Rundfunkübertragung; **geostationary** ~ geostationärer Satellit; **geosynchronous** ~ geosynchroner Satellit; **man-made** ~ künstlicher Satellit; **passive** ~ passiver Satellit; **retrograde** ~ rückläufiger Satellit; **stationary** ~ stationärer Satellit

saturate *v* sättigen *v*

saturation *n* Sättigung *f*, Farbsättigung *f*; ~ **banding** Farbsättigungsstreifigkeit *f*

saw-tooth *n* Sägezahn *m*; ~ **correction** Sägezahnkorrektur *f*; ~ **generator** Sägezahngenerator *m* ~ **signal** sägezahnförmiges Korrektursignal; ~ **signal with colour carrier** Sägezahnsignal mit Farbträger; ~ **with HF mean value** Sägezahn mit HF-Mittelwert

scaffold clamp Rohrklammer *f*; ~ **suspension** Scheinwerfergerüst *n*

scaffolding *n* Gerüst *n*

scale *n* Skala *f*, Maß *n*, Teilung *f*; ~ **model** Trickmodell *n*

scan *v* abtasten *v*; ~ **generator** Ablenkgerät *n*; ~ **linearity** Linearität der Ablenkung; ~ **rings** *n pl* Zeileneinschwinger *m*

scanner *n* Abtaster *m*, Bildabtaster *m*; ~ **area** Abtastraum *m*; **flying-spot** ~ Lichtpunktabtaster *m*, Punktlichtabtaster *m*

scanning *n* Abtastung *f*, Ablenkung *f*; ~ **angle** Abtastwinkel *m*; ~ **beam** Abtaststrahl *m*; ~ **device** Abtasteinrichtung *f*, Bildabtaster *m*; ~ **gap** Abtastspalt *m*;

~ generator Ablenkgenerator *m*; **~ interlace system** Zwischenzeilenverfahren *n*; **~ line** Abtastzeile *f*, Bildzeile *f*, Zeile *f*; **~ linearity** Abtastlinearität *f*; **~ -pattern image** Rasterbild *n*; **~ rate** Bildfolgefrequenz *f*; **~ room** Abtastraum *m*; **~ signal** Abtastsignal *n*; **~ spot** Abtastpunkt *m*, abtastender Lichtpunkt; **~ -system definition** Schärfe des Abtastsystems; **~ time** Abtastzeit *f*, Ablenkzeit *f*; **~ waveform** Abtastsignal *n*; **flying-spot ~** Lichtpunktabtastung *f*, Punktlichtabtastung *f*

scar *n* (F) Schramme *f*

scatter *v* (opt.) zerstreuen *v*; **~ communication** Scatterverbindung *f*; **~ link** Scatterrichtfunkstrecke *f*; **~ radio-relay circuit** Scatterrichtfunkstrecke *f*

scattering *n* Streuung *f*, Zerstreuung *f*

scenario *n* Drehbuch *n*, Buch *n*, Manuskript *n*, Script *n*, Szenarium *n*; **~ editor** (R, TV) Dramaturg *m*

scenario-writer *n* Drehbuchautor *m*

scenarist *n* Drehbuchautor *m*, Filmautor *m*

scene *n* Szene *f*, Bild *n*, Bühne *f*, Schauplatz *m*; **~ excerpt** Szenenausschnitt *m*; **~ hand** Bühnenarbeiter *m*, Baubühnenarbeiter *m*; **~ hands** *n pl* Baubühne *f*; **~ lighting** Szenenbeleuchtung *f*; **~ lighting level** Szenenbeleuchtungsumfang *m*; **~ of action** Schauplatz *m*; **~ painter** Dekorationsmaler *m*; **~ shifter** Bühnenarbeiter *m*; **~ supervisor** Studiomeister *m*; **~ tester** (FP) Szenentester *m*; **automatic ~ marking** automatische Markiervorrichtung **radio ~ marking** drahtlose Markiervorrichtung; **to be the ~ of** .. Schauplatz sein von ...; **to fake a ~** Türken bauen

scenery *n* Bühnenbild *n*, Szenenbild *n*, Dekoration *f*, Dekoı *n*, Bauten *m pl*; **~ and furnishing** Bau und Ausstattung; **~ clamp** Dekoklammer *f*; **~ designer** Bühnenbildner *m*, Szenenbildner *m*; **~ designing** Bühnenbildnerei *f*; **~ illumination** Szenenausleuchtung *f*; **~ operatives** *n pl* Baubühne *f*; **~ set** Dekoration *f*; **~ stock** Baufundus *m*; **~ store** Kulissenfundus *m*, Kulissenhalle *f*

scenic artist Kunstmaler *m*, Prospektmaler *m*; **~ carpenter** Bühnenschreiner *m*, Bühnentischler *m*; **~ carpenter's shop** Bühnenschreinerei *f*, Bühnentischlerei *f*; **~ design*** Bühnenbildnerei* *f*; **~ designer** Bühnenbildner *m*, Szenenbildner *m*; **~ dock** Baubühne *f*; **~ flat** (design) Wand *f*; **~ model discussion** Modellbesprechung *f*; **~ painter** Bühnenmaler *m*; **~ progression** szenischer Ablauf; **~ service crew** Drehbühne *f*; **~ service man** Bühnenarbeiter *m*; **~ services** Baubühne* *f*; **~ truck** Bühnenwagen *m*; **~ unit** (design) Baueinheit *f*; **~ workshop** Bühnenwerkstatt *f*

schedule *v* ins Programm einsetzen **~** *n* (prod.) Disposition *f*, Drehplan *m*, Drehübersicht *f*; **~** *n* (F, thea.) Spielplan *m*; **to be kept in the ~** auf dem Spielplan bleiben; **to resume normal ~s** Programm fortsetzen, Programm übernehmen

scheduled, to be auf dem Spielplan stehen

schematic *n* (US) Schaltung *f*

school broadcast

Schulfunksendung *f*; ~ **broadcasting** Schulfunk *m*; ~ **programme** Schulfunksendung *f* ~ **radio** Schulfunk *m*; ~ **television** Schulfernsehen *n*; ~ **viewer** Fernsehschüler *m*

schools television programme Schulfernsehsendung *f*

Schuko-type coupling piece Schukokupplung *f*

science and arts features Kultur und Wissenschaft; ~ **and features*** Wissenschaft und Technik*

science-fiction film Science-Fiction-Film *m*

scissors shutter Scheitelblende *f*

scoop *n* Scoop *m*

score *v* vertonen *v*; ~ *n* Partitur *f*

score-reading panel Musiklektorat *n*

scoring *n* (F) Musikaufnahme *f*, Vertonung *f*; ~ **stage** Musikstudio *n*, Musikaufnahmeatelier *n*

scrap *n* Abfall *m*, Ausschuß *m*

scraper *n* Filmhobel *m*, Schabemesser *n*

scraping tool Schabemesser *n*

scratch *n* (disc) Kratzer *m*; ~ *n* (F) Bildschramme *f*, Drop-out *m*, Scratch *m*; ~ **on base side** Blankschramme *f*

scratching noise Kratzer *m*

scratchpad memory (SPM) (EDP) Zwischenspeicher *m*

screen *v* abschirmen *v*, verschleiern *v*; ~ *v* (F) ansehen *v*, vorführen *v*; ~ *n* Abschirmung *f*; ~ *n* (video) Raster *m*, Schirmgitter *n*; ~ *n* (F) Bildschirm *m*, Bildwand *f*, Leinwand *f*, Schirm *m*; ~ *n* (cinema) Kintopp *m* (fam.); ~ *n* (design) Wand *f*; ~ **adaptation** Filmbearbeitung *f*, Verfilmung *f*; ~ **author** Filmautor *m*; ~ **brightness** Bildwandhelligkeit *f*, Schirmhelligkeit *f*; ~ **connection** (pict. tube) Schirmwanne *f*; ~ **current** Schirmgitterstrom *m*; ~ **grid** Schirmgitter *n*, Schutzgitter *n*; ~ **-grid current** Schirmgitterstrom *m*; ~ **-grid voltage** Schirmgitterspannung *f*; ~ **image** Schirmbild *n*; ~ **luminance** Bildwandhelligkeit *f*; ~ **out** *v* aussieben *v*; ~ **picture** Schirmbild *n*; ~ **plate** Rasterplatine *f*; ~ **publicity** Kinoreklame *f*; ~ **rights** Verfilmungsrechte *n pl*; ~ **size** Bildschirmformat *n*; ~ **test** (perf.) Probeaufnahme *f*; ~ **time** (F) Laufzeit *f*, Vorführdauer *f*; ~ **voltage** Schirmgitterspannung *f*; **beaded** ~ Perlleinwand *f*; **reflecting** ~ reflektierende Wand; **to** ~ **a film** Film ansehen, Film vorführen; **to make a** ~ **version of** verfilmen *v*

screened aerial abgeschirmte Antenne

screening *n* Abschirmung *f*; ~ *n* (F) Vorführung *f*; ~ **of cutting copy** Schnittvorführung *f*; ~ **of rough cut** Rohschnittvorführung *f*; ~ **room** Vorführraum *m*

screenplay *n* Drehbuch *n*; ~ **writer** Filmautor *m*

screenwriter *n* Drehbuchautor *m*, Filmautor *m*

screw on *v* anflanschen *v*

scrim *n* (lighting) Diffusionsfilter *m*, Gazeschirm *m*, Softscheibe *f*

script *v* texten *v*; ~ *n* Buch *n*, Drehbuch *n*, Filmtext *m*, Manuskript *n*, Script *n*, Sprechertext *m*, Text *m*; ~ **conference** Buchbesprechung *f*; ~ **department** Dramaturgie* *f*; ~ **discussion** Buchbesprechung *f*; ~ **editor** Dramaturg *m*, stofführender Redakteur; ~ **-girl** *n* Ateliersekretärin *f*, Scriptgirl *n*, Script *f*; ~ **library** Wortarchiv *n*; ~ **-reader** *n* Lektor *m*; ~ **unit***

Dramaturgie* *f*, Lektorat *n*; **~ -writer** *n* Drehbuchautor *m*, Texter *m*; **accompanying ~** Begleittext *m*; **to ~ to film** auf Bild texten; **to cut down a ~** Text einstreichen, Text kürzen; **to edit down a ~** Text einstreichen, Text kürzen; **to pad a ~** Text breitwalzen; **to stretch a ~** Text breitwalzen; **to sub down a ~** Text einstreichen, Text kürzen
scripter *n* Texter *m*
scrutinise *v* (R) abnehmen *v*
scrutiny *n* (R) Abnahme *f*
seamstress *n* Näherin *f*
second cameraman zweiter Kameraassistent, Schärfeassistent *m*, Schärfezieher *m*; **~ director** Hilfsregisseur *m*; **~ frequency** Spiegelfrequenz *f*; **~ home set** Zweitempfänger *m*; **~ showing** (TV) Zweitsendung *f*
secondary cell Akkumulatorenzelle *f*; **~ development** Zweitentwicklung *f*; **~ radiator** Sekundärstrahler *m*; **~ receiver** Zweitempfänger *m*; **~ service area** Fernempfangsgebiet *n*; **~ source** Fremdleuchter *m*
second-order harmonic distortion quadratischer Klirrfaktor
second-run theatre (F) Nachaufführungstheater *n*
section *n* Abteilung *f*, Referat *n*; **~ of line** Leitungsabschnitt *m*
sectional view Schnittbilder *n pl*
sector *n* (prog.) Sparte *f*
security officer Sicherheitsbeauftragter *m*
sedecimal *adj* (EDP) sedezimal *adj*, hexadezimal *adj*; **~ number** (EDP) Sedezimalzahl *f*, Hexadezimalzahl *f*
Seeger circlip Seegersicherung *f*
seek time (EDP) Positionierungszeit *f*
segment shutter Sektorenverschluß *m*
select *v* (rushes) ausmustern *v*, auswählen *v*; **to ~ shots** Muster aussuchen
selection *n* Auswahl *f*; **~** *n* (EDP) Selektion *f*; **to make ~ s** Muster aussuchen
selective calling Selektivruf *m*; **~ coupler** Weiche *f*; **~ filter** Selektivfilter *m*; **~ switching** Selektivschaltung *f*
selectivity *n* Trennschärfe *f*
selector *n* (tech.) Wähler *m*; **~ switch** Betriebsartenschalter *m*, Wahlschalter *m*, Funktionswahlschalter *m*, Umschalter *m*, Umschaltgerät *n*
selenium cell Selenzelle *f*; **~ rectifier** Selengleichrichter *m*
self-adhesive *adj* selbstklebend *adj*
self-adjusting motor Selbstregelmotor *m*
self-capacitance *n* Eigenkapazität *f*
self-censorship *n* Selbstkontrolle *f*; **voluntary ~** freiwillige Selbstkontrolle
self-checking *adj* selbstprüfend *adj*
self-excitation *n* Selbsterregung *f*, Selbstaufschaukelung *f*
self-induction *n* Selbstinduktion *f*
self-lacing *n* (proj.) Selbsteinfädelung *f*
self-locking key Selbsthaltetaste *f*; **~ push button** Selbsthaltetaste *f*
self-modulation *n* Eigenmodulation *f*
self-oscillate *v* freilaufen *v*, freischwingen *v*
self-oscillation *n* selbsterregte Schwingung, Selbsterregung *f*, Selbstaufschaukelung *f*
self-regulating motor Selbstregelmotor *m*
self-resonance *n* Eigenresonanz *f*
self-sealing *adj* selbstklebend *adj*
self-synchronisation *n* Eigensynchronisation *f*
self-wiping *n* Selbstreinigung *f*; **~** *adj* selbstreinigend *adj*

selsyn *n* elektrische Welle
semi-close-up (SCU) *n* Halbnahe *f*
semiconductor *n* (electronics) Halbleiter *m*; ~ **diode** Halbleiterdiode *f*
semi-frontal *adj* halbfrontal *adj*
semi-profile *n* Halbprofil *n*
semi-tone *n* Halbton *m*
send *v* (wireless) senden *v*
sender *n* (transmitter) Sender *m*
sending amplifier Sendeverstärker *m*; ~ **circuit** Sendestraße *f*, Sendeweg *m*; ~ **end** Senderseite *f*, Geberseite *f*; ~ **level** Sendepegel *m*; ~ **station** Sendestation *f*
senior *adj* (staff) Gehobener ...; ~ **cameraman** erster Kameramann; ~ **duty editor** Chef vom Dienst (CvD), Dienstleiter *m*, Redakteur vom Dienst, diensthabender Redakteur; ~ **editor** Redaktionsleiter *m*; ~ **engineer** Betriebsingenieur *m*, Betriebsleiter *m*; ~ **film editor** Chefcutter *m*; ~ **member of staff on duty** Dienstleiter *m*; ~ **producer** (drama) Oberspielleiter *m*; ~ **television engineer** Bildingenieur *m*
sensation *n* Empfindung *f*; ~ **of brightness** Helligkeitseindruck *m*
sensing lever Fühlhebel *m*
sensitisation *n* Sensibilisierung *f*
sensitise *v* sensibilisieren *v*
sensitised face Emulsionsebene *f*; ~ **side** Schichtseite *f*, Emulsionsebene *f*
sensitive *adj* empfindlich *adj*
sensitivity *n* (FP) Empfindlichkeit *f*; ~ **control** Empfindlichkeitsregelung *f*; ~ **of the eye** Augenempfindlichkeit *f*; **differential** ~ differentielle Empfindlichkeit; **high** ~ hohe Empfindlichkeit; **low** ~ niedrige Empfindlichkeit; **spectral** ~ **curve** spektrale Hellempfindlichkeitskurve
sensitometer *n* Empfindlichkeitsmesser *m*, Sensitometer *n*
sensitometric *adj* sensitometrisch *adj*; ~ **step wedge** Belichtungskeil *m*; ~ **test strip** Sensitometerstreifen *m*; ~ **wedge** Keilvorlage *f*
sensitometry *n* Sensitometrie *f*
sensor *n* (EDP) Meßwertgeber *m*
separate *v* abtrennen *v*; ~ **excitation** Fremderregung *f*; ~ **head monitoring** Hinterbandkontrolle *f*, Abhören hinter Band; ~ **magnetic sound (Sepmag)** separater Magnetton (SEPMAG); ~ **optical sound (Sepopt)** separater Lichtton (SEPOPT); **two** ~ **magnetic sound tracks (Sepdumag)** separater Magnetton auf zwei Spuren (SEPDUMAG)
separation allowance Trennungsentschädigung *f*; ~ **filter** Trennschleife *f*; ~ **positive** Auszugspositiv *n*; **electrical** ~ elektrische Auftrennung
separator *n* (tape) statisches Band; ~ *n* (diplexer) Frequenzweiche *f*
Sepmag *n* Bildfilm mit Cordband; ~ *n* Zweibandverfahren *n*; ~ **projector** Zweibandprojektor *m*; ~ **telecine** Zweibandabtaster *m*; ~ **telecine system** Zweibandabtastung *f*
sequel *n* Folge *f*
sequence *n* (F, tape) Sequenz *f*, Take *m*; ~ *n* (script) Bild *n*; ~ *n* (prog.) Programmblock *m*; ~ **change-over contact** Folge-Umschaltkontakt *m*; ~ **control** Folgeschaltung *f*; ~ **of events** Ereignisablauf *m*; ~ **of instructions** (EDP) Befehlsfolge *f*; ~ **of operations** Arbeitsfolge *f*; ~ **of pictures** Bildfolge *f*; ~ **of programmes** Programmfolge *f*; ~ **of shots** Einstellungsfolge *f*;

~ **operation** Folgeschaltung *f*; ~ **switch** Stufenschalter *m*

sequential *adj* sequentiell *adj*; ~ **control** (EDP) Folgesteuerung *f*; ~ **process** Sequenzverfahren *n*; ~ **system** Sequenzsystem *n*

serial *n* Fortsetzungsreihe *f*, Fortsetzungsserie *f*; ~ *adj* (EDP) seriell *adj*; ~ **film** Episodenfilm *m*; ~ **hook-up** (US) Hintereinanderschaltung *f*

serial-parallel converter (EDP) Serien-Parallel-Umsetzer *m*

series *n* Serie *f*, Reihe *f*, Folge *f*, Fortsetzungsbericht *m*, Episodenreihe *f*, Episodenserie *f*; ~ *n* (F) Filmserie *f*; ~ **circuit** Reihenkreis *m*; ~ **connection** Serienschaltung *f*, Hintereinanderschaltung *f*; ~ **feed** Serienspeisung *f*; ~ **motor** Hauptstrommotor *m*; ~ **of broadcasts** Sendereihe *f*; ~ **resonance** Serienresonanz *f*; ~ **-resonant circuit** Serienresonanzkreis *m*; ~ **supply** Serienspeisung *f*; ~ **-tuned circuit** Serienresonanzkreis *m*

serious music E-Musik *f* (=Ernste Musik)

serrations *n pl* Mäusezähnchen *n pl*

service *n* Dienst *m*; ~ *n* (facilities) Leistung *f*, Hilfeleistung *f*; ~ *n* (prog.) Programm *n*, Kanal *m*; ~ *n* (transmitter) Versorgung *f*; ~ **area** Empfangsbereich *m*, Empfangsgebiet *n*, Sendebereich *m*, Sendegebiet *n*, Anstaltsbereich *m*, Verbreitungsgebiet *n*, Versorgungsbereich *m*, Versorgungsgebiet *n*; ~ **circuit** Dienstleitung *f*; ~ **contract** Dienstvertrag *m*; ~ **earth** Betriebserde *f*; ~ **instruction** Bedienungsanleitung *f*, Bedienungsvorschrift *f*; ~ **line** (tel.) Dienstleitung *f*; ~ **oscilloscope** Betriebsoszillograf *m*; ~ **range** Sendebereich *m*, Sendegebiet *n*, Anstaltsbereich *m*; ~ **reliability** Betriebssicherheit *f*; **in** ~ in Betrieb; **to put into** ~ in Betrieb nehmen, in Betrieb setzen

servicing area Wartungsraum *m*

servo control Servosteuerung *f*; ~ **motor** Servomotor *m*, Stellmotor *m*; ~ **system** Servosystem *n*

set *v* einstellen *v*, verstellen *v*, richten *v*; ~ *n* (design) Bühnenbild *n*, Bühne *f*, Szenenbild *n*, Szene *f*, Dekoration *f*, Dekor *n*, Aufbauten *n pl*; ~ *n* (batch) Satz *m*; ~ *n* (appar.) Apparat *m*, Gerät *n*, Anlage *f*, Aggregat *n*; ~ *n* (R, TV) Radio *n*, Fernseher *m* (fam.); ~ **design** Bühnenbild *n*, Bühnenbildentwurf *m*; ~ **designer** Bühnenbildner *m*, Szenenbildner *m*, Filmarchitekt *m*; ~ **designing** Bühnenbildnerei *f*; ~ **dresser** Ausstatter *m*; ~ **dressing** Bühnendekoration *f*; ~ **dressings** Dekorationsrequisiten *n pl*, Requisiten *n pl*; ~ **erection** Dekorationsaufbau *m*; ~ **-in** *n* Hintersetzer *m*, Rücksetzer *m*; ~ **light** Dekorationslicht *n*; ~ **lighting** Szenenausleuchtung *f*; ~ **model** Dekorationsmodell *n*; ~ **of lenses** Linsensatz *m*; ~ **on a stand** Standgerät *n*; ~ **point** (EDP) Sollwert *m*; ~ **prefabrication** Dekorationsvorfertigung *f*; ~ **pulse** (EDP) Setzimpuls *m*; ~ **-screw wrench** Inbusschlüssel *m*; ~ **sketch** Bühnenbildentwurf *m*; ~ **striking** Dekorationsabbau *m*; ~ **up** *v* aufbauen *v*, einrichten *v*, errichten *v*, montieren *v*; ~ **up** *v* (cam.) einstellen *v*, voreinstellen *v* **to** ~ **to music** vertonen *v*; **to kill a** ~ (US) abbauen *v*; **to strike a** ~ abbauen *v*

setting *n* Einstellung *f*, Justierung *f*, Regelung *f*, Richten *n*; ~ *n*

(design) Szenenbild *n*, Bühnenbild *n*, Ausstattung *f*, Bauten *m pl*; **~ and properties** Dekoration *f*; **~ and upholstery** Dekoration *f*; **~ construction** Bühnenbau *m*; **~ to music** Vertonung *f*
settings *n pl* Bühnenbauten *m pl*
settlement *n* Abrechnung *f*, Abwicklung *f*
set-up *n* (script) Einstellung *f*; ~ *n* (video) Schwarzabhebung *f*, Schwarzabsetzung *f*; **~ interval** Schwarzabhebung *f*
sexadecimal *adj* (EDP) sedezimal *adj*, hexadezimal *adj*; **~ number** (EDP) Sedezimalzahl *f*, Hexadezimalzahl *f*
sexless connector Zwitterstecker *m*
shade *v* schattieren *v*; ~ *v* (col.) abstufen *v*; ~ *n* Schatten *m*, Schattierung *f*; ~ *n* (col.) Farbton *m*; **~ density** Schattendichte *f*; **~ of grey** Graustufe *f*
shades *n pl* Helligkeitsabstufungen *f pl*
shading *n* Schatten *m*, Schattierung *f*
shadow *n* Schatten *m*; **~ area** abgeschattete Zone, Schattenzone *f*; **~ areas** *n pl* (pict.) Schatten *m*; **~ effect** (pict.) Schatten *m*; **~ mask** (pict. tube) Lochmaske *f*; **~ mask tube** Schattenmaskenröhre *f*, Maskenröhre *f*; **~ scratch** (F) Schramme *f*; **~ zone** abgeschattete Zone, Schattenzone *f*; **cast ~** Schlagschatten *m*; **deep ~** Kernschatten *m*; **even ~** reiner Schatten; **hard ~** Schlagschatten *m*; **heavy ~** Schlagschatten *m*
shape *n* (journ.) Aufbau *m*
sharp *adj* scharf *adj*
sharp-focus lens Hartzeichner *m*
sharpness *n* Schärfe *f*; ~ *n* (pict.) Scharfzeichnung *f*; **~ of vision** Sehschärfe *f*
sheet of music Notenblatt *n*
shield *v* abschirmen *v*; ~ *n* Abschirmung *f*, Schirm *m*
shielding *n* Abschirmung *f*
shift *v* verschieben *v*; ~ *n* Verschiebung *f*; ~ *n* (key) Umtastung *f*; ~ *n* (staff) Schicht *f*; **~ leader** Schichtleiter *m*; **~ of operating point** Arbeitspunktverschiebung *f*; **~ of working point** Arbeitspunktverschiebung *f*; **~ register** (EDP) Schieberegister *n*
shifting register (EDP) Schieberegister *n*
shiny side Glanzseite *f*
shipping* *n* Expedition* *f*, Versandabteilung *f*
shipping office Versandabteilung *f*,
shock-mounted *adj* gefedert *adj*
shoot *v* (F, TV) filmen *v*, drehen *v*, aufnehmen *v*; **to ~ a film** Film drehen; **to ~ for time lapse effect** unterdrehen *v*; **to ~ in sequence** durchdrehen *v*; **to ~ indoors** Innenaufnahme drehen; **to ~ slow-motion** überdrehen *v*; **to ~ with hand-held camera** aus der Hand drehen; **to ~ with low speed** unterdrehen *v*
shooting *n* Dreh *m*, Dreharbeiten *f pl*, Filmaufnahme *f*; **~ angle** Aufnahmewinkel *m*, Kameraeinstellung *f*, Bildwinkel *m*; **~ aperture** Blendenöffnung *f*; **~ day** Drehtag *m*; **~ lens** Aufnahmeobjektiv *n*; **~ order** Drehfolge *f*; **~ period** Drehzeit *f*; **~ plan** (prod.) Disposition *f*, Drehplan *m*, Drehübersicht *f*; **~ ratio** Drehverhältnis *n*; **~ record** Drehbericht *m*; **~ schedule** Aufnahmeplan *m*, Drehplan *m*, Drehübersicht *f*; **~ script** Drehbuch *n*, Buch *n*; **~ script** (cam.) Kamerascript *n*; **~ time** Drehzeit *f*; **chronological ~** chronologischer Dreh
short *n* (F) Kurzfilm *m*

short-circuit *v* kurzschließen *v*; ~ *n* Kurzschluß *m*; ~ **current** Kurzschlußstrom *m*; ~ **flux** Kurzschlußflux *m*; ~ **oscillogram** Kurzschlußoszillogramm *n*; ~ **transmission system** Kurzschlußübertragungsverfahren *n*

short-circuiting plug Kurzschlußstecker *m*

shortening factor Verkürzungsfaktor *m*

short feature film Kurzspielfilm *m*

short film Kurzfilm *m*

shorting bridge Kurzschlußbrücke *f*

short-notice *adj* kurzfristig *adj*

short-range aerial Nahbereichantenne *f*; ~ **fading** Nahschwund *m*; ~ **reception** Nahempfang *m*

short-term *adj* kurzfristig *adj*

short wave Kurzwelle (KW) *f*

short-wave transmitter Kurzwellensender *m*

shot *n* (F, TV) Aufnahme *f*, Bild *n*, Bildaufnahme *f*, Schuß *m*; ~ *n* (F) Szene *f*; ~ *n* (script) Einstellung *f*; ~ **effect** Schrotrauschen *n*; ~ **list** Drehfolge *f*, Inhaltsangabe *f*, Kamerabericht *m*, Shotlist *f*; ~ **noise** (pict.) Grieß *m*, Schrotrauschen *n*; ~ **number** Buchnummer *f*; ~ **to be printed** Kopierer (K) *m*; **extreme long ~ (ELS)** Weiteinstellung *f*; **high-angle ~** Kamera leicht von oben, Schuß von oben; **low-angle ~** Kamera leicht von unten, Schuß von unten; **mute ~** stumme Aufnahme; **to be in ~** im Bild sein, im Blickfeld sein; **to come into ~** ins Bild kommen; **to do a three-quarter ~** halbfrontal aufnehmen; **to get out of ~** aus dem Bild gehen; **to go out of ~** aus dem Bild gehen; **to miss the ~** nicht aufs Bild kommen; **to run through a ~** Szene durchstellen; **to select ~s** Muster aussuchen; **to set up a ~** Szene einrichten; **top ~** Schuß von oben; **very high-angle ~** Kamera von oben; **very long ~ (VLS)** Weiteinstellung *f*; **very low-angle ~** Kamera von unten

shotgun *v* (US) (acceptance) abnehmen *v*

shot/reaction shot Schuß-Gegenschuß *m*

shoulder harness Schultertragriemen *m*; ~ **pod** Schulterstativ *n*; ~ **strap** Tragriemen *m*; ~ **tripod** Schulterstativ *n*

show *v* (F) vorführen *v*; ~ *n* Show *f*, Musikshow *f*, Unterhaltungsprogramm *n*, Unterhaltungssendung *f*, Expedition *f* Veranstaltung *f*, Vorstellung *f*; ~ **workers** (coll.) Drehbühne *f*

showing *n* Vorstellung *f*, Vorführung *f*; **private ~** geschlossene Vorführung; **public ~** offene Vorführung

shrinkage *n* (proj.) Schleifenschwund *m*; ~ *n* (F) Schrumpfung *f*; ~ *n* (mech.) Schwund *m*; ~ **compensation** (F) Schrumpfausgleich *m*

shrinking *n* (F) Schrumpfung *f*

shunt *n* Nebenschluß *m*; ~ **connection** Parallelschaltung *f*; ~ **current** Nebenschlußstrom *m*; ~ **feed** Anzapfspeisung *f*; ~ **line** Nebenschlußleitung *f*; ~ **motor** Nebenschlußmotor *m*; ~ **resistance** Nebenschlußwiderstand *m*

shutter *n* Blende *f*, Verschluß *m*; ~ **aperture** Blendenöffnung *f*; ~ **blade** Blendenflügel *m*; ~ **button** Auslöser *m*; ~ **-phasing device** Blendennachdrehvorrichtung *f*; ~ **release** Auslöser *m*; ~ **speed** Verschlußgeschwindigkeit *f*; ~ **time** Verschlußzeit *f*

side aerial Seitenantenne *f*

sideband *n* Seitenband *n*;

independent ~s unabhängige Seitenbänder; **suppressed ~** unterdrücktes Seitenband
side-cutters *n pl* Seitenschneider *m*
side-cutting pliers *n pl* Seitenschneider *m*
side-inverted *adj* seitenverkehrt *adj*
side light Seitenlicht *n*
side lighting Seitenbeleuchtung *f*, waagerechte Lichtleiste
side-tone *n* (tel.) Nebengeräusch *n*
side wings *n pl* (set) Gasse *f*
sign *n* Marke *f*, Zeichen *n*; **~ off** *v* (US) absagen *v*; **~ off** *v* (coll.) zu senden aufhören; **~ up** *v* (perf.) verpflichten *v*
signal *n* Signal *n*, Zeichen *n*; **~ above black level** Durchstoßen des Schwarzwertes; **~ amplitude** Signalamplitude *f*; **~ cancellation** Frequenzauslöschung *f*; **~ combiner** Signalmischer *m*; **~ conditioning** (EDP) Meßwertaufbereitung *f*; **~ current** Signalstrom *m*, Tonstrom *m*; **~ deviation** Signalhub *m*; **~ edge** Signalflanke *f*; **~ electrode** Signalelektrode *f*; **~ generation** Signalerzeugung *f*; **~ generator** Meßgenerator *m*, Meßsender *m*, Servicegenerator *m*; **~ injection** Signaleinspeisung *f*; **~ input** Signaleinspeisung *f*; **~ level** Signalpegel *m*; **~ mixer** Signalmischer *m*; **~ path** Signalweg *m*; **~ processing** Signalaufbereitung *f*; **~ regenerating** Signalaufbereitung *f*; **~ shaping** Signalaufbereitung *f*, Signalformierung *f*; **~ strength** Signalstärke *f*; **~ voltage** Signalspannung *f*; **black-level ~ voltage** Signalspannung für Szenenschwarz; **coded ~** kodiertes Signal; **colour-servicing ~ generator** Farbservicegenerator *m*; **disabling ~** (EDP) Sperrsignal *n*; **replayed ~** wiedergegebenes Signal; **reproduced ~** wiedergegebenes Signal; **structure of ~** Signalstruktur *f*
signalling *n* Signalisierung *f*; **~ current** Signalisationsstrom *m*; **~ lamp** Signallampe *f*
signal-to-interference ratio Störabstand *m*
signal-to-noise ratio (S/N ratio) Rauschabstand *m*, Störabstand *m* **~ ratio recording** Störaufzeichnung *f*; **unmodulated ~ ratio** Störabstand ohne Modulation
signature tune Erkennungsmelodie *f*, Kennmelodie *f*; **~ tune** (bcast.) Indikativ einer Sendung
silence *n* Ruhe *f*
silencing *n* Geräuschdämpfung *f*
silent *adj* stumm *adj*; **~ film** Stummfilm *m*
silicon capacitor Kapazitätsdiode *f*, Kapazitätsvariationsdiode *f*, Nachstimmdiode *f*
silk *n* Seide *f*; **~ scrim** Seidenblende *f*
silver foil reflector Aufhellblende *f*, Folienblende *f*; **~ halide** Silbersalz *n*; **~ image** Silberbild *n*; **~ screen** Silberschirm *m*
silvered reflector Silberblende *f*, Aufhellblende *f*
simulation *n* (EDP) Nachbildung *f*
simultaneous *adj* gleichzeitig *adj*, simultan *adj*; **~ broadcast** Simultanübertragung *f*; **~ relay** Simultanübertragung *f*; **~ release** (F) Ringstart *m*; **~ system** Simultansystem *n*; **~ transmission** Simultanübertragung *f*
sine-square and rectangular pulse 2T-20T-Impuls *m*
sine-squared pulse Sinusquadratimpuls *m*
sine wave Sinuswelle *f*
sine-wave generator Sinusgenerator *m*

singer *n* Sänger *m*
single-channel *adj* einkanalig *adj*; ~ **aerial** Kanalantenne *f*; ~ **amplifier** Einkanalverstärker *m*
single-ended stage Eintaktstufe *f*
single frame Einzelbild *n*
single-frame exposure Einzelbildaufnahme *f*; ~ **mechanism** Einzelbildschaltung *f*; ~ **motor** Einzelbildmotor *m*; ~ **shooting** Einzelbildaufnahme *f*
single-knob control Einknopfbedienung *f*
single-lamp suspension unit (lighting) Einzelaufhängung *f*
single-perforated film einseitig perforierter Film
single-phase mains supply Lichtnetz *n*; ~ **power supply** Einphasennetz *n*
single-picture taking Zeitrafferaufnahme *f*
single-pole *adj* einpolig *adj*
single sideband (SSB) Einseitenband (ESB) *n*
single socket Einzeldose *f*
single-standard *adj* Einnorm- (in Zus.)
single suspension unit (lighting) Einzelaufhängung *f*
single track Einspur *f*
sinusoidal signal Sinussignal *n*; ~ **wave** Sinuswelle *f*
site *n* Standort *m*; ~ **plan** Lageplan *m*; ~ **supervisor** Bauleiter *m*
sitter *n* Modell *n*
size *n* Format *n*, Größe *f*, Maß *n*; ~ **of picture element** Rastermaß *n*
sizzle *v* knistern *v*; ~ *n* Knattern *n*, Rasseln *n*
skeleton agreement Manteltarifvertrag *m*; ~ **staff** Bereitschaftsdienst *m*
sketch *n* Skizze *f*, Zeichnung *f*, Sketch *m*
skid *n* Andruckkufe *f*
skilled worker Facharbeiter *m*
skin effect Hauteffekt *m*, Skineffekt *m*, Stromverdrängungseffekt *m*
skirting board Fußleiste *f*
skypan *n* Skypan *m*
sky wave Raumwelle *f*
sky-wave service area Fernempfangsgebiet *n*
slapstick *n* Klamotte *f* (fam.)
slash dupe Klatschkopie *f*; ~ **duping** Abklatschen *n*; ~ **print** Klatschkopie *f*
slaving *n* Fremdsynchronisation *f*; ~ **unit** Fremdsynchronisierungseinrichtung *f*
slewing *n* seitlicher Schwenk
slide *n* Diapositiv *n*, Dia *n*, Lichtbild *n*, Standbild *n*; ~ **advertising** Diawerbung *f*; ~ **carrier** Diapositiv-Wechselschlitten *m*; ~ **cassette** Kassettenrahmenträger *m*; ~ **changer** Diapositiv-Wechselschlitten *m*; ~ **mount** Diarahmen *m*; ~ **projector** Diaprojektor *m*, Diawerfer *m*, Bildwerfer *m*; ~ **publicity** Diawerbung *f*; ~ **-rail** *n* Gleitschiene *f*; ~ **scanner** Diaabtaster *m*, Diageber *m*; ~ **sequence** *n* Lichtbildreihe *f*; ~ **switch** Schiebeschalter *m*; ~ **viewer** Bildbetrachter *m*
slide-in unit Einschub *m*
slider *n* (fader) Schleifer *m*
sliding attenuator Flachbahnsteller *m*; ~ **diaphragm** Schiebeblende *f*; ~ **magnet** Schiebemagnet *m*
slip *n* Schlupf *m*; ~ **on** *v* aufstecken *v*
slip-on type filter Aufsteckfilter *m*
slippage of sound to picture Bild-Ton-Versatz *m*
slipping rotor Schleifringläufer *m*
slit *n* (opt.) Spalt *m*; ~ **width** (opt.) Spaltbreite *f*
slit-type shutter Schlitzverschluß *m*
slope *n* (characteristic) Steilheit *f*; ~ **of valve characteristics** Steilheit *f*

slot *n* Nut *f*; ~ *n* (prog.) Termin *m*, Sendezeit *f*; ~ **aerial** Schlitzantenne *f*
slotted grid Rillendecke *f*
slow motion Zeitlupe *f*, Zeitlupentempo *n*, Zeitdehner *m*
slow-motion camera Zeitdehnerkamera *f*; ~ **effect** Zeitlupe *f*; ~ **machine** Slowmotion-Maschine (SMM) *f*; ~ **method** Zeitlupenverfahren *n*; ~ **picture** Zeitdehneraufnahme *f*; **to shoot** ~ überdrehen *v*
slug *v* (agency) betiteln *v*; ~ *n* (news) Arbeitstitel *m*
slur *v* (speech) verschlucken *v*
small lighting stand Babystativ *n*; ~ **part** Nebenrolle *f*
small-part actor Kleindarsteller *m*
smear *v* (pict.) schmieren *v*; ~ *n* (pict.) Fahne *f*
smearing effect Nachzieheffekt *m*
smoke box Rauchkasten *m*; ~ **pot** Nebeltopf *m*, Rauchbüchse *f*
smoothing capacitor Siebkondensator *m*; ~ **circuit** Glättungsschaltung *f*; ~ **factor** Siebfaktor *m*
snap *n* (news) Vorrangmeldung *f*, Blitzmeldung *f*; ~ **contact** Einrastkontakt *m*
snapshot *n* Schnappschuß *m*
snoot *n* Scheinwerfernase *f*, Tubus *m*, Tute *f* (fam.)
snow *n* (pict.) Schnee *m*
soak *v* (FP) aufquellen *v*
soaking *n* (FP) Aufquellen *n*, Einweichung *f*
social affairs *n pl* Sozialpolitik* *f*
socket *n* Buchse *f*, Fassung *f*, Steckdose *f*; ~ **box** Steckkasten *m*; ~ **cleat** Buchsenleiste *f*; ~ **connections** *n pl* Sockelbelegung *f*; ~ **-head screw** Inbusschraube *f*; ~ **-outlet adapter** Mehrfachsteckvorrichtung *f*; **concealed** ~ Unterputzdose *f*; **live** ~ gespeiste Steckdose; **switched** ~ schaltbare Steckdose
sodium thiosulphate Fixiernatron *n*
sodium-vapour lamp Natriumdampflampe *f*
soft *adj* (pict.) weich *adj*; ~ **-edged wipe** Wischblende *f*; ~ **edges** *n pl* Randunschärfe *f*; ~ **focus** Weichzeichnung *f*; ~ **focus filter** (opt.) Softscheibe *f*; ~ **-focus lens** Diffuserlinse *f*, Weichzeichner *m*; ~ **-iron instrument** Weicheiseninstrument *n*; ~ **lens** Softlinse *f*; ~ **source** Flächenleuchte *f*
soften *v* (F) soften *v*; ~ *v* (light) dämpfen *v*
software *n* Software *f*
solar cell Sonnenzelle *f*
solarisation *n* Solarisation *f*
sold out ausverkauft *adj*
solderable *adj* lötbar *adj*
soldered joint Lötstelle *f*; ~ **seam** Lötstelle *f*; ~ **tag block** Lötigel *m*
soldering bushing Lötdurchführung *f*; ~ **gun** Lötpistole *f*; ~ **iron** Lötkolben *m*; ~ **lug** Lötöse *f*; ~ **-lug strip** Lötösenstreifen *m*; ~ **pin** Lötpin *m*, Lötstift *m*; ~ **tag** Lötöse *f*; ~ **-tag strip** Lötösenstreifen *m*
solid piece (design) Baueinheit *f*, Normbauteil *n*
solid-state *adj* (US) transistorisiert *adj*, transistorbestückt *adj*; ~ **circuit** (EDP) Festkörperschaltkreis *m*; ~ **component** (EDP) Festkörper-Bauelement *n*; ~ **device** (EDP) Festkörper-Bauelement *n*
solo performance Solovortrag *m*
soloist *n* Solist *m*
solution *n* Auflösung *f*, Lösung *f*
solvent *n* Lösungsmittel *n*; ~ **power** (chem.) Auflösungsvermögen *n*
song contest Schlagerwettbewerb *m*
songwriter *n* Schlagertexter *m*
sonic *adj* Schall- (in Zus.)
soot and whitewash knochig *adj*, zu hart, zu kontrastreich

sort *v* sortieren *v*
sound *n* Ton *m*, Klang *m*, Laut *m*, Schall *m*; ~ (compp.) Ton- (in Zus.), Schall- (in Zus.); ~ **-absorbing** *adj* schallabsorbierend *adj*, schalldämpfend *adj*; ~ **absorption** Schallabsorption *f*, Schalldämpfung *f*, Schallschluckung *f*; ~ **absorption coefficient** Schallschluckgrad *m*; ~ **advance** Bild-Ton-Versatz *m*; ~ **amplifier** Niederfrequenzverstärker *m*; ~ **and vision transmission** Ton- und Bildübertragung *f*; ~ **archives** *n pl* Lautarchiv *n*, Schallarchiv *n*, Tonarchiv *n*; ~ **attenuation** Geräuschdämpfung *f*; ~ **bank** Lautbank *f*; ~ **bay** Modulationsgestell *n*; ~ **beam** Schallstrahl *m*; ~ **boom** Galgen *m*; ~ **booth** Abhörbox *f*, Abhörkabine *f*, Tonraum *m*; ~ **box** Schallkörper *m*; ~ **branching amplifier** Tonabzweigverstärker *m*; ~ **breakdown** Tonausfall *m*; ~ **broadcasting** Hörfunk *m*, Hörrundfunk *m*, Tonrundfunk *m*; ~ **camera** Tonkamera *f*; ~ **carrier** Tonträger *m*; ~ **change-over dot** Tonüberblendungsstanze *f*; ~ **channel** Tonkanal *m*, Kanal *m*; ~ **channel** (room) Tonstudio *n*; ~ **circuit** Tonleitung *f*; ~ **column** Tonsäule *f*; ~ **component** Tonkomponente *f*; ~ **control** Tonregler *m*, Tonsteller *m*; ~ **control desk** Tonaufnahmepult *n*; ~ **control engineer** Toningenieur *m*; ~ **control room** Tonregie *f*; ~ **copy** Tonkopie *f*; ~ **crew** Aufnahmegruppe *f*; ~ **cue** Stichwort *n*; ~ **current** Tonstrom *m*; ~ **-damping** *adj* schalldämpfend *adj*; ~ **damping** Schalldämpfung *f*; ~ **-deadening** *adj* schalldämpfend *adj*; ~ **deadening** Schalldämpfung *f*; ~ **definition** Klangbestimmung *f*; ~ **distortion** Tonverzerrung *f*; ~ **distribution amplifier** Tonverteilerverstärker *m*; ~ **document** Tondokument *n*; ~ **driver** Tonsteuersender *m*; ~ **dubbing** (F) Tonmischung *f*; ~ **editing** Tonschnitt *m*; ~ **effect** Schalleffekt *m*, Toneffekt *m*; ~ **effects** *n pl* Geräusche *n pl*, Geräuschkulisse *f*; ~ **effects library** Geräuscharchiv *n*; ~ **effects recording** Geräuschaufnahme *f*; ~ **effects studio** Toneffektraum *m*; ~ **effects technician** Geräuschemacher *m*, Geräuschtechniker *m*; ~ **energy** Schallenergie *f*; ~ **engineer** Toningenieur *m*; ~ **engineering** Tontechnik *f*; ~ **exciter lamp** Tonlampe *f*; ~ **fade** Abblende *f*, Abblendung *f*, Ausblende *f*, Tonausblendung *f*, Tonblende *f*; ~ **fader** Tonblende *f*, Tonregler *m*, Tonsteller *m*; ~ **fading** Tonüberblendung *f*; ~ **feed** Tonzuspielung *f*; ~ **field** Schallfeld *n*; ~ **film** Tonfilm *m*; ~ **-film traction** Tonlaufwerk *n*; ~ **filter** Klangfilter *m*; ~ **flash** Tonblitz *m*; ~ **frequency** Tonfrequenz *f*; ~ **gate** Tonschleuse *f*, Tonabtastung *f*; ~ **generator** Schallquelle *f*; ~ **head** Sprechkopf *m*, Tonabnehmer *m*, Tonabtaster *m*, Tonabtasteinrichtung *f*, Tonkopf *m*; ~ **impression** Klangeindruck *m*; ~ **insulation** Schalldichtung *f*, Schalldämmung *f*, Geräuschdämpfung *f*; ~ **intensity** Lautstärke *f*, Schallintensität *f*, Schallstärke *f*, Tonstärke *f*; ~ **is grotty** (coll.) Ton rotzt (fam.); ~ **is out of sync** Ton läuft weg; ~ **join** Tonklebestelle *f*; ~ **level** Tonpegel *m*, Lautstärkepegel *m*; ~ **level check** Tonpegelkontrolle *f*, Tonprobe *f*; ~ **level meter**

Lautstärkemesser *m*; ~ **librarian** Schallarchivar *m*; ~ **library** Lautarchiv *n*, Schallarchiv *n*, Tonarchiv *n*; ~ **lock** Schallschleuse *f*; ~ **maintenance** Tonmeßtechnik *f*; ~ **man** Tonassistent *m*, Tontechniker *m*; ~ **master control** Senderegieton *m*, Tonendkontrolle *f*; ~ **mixer** Tonmischpult *n*; ~ **mixer** (staff) Tontechniker *m*; ~ **mixing** Tonmischung *f*, Tonüberblendung *f*; ~ **mixing amplifier** Tonmischverstärker *m*; ~ **mixing console** Tonmischpult *n*; ~ **mixing desk** Tonaufnahmepult *n*, Tonmischpult *n*; ~ **motion picture** Tonfilm *m*; ~ **negative** Tonnegativ *n*; ~ **negative report** Tonnegativbericht *m*; ~ **network** Tonleitungsnetz *n*; ~ **OB operations** *n pl* Übertragungsdienst Ton; ~ **OB van** Übertragungswagen *m*, Ü-Wagen *m*; ~ **on film (SOF)** Filmton *m*; ~ **on vision** Ton im Bild; ~ **only** nur Ton; ~ **operator** Tontechniker *m*; ~ **pattern** Klangbild *n*; ~ **perspective** Raumwirkung *f*; ~ **pick-up** Schallempfänger *m*, Tonabnehmer *m*, Tonabtaster *m*, Tonabtastung *f*; ~ **pick-up device** Tonabtasteinrichtung *f*; ~ **picture** Hörbild *n*, Tonrelief *n*; ~ **positive** Tonpositiv *n*; ~ **pressure** Schalldruck *m*; ~ **print** Tonkopie *f* ~ **projection** Schallabstrahlung *f*; ~ **projector** Tonprojektor *m*; ~ **-proof** *adj* schalldicht *adj*; ~ **-proof casing** Schallschutzhaube *f*; ~ **-proof covering** schalldichte Hülle; ~ **-proofing** *n* Geräuschdämpfung *f*; ~ **quality** Tonqualität *f*; ~ **radiation** Schallabstrahlung *f*, Schallstrahlung *f*; ~ **radio** Tonfunk *m*; ~ **recorder** Tonaufnahmegerät *n*, Tonaufnahmemaschine *f*, Tonaufzeichnungsanlage *f*; ~ **recording** Schallaufnahme *f*, Schallaufzeichnung *f*, Tonaufnahme *f*, Tonaufzeichnung *f*; ~ **recording** (methods) Tonaufnahmetechnik *f*; ~ **recording** (mus.) Vertonung *f*; ~ **recording and reproducing equipment** Tonaufnahme- und Wiedergabegerät *n*; ~ **recording equipment** Tonaufnahmegerät *n*, Tonaufnahmemaschine *f*, Tonaufzeichnungsanlage *f*; ~ **recording medium** Schallspeicher *m*, Schallträger *m*; ~ **recording studio** Tonatelier *n*, Tonaufnahmestudio *n*, Tonstudio *n*, Schallaufzeichnungsraum *m*; ~ **recording system** Schallaufnahmeverfahren *n*, Tonaufzeichnungsverfahren *n*; ~ **recordist** Tontechniker *m*; ~ **recordist** (F) Tonmeister *m*; ~ **report** Tonbericht *m*; ~ **reproducer** Tonwiedergabegerät *n*; ~ **reproduction** Schallwiedergabe *f*, Tonwiedergabe *f*; ~ **running!** Ton läuft!; ~ **scanning** Tonabtastung *f*; ~ **scanning device** Tonabtasteinrichtung *f*; ~ **scanning head** Tonabtastkopf *m* ~ **scratch** Tonschramme *f*; ~ **script** Tonscript *n*; ~ **section** Tonteil *m*; ~ **signal** Tonsignal *n*; ~ **signal direct synchronisation** Mitnahmesynchronisierung *f*; ~ **signal transmission** Tonsignalübermittlung *f*; ~ **source** Klangquelle *f*, Schallquelle *f*; ~ **spectrum** Klanggemisch *n*; ~ **splice** Tonklebestelle *f*; ~ **stage** (stereo) Basis *f*, Raumvorstellung des Hörers; ~ **-stage width** (stereo) Basisbreite *f*; ~ **start mark** Tonstartmarke *f*; ~ **studio** Tonatelier *n*, Tonaufnahmestudio *n*, Tonstudio *n*, Schallaufzeichnungsraum *m*; **~ switching area** Tonschaltraum *m*; **~ switching error** Tonfehlschaltung *f*; **~ sync** Geräuschsynchronisation *f*; **~ system** Tonsystem *n*; **~ tape** Tonband *n*; **~ tape recording** Tonbandaufnahme *f*; **~ tape width** Tonbandbreite *f*; **~ track** Tonspur *f*, Tonband *n*, Filmton *m*; **~ track advance** Bild-Ton-Versatz *m*; **~ track negative** Tonnegativ *n*; **~ track support** (material) Tonträger *m*; **~ transducer** Schallumwandler *m*; **~ transduction** Schallrückwandlung *f*; **~ transmission** Klangübertragung *f*; **~ transmitter** Tonsender *m*; **~ trap** Tonfalle *f*, Tonsperre *f*; **~ version** Tonfassung *f*; **~ vibration** Tonschwingung *f*; **~ volume** Klangfülle *f*, Lautstärke *f*, Tonstärke *f*, Tonvolumen *n*; **~ wave** Schallwelle *f*; **bad ~ join** fehlerhafte Tonklebestelle; **change in ~ level** Tonpegeländerung *f*; **cut ~ !** Ton aus!; **international ~** internationaler Ton (IT); **international ~ circuit** IT-Leitung *f*, internationale Tonleitung, Begleittonleitung *f*; **international ~ network** internationales Tonleitungsnetz; **international ~ track** internationales Tonband *n* (IT-Band); **jump in ~ level** Tonpegelsprung *m*; **o.k. for ~ !** Ton klar!; **o.k. for ~** Ton in Ordnung; **pure ~** reiner Ton; **take out ~ !** Ton aus!; **to add ~ to a film** vertonen *v*; **to adjust ~ levels** Ton einpegeln; **to dip the ~** abblenden *v*; **to dub ~** Ton unterlegen; **to insulate for ~** schallisolieren *v*; **to lay the ~** Ton unterlegen; **to lay the ~ track** Ton anlegen; **to make a ~ recording** vertonen *v*; **to put ~ to picture** Ton anlegen; **turn over ~ !** Ton ab!; **variation in ~ level** Tonpegelschwankung *f*; **well-balanced ~ mix** ausgewogenes Tongemisch

sounding board Schallwand *f*

soup, it's in (coll.) (FP) der Film schwimmt

source *n* Quelle *f*, Quellpunkt *m*; **~ impedance** Quellwiderstand *m*; **~ language statement** (EDP) Primäranweisung *f*; **~ of interference** Störspannungsquelle *f*; **~ statement** (EDP) Primäranweisung *f*

space *n* Raum *m*; **~ charge** Raumladung *f*; **~ -charged grid** Raumladungsgitter *n*; **~ satellite** Raumsatellit *m*

spaced-microphone stereo Intensitäts- und Phasenstereofonie *f*

spacer ring Distanzring *m*

spacing *n* (F) Blankfilm *m*, Blindfilm *m*

spare *n* Ersatzteil *n*; **~ apparatus** Reservegerät *n*; **~ battery** Ersatzbatterie *f*; **~ circuit** Reserveleitung *f*; **~ part** Ersatzteil *n*; **~ set** Ersatzgerät *n*

spark *n* Funke *m*; ~ *n* (coll.) (lighting staff) Beleuchter *m*; **~ absorber** Funkenlöscher *m*; **~ arrester** Funkenlöscher *m*; **~ extinguisher** Funkenlöscher *m*; **~ gap** Funkenstrecke *f*; **~ screen** Funkenschutzschirm *m*

sparking *n* Funkenstörung *f*

sparkle *v* flimmern *v*

sparks *n pl* (coll.) (lighting staff) Beleuchtertrupp *m*

spatial effect Raumwirkung *f*

speak *v* sprechen *v*; **to ~ to camera** im On sprechen

speaker *n* (R, TV) Sprecher *m*, Rundfunksprecher *m*; ~ *n* (loudspeaker) Lautsprecher *m*;

~ **cone** Lautsprecherkonus *m*
speaking clock announcement Zeitansage *f*
special *n* (TV, R) Sondersendung *f*, Sonderbericht *m*, Special *n*; ~ *n* (design) Versatzstück *n*, Dekorationsversatzstück *n*; ~ **announcement** (R) Rundfunkdurchsage *f*, Sondermeldung *f*; ~ **circuit** Sonderleitung *f*; ~ **correspondent** Sonderberichterstatter *m*; ~ **effect** Trick *m*, Trickeffekt *m*; ~ **effects** *n pl* Spezialeffekt *m*, Trick *m*; ~ **effects desk** Trickpult *n*; ~ **effects film** Trickfilm *m*; ~ **effects generator** Trickmischer *m*; ~ **effects lighting** Effektbeleuchtung *f*; ~ **effects man** Pyrotechniker *m*; ~ **effects mixer** Trickmischer *m*; ~ **effects section** Trickabteilung *f*; ~ **field** Sachgebiet *n*; ~ **report** Sonderbericht *m*
specialist *n* Fachmann *m*, Sachverständiger *m*, Experte *m*; ~ **correspondent** Fachjournalist *m*, Fachredakteur *m*, Redakteur *m*
speciality *n* Fachgebiet *n*, Sachgebiet *n*
specifications *n pl* Pflichtenheft *n*
spectacular *n* (F) Ausstattungsfilm *m*
spectator *n* Zuschauer *m*
spectral analysis Spektralzerlegung *f*; ~ **colour** Spektralfarbe *f*; ~ **component** Spektralkomponente *f*, Spektralanteil *m*; ~ **curve** Spektralverteilungskurve *f*, Spektralkurvenzug *m*; ~ **line** Spektrallinie *f*; ~ **re-emission** Remissionsumfang *m*; ~ **region** Spektralbereich *m*; ~ **response** Farbempfindlichkeit *f*; ~ **sensitivity** Spektralempfindlichkeit *f*; ~ **sensitivity curve** spektrale Hellempfindlichkeitskurve
spectrogram *n* Spektrogramm *n*
spectroscope *n* Spektroskop *n*
spectrum *n* Spektrum *n*; ~ **line** Spektrallinie *f*; **continuous** ~ kontinuierliches Spektrum; **luminous** ~ sichtbares Spektrum; **visible** ~ sichtbares Spektrum
specular *n* Weißspitze *f*
speech band Sprachband *n*; ~ **circuit** Sprechleitung *f*; ~ **communication** Sprechverbindung *f*; ~ **current** Sprechstrom *m*; ~ **frequency** Sprechfrequenz *f*; ~ **frequency range** Sprachfrequenzbereich *m*; ~ **line** Sprechleitung *f*; ~ **recording** Sprachaufnahme *f*
speed *n* Geschwindigkeit *f*; ~ *n* (FP) Empfindlichkeit *f*; ~ **change** Geschwindigkeitsänderung *f*; ~ **controller** Geschwindigkeitsregler *m*; ~ **error** Geschwindigkeitsfehler *m*; ~ **fluctuation** Geschwindigkeitsschwankung *f*; ~ **governor** Geschwindigkeitsregler *m*; ~ **ratio** Übersetzungsverhältnis *n*; ~ **regulator** Geschwindigkeitsregler *m*; ~ **selector** (recorder) Bandgeschwindigkeitsumschalter *m*; ~ **variation** Geschwindigkeitsabweichung *f*; **continuous** ~ **variation** stufenlose Geschwindigkeitsänderung; **controlled** ~ steuerbare Geschwindigkeit; **high** ~ hohe Empfindlichkeit; **low** ~ niedrige Empfindlichkeit; **variable** ~ veränderliche Geschwindigkeit
speeded-up action Zeitraffer *m*
speedometer *n* Tachometer *m*
sphere of responsibility Ressort *n*
spider *n* Stativspinne *f*, Spinne *f*
spike *v* (coll.) (news) Nachricht unter den Tisch fallen lassen

(fam.)
spill light Streulicht *n*, Nebenlicht *n*
spirit level Wasserwaage *f*, Libelle *f*
splash *n* Spratzer *m*
splash-proof *adj* spritzwasserdicht *adj*
splice *v* kleben *v*; ~ *v* (tape) zusammenschneiden *v*; ~ *n* Klebestelle *f*; **faulty ~** fehlerhafte Klebestelle; **manual ~** mechanische Klebestelle; **to ~ leader sticker** Startband kleben (nach Bandgeschwindigkeit); **to ~ 1 7/8"/sec** (grey) Startband kleben 4,75 cm (grau); **to ~ 3 3/4"/sec** (green) Startband kleben 9,5 cm (grün); **to ~ 7 1/2"/sec** (blue) Startband kleben 19 cm (blau); **to ~ 15"/sec** (red) Startband kleben 38 cm (rot); **to ~ 30"/sec** (white) Startband kleben 76 cm (weiß)
splicer *n* Klebelade *f*, Klebepresse *f*, Schneidelehre *f*
splicing *n* Kleben *n*; **~ bench** Klebetisch *m*; **~ cement** Filmkitt *m*; **~ girl** Filmkleberin *f*, Kleberin *f*; **~ patch** Unterkleber *m*; **~ press** Klebelade *f*, Klebepresse *f*, Schneidelehre *f*; **~ table** Klebetisch *m*; **~ tape** (VTR) Videoklebeband *n*; **~ tape** (F, sound) Klebeband *n*
split *v* knicken *v*; **~ -field rangefinder** Schnittbildentfernungsmesser *m*; **~ film** Spaltfilm *m*; **~ -image rangefinder** Schnittbildentfernungsmesser *m*; **~ phase** Hilfsphase *f*; **~ picture** Teilbild *n*; **~ screen** geteiltes Bild
splitter *n* (cable) Peitsche *f*
splitting of spectrum Zerlegung des Spektrums
spoken word broadcast Wortsendung *f*; **~ word programme** Wortprogramm *n*, Wort* *n*
spokesman *n* Sprecher *m*
sponsored broadcast Sponsorsendung *f*, gesponsorte Sendung; **~ programme** Werbesendung *f*, Sponsorsendung *f*, gesponsorte Sendung; **~ television** (US) Werbefernsehen *n*
spool *v* auftrommeln *v*, spulen *v*; ~ *n* Rolle *f*, Spule *f*, Akt *m*, Aktrolle *f*; **~ off** *v* abtrommeln *v*; **~ (up)** *v* aufspulen *v*, aufwickeln *v*; **~ with side plates** Spule mit Seitenflanschen; **lower ~** (proj.) Aufwickelspule *f*; **upper ~** Abwickelspule *f*, Abwickeltrommel *f*
spooling *n* Wicklung *f*; **~ system** Abwickelsystem *n*
sport *n* Sport *m*
sportcast *n* (US) Sport *m*, Sportsendung *f*
sporting event Sportveranstaltung *f*
sports and events* (TV) Sport* *m*; **~ broadcast** Sportsendung *f*; **~ commentator** Sportkommentator *m*; **~ editor** Sportredakteur *m*; **~ event** Sportveranstaltung *f*; **~ film** Sportfilm *m*; **~ journalist** Sportredakteur *m*; **~ news programmes*** *n pl* Sport* *m*, Sportfunk *m*; **~ reporter** Sportreporter *m*; **~ reporting** Sport *m*
spot *n* (light) Spotlicht *n*, Spot *m* (fam.); ~ *n* (advert.) Durchsage *f*, Spot *m*; ~ *n* (coll.) (prog.) Sendezeit *f*; **~ brightness** Lichtpunkthelligkeit *f*, Punkthelligkeit *f*; **~ effects** Geräuscheffekte *m pl*; **~ focus** Punktschärfe *f*; **~ photometer** Partialbelichtungsmesser *m*, Fotospotmeter *n*, Spotmeter *n*; **~ -wobble** *v* Schärfe wobbeln; **~ wobble** Wobbeln des Strahlstroms; **~ -wobbled** *adj* zeilenfrei *adj*; **to be on the ~** vor

der Kamera auftreten
spotlight *n* Scheinwerter *m*, Spotlicht *n*, Spot *m* (fam.); ~ **lamp** Scheinwerferlampe *f*; ~ **lens** Scheinwerferlinse *f*; ~ **meter** Punktlichtmesser *m*
spotmeter *n* Fotospotmeter *n*
spotting box Lichtkasten *m*, Lichtfeld *n*
spray development Sprühentwicklung *f*; ~ **gun** Spritzpistole *f*; ~ **painter** Spritzlackierer *m*; ~ **processor** Sprühentwicklungsmaschine *f*; ~ **watering** Sprühwässerung *f*
spring mechanism Federwerk *n*; ~ **strip** Federleiste *f*; ~ **tension** Federspannung *f*
sprocket *n* Zahntrommel *f*; ~ **hole** Perforationsloch *n*; ~ **holes** *n pl* Perforation *f*; ~ **marking** (F) Rädern *n*; ~ **wheel** Schaltrolle *f*, Zahntrommel *f*
sprung *adj* gefedert *adj*
spur feeder (aerial) Zweigleitung *f*
spurious printing (F) Kopiereffekt *m*; ~ **radiation** Störstrahlung *f*; ~ **signal** Störsignal *n*; ~ **signal compensation** Störsignalkompensation *f*
sputter *n* Spratzer *m*
square pulse Rechteckimpuls *m*; ~ **tube** Vierkanttubus *m*; ~ **wave signal** Rechtecksignal *n*
squelch circuit Geräuschsperre *f*
squirrel cage motor Käfigläufer *m*
stabilisation *n* Stabilisierung *f*; ~ **of rotation** (sat.) Drehstabilisierung *f* ~ **of spin** (sat.) Spinstabilisierung *f*
stabiliser *n* Konstanthalter *m*, Regler *m*
stabilising amplifier Stabilisierverstärker *m*
stability *n* Konstanz *f*
staccato *adv* abgehackt *adv*
stacker truck Hubstapler *m*
staff *n* Belegschaft *f*, Personal *n*, Stab *m*; ~ **administration*** Personalabteilung *f*; ~ **duty sheet** Dienstplan *m*; ~ **engineer** Betriebstechniker *m*; ~ **maintenance worker** Betriebshandwerker *m*; ~ **medical adviser** Betriebsarzt *m*; ~ **medical officer** Betriebsarzt *m*; ~ **nursing sister** Betriebsschwester *f*; ~ **on call** Sendebereitschaft *f*, Betriebsbereitschaft *f*; ~ **set** (rec.) Dienstgerät *n*; ~ **training** Ausbildungswesen *n*; ~ **training school** Nachwuchsstudio *n*; **artistic** ~ künstlerisches Personal; **member of** ~ Angestellter *m*; **member of unestablished** ~ Zeitvertragsinhaber *m*
stage *v* (play) herausbringen *v*, inszenieren *v*; ~ *n* Bühne *f*; ~ *n* (platform) Podest *n*; ~ *n* (ampl.) Stufe *f*; ~ **decorations** *n pl* Bühnendekoration *f*; ~ **direction** Regieanweisung *f*; ~ **flat** (design) Bauelement *n*; ~ **-fright** *n* Lampenfieber *n*; ~ **hand** Atelierarbeiter *m*, Bühnenarbeiter *m*; ~ **hands** *n pl* Bühnenpersonal *n*, Bühne *f* (fam.) ~ **hands' foreman** Bühnenvorarbeiter *m*; ~ **left** bühnenlinks *adv*; ~ **lift** Hebebühne *f*; ~ **machinery** Bühnenmaschinerie *f*; ~ **manager (SM)** Aufnahmeleiter *m*; ~ **manager (SM)** (thea.) Inspizient *m*; ~ **right** bühnenrechts *adv*; ~ **waggon** Bühnenwagen *m*
staging *n* (thea.) Inszenierung *f*, Regie *f*
staircase signal Graukeilsignal *n*; ~ **test chart** Graukeiltestvorlage *f*
stamp *n* Stanze *f*
stamper *n* (disc) Matrize *f*
stand *n* Ständer *m*, Stativ *n*, Gestell *n*, Untergestell *n*; ~ **by!** (cam.) Achtung, Aufnahme!,

Ausgangsposition!; **~ in** *v* (perf.) doubeln *v*
standard *n* Norm *f*; **~ component** Normbauteil *n*; **~ equipment** Standardausrüstung *f*; **~ format** Normalformat *n*; **~ frequency** Normalfrequenz *f*, Prüffrequenz *f*; **~ frequency generator** Normalfrequenzgenerator *m*; **~ frequency satellite service** Normalfrequenzfunkdienst mit Satelliten; **~ gauge** Normalfilmformat *n*; **~ -gauge film** Normalfilm *m*; **~ -gauge stock** Normalfilm *m*; **~ level generator** Pegelgeber *m*; **~ level tape** Pegelband *n*; **~ magnetic tape** Bezugsband *n*, Magnetbezugsband *n*; **~ print** Standardkopie *f*; **~ rack cabinet** Normschrank *m*; **~ replay chain** Normalwiedergabekette *f*; **~ resistor** Widerstandsnormal *n*; **~ signal generator** Bezugsgenerator *m*; **~ specifications** *n pl* Norm *f*, Pflichtenheft *n*; **~ tape** Normband *n*, Normbezugsband *n*, Bezugsband *n*, Testband *n*; **tentative ~** Vornorm *f*
standardisation committee Normenausschuß *m*
standardise *v* eichen *v*, normen *v*
standards committee Normenausschuß *m*; **~ conversion** Normenwandlung *f*; **~ conversion equipment** Normenwandler *m*; **~ converter** Normenwandler *m*; **~ for measurement of magnetic tapes** Richtlinien zum Einmessen von Schallträgern
stand-by *n* Bereitschaft *f*; **~** *n* (prog.) Reserve *f*; **~ programme** Reserveprogramm *n*, Ersatzsendung *f*; **~ service** Bereitschaftsdienst *m*, Reservebetrieb *m*; **~ stage team** Bühnenwache *f*; **~ transmitter** Ersatzsender *m*, Füllsender *m*; **at ~** in Bereitschaft
stand-in *n* Doubel *n*
standing wave Stehwelle *f*
stand microphone Stützmikrofon *n*
stand-off insulator Abstandsisolator *m*
standstill *n* Stillstand *m*
staple *v* antuckern *v* (fam.)
star *v* (perf.) herausstellen *v*; **~** *n* Star *m*, Hauptdarsteller *m*; **~ connection** Sternsystem *n*; **~ -delta** *n* Stern-Dreieck *n*; **~ distributing system** Sternverteilungssystem *n*; **~ indicator** Kleeblattschauzeichen *n*; **~ system** Sternsystem *n*
starlet *n* Filmsternchen *n*
starring ... in der Hauptrolle ...
start *v* (cam.) einschalten *v*; **~** *n* Start *m*; **~** (appar.) ein; **~ leader** Startband *n*, Startvorspann *m*; **~ mark** Startmarke *f*, Startmarkierung *f*, Startzeichen *n*, Einlegemarke *f*; **~ of shooting** Drehbeginn *m*; **~ of switching sequence** Schaltanfang *m*; **~ of transmission** Sendebeginn *m*; **~ pulse** Startauslösezeichen *n*; **~ release signal** Startauslösezeichen *n*; **~ up** *v* (motor) anlaufen *v*; **~ up** *v* in Betrieb nehmen, in Betrieb setzen; **flying ~** fliegender Start; **non-sync ~** asynchroner Start; **ready to ~ ?** Studio klar?; **to ~ studio work** ins Atelier gehen; **to lace up to ~ mark** auf Startmarkierung einlegen; **to make ~ marks** Film einstarten, einstarten *v*, Startmarkierungen anbringen
starter resistor Anlaßwiderstand *m*; **~ rheostat** Anlaßwiderstand *m*
starting blip Auslösezeichen *n*; **~ current** Anlaufstrom *m*; **~ hum** Einschaltbrumm *m*; **~ mark** Startauslösezeichen *n*; **~ panel**

Einschaltfeld *n*; ~ **signal** Startauslösezeichen *n*; ~ **time** Anfangszeit *f*; ~ **torque** Anlaufmoment *m*

start-up *n* (transmitter) Inbetriebnahme *f*

state *n* Zustand *m*; ~ **broadcasting authority** Staatsrundfunk *m*; ~ **of charge** Ladungszustand *m*

statement *n* Presseverlautbarung *f*, Verlautbarung *f*, Mitteilung *f*, Statement *n*; ~ *n* (EDP) Anweisung *f*; ~ **of contents** Inhaltsangabe *f*

static *n* statisches Rauschen; ~ **caption** Standtitel *m*; ~ **induction** Influenz *f*; ~ **suppression** Entstörung *f*

station *n* Anstalt *f*, Sender *m*, Station *f*; ~ **announcement** Stationsansage *f*; ~ **caption** Stationskennzeichen *n*, Stationsdia *n*; ~ **identification** Stationskennung *f*; ~ **identification signal** Erkennungszeichen *n*, Indikativ *n*, Pausenzeichen *n*; ~ **identification slide** Senderdia *n*, Stationsdia *n*; ~ **manager** Studioleiter *m*; **attended** ~ bemannte Station; **commercial** ~ kommerzielle Station; **control** ~ betriebsführendes Amt; **directing** ~ betriebsführendes Amt; **mobile** ~ fahrbarer Sender, beweglicher Sender; **remote-switched** ~ ferngeschaltete Station; **semi-attended** ~ nicht ständig besetzte Station; **to pick up a** ~ Sender bekommen, Sender einfangen; **to tune in to a** ~ Sender einstellen; **unattended** ~ unbemannte Station

stationary wave test set Stehwellenmeßgerät *n*

stay *v* (mast) abspannen *v*, verankern *v*, verspannen *v*; ~ *n* (mast) Pardune *f*, Abspannseil *n*; ~ *n* (design) Blendenstrebe *f*, Blendenstütze *f*

steerable radio link drehbares Funkfeld

steerer *n* Kamerafahrer *m*, Dollyfahrer *m*

steering lever Steuerhebel *m*

step *n* Stufe *f*; ~ **down** *v* (elec.) heruntertransformieren *v*; ~ **function** Sprungfunktion *f*; ~ **function response** Sprungkennlinie *f*; ~ **function signal** Sprungsignal *n*; ~ **-ladder** *n* Stehleiter *f*; ~ **printer** Schrittkopiermaschine *f*; ~ **switch** Stufenschalter *m*; ~ **up** *v* (elec.) herauftransformieren *v*; ~ **wedge** Belichtungskeil *m*, Graukeil *m*, Grauskala *f*, Keilvorlage *f*, Stufenkeil *m*

step-by-step motion Schrittlauf *m*; ~ **switch** Schrittschaltwerk *n*

stepped photometric absorption wedge Stufenkeil *m*

stepping motion Schrittlauf *m*; ~ **motor** Schrittmotor *m*

stereo *n* Stereo *n*, Stereofonie *f*; ~ *adj* stereo *adj*, stereofon *adj*, stereofonisch *adj*; ~ **broadcast** Stereosendung *f*; ~ **-capable** *adj* stereotüchtig *adj*; ~ **decoder** Stereodekoder *m*; ~ **effect** Raumeffekt *m*; ~ **information** (coll.) (stereo) Richtungsinformation *f*; ~ **layout** Raumvorstellung des Hörers; ~ **operation** Stereosendebetrieb *m*; ~ **picture** (coll.) Raumvorstellung des Hörers; ~ **programme** Stereoprogramm *n*; ~ **radio** (coll.) Rundfunkstereofonie *f*; ~ **rebroadcast receiver** Stereoballempfänger *m*; ~ **rebroadcast transmitter** Stereoumsetzer *m*; ~ **receiver** Stereoempfänger *m*; ~ **recording** Stereoaufzeichnung *f*; ~ **relay transmitter** Stereoumsetzer *m*; ~ **reproduction** Stereowiedergabe *f*; **~ signal** Stereosignal *n*; **~ sound** Stereofonie *f*, Raumton *m*; **~ studio** Stereostudio *n*; **~ transmission** Stereosendung *f*; **~ transmission system** stereofone Übertragungsanlage; **~ transmitter operation** Stereosendebetrieb *m*; **~ transposer** Stereoumsetzer *m*; **~ tuner** Stereoempfänger *m*

stereophonic *adj* stereo *adj*, stereofon *adj*, stereofonisch *adj*; **~ effect** Raumwirkung *f*; **AB ~ recording process** Stereoaufnahmeverfahren AB; **XY and MS ~ recording process** Stereoaufnahmeverfahren XY und MS

stereophony *n* Stereo *n*, Stereofonie *f*

stereoscope *n* Stereoskop *n*

sticking *n* (pict.) Einbrennen *n*, eingebranntes Bild

stick-on cardboard Aufklebekarton *m*

still *n* Aufnahme *f*, Foto *n*, Fotografie *f*, Lichtbild *n*; ~ *n* (F) Standbild *n*, Standfoto *n*, Werkaufnahme *f*; **~ copy** Standbildverlängerung *f*, Standkopie *f*, weiterkopiertes Einzelbild; **~ frame** Standbild *n*; **~ picture** Standbild *n*, Standfoto *n* **~ projector** Bildprojektor *m*, Bildwerfer *m*

stills cameraman Standfotograf *m*; **~ library** Fotoarchiv *n*, Fotostelle *f* **~ man** (coll.) Bildberichterstatter *m*, Bildreporter *m*, Standfotograf *m*; **~ photographer** Standfotograf *m*, Fotograf *m*

stirring device (FP) Rührwerk *n*

stock *n* (material) Film *m*, Rohfilm *m*, Rohfilmmaterial *n*; ~ *n* (store) Fundus *m*; **~ -keeper** *n* Requisitenmeister *m*, Fundusverwalter *m*; **~ scenery part** Fundusteil *n*; **~ shot** Archivaufnahme *f*; **~ shots** *n pl* Fremdfilmmaterial *n*; **non-exposed ~** unbelichteter Film; **raw ~** unbelichteter Film

Stockholm plan Stockholmer Wellenplan

stop *n* Stillstand *m*; ~ *n* (lens) Blende *f*

stop! (appar.) aus!, Stopp!

stop bath (FP) Stoppbad *n*, Unterbrechungsbad *n*; **~ -camera effect** Stopptrick *m*; **~ condition** (EDP) Haltbedingung *f*; **~ down** *v* abblenden *v*, Blende schließen; **~ frame** Standbildverlängerung *f*, Standkopie *f*, weiterkopiertes Einzelbild; **~ -frame animation** Phasentrick *m*; **~ -frame mechanism** Einzelbildschaltung *f* **~ -frame motor** Einzelbildmotor *m*; **~ -frame rostrum** Tricktisch *m*, Trickbank *f*; **~ -frame shooting** Einzelbildaufnahme *f*; **~ framing** Standkopieren *n*; **~ instruction** (EDP) Stoppbefehl *m*; **~ motion** Zeitraffer *m*, Zeitrafferaufnahme *f*, Einergang *m*; **~ -motion camera** Zeitraffer *m*; **~ -motion effect** Zeitraffung *f*; **~ press** letzte Meldung; **~ setting** Blendeneinstellung *f*

stopper *n* Stöpsel *m*

stopping device Stillstandvorrichtung *f*; **~ time** Nachlaufzeit *f*

stopping-down *n* Abblende *f*, Abblendung *f*, Ausblende *f*

stopwatch *n* Stoppuhr *f*

storage *n* Lagerung *f*, Speicherung *f*, Archivierung *f*; **~ address** (EDP) Speicheradresse *f*; **~ camera tube** Speicherröhre *f*; **~ capacity** (EDP) Speicherkapazität *f*; **~ cell** (EDP) Speicherzelle *f*; **~ cycle** (EDP) Speicherzyklus *m*; **~ element** (EDP) Speicherzelle *f*; **~ plate** (orthicon) Glashaut *f*, Speicherplatte *f*; **~ protection** (EDP) Speicherschutz *m*; **~ relay**

Speicherrelais *n*; ~ **system** Speichersystem *n*; ~ **tank** Vorratsgefäß *n*; ~ **target** Speicherplatte *f*; ~ **time** Speicherzeit *f*; ~ **-type camera tube** Bildspeicherröhre *f*, Speicherröhre *f*; ~ **unit** (EDP) Speicherzelle *f*; **protected ~ area** (EDP) geschützter Speicher

store *v* lagern *v*; ~ *n* Lager *n*, Magazin *n*, Speicher *m*, Abstellraum *m*; ~ *n* (EDP) Speicher *m*; ~ **-keeper** *n* Lagerist *m*; ~ **location** (EDP) Speicherplatz *m*; **active** ~ (EDP) Aktivspeicher *m*; **auxiliary** ~ (EDP) Hintergrundspeicher *m*; **backing** ~ (EDP) Hintergrundspeicher *m*; **bulk** ~ (EDP) Großraumspeicher *m*; **computing** ~ (EDP) Arbeitsspeicher *m*, Hauptspeicher *m*, Primärspeicher *m*; **core** ~ (EDP) Kernspeicher *m*; **delay-line** ~ (EDP) Laufzeitspeicher *m*; **disc** ~ (EDP) Plattenspeicher *m*; **electrostatic** ~ (EDP) Ladungsspeicher *m*; **external** ~ (EDP) externer Speicher; **fast** ~ (EDP) Speicher mit schnellem Zugriff; **fixed** ~ (EDP) Festwertspeicher *m*; **general** ~ (EDP) Arbeitsspeicher *m*, Hauptspeicher *m*, Primärspeicher *m*; **high-speed** ~ (EDP) Speicher mit schnellem Zugriff; **intermediate** ~ (EDP) Zwischenspeicher *m*; **internal** ~ (EDP) interner Speicher; **magnetic core** ~ (EDP) Kernspeicher *m*; **magnetic disc** ~ (EDP) Magnetplattenspeicher *m*; **magnetic drum** ~ (EDP) Magnettrommelspeicher *m*; **magnetic tape** ~ (EDP) Magnetbandspeicher *m*, Bandspeicher *m*; **non-volatile** ~ (EDP) permanenter Speicher; **permanent** ~ (EDP) permanenter Speicher; **random-access** ~ (EDP) Speicher mit direktem Zugriff, Speicher mit wahlfreiem Zugriff; **rapid** ~ (EDP) Speicher mit schnellem Zugriff; **read-only** ~ (EDP) Festwertspeicher *m*; **sequential-access** ~ (EDP) Speicher mit sequentiellem Zugriff; **slow** ~ (EDP) langsamer Speicher; **slow-access** ~ (EDP) langsamer Speicher; **temporary** ~ (EDP) Zwischenspeicher *m*; **thin-film** ~ (EDP) Dünnfilmspeicher *m*; **working** ~ (EDP) Arbeitsspeicher *m*, Hauptspeicher *m*, Primärspeicher *m*; **zero-access** ~ (EDP) Speicher mit schnellem Zugriff

stores* *n pl* Lager* *n*

stores manager Lagerverwalter *m*

story *n* (journ.) Beitrag *m*, Bericht *m*, Reportage *f*, Story *f*; ~ *n* (F) Inhaltsangabe *f*, Stoff *m*; ~ **-board** *n* Ablaufplan *m*, Storyboard *n*; ~ **line** Handlungsablauf *m*; **to be on a** ~ am Ball sein; **to drop a** ~ Nachricht kippen (fam.), Nachricht sterben lassen (fam.); **to kill a** ~ Nachricht kippen (fam.), Nachricht sterben lassen (fam.)

straight amplifier Geradeausverstärker *m*; ~ **-circuit receiver** Geradeausempfänger *m*; ~ **-forward projection** Geradeausprojektion *f*; ~ **piece** (journ.) Statement *n*; ~ **read** Wortmeldung *f*; ~ **receiver** Geradeausempfänger *m*

straightener *n* Gleichrichter *m*

strain *n* (mech.) Beanspruchung *f*, Belastung *f*

strand *n* (prog.) Leiste *f*

strap *n* Gurt *m*

stratum *n* Schicht *f*

stray light Nebenlicht *n*, Streulicht *n*; ~ **radiation** Störstrahlung *f*

streak *n* (F, TV) Fahne *f*, Schliere *f*, Streifen *m*

streaking *n* Fahnenziehen *n*, Nachzieheffekt *m*, Nachziehen *n*, Nachziehfahne *f*; ~ **test pattern** Nachziehtestbild *n*

stress *n* (mech.) Beanspruchung *f*, Belastung *f*

stretch *v* (black) dehnen *v*

striation *n* (video) Streifen *m*

strike *n* (set) Abbau *m*; ~ ! (set) gestorben!; ~ **out** *v* (script) herausstreichen *v*; **to ~ a set** abbauen *v*

stringer *n* fester freier Mitarbeiter, Korrespondent *m*

strip board Latte *f*; ~ **of foil** (VTR) Klebeband *n*

stripe *v* randbespuren *v*

striping *n* (F) Bespurungsverfahren *n*; ~ **process** Bespurung *f*; ~ **sound track** Filmbespurung *f*

striplight *n* Soffittenleuchte *f*

striplights *n pl* Fußrampe *f*

stripping pliers *n pl* Abisolierzange *f*

strobe line Horizontalbalken *m*

strobing *n* stroboskopischer Effekt

stroboscope *n* Stroboskop *n*

stroboscopic interference stroboskopischer Effekt

structural engineer Bauingenieur *m*; ~ **return loss** Rückflußdämpfung *f*

structure of signal Signalstruktur *f*

structure-borne vibration Körperschall *m*

stub *n* Stichleitung *f*; ~ **cable** Stichleitung *f*; ~ **line** Stichleitung *f*

stud driver Bolzensetzwerkzeug *n*

studio *n* Studio *n*, Atelier *n*; ~ *n* (bcast.) Senderaum *m*, Sendestudio *n*; ~ **allocation** Atelierdisposition *f*, Studiodisposition *f*, Disposition *f*; ~ **allocations schedule** Studiobelegungsplan *m*; ~ **annex** Nebenstudio *n*; ~ **area** Ateliergelände *n*, Gelände *n*; ~ **attendant** Studiowart *m*; ~ **bookings** *n pl* Studiobelegungsplan *m*, Studiodisposition *f*, Disposition *f*; ~ **bookings*** Dispositionsbüro *n*; ~ **broadcast** Studiosendung *f*; ~ **building day** Bautag *m*; ~ **buildings** Ateliergebäude *n*; ~ **camera** Atelierkamera *f*; ~ **console** Bedienungswanne *f*; ~ **director** Studioregisseur *m*; ~ **electrician** *n* Beleuchter *m*; ~ **engineering** Studiotechnik *f*; ~ **equipment** Studioausrüstung *f*; ~ **fitter** Bühnenschlosser *m*; ~ **flat** Studioebene *f*; ~ **gallery** Rundgang *m*; ~ **hand** Studiohilfe *f* ~ **layout** Studioanlage *f*; ~ **lighting** Studiobeleuchtung *f*; ~ **lining** Studioauskleidung *f*; ~ **management** Atelierleitung *f*, Aufnahmeleitung *f*; ~ **manager (SM)** Aufnahmeleiter *m*, Inspizient *m*; ~ **metalworker** Bühnenschlosser *m*; ~ **monitor** Studioempfänger *m*; ~ **photographer** Standfotograf *m*; ~ **plan** Studiogrundriß *m*, Szenenbauplan *m*; ~ **planning*** Studioplanung* *f*; ~ **production** Studioproduktion *f*; ~ **ready?** Studio klar?; ~ **rent** Ateliermiete *f* ~ **scenery** Dekor *n*; ~ **shot** Atelieraufnahme *f*, Innenaufnahme *f*; ~ **staff** Studiobelegschaft *f*; ~ **treatment** Studioauskleidung *f*; ~ **usage** Studiobelegung *f*; ~ **with reverberation** Studio mit Nachhall; **current affairs ~** aktuelles Studio; **dead ~** nachhallfreies Studio, schalltotes Studio; **large ~** (R) Sendesaal *m*; **mobile ~** fahrbares Studio

studios *n pl* Ateliergebäude *n*; ~ *n pl* Gelände *n*

stunt effect Trickeffekt *m*

stuntman *n* Sensationsdarsteller *m*,

Stuntman *m*, Kaskadeur *m*
stylus *n* Abspielnadel *f*; ~ **force** Auflagekraft *f*; ~ **printer** (EDP) Matrixdrucker *m*; ~ **tip** Abtastnadel *f*
sub CR (coll.) Nebenregie *f*
subcarrier *n* Hilfsträger *m*, Zwischenträger *m*
sub-channel *n* Hilfskanal *m*
sub-control room Nebenregie *f*
subdivision *n* Unterteilung *f*
sub-edit *v* (news) redigieren *v*
sub-editing *n* Redaktion *f*
sub-editor *n* Nachrichtenredakteur *m*, Redakteur *m*, Texter *m*
sub-editor/script-writer *n* (TV) Nachrichtenredakteur *m*
sub-harmonic generator Frequenzteiler *m*; ~ **oscillation** Unterschwingung *f*
subject *n* Thema *n*, Stoff *m*; ~ *n* (speciality) Sachgebiet *n*; ~ *n* (F) Aufnahmegegenstand *m*; ~ **matter** Stoff *m*
subliminal modulation unterschwellige Modulation
submarine cable Unterseekabel *n*
subroutine *n* (EDP) Unterprogramm *n*
subscriber *n* (tel.) Teilnehmer *m*; ~ **trunk dialling installation (STD)** Telefonselbstwählanlage *f*
subsistence allowance Tagegeld *n*
substandard film Schmalfilm *m*; ~ **film spool** Schmalfilmspule *f*; ~ **size** Schmalfilmformat *n*
substitute item Reservebeitrag *m*; ~ **programme** Ersatzsendung *f*
substrate *n* (F, tape) Träger *m*
subterranean *adj* unterirdisch *adj*
subtitle *v* untertiteln *v*; ~ *n* Fußtitel *m*, Untertitel *m*
subtitler *n* Fußtitelmaschine *f*
subtitling *n* Untertiteln *n*; ~ **machine** Fußtitelmaschine *f*
succeed *v* (prog.) einschlagen *v*
suitable for filming drehbar *adj*; ~ **for printing** (FP) kopierfähig *adj*
summary *n* Übersicht *f*, Überblick *m*, Zusammenfassung *f*
sunshade *n* Gegenlichtblende *f*, Sonnenblende *f*, Sonnenschutz *m*, Sonnentubus *m*
sunshield *n* Sonnenschutz *m*, Sonnenblende *f*
sun visor Sonnenblende *f*
super *n* (coll.) Durchblendung *f*, Einblendung *f*; ~ *n* (extra) Komparse *m*, Statist *m*
supercoat *n* Gelatineschutzschicht *f*
superhet *n* (fam.) Überlagerungsempfänger *m*
superheterodyne receiver Überlagerungsempfänger *m*
super-high frequency (SHF) superhohe Frequenz
supericonoscope *n* Super-Ikonoskop *n*
superimpose *v* durchblenden *v*, einblenden *v*; ~ *v* (FP) einkopieren *v*; ~ *v* (pict.) überblenden *v*
superimposed interference Störüberlagerung *f*
superimposing *n* Einkopierung *f*; ~ **head** Mischkopf *m*
superimposition *n* Überblendung *f*, Überblenden *n*, Durchblendung *f*, Trickeinblendung *f*; ~ *n* (exposure) Doppelbelichtung *f*; ~ *n* (freq.) Überlagerung *f*
supernumerary *n* Aushilfskraft *f*; ~ *n* Komparse *m*, Statist *m*
superorthicon *n* Super-Orthikon *n*
superposition *n* Einblendung *f*, Überblendung *f*, Überblenden *n*
supers *n pl* Komparserie *f*, Statisterie *f*
supervise *v* überwachen *v*
supervision *n* Überwachung *f*
supervisor's office Betriebsbüro *n*
supervisory body Aufsichtsgremium *n*
supplement *n* Zugabe *f*, Zusatz *m*
supply *v* (elec.) speisen *v*; ~ *n* (elec.) Speisung *f*, Zuführung *f*,

Versorgung *f*; ~ **cable** Anschlußkabel *n*; ~ **line** Zuführung *f*, Zuführungsleitung *f*; ~ **programme** Zulieferprogramm *n*; ~ **reel** Abwickelspule *f*, Abwickeltrommel *f*, Vorwickelrolle *f*; ~ **spool** Abwickelspule *f*, Abwickeltrommel *f*; ~ **unit** Speisegerät *n*

support *n* Gestell *n*, Ständer *m*, Stativ *n*; ~ *n* (HF) Träger *m*; ~ *n* (F) Schichtträger *m*, Träger *m*; ~ **mast** (carrier) Antennenmast *m*; **ceramic** ~ keramischer Stützpunkt

supporting film Beifilm *m*; ~ **flange** Auflageflansch *m*; ~ **programme** Beiprogramm *n*; ~ **role** Nebenrolle *f*; ~ **strap** Haltebügel *m*

suppress *v* (news) totschweigen *v*, unterdrücken *v*; ~ *v* (blanking) zutasten *v*; **to** ~ **noise** entstören *v*

suppressed-carrier modulation Amplitudenmodulation mit unterdrücktem Träger, Modulation mit unterdrücktem Träger

suppression *n* (blanking) Austastung *f*, Zutastung

suppressor grid Bremsgitter *n*

surface induction Oberflächeninduktion *f*; ~ **noise** (disc) Eigengeräusch *n*, Grundgeräusch *n*, Nadelgeräusch *n*, Schramme *f*; ~ **socket** Aufputzdose *f*; ~ **wave** Bodenwelle *f*

surge arrester Überspannungsschutz *m*; ~ **impedance** Wellenwiderstand *m*

surgery *n* betriebsärztliche Dienststelle

survey *n* Überblick *m*, Übersicht *f*

susceptance *n* Blindleitwert *m*, Leitwert *m*

susceptibility to interference Störanfälligkeit *f*; ~ **to trouble** Störanfälligkeit *f*

suspension *n* Aufhängung *f*; ~ **chain** Befestigungskette *f*; ~ **cord** Befestigungsleine *f*; ~ **unit** Hängestück *n*

sustained *adj* ungedämpft *adj*

swallow *v* verschlucken *v*

swan neck Schwanenhals *m*, Gänsegurgel *f*

swan-neck microphone Schwanenhalsmikrofon *n*

sweep *v* ablenken *v*, durchlaufen *v*, wobbeln *v*; ~ *n* Ablenkung *f*, Abtastung *f*, Durchlauf *m*, Durchlaufgeschwindigkeit *f*, Zeitablenkung *f*; ~ **circuit** Ablenkschaltung *f*; ~ **frequency** Wobbelfrequenz *f*; ~ **-frequency signal generator** Wobbler *m*, Wobbelgenerator *m*, Wobbelmeßsender *m*; ~ **generator** Ablenkgenerator *m*, Kippgerät *n*, Zeitablenkgenerator *m*; ~ **linearity** Linearität der Ablenkung; ~ **magnification** (CRO) Zeitdehnung *f*; ~ **time** Ablenkzeit *f*; ~ **transformer** Kipptransformator *m*; ~ **unit** (TV rec.) Ablenkeinheit *f*; ~ **voltage** Kippspannung *f*; ~ **width** Frequenzhub eines Wobblers

sweeping *n* Wobbeln *n*, Wobbelung *f*; ~ **coil** Ablenkspule *f*

swish pan Reißschwenk *m*

switch *v* (to) schalten *v* (auf); ~ *v* (video) schneiden *v*, umschneiden *v*; ~ *n* Schalter *m*; ~ **box** Schaltkasten *m*; ~ **desk** Schaltpult *n*; ~ **enclosure** Schaltkasten *m*; ~ **in** *v* (voltage) einschalten *v*; ~ **jack** Schaltbuchse *f*; ~ **off** *v* abschalten *v*, ausschalten *v*; ~ **on** *v* einschalten *v*, zuschalten *v*; ~ **over** *v* umschalten *v*; ~ **-over** *n* Umschaltung *f*; ~ **panel** Schaltfeld *n*, Schalttafel *f*, Schaltbrett *n*; **centrifugal** ~ Fliehkraftschalter *m* **main** ~ Hauptschalter *m*; **to** ~ **into**

circuit schalten *v*
switchable *adj* umschaltbar *adj*
switchboard *n* Schalttafel *f*, Schaltbrett *n*, Schaltpult *n*; **~ attendant** Schaltwart *m*; **~ operator** Telefonist *m*
switchgear *n* Schaltgerät *n*
switching *n* Umschaltung *f*; **~** *n* Schaltungstechnik *f*; **~ algebra** (EDP) Schaltalgebra *f*; **~ area** Schaltraum *m*; **~ break** Schaltstörung *f*; **~ centre** Schaltzentrale *f*; **~ diode** Schaltdiode *f*; **~ error** Schaltfehler *m*, Fehlschaltung *f*; **~ flash** Blitzschaltung *f*, Blitzumschaltung *f*; **~ frequency** Schaltfrequenz *f*, Umschaltfrequenz *f*; **~ level** Schaltebene *f*; **~ matrix** Umschaltautomatik *f*; **~ -off** *n* Abschaltung *f*, Ausschaltung *f*, Ausschalten *n*; **~ -off of programme** (transmitter) Programmabschaltung *f*; **~ -on** *n* Einschaltung *f*; **~ panel** Schaltfeld *n*; **~ period** (transmitter) Umschaltpause *f*; **~ position** Schaltstelle *f*; **~ room** Schaltraum *m*; **~ time** Schaltzeit *f*, Umschaltzeit *f*; **~ to common programme** (transmitter) Zusammenschaltung *f*; **number of ~ operations in given period** Schalthäufigkeit *f*
swivel *v* schwenken *v*; **~ arm** Schwenkarm *m*
swivelling *adj* schwenkbar *adj*
swivel-mounted *adj* schwenkbar *adj*
syllabus *n* Lehrplan *m*, Studienplan *m*
symbolic language (EDP) Symbolsprache *f*; **~ programming language** (EDP) Symbolsprache *f*
symmetrical *adj* symmetrisch *adj*
symmetrise *v* symmetrieren *v*
symmetry axis Symmetrieachse *f*
symphony orchestra Sinfonieorchester *n*
sync *adj* (coll.) synchron *adj*; **~ advance** Bild-Ton-Versatz *m*; **~ amplitude** Synchronimpulsamplitude *f*, Synchronsignalwert *m*; **~ cross** Startkreuz *n*, Bildstartmarke *f*; **~ level** Synchronwert *m*; **~ mark** Startimpuls *m*, Synchronmarke *f*, Synchronzeichen *n*; **~ pip** Kennimpuls *m*; **~ plop** Kennimpuls *m*, Startimpuls *m*; **~ pulse** Synchronimpuls *m*; **~ -pulse generator** synchronisierter Taktgeber; **~ -pulse regenerator** Regenerator *m*; **~ pulse system** Takthaushalt *m*; **~ regenerator** Impulsregeneriergerät *n*; **~ separator** Separator *m*; **~ signal** Synchronisationssignal *n*; **~ start** Synchronstart *m*; **~ up** *v* anlegen *v*, Bildband und Tonband auf gleiche Länge ziehen, hinziehen *v* **in ~** (coll.) synchron *adj*; **to ~ up with music** Musik unterlegen
synchro-link *n* elektrische Welle
synchronisation *n* Synchronisation *f*, Synchronisierung *f*; **~ pulse** Synchronimpuls *m*; **~ signal** Synchronsignal (S-Signal) *n*
synchronise *v* synchronisieren *v*
synchronised *adj* synchronisiert *adj* **~ generator** synchronisierter Taktgeber; **~ network** Synchronnetz *n*; **~ pulse generator (SPG)** synchronisierter Taktgeber; **~ transmitter** Gleichwellensender *m*
synchroniser *n* Synchronabziehtisch *m*, Synchronisator *m*, Synchronumroller *m*, Hesselbach *m* (fam.)
synchronising *n* Synchronisieren *n*; **~ cue** Synchronzeichen *n*; **~ level** Synchronwert *m*; **~ mark** Synchronmarke *f*, Synchronzeichen *n*; **~ -pulse**

generator Impulsgeber *m*, Impulsgenerator *m*; ~ **-pulse separation** Impulstrennung *f*; ~ **signal** Gleichlaufsignal *n*; ~ **-signal generator** Impulsgeber *m*, Impulsgenerator *m*; ~ **unit** Synchronisator *m*, Hesselbach *m* (fam.); **field ~ pulse** Vertikalsynchronimpuls *m*; **vertical ~ pulse** (US) Vertikalsynchronimpuls *m*

synchronism *n* Synchronität *f*, Gleichlauf *m*, Übereinstimmung *f*; **in ~** synchron *adj*

synchronous *adj* synchron *adj*; ~ **converter** Synchronumrichter *m* ~ **demodulator** Synchrondemodulator *m*; ~ **detector** Produktdetektor *m*; ~ **motor** Synchronmotor *m*; ~ **orbit** (sat.) Synchronbahn *f*; ~ **picture** Synchronbild *n*; ~ **recording** Mehrsignalaufzeichnung *f*; ~ **running** Synchronlauf *m*; ~ **satellite** Synchronsatellit *m*; ~ **sound** Synchronton *m*

synopsis *n* Exposé *n*, Inhaltsangabe *f*, Synopsis *f*, Zusammenfassung *f*

synthetic *adj* künstlich *adj*; ~ **resin varnish** Kunstharzlack *m*

system *n* System *n*, Verfahren *n*; ~ **analysis** (EDP) Systemanalyse *f*; ~ **configuration** (EDP) Anlagenausstattung *f*; **carrier-frequency ~** trägerfrequentes System (TF-System); **field-sequential ~** rasterfrequentes System; **line-sequential ~** zeilenfrequentes System; **point-sequential ~** punktfrequentes System

T

table microphone Tischmikrofon *n*; ~ **model** Tischgerät *n*; ~ **of subjective grades** (EBU) Bewertungstabelle *f*; ~ **set** Tischgerät *n*

tachometer *n* (F) Tachometer *m*; ~ **disc** (VTR) Tachoimpulsrad *n*

tackle-line *n* Seilzug *m*

tact *n* Takt *m*

tag block Igel *m*

tail leader (F) Nachlauf *m*

tailoress *n* Damenschneiderin *f*

tailoring *n* Schneiderei *f*

take *v* (F, tape) aufnehmen *v*, taken *v*; ~ *n* (F, tape) Aufnahme *f*, Take *m*; ~ *n* (pict.) Bildaufnahme *f*; ~ **down** *v* (telephoned news item) aufnehmen *v*; ~ **down** *v* (light) herunterregeln *v*, zurücknehmen *v*; ~ **in** *v* (FP) ansaugen *v*; ~ **number** Takenummer *f*; ~ **on** *v* (staff) einstellen *v*; ~ **up** *v* (reel) aufspulen *v*, aufwickeln *v*; **dud ~** schlechte Aufnahme; **mute ~** stumme Aufnahme; **to ~ a film** Film drehen; **to ~ apart** auseinandernehmen *v*; **to ~ bearings** peilen *v*; **to ~ on lease** mieten *v*

take-up magazine Aufwickelkassette *f*; ~ **plate** Aufwickelteller *m*; ~ **reel** Aufwickelspule *f*, Nachwickelrolle *f*; ~ **speed** Aufwickelgeschwindigkeit *f*; ~ **spool** Aufwickelspule *f*, Nachwickelrolle *f*; ~ **system** Aufwickelsystem *n*

taking angle Aufnahmewinkel *m*; ~ **lens** Aufnahmeobjektiv *n*; ~ **mask** (cam.) Bildfensterabdeckung *f*, Bildfenstereinsatz *m*; ~ **of bearings** Peilung *f*; ~ **out of service** Außerbetriebnahme *f*

talk *n* (R) Bericht *m*

talkback *n* Gegensprechanlage *f*; ~ **arrangement** Kommandoanlage *f*; ~ **circuit** Gegensprechanlage *f*,

Rücksprechleitung *f*, Regieleitung *f*; ~ **microphone** Gegensprechmikrofon *n*, Kommandomikrofon *n*; ~ **speaker** Kommandolautsprecher *m*; ~ **system** Kommandoanlage *f*
talkie *n* (coll.) Tonfilm *m*
talks-writer *n* (TV, R) Chronist *m*
talk-up *n* (journ.) Absprache *f*
tally light Signallampe *f*
tandem connection Hintereinanderschaltung *f*; ~ **potentiometer** Tandempotentiometer *n*
tank *n* (FP) Gefäß *n*, Tank *m*, Trog *m*, Küvette *f*; ~ *n* (thea.) versenkbare Bühne; ~ **circuit** Schwingkreis *m*; ~ **draining** Tankentleerung *f*
tap *n* Anzapfung *f*
tape *v* Band aufzeichnen, aufzeichnen *v*, aufnehmen *v*; ~ *v* (video) (coll.) MAZ aufzeichnen, mazen *v* (fam.); ~ *n* Band *n*; ~ **base** Magnetschichtträger *m*, Schichtträger *m*, Träger *m*; ~ **break** Bandriß *m*; ~ **card** (EDP) Lochstreifenkarte *f*; ~ **cartridge** Bandkassette *f*; ~ **cassette** Bandkassette *f*; ~ **cassette** (sound) Tonbandkassette *f*; ~ **coating** Bandbeschichtung *f*; ~ **copy** Bandkopie *f*, Tochterband *n*; ~ **curling** Bandverformung *f*, Magnetbandverformung *f*; ~ **curvature** Bandverdehnung *f*; ~ **deck** Abspielerchassis *n*, Platine mit Bandmaschine, Laufwerkplatte *f*; ~ **deformation** Bandverformung *f*, Magnetbandverformung *f*; ~ **drive capstan** Bandtrieb *m*; ~ **edit** Bandschnitt *m*; ~ **edit** (EDP) Bandauszug *m*; ~ **editing** Bandbearbeitung *f*, Bandschnitt *m*; ~ **editor** Cutter *m*, Cutterin *f*, Schnittmeister *m*; ~ **error** Bandfehler *m*; ~ **feed** (EDP) Bandbewegung *f*; ~ **flux** Bandfluß *m*; ~ **for editing** Schnittmaterial *n*; ~ **guidance** Spurhaltung *f*; ~ **guide** Bandführung *f*; ~ **guides** *n pl* Bandführungsvorrichtung *f*; ~ **guiding** Bandführung *f*; ~ **ident** (coll.) Kennungsband *n*; ~ **insert** Bandbeitrag *m*; ~ **join** (F) Bildunterkleber *m*; ~ **leader** Vorlaufband *n*, Startband *n*; ~ **library** Bandarchiv *n*; ~ **lifter** Bandabheber *m*; ~ **loop** endloses Band; ~ **loop cartridge** Endlos-Bandkassette *f*; ~ **loop cassette** Endlos-Bandkassette *f*; ~ **machine** Bandmaschine *f*, Bandgerät *n*; ~ **noise** Bandrauschen *n*, Raumstatik *f*; ~ **-numbering machine** Numeriermaschine für Bänder; ~ **perforator** (EDP) Lochstreifenlocher *m*; ~ **plate** Bandteller *m*; ~ **pressure** Bandandruck *m*; ~ **pressure fault** Bandandruckfehler *m*; ~ **punch** (EDP) Lochstreifenstanzer *m*; ~ **recorder** Bandspieler *m*, Magnettongerät *n*, Magnetofon *n*, Magnetofongerät *n*, Tonbandgerät *n*, Tonbandmaschine *f*; ~ **recording** Bandaufnahme *f*, Bandaufzeichnung *f*; ~ **recording enthusiast** Tonbandamateur *m*, Tonbandfreund *m*; ~ **reel** Bandspule *f*; ~ **run** Bandlauf *m*; ~ **scratch** Schramme *f*; ~ **speed** Bandgeschwindigkeit *f*, Durchlaufgeschwindigkeit *f*; ~ **spool** Bandspule *f*; ~ **store** (VTR) Bildbandarchiv *n*; ~ **tension** Bandzug *m*; ~ **tension cut-out switch** Bandzugschalter *m*; ~ **-tension lever** Fühlhebel *m*; ~ **transport** Bandtransport *m*, Bandbewegung *f*, Tonbandtransport *m*; ~ **travel** Tonbandlauf *m*; ~ **travel direction** Bandlaufrichtung *f*; ~ **width** Bandbreite *f*; **clean** ~ Leerband *n*;

coated ~ beschichtetes Magnetband; **endless** ~ endloses Band; **mechanically coupled ~ recorder** Duplex-Cordanlage *f*, Duplexmaschine *f*; **perforated** ~ perforiertes Band; **recorded** ~ bespieltes Band; **regulation of ~ tension** Bandzugregelung *f*; **to cut a** ~ Band trennen; **to mark a** ~ Band randnumerieren; **to play a** ~ Band abfahren; **unperforated** ~ unperforiertes Band; **unrecorded** ~ unbespieltes Band

tapping *n* Anzapfung *f*

target *n* (light) Blende *f*; ~ *n* (pick-up tube) Bildschirm *m*, Target *n*

taxable *adj* gebührenpflichtig *adj*

teaching aids Lehrmittel *n pl*

team *n* Team *n*, Stab *m*

tear *n* Riß *m*, Filmriß *m*

tearing *n* Zerreißen *n*

technical arrangements *n pl* Disposition *f*; ~ **assistance** technische Hilfe; ~ **coordination circuit** Technikkoordinationsleitung *f*; ~ **director** (US) technischer Direktor; ~ **equipment** Betriebseinrichtung *f*; ~ **facilities** *n pl* technische Hilfe; ~ **log** Sendeprotokoll *n*; ~ **monitoring service** Empfangsdienst *m*; ~ **operations*** Betriebsabwicklung* *f*, Betriebszentrale *f*; ~ **operations manager (TOM)** Produktionsingenieur *m*, Programmingenieur *m*, Sendeingenieur *m*, Ingenieur vom Dienst (IvD); ~ **superintendent** Betriebsleiter *m*; ~ **support** technische Hilfe

technician *n* Techniker *m*

technicolor *n* additives Farbfilmverfahren

technique *n* Verfahren *n*

telecast *v* (US) senden *v*

telecine (TK) *n* Filmabtaster *m*, Filmgeber *m*, Filmübertragungsanlage *f*; ~ **area** Filmabtasterraum *m*, Filmgeberraum *m*, Abtastraum *m* ~ **insert** Filmeinspielung *f*; ~ **machine** Filmabtaster *m*, Filmgeber *m*

telecommunications *n pl* Fernmeldewesen *n*, Fernmeldetechnik *f*; ~ **centre** Fernmeldezentrum *n*; ~ **engineer** Fernmeldetechniker *m*; ~ **engineering** Fernmeldetechnik *f* ~ **office** Fernmeldeamt *n*; ~ **satellite** Fernmeldesatellit *m*

telecontrol *n* Fernsteuerung

telefilm *n* (US) Fernsehfilm *m*

telegenic *adj* telegen *adj*

telemetrical data Fernmeßdaten *n pl*

telephone answering service Auftragsdienst *m*; ~ **channel** Telefoniekanal *m*; ~ **connection** Telefonverbindung *f*, Telefonanschluß *m*; ~ **jack** Telefonbuchse *f*; ~ **maintenance crew** Telefonwartung* *f*; ~ **receiver** Telefonhörer *m*; ~ **switchboard** Telefonzentrale *f*; ~ **traffic** Telefonsprechverkehr *m*; **temporary ~ connection** Fernsprechzeitanschluß *m*

telephony *n* Telefoniebetrieb *m*

telephoto lens Fernbildlinse *f*, Teleobjektiv *n*, Tüte *f* (fam.); ~ **picture** Fernaufnahme *f*

teleplayer *n* Fernsehfilm-kassettenwiedergabegerät *n*

teleprint *v* über den Fernschreiber laufen lassen, über den Ticker laufen lassen; ~ *n* Fernschreiben *n*

teleprinter *n* Fernschreiber *m*; ~ **message** Fernschreiben *n*; ~ **network** Fernschreibnetz *n*; ~ **operator** Fernschreiber *m* (Person); ~ **service** Fernschreibstelle *f*

teleprompter *n* Teleprompter *m*
telerecord *v* fazen *v* (fam.)
telerecorder *n* Bildaufzeichnungsgerät *n*
telerecording (TR) *n* Fernsehaufzeichnung *f*, Fernsehaufnahme *f*; ~ *n* (EFR) Filmaufzeichnung (FAZ) *f*; ~ **equipment** FAZ-Anlage (FAZ) *f*
telescope *n* Teleskop *n*
telescopic *adj* ausziehbar *adj*; ~ **aerial** Teleskopantenne *f*, ausziehbare Antenne; ~ **arm** Teleskoparm *m*; ~ **column** Teleskopsäule *f*; ~ **mast** Teleskopmast *m*
teletype *n* Fernschreiber *m*
teletyper *n* Fernschreiber *m*
teletypewriter *n* Fernschreiber *m*
televise *v* über Fernsehen ausstrahlen, senden *v*
televised lesson Fernsehlektion *f*
television (TV) *n* Fernsehen (FS) *n*, Sehfunk *m*; ~ *n* (coll.) Fernsehapparat *m*, Fernsehempfänger *m*, Fernsehempfangsgerät *n*, Fernsehgerät *n*, Fernseher *m* (fam.), Guckkasten *m* (fam.), Mattscheibe *f* (fam.); ~ (compp.) (TV) Fernseh- (in Zus.); ~ **adaptation** Fernsehbearbeitung *f*; ~ **address** Fernsehansprache *f*; ~ **advertisement** Fernsehreklame *f*; ~ **advertising** Fernsehreklame *f*, Fernsehwerbung *f*; ~ **advisory council** Fernsehbeirat *m* (ARD); ~ **aerial** Fernsehantenne *f*; ~ **and radio station** Rundfunk- und Fernsehstation; ~ **announcer** Fernsehansager *m*; ~ **apparatus for the rectification of indifferent film (TARIF)** Farbkorrektureinrichtung für stichige Filme; ~ **archives** *n pl* Fernseharchiv *n*; ~ **audience** Fernsehpublikum *n*; ~ **audience survey** Zuschauerbefragung *f*; ~ **broadcast** Fernsehsendung *f*; ~ **broadcasting** Fernsehrundfunk *m*; ~ **budget** Fernsehhaushalt *m*; ~ **camera** Fernsehkamera *f*, Fernsehaufnahmekamera *f*; ~ **camera truck** (US) Fernsehaufnahmewagen *m*; ~ **cameraman** E-Kameramann *m*; ~ **car** Aufnahmewagen *m*, Bildaufnahmewagen *m*, Fernsehaufnahmewagen *m*; ~ **cartridge** Fernsehkassette *f*; ~ **cassette** Fernsehkassette *f*; ~ **cassette player** Fernsehfilmkassettenwiedergabegerät *n*; ~ **centre** Fernsehkomplex *m*, Fernsehzentrum *n*; ~ **chain** Übertragungskette *f*; ~ **channel** Fernsehkanal *m*; ~ **channel using lower sideband** Fernsehkanal mit spiegelbildlicher Lage der Träger; ~ **channel using upper sideband** Fernsehkanal mit normaler Lage der Träger; ~ **circuit** Fernsehleitung *f*; ~ **column** (press) Fernsehkritik *f*; ~ **contest** Fernsehwettbewerb *m*; ~ **corporation** Fernsehanstalt *f*, Fernsehgesellschaft *f*; ~ **council** Fernsehrat *m* (ZDF); ~ **course** Fernsehkursus *m*; ~ **coverage** Fernsehberichterstattung *f*; ~ **coverage** (tech.) Fernsehversorgung *f*; ~ **current affairs programmes** *n pl* Zeitgeschehen *n*; ~ **debate** Fernsehdiskussion *f*; ~ **director** Fernsehregisseur *m*; ~ **directorate** Fernsehdirektion *f*, Programmdirektion Fernsehen; ~ **distribution circuit** Fernsehmodulationsleitung *f*, Fernsehverteilleitung *f*; ~ **distribution satellite** Fernsehverteilersatellit *m*; ~ **drama** Fernsehspiel *n*; ~ **drama library** Fernsehspielarchiv *n*; ~ **engineering** Fernsehtechnik *f*;

~ engineering operations Betriebstechnik Fernsehen; **~ event** Fernsehveranstaltung *f*; **~ film** Fernsehfilm *m*; **~ film cartridge** Fernsehfilmkassette *f*; **~ film cassette** Fernsehfilmkassette *f*; **~ film studios*** *n pl* Filmproduktionsbetrieb* *m*; **~ financed from licence fees** Gebührenfernsehen *n*; **~ franchise** Fernsehlizenz *f*; **~ graticule** Fernsehkasch *m*; **~ home** (audience research) Fernsehhaushalt *m*; **~ image** Fernsehbild *n*; **~ installation** Fernsehanlage *f*, Fernsehübertragungsanlage *f*; **~ journalist** Fernsehjournalist *m*; **~ licence** Fernsehgenehmigung *f*; **~ licence fee** Fernsehgebühr *f*; **~ licence-holder** Fernsehteilnehmer *m*; **~ light entertainment** Fernsehunterhaltung *f*; **~ link** Fernsehstrecke *f*, Fernsehübertragungsstrecke *f*; **~ magazine** Fernsehzeitschrift *f*; **~ monitor** Bildkontrollempfänger *m*, Bildmonitor *m*, Monitor *m*; **~ musical** Fernsehmusical *n*; **~ network** Fernsehnetz *n*; **~ news** Fernsehnachrichten *f pl*, Nachrichten *f pl*; **~ news commentator** Fernsehpublizist *m*; **~ OB link** Fernsehzubringerleitung *f*; **~ OB operations** *n pl* Übertragungsdienst Bild; **~ OB van** Fernsehaufnahmewagen *m*; **~ opera** Fernsehoper *f*; **~ operations and maintenance*** Fernsehbetriebstechnik* *f*; **~ output** Fernsehproduktion *f*; **~ panel discussion** Fernsehdiskussion *f*; **~ picture** Fernsehbild *n*; **~ picture projector** Fernsehbildprojektor *m*; **~ play** Fernsehspiel *n*; **~ prize** Fernsehpreis *m*; **~ producer** Fernsehproduzent *m*; **~ production** Fernsehinszenierung *f*, Fernsehproduktion *f*; **~ programme** Fernsehprogramm *n*, Fernsehsendung *f*; **~ programme committee** Fernsehrat *m* (ARD); **~ programme company** Werbefernsehgesellschaft *f*; **~ programme correspondence*** Zuschauerpost* *f*; **~ programme directors' committee** Fernsehprogrammkommission *f* (ARD); **~ programme exchange circuit** Fernsehaustauschleitung *f* **~ programmes preview** Schrifttafel *f*; **~ pundit** (coll.) Fernsehpublizist *m*; **~ receiver** Fernsehapparat *m*, Fernsehempfänger *m*, Fernsehempfangsgerät *n*, Fernsehgerät *n*, Fernseher *m* (fam.), Guckkasten *m* (fam.), Mattscheibe *f* (fam.); **~ reception** Fernsehempfang *m*; **~ recording** Fernsehaufnahme *f*; **~ recording equipment** Bildaufzeichnungsgerät *n*; **~ relay link** Fernsehstrecke *f*, Fernsehübertragungsstrecke *f*; **~ report** Fernsehbericht *m*; **~ reporter** Fernsehreporter *m*; **~ rights** Fernsehrechte *n pl*; **~ satellite** Fernsehsatellit *m*; **~ scanning device** Bildabtaster *m*; **~ screen** Fernsehschirm *m*, Bildschirm *m*; **~ scripts unit** Fernsehdramaturgie* *f*; **~ service** Fernsehdienst *m*; **~ set** Fernsehapparat *m*, Fernsehempfänger *m*, Fernsehempfangsgerät *n*, Fernsehgerät *n*, Fernseher *m* (fam.), Guckkasten *m* (fam.), Mattscheibe *f* (fam.); **~ show**

Fernsehveranstaltung *f*, Unterhaltungsprogramm *n*, Unterhaltungssendung *f*; **~ signal** Fernsehsignal *n*; **~ sound operations*** *n pl* Fernsehbetrieb Ton*; **~ sound transmitter** Fernsehtonsender *m*; **~ sports news** *n pl* Sportschau *f*; **~ standard** Fernsehnorm *f*; **~ station** Fernsehsender *m*, Fernsehstation *f*, Fernsehanstalt *f*, Fernsehgesellschaft *f*; **~ studio** Fernsehstudio *n*; **~ switching area** Fernsehschaltraum *m*; **~ switching network centre** Sternpunkt *m*; **~ synchronising signals** Fernsehtaktgeberimpulse *m pl*; **~ tape recorder** Magnetbildaufzeichnungsanlage *f* **~ teacher** Fernsehlehrer *m*; **~ technology** Fernsehtechnik *f*; **~ telephone** Fernsehtelefon *n*; **~ tower** Fernsehturm *m*; **~ translator** Fernsehumsetzer *m*, Fernsehkanalumsetzer *m*; **~ transmission** Fernsehübertragung *f*, Fernsehsendung *f*, Bildschirmübertragung *f*, Fernsehausstrahlung *f*; **~ transmission circuit** Fernsehübertragungsstrecke *f*; **~ transmitter** Fernsehsender *m*, Fernsehstation *f*; **~ transposer** Fernsehkanalumsetzer *m*; **~ tube** Fernsehröhre *f*, Bildwiedergaberöhre *f*; **~ version** Fernsehfassung *f*; **independent ~** (GB) kommerzielles Fernsehen; **large-screen ~ projector** Fernsehgroßbildprojektor *m*; **live ~ broadcast** Fernsehdirektübertragung *f*; **100-perforation ~ film** FS-Film /100 Perforationslöcher; **portable ~ transmitter** tragbarer Fernsehsender; **sponsored ~** (US) Werbefernsehen *n*; **to watch ~** fernsehen *v*; **wired ~** Drahtfernsehen *n*

telex *n* Fernschreiben *n*; **~** *n* (appar.) Fernschreiber *m*; **~ message** Fernschreiben *n*; **~ operator** Fernschreiber *m*; **to put on ~** über den Fernschreiber laufen lassen, über den Ticker laufen lassen

temperature change Temperaturänderung *f*; **~ constant** Temperaturkonstante *f* **~ dependence** Temperaturabhängigkeit *f*; **~ drift** Temperaturdrift *f*; **~ range** Temperaturbereich *m*; **~ response** Temperaturgang *m*; **~ stability** Temperaturfestigkeit *f*; **~ variation** Temperaturschwankung *f*

temporary *n* Hilfskraft *f*; **~ help** Hilfskraft *f*; **~ stop** (sound tape) Kurzstopp *m*; **~ telephone connection** Fernsprechzeitanschluß *m*

tendency to oscillate Schwingneigung *f*; **~ to regenerate** Rückkopplungsneigung *f*

ten-light *n* Ten-light *n*

tension *n* Spannung *f*; **~ measuring device** Bandzugwaage *f*; **~ roller** Spannrolle *f*

term of office Amtsdauer *f*

terminal *n* (line) Leitungsendpunkt *m*, Endpunkt *m*, Endstelle *f*; **~** *n* (elec.) Klemme *f*, Anschlußklemme *f*; **~** *n* (EDP) Datenstation *f*; **~ block** Klemmleiste *f*; **~ board** Anschlußplatte *f*, Klemmleiste *f*; **~ box** Anschlußkasten *m*, Klemmkasten *m*, Verteilerkasten *m*; **~ point** Leitungsendpunkt *m*, Endpunkt *m*, Endstelle *f*; **~ procedure** Schlußablauf *m*;

~ **strip** Anschlußleiste *f*, Klemmleiste *f*; **international ~** internationaler Endpunkt
terminate *v* (tech.) abschließen *v*
terminating point (line) Endpunkt *m*, Endstelle *f*; **~ resistance** Abschlußwiderstand *m*
termination *n* (tech.) Abschluß *m*; **~ box** Enddose *f*
terms of employment Arbeitsverhältnis *n*
terrestrial *adj* terrestrisch *adj*; **~ magnetic field** Erdmagnetfeld *n*; **~ radio communication** terrestrischer Funkverkehr; **~ radio station** Bodenfunkstelle *f*
test *n* Test *m*, Prüfung *f*, Probe *f*; **~** *n* (meas.) Messung *f*; **~ adapter** Prüfadapter *m*; **~ and measurements** *n pl* Prüffrequenz- und Meßverfahren; **~ assembly** Meßplatz *m*; **~ bay** Meßgestell *n*; **~ card** Testbild *n*, Prüfbild *n*; **~ card** (TV cam.) Einstelltestbild *n* **to put out ~card** Testbild aufschalten **~ certificate** Abnahmebericht *m*, Abnahmeprotokoll *n*; **~ certificate** (meas.) Meßprotokoll *n*; **~ chart** Auflösungstestbild *n*, Testbild *n*, Prüfbild *n*; **~ circuit** Meßschaltung *f*; **~ colour** Testfarbe *f*; **~ contact strip** Messerleiste *f*; **~ demodulator** Meßdemodulator *m*; **~ department** Prüffeld *n*; **~ engineer** Meßingenieur *m*, Prüffeldingenieur *m*; **~ equipment bay** Meßgestell *n*; **~ film** Testfilm *m*, Prüffilm *m*, Probefilm *m*, Meßfilm *m*; **~ frequency** Prüffrequenz *f*; **~ jack** Meßbuchse *f*; **~ key** Prüftaste *f*; **~ level** Meßpegel *m*; **~ line** (coll.) Prüfzeile *f*; **~ line inserter** Prüfzeileneinmischer *m*; **~ methods** *n pl* Meßtechnik *f*; **~ mode** (EDP) Testbetrieb *m*; **~ object** Meßobjekt *n*; **~ oscillator** Meßsender *m*; **~ output** Meßausgang *m*; **~ pattern** Testbild *n*, Prüfbild *n*; **~ pattern** (TV set) Einstelltestbild *n*; **~ pattern generator** Testbildgeber *m*; **~ period** (line) Vorschaltzeit *f*, Vorlaufzeit *f*; **~ point** Meßpunkt *m*, Meßsendereinkopplungspunkt *m*; **~ print** Positivmuster *n*; **~ report** Prüfbericht *m*; **~ result** Meßergebnis *n*; **~ rig** Meßplatz *m*; **~ set-up** Meßplatz *m*; **~ shot** Probeaufnahme *f*; **~ shot** (TV) kalte Probe; **~ signal** Meßsignal *n*, Prüfsignal *n*, Testsignal *n*; **~ signal generator** Prüfsignalgeber *m*; **~ signal key** Prüftaste *f*; **~ socket** Meßbuchse *f*, Prüfbuchse *f*; **~ strip** Probestreifen *m*, Testfilm *m*, Versuchsstreifen *m*; **~ switch** Meßschalter *m*; **~ take** Probeaufnahme *f*; **~ tape** Bezugsband *n*, Magnetbezugsband *n*, Testband *n* **~ tone** Prüfton *m*; **~ transmission** Probesendung *f*; **~ transmission** (tech.) Testsendung *f*; **~ voltage** Meßspannung *f*; **~ wedge** Besenkeil *m*
testing *n* Messung *f*, Prüfung *f*
tête-bêche, channels in spiegelbildliche Fernsehkanäle
tetrode *n* Tetrode *f*
text *n* Text *m*
that's all! (filming, recording) gestorben! (fam.)
theatre *n* Theater *n*, Schauplatz *m*; **~ live transmission** Theaterübertragung *f*; **~ recording** Theateraufzeichnung *f*; **~ screen** (F) Bildwand *f*; **direct broadcast from ~** Theaterübertragung *f*; **to record a ~ production** abfotografieren *v*
theatre-goer *n* Besucher *m*
theme music Themamusik *f*
thermal circuit-breaker Thermoschutzschalter *m*;

~ **conductivity** Wärmeleitwert *m*; ~ **rays** Wärmestrahlen *m pl*
thermistor *n* Thermistor *m*, Thernewid *m*
thermocouple *n* Thermokreuz *n*
thermomagnetic *adj* thermomagnetisch *adj*
thermoplastic machine Tiefziehpresse *f*
thermostat *n* Thermostat *m*
thin-emulsion film Dünnschichtfilm *m*
thin-film component Dünnfilmbaustein *m*; ~ **technique** Dünnfilmtechnik *f*
third-order harmonic distortion kubischer Klirrfaktor
Thomson filter Thomsonfilter *m*
thread *n* Gewinde *n*; ~ **of screw** Windung *f*; ~ **up** *v* (cam.) einlegen *v*; **to ~ a film** Film einlegen
threaded stud Gewindestift *m*
threading *n* (cam.) Filmeinlegen *n*
three-colour method Dreifarbenverfahren *n*; ~ **process** Dreifarbensystem *n*, Dreifarbenverfahren *n*
three-gun colour tube Dreistrahlröhre *f*
three-phase circuit Drehstromnetz *n*; ~ **current** Drehstrom *m*; ~ **distribution system** Sternverteilungssystem *n*; ~ **four-wire network** Dreiphasennetz *n*; ~ **mains supply** Kraftnetz *n*; ~ **synchronous motor** Drehstromsynchronmotor *m*; ~ **three-wire network** Dreiphasennetz *n*
three-pole *adj* dreipolig *adj*
threshold *n* Schwelle *f*; ~ **level** Schwellwert *m*; ~ **of discrimination** Unterscheidungsschwelle *f*; ~ **of pain** Schmerzschwelle *f*; ~ **of sensation** Reizschwelle *f*; ~ **of stimulation** Reizschwelle *f*; ~ **value** Schwellwert *m*
thriller *n* (coll.) Kriminalfilm *m*, Krimi *m* (fam.)
throat microphone Kehlkopfmikrofon *n*
through-connection junction box (aerial) Durchgangsdose *f*
through-dialling *n* (tel.) Durchwahl *f*
throw *n* Projektionsentfernung *f*
ticker *n* (coll.) Fernschreiber *m*, Ticker *m* (fam.)
ticket office Veranstaltungsbüro *n*
tidy up *v* (coll.) (tape) nachschneiden *v*
tie line Rangierleitung *f*
tight, too (pict.) zuwenig Luft
tighten up *v* (script) einstreichen *v*, zusammenstreichen *v*, raffen *v*; ~ **up** *v* (zoom) nachziehen *v*
tilt *v* kippen *v*, neigen *v*, senkrecht schwenken; ~ *n* senkrechter Schwenk, Senkrechtschwenk *m*; ~ **angle** Neigungswinkel *m*; ~ **head** Neigekopf *m*; ~ **shot** (cam.) Draufsicht *f*; **to ~ the camera** Kamera kippen
tilting *n* senkrechter Schwenk, Senkrechtschwenk *m*; ~ **mirror** Drehspiegel *m*
timbre *n* Klangfarbe *f*, Tonfarbe *f*
time *v* die Zeit nehmen *v*, abstoppen *v*, mitstoppen *v*, stoppen *v*, durchstoppen *v timen v*, austimen *v*; ~ *v* (US) (FP) entzerren *v*; ~ *n* Zeit *f*; ~ *n* (beat) Takt *m*; ~ **announcement** (R) Zeitansage *f*; ~ **base** Zeitbasis *f*, Zeitablenkung *f*; **triggered ~ base** getriggerte Zeitbasis, angestoßene Zeitbasis; ~ **-base deflection** Zeitablenkung *f*; ~ **-base error correction** (VTR) Zeitfehlerkorrektur *f*; ~ **-base generator** Zeitablenkgenerator *m*, Ablenkgenerator *m*; ~ **calibration** Zeiteichung *f*; ~ **check** (R) Zeitansage *f*; ~ **-constant** *n*

Zeitkonstante *f*; **~ delay** Schaltverzögerung *f*; **~ -division multiplex decoder** Zeitmultiplexdekoder *m*; **~ exposure** Zeitaufnahme *f*; **~ for reversal** Umschaltzeit *f*; **~ lag** Zeitversatz *m*, Verzögerung *f*; **~ lapse** Zeitraffer *m*; **~ -lapse equipment** Zeitraffer *m*; **~ -lapse motion camera** Zeitraffer *m*; **~ -lapse shooting** Zeitrafferaufnahme *f*; **~ leap** Zeitsprung *m*; **~ -lens** *n* Zeitlupe *f* **~ -link** *n* Zwischentitel *m*; **~ marker** Zeitmarke *f*; **~ -marker generator** Zeitmarkengenerator *m*; **~ of transmission** Sendezeit *f*; **~ pips** *n pl* Zeitzeichen *n*; **~ recorder** Zeitzähler *m*; **~ -schedule** *n* Zeitplan *m*; **~ -sharing mode** (EDP) Teilnehmerbetrieb *m* **~ shift** Zeitverschiebung *f*; **~ shot** Zeitaufnahme *f*; **~ signal** Zeitzeichen *n*; **~ -table** *n* Zeitplan *m*, Dienstplan *m*

timer *n* (FP) Lichtbestimmer *m*, Belichtungsuhr *f*; ~ *n* (US) (FP) Entzerrer *m*

timing *n* Laufzeit *f*; ~ *n* Timing *n*, Zeitfestsetzung *f*; ~ *n* (FP) Lichtbestimmung *f*; ~ *n* (US) (FP) Entzerrung *f*; **~ pulse** Zeitimpuls *m*, Taktimpuls *m*

tint *n* Farbton *m*

tinting *n* Einfärbung *f*; **~ equipment** Einfärbgerät *n*

tip *n* Hinweis *m*, Tip *m*, Wink *m*, Aizes *m pl* (fam.); **~ engagement** Kopfeindringtiefe *f*; **~ of synchronising pulses** Impulsboden *m*; **~ penetration** Kopfeindringtiefe *f*; **~ projection** Kopfvorsprung *m*, Kopfvorstand *m*

tip-off *n* Hinweis *m*, Tip *m*, Wink *m*

tissues *n pl* (make-up) Abschminkpapier *n*

title *v* betiteln *v*, titeln *v*; ~ *n* Titel *m* **~ background** Titeluntergrund *m*; **~ card** Titelvorlage *f*; **~ lettering** Titelschrift *f*; **~ -link** *n* Zwischentitel *m*; **~ music** Titelmusik *f*; **~ negative** Titelnegativ *n*; **~ positive** Titelpositiv *n*; **~ printer** Titelgerät *n*, Titelmaschine *f*; **~ role** Titelrolle *f*; **~ roll** Titelrolle *f*; **~ sequence** Titelliste *f*; **~ strip** Titelband *n*; **moving ~** wandernder Titel; **overlay ~** einkopierter Titel; **superimposed ~** einkopierter Titel; **to fade in ~ music** Titelmusik aufziehen; **to mount ~** Titel aufziehen; **working ~** Arbeitstitel *m*, vorläufiger Titel, Werktitel *m*

titler *n* Titelgerät *n*, Titelmaschine *f*

titles *n pl* Filmvorspann *m*; **~ easel** Titelständer *m*; **~ planning meeting** Titelkonferenz *f*; **roller ~** *n pl* rollender Titel; **to mount ~** Titel aufziehen

titling artist Titelanfertiger *m*, Titelzeichner *m*; **~ bench** Titelbank *f*

titling-bench work Titelaufnahme *f*

toggle change-over switch Kippumschalter *m*; **~ switch** Kippschalter *m*

tolerance *n* Toleranz *f*, Spielraum *m*; ~ *n* Verträglichkeit *f*; **~ zone** Toleranzfeld *n*

tonal value Grauwert *m*

tonality *n* Klangfarbe *f*, Tonung *f*

tone *v* (col.) abstufen *v*; ~ *n* Klang *m*, Laut *m*, Ton *m*, Tonung *f*, Abstimmton *m*; ~ *n* (col.) Farbton *m*; **~ colour** Klangfarbe *f*; **~ control** Klangblende *f*, Klangregler *m*, Klangfarbenregelung *f*; **~ correction** Klangfarbenkorrektur *f*; **~ frequency run** Wobbelton *m*; **~ quality** Klangfarbe *f*, Tonqualität *f*; **~ wheel** (VTR)

Tachoimpulsrad *n*; **to send ~** Meßton aufschalten
tongue *n* (mus.) Zunge *f*
toothed wheel Zahnrad *n*; **~ wheel rim** Zahnkranzrolle *f*
top cut Höhenabschwächung *f*; **~ -cut filter** Höhensperre *f*; **~ feed** Höheneinspeisung *f*; **~ frequencies** hohe Tonfrequenzen; **~ light** Oberlicht *n*; **~ lighting** senkrechte Lichtleiste, Oberlicht *n*
topic *n* Thema *n*
topical *adj* zeitnah *adj*, aktuell *adj*; **~ comment** Zeitkritik *f*; **~ events** Aktualitäten *f pl*; **~ magazine** (prog.) Umschau *f*; **of ~ interest** aktuell *adj*
toroidal core (EDP) Ringkern *m*; **~ transformer** Ringübertrager *m*
torque *n* Drehmoment *m*
torque-limiter *n* Drehmomentbegrenzer *m*
total circulating capacity Umlaufmenge *f*; **~ dubbing** Vollsynchronisation *f*; **~ harmonic distortion factor** Gesamtklirrfaktor *m*
touch up *v* retuschieren *v*
touring cinema Wanderkino *n*
town mains *n pl* Stadtnetz *n*
trace *n* Spur *f*
traced design Pause *f*
tracing *n* Pause *f*
track *n* (shot) Fahraufnahme *f*, Fahrt *f*; **~** *n* (dolly) Laufschiene *f*; **~** *n* (tape) Spur *f*, Band *n*; **~ configuration** Spurnormen *f pl*; **~ dolly** Schienenwagen *m*; **~ in** *v* Kamera vorwärts fahren, vorwärts fahren, vorfahren *v*; **~ -in** *n* (cam.) Vorfahrt *f*; **~ out** *v* Kamera rückwärts fahren, rückwärts fahren; **~ placement** Spurlage *f*; **~ position** Spurlage *f*; **~ -round** *n* Kreisfahrt *f*; **~ width** Spurbreite *f*; **~ width** (cam.) Abtastbreite *f*
tracker *n* Kamerafahrer *m*, Dollyfahrer *m*
tracking *n* (sync) Gleichlauf *m*; **~ back** Kamerafahrt rückwärts, Rückfahrt *f*; **~ in** Kamerafahrt vorwärts; **~ line** Kameraweg *m*; **~ out** Kamerafahrt rückwärts, Rückfahrt *f*; **~ shot** Fahraufnahme *f*, Fahrt *f*
trade showing (F) Interessentenvorführung *f*
traffic by satellite Satellitenverkehr *m*; **~ news** (R) Verkehrshinweise *m pl*
tragedy *n* Tragödie *f*
trail *v* (R, TV) ankündigen *v*
trailer *n* (F) Vorschau *f*; **~** *n* (prog.) Programmankündigung *f*, Trailer *m*; **~** *n* (tape) Endband *n*; **~ statement** (EDP) Endanweisung *f*; **~ tape** Endband *n*; **to attach ~ tape** Endband kleben
trailing edge Rückflanke *f*
trainee *n* Praktikant *m*, Volontär *m*
training film Lehrfilm *m*, Erziehungsfilm *m*; **~ studio** Versuchsstudio *n*
trajectory *n* Flugbahn *f*
transceiver *n* Sendeempfangsgerät *n*
transcoder *n* Farbnormwandler *m*, Farbumkodierer *m*, Transkoder *m*, Umkodierer *m*
transcoding *n* Transkodierung *f*, Umkodierung *f*, Dekodierung *f*
transconductance *n* (tube) Steilheit *f*
transcribe *v* (script) ausschreiben *v*; **~** *v* (tape) überspielen *v*
transcription *n* (tape) Tonaufnahme *f*, Überspielung *f*; **~ service** Transkriptionsdienst *m*
transduced gain Übertragungsleistungsverstärkung *f*
transducer *n* Wandler *m*, Transduktor *m*
transfer *v* überspielen *v*,

umschneiden *v*, umspielen *v*; ~ *n* Überspielung *f*, Umschneiden *n*, Umschnitt *m*, Umspielung *f*; **~ characteristic curve** Schwärzungskurve *f*; **~ constant** Übertragungskonstante *f*; **~ function** Übertragungsfunktion *f* **~ impedance** Kopplungswiderstand *m*; **~ of rights** Rechteübertragung *f*; **~ resistance** Übergangswiderstand *m*; **magnetic ~** Überspielung von Licht- auf Magnetton; **optical ~** Überspielung von Magnet- auf Lichtton

transform *v* umwandeln *v*, umsetzen *v*

transformation *n* Umwandlung *f*, Umsetzung *f*; **~ ratio** Übersetzungsverhältnis *n*

transformer *n* Transformator *m*, Trafo *m* (fam.), Übertrager *m*; **~ station** Transformatorstation *f*; **~ trailer** Transformatorwagen *m*; **~ truck** Transformatorwagen *m*; **balanced ~** Symmetrieübertrager *m*; **balanced-to-unbalanced ~** Symmetrierglied *n*; **continuously variable ~** Stelltransformator *m*; **differential ~** Differentialübertrager *m*; **rotary ~** rotierender Transformator, rotierender Übertrager

transient distortion Verzerrung durch Ein- und Ausschwingvorgänge; **~ response** Flankenwiedergabe *f*, Sprungkennlinie *f*

transistor *n* Transistor *m*; **~ socket** Transistorfassung *f*

transistorisation *n* Transistorisierung *f*

transistorise *v* transistorisieren *v*

transistorised *adj* transistorisiert *adj*, transistorbestückt *adj*; **~ receiver** Transistorempfänger *m*

transit circuit Transitleitung *f*; **~ time** Ansprechzeit *f*, Durchlaufzeit *f*, Laufzeit *f*; **~ -time distortion** Laufzeitverzerrung *f*

transition *n* Übergang *m*; ~ *n* (F) Übergangsszene *f*; **~ frequency** Sprungfrequenz *f*, Übergangsfrequenz *f*; **~ point** (elec.) Kippunkt *m*; **~ resistance** Übergangswiderstand *m*; **~ scene** Übergangsszene *f*

translation *n* (transmitter) Umsetzung *f*

translator *n* (transmitter) Umsetzer *m*

translucent screen Rückproschirm *m*

transmission *n* Sendung *f*, Rundfunksendung *f*; ~ *n* (tech.) Übertragung *f*, Übermittlung *f*, Ausstrahlung *f*, Abstrahlung *f*; ~ *n* (mech.) Übersetzung *f*; ~ *n* (transmittance) Durchlässigkeit *f*; **~ area** Sendebereich *m*, Sendegebiet *n*, Anstaltsbereich *m*; **~ capacity** Übertragungskapazität *f*; **~ chain** Übertragungskette *f*; **~ channel** Übertragungskanal *m*, Übertragungsweg *m*; **~ characteristic** Durchlaßkurve *f*; **~ circuit** Sendestraße *f*, Sendeweg *m*, Übertragungsleitung *f*; **~ coefficient** Übertragungskoeffizient *m*; **~ constant** Übertragungskonstante *f*; **~ copy** Sendekopie *f*, Abnahmekopie *f*; **~ costs** Übertragungskosten *plt*; **~ distortion** Übertragungsverzerrung *f*; **~ fault** Übertragungsfehler *m*; **~ gamma** Kontrastübertragungsfunktion (KÜF) *f*; **~ label** Sendepaß *m*; **~ level** Übertragungspegel *m*; **~ line** Übertragungsleitung *f*, Zubringerleitung *f*, Zubringer *m* (fam.); **~ line** (aerial) Antennenleitung *f*; **~ loss** Durchgangsdämpfung *f*,

Übertragungsverlust *m*; **~ -measuring set** Pegelmesser *m*; **~ medium** Übertragungsweg *m*; **~ method** Übertragungsverfahren *n*; **~ monitor** Hauptmonitor *m*; **~ of pre-recorded material** Bandsendung *f*; **~ of sports event** Sportübertragung *f*; **~ path** Übertragungsweg *m*; **~ primaries** Übertragungsprimärvalenzen *f pl*; **~ print** (F) Sendekopie *f*, Abnahmekopie *f*; **~ process** Sendeverfahren *n*; **~ range** Reichweite *f*, Sendebereich *m*, Anstaltsbereich *m*, Sendegebiet *n*; **~ ratio** Übersetzungsverhältnis *n*; **~ rights** Übertragungsrechte *n pl*, Senderechte *n pl*; **~ satellite** Übertragungssatellit *m*; **~ schedule** Sendeplan *m*, Sendeablaufplan *m*; **~ standard** Übertragungsnorm *f*; **~ switch** Sendeschalter *m*; **~ system** Übertragungssystem *n*, Übertragungsverfahren *n*; **~ tape** Sendeband *n*, Sendekopie *f*, Abnahmekopie *f*, Sendetonband *n* **~ time** Sendezeit *f*, Übertragungszeit *f*, Übermittlungsdauer *f*; **~ tower** Senderturm *m*; **~ via satellite** Satellitenfunk *m*; **acoustic ~ system** akustisches Übertragungssystem; **checked for ~** zur Sendung; **radio ~** (WT) drahtlose Übertragung; **sequential ~** sequentielle Übertragung; **stereo ~ system** stereofone Übertragungsanlage; **to run a ~** Sendung fahren

transmit *v* senden *v*, übertragen *v*, ausstrahlen *v*, abstrahlen *v*, übermitteln *v*; ~ *v* (mech.) übersetzen *v*; **to ~ over closed circuit** überspielen *v*

transmittance *n* Durchlässigkeit *f*, Transmittanz *f*

transmitted energy Strahlungsenergie *f*; **~ modulation** Sendemodulation *f*

transmitter *n* Sender *m*; **~ amplifier** Senderverstärker *m*; **~ chain** Senderkette *f*; **~ complex** Senderkomplex *m*, Senderanlage *f*; **~ control room** Senderbetriebszentrale *f*; **~ distribution network** Sendeschiene *f*; **~ engineer** Senderingenieur *m*, Sendertechniker *m*; **~ engineering** Senderbetriebstechnik *f*, Sendertechnik *f*; **~ equipment** Senderausrüstung *f*; **~ mast** Sendemast *m*; **~ network** Sendergruppe *f*, Sendernetz *n*; **~ operations** *n pl* Senderbetrieb *m*; **~ output** Senderausgang *m*; **~ output power** Senderleistung *f*; **~ power** Senderleistung *f*; **~ selection** Senderwahl *f*; **~ site** Senderstandort *m*; **~ technician** Sendetechniker *m*; **~ tuning** Senderabstimmung *f*; **colour-capable ~** farbtüchtiger Fernsehsender; **mobile ~** fahrbarer Sender, beweglicher Sender; **portable ~** tragbarer Sender; **to receive a ~** Sender bekommen, Sender einfangen

transmitting aerial Sendeantenne *f* **highly directional ~ aerial** Sendeantenne mit sehr ausgeprägter Strahlungskeule

transmitting end Senderseite *f*, Geberseite *f*; **~ frequency** Sendefrequenz *f*; **~ frequency range** Sendeband *n*; **~ installation** Sendeanlage *f*; **~ microphone** Sendemikrofon *n*; **~ power** Sendeleistung *f*; **~ station** Sendeanlage *f*, Sendestation *f*, Senderanlage *f*, Senderkomplex *m*; **~ system** Sendeverfahren *n*

transparency *n* Durchsichtigkeit *f*, Transparenz *f*; ~ *n* (slide) Diapositiv *n*, Dia *n*, Lichtbild *n*;

~ **cassette** Kassettenrahmenträger *m*; ~ **effect** Nachzieheffekt *m*; ~ **mount** Diarahmen *m*
transparent colour Lasurfarbe *f*; ~ **ink** Lasurfarbe *f*; ~ **screen** Transparenzschirm *m*
transponder *n* Transponder *m*
transport* *n* Fahrbereitschaft* *f*
transport manager Fahrdienstleiter *m*; ~ **mechanism** Laufwerk *n*; ~ **officer** Fahrbereitschaftsleiter *m* ~ **roller** Transportrolle *f*
transpose *v* umsetzen *v*
transverse head Transversalkopf *m*; ~ **magnetisation** Transversalmagnetisierung *f*, Quermagnetisierung *f*; ~ **recording** Querschriftaufzeichnung *f*, Querspuraufzeichnung *f*, Transversalaufzeichnung *f*; ~ **scan** Querschriftaufzeichnung *f*, Querspuraufzeichnung *f*; ~ **signal** Transversalwelle *f*; ~ **wave** Querwelle *f*
trap *n* Falle *f*; ~ **amplifier** Trennverstärker *m*; ~ **circuit** Bildfalle *f*
trapdoor *n* Versenkvorrichtung *f*
trapezium distortion Trapezverzerrung *f*
trap-valve amplifier Trennverstärker *m*
travel *n* (appar.) Lauf *m*; ~ **allowances** Reisespesen *plt*; ~ **allowances clerk** Reisekostenstelle *f*; ~ **authorisation** Dienstreiseauftrag *m*; ~ **diary** Reisetagebuch *n*; ~ **direction** (tape) Bandlaufrichtung *f*; ~ **expenses** Reisekosten *plt*; ~ **expenses claim** Reisekostenabrechnung *f*; ~ **ghost** ziehende Blende; **application for ~ allowances** Reisekostenantrag *m*; **application for ~ authorisation** Dienstreiseantrag *m*
travelling matte process Travelling-Matte-Verfahren *n*, Wandermaskenverfahren *n*; ~ **shot** Fahraufnahme *f*, Fahrt *f*, Kamerafahrt *f*
travelling-wave tube (TWT) Wanderfeldröhre *f*
travelogue *n* Reisebericht *m*; ~ *n* (F) Reisefilm *m*
traverse *v* (elec.) durchlaufen *v*
tray *n* Trog *m*
treat *v* (story) aufziehen *v*, bearbeiten *v*
treatment *n* (F) Bearbeitung *f*, Verarbeitung *f*; ~ *n* (script) Treatment *n*
treble *n* Hochton *m*, Höhen *f pl*; ~ **attenuation** Höhenabschwächung *f*; ~ **boost** Höhenanhebung *f*; ~ **correction** Höhenentzerrung *f*; ~ **cut** Höhenabschwächung *f*; ~ **equalisation** Höhenentzerrung *f* ~ **loudspeaker** Hochtonlautsprecher *m*
trebles *n pl* hohe Tonfrequenzen
triac *n* (elec.) Triac *m*
triad *n* Dreiklang *m*
trial *n* Probe *f*; ~ **programme** Testsendung *f*; ~ **shot** Probeaufnahme *f*; ~ **take** heiße Probe
trichromatic coefficients Farbwertanteile *m pl*; ~ **process** Dreifarbenverfahren *n*; ~ **response** Farbmischkurven *f pl*
trick button Tricktaste *f*
tricolour system Dreifarbensystem *n*
trigger *v* ansteuern *v*, anstoßen *v*, triggern *v*; ~ *n* Trigger *m*; ~ **circuit** (EDP) Kippschaltung *f*; **bistable ~** (EDP) bistabiler Multivibrator, bistabile Kippschaltung, Flip-Flop-Schaltung *f*
trim *v* kürzen *v*, überarbeiten *v*, zusammenstreichen *v*
trimmer *n* Trimmer *m*

trimming *n* Feineinstellung *f*; **~ apparatus** Nachstimmgerät *n*; **~ filter** Korrekturfilter *m*; **~ potentiometer** Trimmpotentiometer *n*; **~ resistor** Trimmwiderstand *m*
trims *n pl* (F) Schnittmaterial *n*; **~ bin** Galgen *m*, Filmgalgen *m*; **to hang up ~** an den Filmgalgen hängen
trip *v* auslösen *v*; **~ button** Auslösetaste *f*
triple *n* Tripel *n*
triplet *n* Tripel *n*
tripod *n* Dreifuß *m*, Stativ *n*; **~ base** Stativspinne *f*; **~ dolly** Stativfahrwagen *m*; **~ extension** Stativverlängerung *f*; **~ head** Stativkopf *m*; **collapsible ~** ausziehbarer Dreifuß; **extensible ~** ausziehbarer Dreifuß; **telescopic ~** ausziehbares Stativ; **wooden ~** Holzstativ *n*
tristimuli, chromatic trichromatische Farbkoeffizienten
tristimulus values Farbwerte *m pl*; **~ values monitor** Farbwertkontrollgerät *n*, Farbwertoszillograf *m*, Farbwertoszilloskop *n*
trolley *n* Laufkatze *f*
troop *n* Ensemble *n*
trouble-hunting *n* Fehlersuche *f*
trouble-shooting *n* Fehlersuche *f*, Störungsbeseitigung *f*
trough *n* Trog *m*
truck shot Fahraufnahme *f*, Fahrt *f*
true value Istwert *m*
trunk distributing frame (US) Hauptverteiler *m*; **~ line** Fernleitung *f*, Stammleitung *f*, Verbindungskabel *n*; **~ line distribution** Stammleitungsverteilung *f*; **~ -line system** Fernleitungsnetz *n*; **~ network** Fernleitungsnetz *n*
truth table (EDP) Funktionstabelle *f*, Wertetabelle *f*, Wahrheitstabelle *f*
try-out *n* (thea.) Vorpremiere *f*
tube *n* Röhre *f*; **~ holder** Röhrensockel *m*; **~ pole** Rohrmast *m*; **~ receiver** Röhrenempfänger *m*; **implosion-proof ~** implosionsgeschützte Röhre
tubular lamp Soffittenleuchte *f*; **~ mast** Rohrmast *m*; **~ scaffolding** Rohrgerüst *n*
Tuchel-type plug Tuchel *m* (fam.)
tulle *n* Tüll *m*
tumbler switch Kippschalter *m*
tumbling *n* (sat.) Taumeln *n*
tune *v* abstimmen *v*; **~ in** *v* abstimmen *v*; **~ in** *v* (rec.) einstellen *v*; **~ out** *v* entkoppeln *v*; **~ out** *v* (jammer) ausblenden *v*; **~ to** *v* abstimmen *v*; **to ~ to zero beat frequency** einpfeifen *v*
tuned amplifier Resonanzverstärker *m*; **~ circuit** Schwingkreis *m*
tuner *n* Abstimmvariometer *n*, Tuner *m*
tungsten *n* Wolfram *n*; **~ lamp** Nitraphotlampe *f*; **~ light** Kunstlicht *n*, Panlicht *n*
tuning *n* Abstimmung *f*; **~** *n* (rec.) Senderwahl *f*; **~ circuit** Abstimmkreis *m*; **~ device** Abstimmvorrichtung *f*; **~ fork** Stimmgabel *f*; **~ -in** *n* Abstimmung *f*; **~ note** Abstimmton *m*; **~ -out** *n* Entkopplung *f*; **~ -out** *n* (jammer) Ausblenden *n*, Ausblendung *f*; **~ range** Abstimmbereich *m*, Empfangsbereich *m*, Empfangsgebiet *n*; **~ variometer** Abstimmvariometer *n*; **automatic ~** automatische Scharfabstimmung
tunnel diode Tunneldiode *f*
tunnel-diode pre-amplifier Vorverstärker mit Tunneldiode
turbidity *n* (FP) Trübung *f*
turbulence *n* Strudelbewegung *f*

turn *n* Windung *f*; ~ **off** *v* ausschalten *v*; ~ **on** *v* anstellen *v*; ~ **over!** (cam.) Kamera ab!; ~ **up** *v* (fader) aufziehen *v*; **in** ~ wechselweise *adv*
turning moment Drehmoment *m*
turning-off *n* Ausschalten *n*, Ausschaltung *f*
turn-over frequency Übergangsfrequenz *f*
turnstile aerial Kreuzdipol *m*
turntable *n* Schallplattenteller *m*, Plattenteller *m*, Teller *m*; ~ *n* (appar.) Plattenmaschine *f*, Plattenspieler *m*; ~ *n* (deck) Platine mit Bandmaschine, Plattenspielerchassis *n*; ~ **motor** Plattenspielermotor *m*
turret rotation Revolverkopfdrehung *f*
turtle *n* (coll.) Babystativ *n*
TV reporter Bildreporter *m*
tweeter *n* (coll.) Hochtonlautsprecher *m*
twin lead Bandleitung *f*, Flachkabel *n*; ~ **station** Partneranstalt *f*; ~ **stock** Zweiebenenantenne *f*; ~ **-stock aerial** Zweiebenenantenne *f*; ~ **track** Doppelspur *f*; ~ **-track recorder** Doppelspur-Tonbandgerät *n*; ~ **-track tape recorder** Zweispurmaschine *f*
twinning *n* (stations) Partnerschaft *f*
twist *v* verdrillen *v*; ~ *n* Windung *f*
two-blade shutter Zweiflügelblende *f*
two-channel *adj* zweikanalig *adj*
two-level aerial Zweietagenantenne *f*
two-phase mains *n pl* Zweiphasennetz *n*
two-pole *adj* zweipolig *adj*; ~ **plug** Stöpsel *m*
two-port network Vierpol *m*
two-shot *n* Zweiereinstellung *f*
two-track recorder Doppelspur-Tonbandgerät *n*
two-way intercommunication system Gegensprechanlage *f*
two-wing shutter Zweiflügelblende *f*
two-wire circuit Zweidrahtleitung *f*
type *n* Modell *n*; ~ **face** Schriftbild *n*; ~ **of broadcast** Funkform *f*, Sendeform *f*; ~ **of production** Produktionsart *f*; ~ **of programme** Programmsparte *f*; ~ **of radio** Sendeform *f*
typing pool Schreibbüro *n*

U

U-certificate *adj* jugendfrei *adj*
UHF band Dezimeterwellenbereich *m*; ~ **television transmitter** UHF-Fernsehsender *m*
ultra-hard *adj* ultrahart *adj*
ultra-high frequencies (UHF) Dezimeterwellen (UHF) *f pl*; ~ **frequency (UHF)** ultrahohe Frequenz (UHF), Ultrakurzwelle *f* (UKW)
ultra-linear circuit Ultralinearschaltung *f*
ultrasonic *adj* Ultraschall- (in Zus.); ~ **delay line** Ultraschalleitung *f*
ultrasonics *n* Ultraschall *m*
ultra-sound *n* Ultraschall *m*
ultra-violet filter Ultraviolettfilter *m*
umbrella-type aerial Gitterantenne *f*
unabridged *adj* ungekürzt *adj*
unblanking circuit (TV) Zündkreis *m*; ~ **pulse** Helltastimpuls *m*
unbreakable *adj* unzerbrechlich *adj*
unclamped *adj* ungetastet *adj*
uncoated *adj* unbeschichtet *adj*
uncoil *v* abspulen *v*
uncoloured *adj* ungefärbt *adj*
unconnected *adj* nicht eingeschaltet *adj*
uncouple *v* (mech.) entkuppeln *v*

uncoupling *n* (mech.) Entkupplung *f*
uncut *adj* ungeschnitten *adj*; **~ tape** (R) Schnittmaterial *n*
undamped *adj* ungedämpft *adj*
undelayed *adj* unverzögert *adj*
undercurrent relay Unterstromrelais *n*
underdevelopment *n* Unterentwicklung *f*
underexpose *v* unterbelichten *v*
underexposure *n* Unterbelichtung *f*
underframe *n* Untergestell *n*
underground *adj* unterirdisch *adj*; **~ cable** Erdkabel *n*
underlay *v* (sound) unterschneiden *v*; **~** *n* Filmeinblendung *f*, Filminsert *m*, Unterschnitt *m*
underlength *n* Unterlänge *f*
underload relay Unterspannungsrelais *n*
undermodulate *v* untermodulieren *v*
undermodulation *n* Untermodulierung *f*, unvollständige Modulation
underrun *v* (prog.) Sendezeit unterschreiten; **~** *n* Zeitunterschreitung *f*
underrunning voltage Unterspannung *f*
underscripted *adj* zuviel Luft
underspeed *n* zu niedrige Geschwindigkeit
understudy *v* (perf.) einspringen *v*; **~** *n* Ersatzbesetzung *f*
undervoltage *n* Unterspannung *f*; **~ relay** Unterspannungsrelais *n*
underwater filming Unterwasseraufnahme *f*; **~ shot** Unterwasseraufnahme *f*
unedited *adj* ungeschnitten *adj*; **~** *adj* (script) unredigiert *adj*; **~ commentary** Originalbeitrag *m*
unestablished staff contract Zeitvertrag *m*
unexposed *adj* unbelichtet *adj*
unfair comparative advertising Wettbewerbsverzerrung *f*
unfit for transmission (take) wertlos *adj*
unfold *v* aufklappen *v*
ungraded *adj* unbewertet *adj*
ungrounded *adj* ungeerdet *adj*; **~** *adj* erdfrei *adj*
unidirectional link gerichtete Verbindung
unilateral *n* (TV) unilaterale Sendung; **~** *adj* unilateral *adj*
unipolar *adj* einpolig *adj*
uni-pulse signal Kombinationssignal *n*
uniselector *n* Drehwähler *m*
unit *n* Abteilung *f*; **~** *n* Einheit *f*; **~** *n* (appar.) Gerät *n*; **interchangeable ~** austauschbare Einheit; **plug-in ~** steckbare Einheit
universal drive Universalgetriebe *n*
univibrator *n* Univibrator *m*
unlace *v* (proj.) auslegen *v*; **to ~ a film** Film auslegen
unlicensed listener Schwarzhörer *m*; **~ viewer** Schwarzseher *m*
unlimited *adj* unbegrenzt *adj*, unbeschränkt *adj*
unload *v* (cam.) auslegen *v*; **to ~ a camera** Film auslegen
unlocked, to become (pict.) durchfallen *v*
unlocking *n* (of a circuit) Entriegelung *f* (eines Schaltkreises)
unmasked *adj* (neg.) unmaskiert *adj*
unmodulated *adj* unmoduliert *adj*
unpaid trainee Hospitant *m*
unpolished script Rohfassung *f*
unsatisfactory recording schlechte Aufnahme
unsharp *adj* unscharf *adj*
unsharpness *n* Unschärfe *f*; **~ due to movement** Bewegungsunschärfe *f*
unskilled staff Betriebshelfer *m*; **~ worker** Hilfsarbeiter *m*
unsoldering *n* Auslöten *n*; **~ set** Entlötgerät *n*, Entlötpistole *f*
unspool *v* abspulen *v*

unsuitable for young people jugendungeeignet *adj*
unthread *v* (cam.) auslegen *v*; **to ~ a film** Film auslegen
unusable *adj* unbrauchbar *adj*, wertlos *adj*
unwanted modulation Störmodulation *f*
unweighted *adj* unbewertet *adj*; **~ signal-to-noise ratio** Fremdspannungsabstand *m*
unwind *v* abspulen *v*, abtrommeln *v*
unwinding *n* (cable) Abwicklung *f*
up-date *v* aktualisieren *v*
upholsterer *n* Dekorateur *m*, Deko *m* (fam.)
upkeep servicing Wartung *f*
up-link *n* (sat.) Aufwärtsverbindung *f*; **~ frequency** (sat.) Aufwärtsfrequenz *f*
upright format Hochformat *n*; **~ size** Hochformat *n*
upstage *n* Hintergrund *m*
upstream *adj* vorgeschaltet *adj*, stromaufwärts *adj*
usable *adj* einsatzfähig *adj*
usage fee Benutzungsgebühr *f*
use *n* Verwertung *f*
useful range Nutzbereich *m*
user programme (EDP) Anwenderprogramm *n*, Benutzerprogramm *n*
usufructuary *n* Nutzungsberechtigter *m*
utilisation *n* Verwertung *f*

V

vacuum *n* Vakuum *n*; **~ guide** Vakuumführungsschuh *m*, Kopfschuh *m*; **~ lamp** Vakuumlampe *f*; **~ tape guide** Bandführungsschuh *m*
vacuum-tube voltmeter (VTVM) (US) Röhrenvoltmeter *n*
valency electron Valenzelektron *n*
valve *n* (tube) Röhre *f*; **~** *n* Vektorventil *n*; **~ base** Röhrensockel *m*; **~ base connections** *n pl* Sockelbelegung *f*; **~ receiver** Röhrenempfänger *m*; **~ set** Röhrenempfänger *m*; **~ socket** Röhrensockel *m*; **~ voltmeter** Röhrenvoltmeter *n*; **deaf ~** taube Röhre
vapour cooling Verdampfungskühlung *f*
variable-area sound track Zackenschrift *f*
variable attenuator Dämpfungsregler *m*; **~ correction unit (VCU)** Tonblende *f*; **~ cycle operation** (EDP) Asynchronbetrieb *m*; **~ -density sound recording** Sprossenschrift *f*; **~ -density track** Sprossenschrift *f*; **~ focus lens** Objektiv mit veränderlicher Brennweite, Multifokusobjektiv *n*; **~ resistance** Regelwiderstand *m*; **~ resistor** Regelwiderstand *m*, Stellwiderstand *m*; **~ video attenuator** BA-Regler *m*
variation *n* (tech.) Schwankung *f*; **~ frequency** Schwankungsfrequenz *f*; **~ in amplitude-frequency response** Frequenzgangabweichung *f*; **~ in running speed** (F) Filmzugsschwankung *f*
variations in density Dichteschwankungen *f pl*
varicap *n* (coll.) Kapazitätsdiode *f*, Kapazitätsvariationsdiode *f*, Nachstimmdiode *f*
variety artist Unterhaltungskünstler *m*
variometer *n* Variometer *n*; **~ tuning** Variometerabstimmung *f*
varistor *n* Varistor *m*, spannungsabhängiger Widerstand, VDR-Widerstand *m*
varnish, clear Lasurfarbe *f*

varnishing *n* Lackieren *n*
vat *n* Trog *m*
vault *n* (F) Filmtresor *m*
vector *n* Vektor *m*; ~ **diagram** Vektordiagramm *n*; ~ **quantity** Vektor *m*
vectorscope *n* Vektorskop *n*, Vektoroszilloskop *n*, Pegelvektorskop *n*
vehicle workshop Kraftfahrzeugwerkstatt *f*
veil *v* (FP) verschleiern *v*
veiling *n* (FP) Schleier *m*; **chemical** ~ (FP) Niederschlag *m*
velocilator *n* Kamerawagen *m*
velocity *n* Geschwindigkeit *f*; ~ **factor** Verkürzungsfaktor *m*; ~ **of propagation** Fortpflanzungsgeschwindigkeit *f*
velocity-modulated tube Laufzeitröhre *f*
velvet pad Samtkufe *f*
venetian blinds *n pl* Jalousieeffekt *m*
venetian-blind pattern jalousieartiges Störmuster; ~ **shutter** Gitterblende *f*
venetian shutter Jalousieblende *f*
ventilation *n* Lüftung *f*; ~ **system** Belüftungsanlage *f*, Entlüftungsanlage *f*
venue *n* Schauplatz *m*
vernier *n* Nonius *m*
version *n* Fassung *f*; **abridged** ~ Kurzfassung *f*; **dubbed** ~ synchronisierte Fassung; **short** ~ Kurzfassung *f*
vertical blanking pulse (US) Vertikalaustastimpuls *m*; ~ **definition** Vertikalauflösung *f*; ~ **deflection coil** Vertikalablenkspule (V-Ablenkspule) *f*; ~ **frequency** (50 or 60 Hz) Bildfrequenz *f*; ~ **frequency** (US) Vertikalfrequenz (V-Frequenz) *f*; ~ **hold** Bildfangregler *m*, Bildfang *m*, Bildsynchronisation *f*; ~ **lock** Bildfangregler *m*, Bildfang *m*; ~ **pulse** (US) Vertikalimpuls (V-Impuls) *m*, Halbbildimpuls *m*; ~ **pulse separator** V-Separator *m*; ~ **rewinder** Vertikalumroller *m*; ~ **saw-tooth** Vertikalsägezahn *m*; ~ **sweep** Bildablenkung *f*; ~ **sync pulse** Bildsynchronimpuls *m*, Bildwechselimpuls *m*; ~ **synchronising pulse** Bildgleichlaufimpuls *m*, Bildsynchronimpuls *m*, Bildwechselimpuls *m*; ~ **synchronising pulse** (US) Vertikalsynchronimpuls
very close shot (VCS) ganz groß, ganz nah; ~ **high frequency (VHF)** sehr hohe Frequenz, Ultrakurzwelle *f* (UKW); ~ **-high-frequency band (VHF band)** Ultrakurzwellenbereich *m*; ~ **long shot (VLS)** Weiteinstellung *f*; ~ **low frequency (VLF)** Längstwellenfrequenz *f*
very-short-distance shooting Detailaufnahme *f*
vestigial sideband Restseitenband *n*; ~ **sideband transmission** Restseitenbandübertragung *f*
VFR equipment Electronic-Cam (E-Cam) *f*
VHF television transmitter VHF-Fernsehsender *m*
vibrating reed meter Vibrationsmesser *m*
vibration *n* Schwingung *f*; ~ **frequency** Schwingungszahl *f*
vibrator *n* Vibrator *m*, Zerhacker *m*
video *n* Video *n*; ~ *n* (US) Fernsehen (FS) *n*; ~ *adj* Bild- (in Zus.); ~ *adj* (US) Fernseh- (in Zus.); ~ **adjustment** Bildsignalabgleich *m*; ~ **amplifier** VF-Verstärker *m*, Videoverstärker *m*; ~ **apparatus room** Videogeräteraum *m*; ~ **attenuator** Bildregler *m*; ~ **bus** (US) Fernsehaufnahmewagen *m*; ~ **cable** Videokabel *n*; ~ **check**

Videokontrolle *f*; **~ circuit** Bildleitung (BL) *f*; **~ control** Bildregie *f*; **~ data terminal** (EDP) Datensichtgerät *n*; **~ disc** Bildplatte *f*, Bildschallplatte *f*, Videoplatte *f*; **~ display** (EDP) Sichtgerät *n*; **~ distributor** Videoverteiler *m*; **~ effects mixer** Bildmischer am Trickpult; **~ engineering** Bildtechnik *f*; **~ film camera** kombinierte Film/E-Kamera, Electronic-Cam *f* **~ -frequency** *adj* videofrequent *adj*; **~ frequency (VF)** Videofrequenz *f* (VF); **~ gain** Bildsignalverstärkung *f*; **~ head** Videokopf *m*; **~ head assembly** Kopfradaggregat *n*, Kopfradeinheit *f*; **~ information** Videoinformation *f*; **~ matrix** Filterkreuzschiene *f*, Videofilterkreuzschiene *f*, Videoverteiler *m*; **~ mixer** Bildmischer *m*, Bildmischpult *n*; **~ mixing** Bildmischung *f*; **~ mixing desk** Bildmischpult *n*; **~ monitor point** Video-Überwachungsstelle *f*; **~ monitoring and mixing desk** Bildmischpult *n*; **~ monitoring circuit** Bildkontrolleitung *f*; **~ noise** Bildrauschen *n*; **~ operations*** *n pl* Fernsehbetrieb Bild*; **~ operator** Videotechniker *m*; **~ quality control** Videomeßdienst *m*; **~ recorder/reproducer** Magnetbildaufzeichnungs- und Wiedergabeanlage *f*; **~ recording** Videoaufzeichnung *f*; **~ signal** Bildsignal *n* (B-Signal), Videosignal *n*; **~ signal without sync pulse** Bildaustastsignal (BA-Signal) *n*, Bildsignal mit Austastung; **~ spool** Videomagnetspule *f*; **~ switch** Hartschnittschalter *m*, Videoumschalter *m*; **~ tape** Bildband *n*, Videomagnetband *n*, Videotape *n*; **~ tape bandwidth** Bildbandbreite *f*; **~ tape cartridge** Bildbandkassette *f*, Bildkassette *f*; **~ tape cassette** Bildbandkassette *f*, Bildkassette *f*, Videobandkassette *f*; **~ tape library** Bildbandarchiv *n*; **~ tape machine** Bildbandgerät *n*; **~ tape recorder (VTR)** Magnetbildaufzeichnungsanlage *f*, Bildbandgerät *n*, MAZ *f* (fam.); **~ tape recording (VTR)** Magnetbildaufzeichnung (MAZ) *f*, magnetische Bildaufzeichnung (MAZ); **~ tape reproducer** Magnetbildwiedergabeanlage *f*; **~ techniques** *n pl* Videofrequenztechnik *f*; **~ telephone** (US) Fernsehtelefon *n* **~ telephony** Fernsehtelefonie *f*; **~ test signal generator** Videoprüfsignalgeber *m*; **~ track** Bildspur *f*, Videospur *f*; **~ viewer** (US) Fernseher *m*, Fernsehzuschauer *m*; **composite ~ signal** zusammengesetztes Bildsignal; **composite ~ waveform** zusammengesetztes Bildsignal

vidicon *n* Bildaufnahmeröhre *f*, Vidikon *n*

view *v* ansehen *v*; **to ~ a film** Film ansehen

viewer *n* Betrachter *m*; **~** *n* (TV) Fernsehzuschauer *m*, Fernseher *m*, Zuschauer *m*, Seher *m* (fam.)

viewer's letters* *n pl* Zuschauerpost* *f*

viewfinder *n* Bildsucher *m*, Motivsucher *m*, Sucher *m*; **~ brightness** Lichtstärke eines Suchers; **~ eyepiece** Sucherokular *n*; **~ frame** Sucherkasch *m*, Sucherrahmen *m*; **~ lens** Sucherobjektiv *n*; **~ window** Sucherfenster *n*; **bright ~** lichtstarker Sucher; **electronic ~** elektronischer Sucher; **optical ~** optischer Sucher

viewing *n* (F) Filmvorführung *f*, Vorführung *f*; **~ angle** Gesichtswinkel *m*; **~ date** Vorführtermin *m*; **~ figure** (TV) Sehbeteiligung *f*; **~ lens** Sucherobjektiv *n*; **~ magnifier** Sucherlupe *f*; **~ print** Vorführkopie *f*; **~ screen** Betrachtungsschirm *m*; **~ storage tube** Sichtspeicherröhre *f*; **~ theatre** Vorführkino *n*, Vorführraum *m*

vignette *n* Kasch *m*, Maske *f*, Schablonenblende *f*, Schattenraster *m*, Scheinwerfervignette *f*, Vignette *f* ~ *n* (journ.) Glosse *f*

vignetting *n* Vignettierung *f*

vintage movies *n pl* (coll.) Kintopp *m* (fam.)

Vinten tripod Vintenstativ *n*

violinist of first desk erste Geige

virgin tape Frischband *n*

virtual focus Zerstreuungspunkt *m*; **~ image** (opt.) Luftbild *n*; **~ image plane** Luftbildebene *f*

visibility *n* Sichtbarkeit *f*

vision *n* Bild *n*; ~ (compp.) Bild- (in Zus.); **~ and sound switching area** Bild- und Tonschaltraum *m*; **~ break** Bildausfall *m*; **~ breakdown** Bildstörung *f*, Störung *f*; **~ carrier** Bildträger *m*; **~ check receiver** Bildkontrollempfänger *m*, Bildmonitor *m*, Monitor *m*; **~ circuit** Bildleitung (BL) *f*; **~ circuit network** Bildleitungsnetz *n*; **~ control** Bildregie *f*, Kamerasignalüberwachung *f*; **~ control circuit** Bildkontrolleitung *f*; **~ control desk** Bildregiepult *n*, Summenbedienpult *n*; **~ control engineer** Bildingenieur *m*; **~ control operator** (TV) Kameratechniker *m*; **~ control room** Bildkontrollraum *m*, Bildregieraum *m*; **~ controller** Bildtechniker *m*; **~ effects mixer** Bildmischer am Trickpult; **~ fader** Bildregler *m*; **~ frequency** Bildträgerfrequenz *f*; **~ howl-round** optische Rückkopplung; **~ identification** Bildkennung *f*; **~ item** (coll.) gesprochene Nachricht; **~ master control** Senderegiebild *n*; **~ mixer** (operator) Bildmischer *m*, Einblender *m*; **~ mixer** (appar.) Bildmischer *m*, Bildmischpult *n*; **~ mixer's desk** Trickpult *n*; **~ mixing** Bildmischung *f*; **~ -mixing apparatus** Bildmischeinrichtung *f*; **~ -mixing panel** Bildmischeinrichtung *f*; **~ network** Bildleitungsnetz *n*; **~ operator** Kameratechniker *m*; **~ pick-up** (US) Fernsehaufnahme *f*; **~ pilot frequency** Bildsteuersender *m*; **~ radio link** Bildfunkstrecke *f*; **~ recording** Bildaufzeichnung *f*; **~ signal** Bildsignal (B-Signal) *n*; **~ story** (coll.) Wortmeldung *f*; **~ switcher** Bildmischer *m*; **~ switching** Bildschnitt *m*, Bildwechsel *m*; **~ switching centre** Bildschaltraum *m*, Bildsternpunkt *m*, Bildstern *m*; **~ transmitter** Bildsender *m*, Fernsehbildsender *m*; **out of ~ (OOV)** im Off; **to be in ~** im Bild sein

vision/sound combining unit Bild-Ton-Weiche *f*; **~ diplexer** Bild-Ton-Weiche *f*

visitor *n* Besucher *m*

visitors service* Empfangsdienst* *m*

visphone *n* Bildtelefon *n*

vista shot (US) Fernaufnahme *f*, Gesamtaufnahme *f*

visual *adj* optisch *adj*, Bild- (in Zus.) **~ aid** Schaubild *n*, Schautafel *f*, Grafik *f*, grafische Darstellung,

Illustration *f*; ~ **aids** *n pl* Anschauungsmaterial *n*; ~ **check** Sichtprüfung *f*; ~ **communication** Sichtverbindung *f*; ~ **contact** Sichtverbindung *f*; ~ **display** Lichtzeigeranzeige *f*; ~ **field** Gesichtsfeld *n*; ~ **indicator** Sichtgerät *n*; ~ **monitor** Sichtgerät *n*; ~ **recording** Bildaufnahme *f*, Bildaufzeichnung *f*; ~ **recording** (contract) Bildträger *m*; ~ **signal** Sichtzeichen *n*; ~ **tape** Textband *n* ~ **tape projector** Textbandprojektor *m*

visualise *v* sichtbar machen

vocal *n* Gesangsstimme *f*; ~ **score** Vokalwerk *n*; ~ **work** Vokalwerk *n*

voice *n* Stimme *f*; ~ **coil** (loudspeaker) Schwingspule *f*; ~ **connection** Sprechverbindung *f*; ~ **contact** Sprechkontakt *m*; ~ **current** Sprechstrom *m*; ~ **dubbing** Doubeln *n*; ~ **frequency** Sprechfrequenz *f*, Tonfrequenz *f*; ~ **frequency range** Sprachfrequenzbereich *m*; ~ **recording** Sprachaufnahme *f*; ~ **sync** Gesangssynchronisation *f*; ~ **tape** Musikband für Gesangssynchronisation; ~ **test** Sprechprobe *f*, Stimmprobe *f*, Mikrofonprobe *f*; **to give more** ~ mehr Stimme geben

voice-over *n* Off-Kommentar *m*; ~ *n* (speaker) Off-Sprecher *m*; ~ **script** Off-Text *m*

voltage *n* Spannung *f*, Spannungswert *m*; ~ **amplification** Spannungsverstärkung *f*; ~ **amplifier** Spannungsverstärker *m*; ~ **between lines** verkettete Spannung; ~ **calibration** Spannungseichung *f*; ~ **change-over switch** Spannungsumschalter *m*; ~ **comparison** Spannungsvergleich *m*; ~ **control** Spannungssteller *m*, Spannungsregler *m* (fam.); ~ **-dependent resistor (VDR)** spannungsabhängiger Widerstand, VDR-Widerstand *m*; ~ **divider** Spannungsteiler *m*; ~ **drop** Spannungsabfall *m*; ~ **gain** Spannungsverstärkung *f*; ~ **level** Spannungswert *m*; ~ **loop** Spannungsbauch *m*; ~ **maximum** Spannungsbauch *m*; ~ **minimum** Spannungsknoten *m*; ~ **multiplier** Spannungsvervielfacher *m*; ~ **negative feedback** Spannungsgegenkopplung *f*; ~ **node** Spannungsknoten *m*; ~ **probe** Spannungsfühler *m*; ~ **rating** Spannungsfestigkeit *f*; ~ **regulator** Spannungssteller *m*, Spannungsregler *m* (fam.); ~ **selector** Spannungswähler *m*; ~ **selector switch** Spannungsumschalter *m*; ~ **stabiliser** Spannungskonstanthalter *m*; ~ **tester** Spannungsprüfer *m*; ~ **to neutral** Sternspannung *f*; ~ **transformer** Spannungswandler *m*; **weighted** ~ bewertete Spannung; **without** ~ spannungslos *adj*

voltmeter *n* Spannungsmesser *m*

volume *n* Lautstärke *f*, Schallvolumen *n*; ~ **control** Lautstärkeregelung *f*, Lautstärkeregler *m* (LR); ~ **expander** Expander *m*; ~ **indicator** Aussteuerungsmesser *m*, Lautstärkemesser *m*, Volumenanzeiger *m*; ~ **level** Lautstärkepegel *m*; ~ **range** Lautstärkeumfang *m*; ~ **unit meter** VU-Meter *n*; **automatic** ~ **control (AVC)** automatische Lautstärkeregelung (ALR)

volumeter *n* VU-Meter *n*

VT *v* MAZ aufzeichnen, mazen *v*

(fam.); ~ **area** MAZ-Raum *m*; ~ **control** MAZ-Kontrolle *f*; ~ **cubicle** MAZ-Raum *m*; ~ **edit pulse** MAZ-Schneideimpuls *m*; ~ **editing** MAZ-Schnitt *m*; ~ **editing system** MAZ-Schneideeinrichtung *f*; ~ **editor** MAZ-Cutter *m*; ~ **engineer/editor** MAZ-Techniker *m*; ~ **insert** Bandbeitrag *m*; ~ **log** Bandbegleitkarte *f*, Bandkontrollkarte *f*; ~ **operator** MAZ-Techniker *m*; ~ **recording** (item) MAZ-Material *n*; ~ **room** MAZ-Raum *m*

VTR *v* MAZ aufzeichnen, mazen *v* (fam.); ~ **allocation** MAZ-Disposition *f*; ~ **control** MAZ-Kontrolle *f*; ~ **summary** zusammenfassender MAZ-Bericht *m*; **roll ~ !** MAZ ab!

VU-meter *n* VU-Meter *n*

W

wages *n pl* Lohn *m*

waiting time Wartezeit *f*

walkie-talkie *n* Funksprechgerät *n*, Handfunksprechgerät *n*, tragbares Sprechfunkgerät, Walkie-Talkie *n*

walk-on *n* Komparse *m*, Statist *m*; ~ **fee** Komparsengage *f*

walk-through *n* Probedurchlauf *m*, Drehprobe *f*

wall *n* Wand *f*; ~ **outlet** Wandsteckdose *f*; ~ **socket** Wandsteckdose *f*; **absorbing ~** absorbierende Wand, schluckende Wand; **reflecting ~** reflektierende Wand; **sound-absorbing ~** absorbierende Wand, schluckende Wand

wanted modulation Nutzmodulation *f*; ~ **signal** Nutzsignal *n*

wanted-signal transmitter Nutzsender *m*

wardrobe *n* Garderobe *f*

wardrobe* *n* Gewandmeisterei *f*

wardrobe supervisor Gewandmeister *m*

warming-up time Aufwärmzeit *f*

warm-up *n* (tube) Einbrennen *n*; ~ **time** Einlaufzeit *f*

warning arrow Warnpfeil *m*; ~ **light** Rotlicht *n*; ~ **sign** Achtungszeichen *n*

wash *v* waschen *v*; ~ **dissolve** Wellenblende *f*

washer *n* Unterlegscheibe *f*

washing plant Waschanlage *f*; ~ **tank** Waschanlage *f*

waste *n* Abfall *m*, Ausschuß *m*, Verschnitt *m*

watch *v* überwachen *v*

watchman *n* Wachmann *m*

water-bath *n* Wasserbad *n*

water down *v* (script) abschwächen *v*

water-cooling *n* Wasserkühlung *f*

watered silks effect Riffelmuster *n*, Moiré *n*

water stain Wasserfleck *m*

watt, 750 ~ pup Dreiviertel-KW *n*; **500 ~ pup** Halb-KW *n*

wattage *n* (elec.) Leistung *f*

wattless power Blindleistung *f*

wave *n* Welle *f*; ~ **crest** Wellenberg *m*; ~ **flicker** Zwischenzeilenflimmern *n*; ~ **impedance** Wellenwiderstand *m* ~ **loop** Wellenbauch *m*; ~ **propagation** Wellenausbreitung *f*; ~ **range** Wellenbereich *m*, Wellenband *n*; ~ **train** Wellenzug *m*; ~ **trap** Sperrkreis *m*; ~ **trough** Wellental *n*; **electromagnetic ~** elektromagnetische Welle; **longitudinal ~** Längswelle *f*; **progressive ~** fortschreitende Welle; **standing ~** stehende Welle; **transverse ~** Querwelle *f*; **travelling ~** fortschreitende Welle

waveband *n* Wellenbereich *m*, Wellenband *n*; ~ **filter** Bandfilter *m*, Bandpaß *m*, Bandpaßfilter *m*
waveform *n* Wellenform *f*, Kurvenform *f*
wavefront *n* Signalflanke *f*
waveguide *n* Hohlleiter *m*
wavelength *n* Wellenlänge *f*; ~ **announcement** Wellenangaben *f pl*; ~ **scale** Wellenlängenskala *f*; ~ **spectrum** Wellenlängenspektrum *n*; **complementary** ~ kompensative Wellenlänge; **dominant** ~ dominierende Wellenlänge, farbtongleiche Wellenlänge
wavemeter *n* Wellenlängenmesser *m*
wax disc Wachsplatte *f*; ~ **recording** Wachsaufnahme *f*
weak *adj* (neg.) weich *adj*; ~ *adj* (pict.) flau *adj*; ~ **current** Schwachstrom *m*
weaken *v* abschwächen *v*
weather chart Wetterkarte *f*; ~ **forecast** Wettervorhersage *f*; ~ **map** Wetterkarte *f*; ~ **report** Wetterbericht *m*
wedge *n* Besenkeil *m*; ~ **plate** Keilplatte *f*; ~ **range-finder** Keilentfernungsmesser *m*
weekend programme Wochenendprogramm *n*
weekly news magazine Wochenrückblick *m*; ~ **-paid staff** Lohnempfänger *m pl*; ~ **round-up** Wochenquerschnitt *m*; ~ **summary** Wochenquerschnitt *m*
weight of pick-up head Auflagegewicht *n*
weighted *adj* (tech.) bewertet *adj*; ~ **signal-to-noise ratio** Geräuschabstand *m*
weighting network Bewertungsfilter *m*
welfare* *n* Sozialwerk* *n*
well-focused *adj* scharf *adj*
western *n* Wildwestfilm *m*, Western *m*
wet *v* anfeuchten *v*; ~ **printing** Feuchtkopierung *f*
wetting agent Netzmittel *n*
whip aerial Peitschenantenne *f*; ~ **pan** Reißschwenk *m*
whistle *v* zischen *v*
whistling *n* Zischen *n*
white *n* Weiß *n*; ~ *adj* weiß *adj*; ~ **balance** Weißabgleich *m*, Weißbalance *f*; ~ **crushing** Weißwertstauchung *f*, Helligkeitsüberstrahlung *f*; ~ **distortion** Weißentzerrung *f*; ~ **film** Weißfilm *m*; ~ **leader** Weißfilm *m*; ~ **level** Weißpegel *m*, Weißwert *m*; ~ **-level clipper** Weißwertbegrenzer *m*; ~ **-level clipping** Weißwertbegrenzung *f*; ~ **-level control** Weißwertregelung *f*; ~ **-level limiter** Weißwertbegrenzer *m*; ~ **-level limiting** Weißwertbegrenzung *f*; ~ **line** Weißzeile *f*; ~ **noise** Weißton *m*, weißes Rauschen; ~ **non-linearity** Weißkrümmung *f*; ~ **spacing** Weißfilm *m*; ~ **spike** Weißspitze *f*; ~ **tape** Weißband *n*; **adjustment of ~ balance** Weißtonregelung *f*; **adjustment of ~ level** Weißwertregelung *f*; **clear** ~ gesättigtes Weiß; **glaring** ~ knallig weiß; **overmodulation of ~ level** Weißwertübersteuerung *f*; **pure** ~ reines Weiß
whiter than white ultraweiß *adj*
whites, to burn out the Weiß übersteuern
white-to-black step Weißschwarzsprung *m*
wide, too (pict.) zuviel Luft
wide angle Breitenwinkel *m*
wide-angle lens Weitwinkelobjektiv *n*; ~ **range** Weitwinkelbereich *m*
wide band Breitband *n*
wide-band aerial Breitbandantenne *f*, Allbereichantenne *f*; ~ **amplifier** Breitbandverstärker *m*,

Allbereichverstärker *m*, Mehrbereichverstärker *m*; **~ circuit** Breitbandkreis *m*; **~ distributor** Mehrbereichverteiler *m*; **~ technique** Breitbandtechnik *f*

wide coverage ausführliche Berichterstattung

wide-coverage transmitter Großflächensender *m*

wide-gauge film Breitfilm *m* (70 mm)

widen out *v* (zoom) aufziehen *v* (Zoom); **~ out** *v* (filming) Luft geben

wide-response microphone Breitbandmikrofon *n*

wide screen Breitwand *f*

wide-screen film Breitbildfilm *m*; **~ picture** *n* Breitbildfilm *m*

width control Bildbreitenregler *m*; **~ of cut** Schnittweite *f*

wig *n* Perücke *f*, Haarteil *n*; **~ -maker** *n* Perückenmacher *m*; **~ store** Perückenfundus *m*

wild noise Nebengeräusch *n*; **~ track effects** Atmosphäre *f*, Atmo *f* (fam.)

winch *n* Winde *f*

winch-base *n* Windeständer *m*

wind *v* spulen *v*; **~ bag** (micr.) Windschutz *m*; **~ band** Blasorchester *n*; **~ gag** Nahbesprechungsschutz *m*; **~ -loading** *n* (aerial) Windlast *f*; **~ shield** (micr.) Windschutz *m*; **~ (up)** *v* aufspulen *v*, aufwickeln *v*; **~ -up stand** Kurbelstativ *n*

winding *n* (spool) Wicklung *f*; ~ *n* (mech.) Windung *f*

winding-off *n* (cable) Abwicklung *f*

window *n* (sat.) Satellitenfenster *n*

window-frame aerial Fensterantenne *f*

window-mounted aerial Fensterantenne *f*

window-mounting *n* (aerial) Fensterbefestigung *f*

wing *n* (thea.) Kulisse *f*; **~ aerial** (vehicle) Kotflügelantenne *f*

wipe *v* (fade) blenden *v*; ~ *v* (tape) löschen *v*; ~ *n* (fade) Blende *f*, Trickblende *f*

wiper *n* (fader) Schleifer *m*

wiping *n* (tape) Löschung *f*; **~ head** Löschkopf *m*

wire *v* schalten *v*, verdrahten *v*; ~ *n* (elec.) Leitung *f*; **~ distribution service** Kabelfernsehen *n*; **~ -lattice guard** Schutzgrill *m*; **~ line** Drahtleitung *f*; **~ picture** Telefoto *n*; **~ picture office** Telefotostelle *f*; **~ printer** (EDP) Matrixdrucker *m*; **~ service** (US) Nachrichtenagentur *f*; **~ strippers** *n pl* Abisolierzange *f*; **~ -wound resistor** Drahtwiderstand *m*; **solid twin-connection ~** Rangierleitung *f*

wired broadcasting Drahtfunk *m*; **~ gauze filter** Drahtgazefilter *m*; **~ radio** Drahtfunk *m*; **~ television** Drahtfernsehen *n*

wireless *n* Rundfunkapparat *m*, Rundfunkempfänger *m*, Rundfunkgerät *n*, Radio *n*; ~ *adj* drahtlos *adj*; **~ set** Rundfunkapparat *m*, Rundfunkempfänger *m*, Rundfunkgerät *n*, Radio *n*; **~ telegraphy (WT)** drahtlose Telegrafie

wireman *n* Elektriker *m*

wiring *n* Verdrahtung *f*, Verkabelung *f*, Drahtleitung *f*, Schaltung *f*, Beschaltung *f*; **~ capacity** Schaltungskapazität *f*; **~ diagram** Schaltbild *n*, Schaltplan *m*, Schaltschema *n*, Verdrahtungsplan *m*, Verkabelungsplan *m*; **~ diagram of building** Bauschaltplan *m*; **~ side** Verdrahtungsseite *f*

wobble *v* wobbeln *v*; **~ frequency** Wobbelfrequenz *f*

wobbling *n* Wobbeln *n*, Wobbelung *f*
wobbulate *v* wobbeln *v*
wobbulated RF signal Hochfrequenzwobbelsignal *n*
wobbulation *n* Wobbeln *n*, Wobbelung *f*
wobbulator *n* Wobbler *m*, Wobbelgenerator *m*, Wobbelmeßsender *m*
wooden tripod Holzstativ *n*
woofer *n* (coll.) Baßlautsprecher *m*, Tieftonlautsprecher *m*
word *v* abfassen *v*; ~ **cue** Stichwort *n*; ~ **length** (EDP) Wortlänge *f*
work on *v* (F) bearbeiten *v*; ~ **print** Arbeitskopie *f*, Schnittkopie *f*
working aperture Blendenöffnung *f* ~ **characteristic** Arbeitskennlinie *f*; ~ **clothes** *n pl* Arbeitskleidung *f*; ~ **condition** Betriebszustand *m*; ~ **costs** Betriebskosten *plt*; ~ **day** Arbeitstag *m*; ~ **drawing** Bauplan *m*; ~ **frequency** Betriebsfrequenz *f* ~ **hours** *n pl* Arbeitszeit *f*, Betriebszeit *f*; ~ **light** Baulicht *n*; ~ **order** Betriebszustand *m*; ~ **plan** Arbeitsfoto *n*; ~ **point** Arbeitspunkt *m*; ~ **point** (tube) Betriebszustand *m*; ~ **process** Arbeitsgang *m*; ~ **programme** (EDP) Arbeitsprogramm *n*; ~ **resistance** Arbeitswiderstand *m*; ~ **resistor** Arbeitswiderstand *m*; ~ **script** Rohfassung *f*; ~ **temperature** Betriebstemperatur *f*; ~ **title** Arbeitstitel *m*, vorläufiger Titel, Werktitel *m*; **good ~ order** stabiler Betrieb; **in good ~ order** einsatzfähig *adj*
works council Betriebsrat *m*
workshop manager Werkstattmeister *m*
world distribution Weltvertrieb *m*; ~ **première** Welturaufführung *f*
worm *n* Schnecke *f*; ~ **drive gear** Schneckengetriebe *n*; ~ **drive reduction ratio** Schneckengang *m*
worm's-eye view Froschperspektive *f*
wow *n* Heuler *m*, Jaulen *n*, langsame Tonhöhenschwankungen
wrap *v* lötlos verdrahten; ~ **it up!** (take) gestorben! (fam.)
wrapped jointing lötlose Verdrahtung
wrapping *n* Wicklung *f*
write head (EDP) Schreibkopf *m*; ~ **instruction** (EDP) Schreibbefehl *m*; ~ **lockout** (EDP) Schreibsperre *f*
writer *n* Verfasser *m*, Autor *m*; ~ *n* (R talks) Chronist *m*; ~ *n* (F) Drehbuchautor *m*; ~ **of dialogue scripts** Dialogautor *m*
written band Textband *n*; ~ **-band projector** Textbandprojektor *m*

X

X-certificate *adj* nicht jugendfrei
xenon lamp Xenonlampe *f*
XY and MS stereophonic recording process Stereoaufnahmeverfahren XY und MS

Y

yagi *n* (coll.) Yagiantenne *f*; ~ **aerial** Yagiantenne *f*
yellow *n* Leerbandteil *n*; ~ **fog** Gelbschleier *m*
youth broadcasting Jugendfunk* *m*; ~ **film** Jugendfilm *m*; ~ **programmes** *n pl* Jugendfunk* *m*
Y-signal *n* Y-Signal *n*

Z

Zener diode Zenerdiode *f*; ~ **effect** Zenereffekt *m*

zero *n* Nullpunkt *m*; ~ **-beat frequency** Schwebungsnull *f*; ~ **level** Nullpegel *m*; ~ **-level clamping** Nulltastung *f*; ~ **reset** Nullrückstellung *f*; ~ **time** Nullzeit *f*

zip pan Reißschwenk *m*

zone *n* Zone *f*, Bereich *m*; ~ **of sharpness** Tiefenschärfebereich *m*; **achromatic** ~ achromatischer Bereich

zoom *v* Gummilinse ziehen, Linse fahren, zoomen *v*, fahren *v*; ~ *n* optische Fahrt; ~ **angle indication** Bildwinkelanzeige *f*; ~ **handle** Brennweitenbügel *m*; ~ **in** *v* Gummilinse zuziehen; ~ **indicator** Bildwinkelanzeiger *m*; ~ **lens** Gummilinse *f*, Objektiv mit veränderlicher Brennweite, Vario-Objektiv *n*, Varioptik *f*, Zoom *m*, Transfokator *m*; ~ **out** *v* Gummilinse aufziehen, aufziehen *v*; ~ **travel** Zoomfahrt *f*

zoomfinder *n* Mehrfachsucher *m*

zooming *n* Zoomen *n*